CONQUERING
GOTHAM

*This book was donated to
the Richmond Public Library
by the Friends of the Richmond Public Library*

ALSO BY JILL JONNES

Empires of Light: Edison, Tesla, Westinghouse
and the Race to Electrify the World

South Bronx Rising: The Rise, Fall, and Resurrection of
an American City

Hep-Cats, Narcs, and Pipe Dreams: A History of
America's Romance with Illegal Drugs

CONQUERING
GOTHAM

———

A GILDED AGE EPIC:
THE CONSTRUCTION OF
PENN STATION AND ITS TUNNELS

———

JILL JONNES

VIKING

VIKING
Published by the Penguin Group
Penguin Group (USA) Inc., 375 Hudson Street, New York, New York 10014, U.S.A.
Penguin Group (Canada), 90 Eglinton Avenue East, Suite 700, Toronto, Ontario
M4P 2Y3 (a division of Pearson Penguin Canada Inc.)
Penguin Books Ltd, 80 Strand, London WC2R 0RL, England
Penguin Ireland, 25 St. Stephen's Green, Dublin 2, Ireland (a division of Penguin Books Ltd)
Penguin Books Australia Ltd, 250 Camberwell Road, Camberwell, Victoria 3124, Australia
(a division of Pearson Australia Group Pty Ltd)
Penguin Books India Pvt Ltd, 11 Community Centre, Panchsheel Park,
New Delhi – 110 017, India
Penguin Group (NZ), 67 Apollo Drive, Mairangi Bay, Auckland 1311, New Zealand
(a division of Pearson New Zealand Ltd)
Penguin Books (South Africa) (Pty) Ltd, 24 Sturdee Avenue,
Rosebank, Johannesburg 2196, South Africa

Penguin Books Ltd, Registered Offices: 80 Strand, London WC2R 0RL, England

First published in 2007 by Viking Penguin, a member of Penguin Group (USA) Inc.

1   3   5   7   9   10   8   6   4   2

Copyright © Jill Jonnes, 2007
All rights reserved

Illustration credits appear on page 369.

LIBRARY OF CONGRESS CATALOGING-IN-PUBLICATION DATA
Jonnes, Jill
Conquering Gotham : a Gilded Age epic : the construction of Penn Station
and its tunnels / Jill Jonnes.
Includes bibliographical references and index.
p.   cm.
ISBN 978-0-670-03158-0
1. Pennsylvania Station (New York, N.Y.)—History—20th century. 2. Tunneling—
New York (State)—New York—History—2oth century. 3. Railroad stations—New York
(State)—New York—History—20th century. 4. Historic buildings—New York (State)—
New York—History—20th century. I. Title.
TF302.N7J66 2006
385.3'14097471—dc22   2006050171

Printed in the United States of America
Designed by Nancy Resnick

For John Ross, Clare Romano Ross,
and Tim Ross

"Rich, hemm'd thick all round with sailships and steamships, an
island sixteen miles long, solid-founded . . .
The countless masts, the white shore-steamers, the lighters, the
ferry-boats, the black sea-steamers, well-model'd
The down-town streets, the jobbers' houses of business, the houses
of business of the ship-merchants and money-brokers, the
river-streets . . .
City of hurried and sparkling waters! City of spires and masts!
City nestled in bays! My city!"

—Walt Whitman, "Mannahatta," 1881

CONTENTS

LIST OF ILLUSTRATIONS

PART I

HOW SHALL WE REACH GOTHAM?

As a Gilded Age United States of great fortunes and booming commerce enters the twentieth century, the rich, sprawling railroad empires—the nation's first great corporations—are an unparalleled power unto themselves. None is more powerful than the Pennsylvania Railroad (PRR), its thousands of miles of track serving the nation's biggest cities and monopolizing the industrial heartland. For thirty years the Pennsylvania Railroad has sought some means—other than its huge fleet of ferries from New Jersey—to bring tens of millions of passengers straight into waterlocked Manhattan, America's commercial heart and most important city. In 1900, there is no bridge or tunnel that spans the Hudson River.

In the first half of this epic history, PRR president Alexander Cassatt, a cultured, steely engineer, fights to find way to get his railroad across the mile-wide Hudson. Solution finally in hand, Cassatt and his railroad prepare to embark on the most monumental and consequent engineering feat of the age, an enterprise that will forever transform the physical and psychological geography of Gotham. And yet, Tammany-run New York's most corrupt politicians and robber barons seek to derail his plans. Like President Theodore Roosevelt, Cassatt believes in an America of such dynamism and promise he sees no reason to truckle to "successful dishonesty." When the battle is joined, it becomes yet another chapter in the ongoing war over whether the United States will be an honorable republic or a corrupt plutocracy.

ONE

"WE MUST FIND A WAY TO CROSS"

Alexander J. Cassatt, president of the Pennsylvania Railroad, arose from the plush chair in his Pullman Palace car sitting room, checking the time on his gold pocket watch. The train was slowing, approaching the railroad's Jersey City station and ferry depot, and billows of steam smoke floated past. The black porter and chef bustled about, the aroma of good coffee lingered, and Tiffany lamps set the polished wood paneling aglow. Cassatt, well over six feet tall, wore a dark old-fashioned frock coat, vest, starched white high-collar shirt, and cravat. As he and several of his PRR officers debarked onto the platform they were enveloped by the sooty clangor of their road's Jersey City Exchange Place Terminal. On this morning in late May 1901, the men strode briskly, joining the impatient tide of travelers and commuters in the new depot, which, with its cavernous, arched glass-ceilinged train shed, rebuilt after a bad fire, had been hailed by the *New-York Tribune* as "one of the handsomest and most commodious in the world."

Uniformed porters maneuvered steamer trunks and valises, while a sea of dark-suited men sporting derbies and young women in Gibson-style shirtwaists and broad-brimmed hats hurried to board one of the railroad's double-decker ferries, huge rumbling boats bound for Manhattan. On the lower decks, one could see and smell horses pulling express wagons and drays up the gangways, jostling into place. On the upper deck, the reek of locomotive coal smoke gave way to the pungent scent of the river. The gigantic ferries named for the road's far-flung empire— the *Philadelphia*, the *Pittsburgh*, the *St. Louis*—were painted a signature Tuscan red, and emblazoned with the PRR's proud keystone crest. As the commuter throng pressed onto the Cortlandt Street ferry, a sign admonished passengers: "Gentlemen will not, others must not, spit on the floor." The freshening river breezes riffled Cassatt's thinning sandy hair and drooping mustache as he angled to the front of the open deck, his intelligent blue-gray eyes calmly sizing things up. Cassatt's aura of authority was tempered by a laconic reserve, a slight stoop, and hint of melancholy. Little known to the general public, Alexander J. Cassatt had long been viewed by his peers as the "most brilliant railroad official in this country." With American railroads at the apogee of their importance and influence—the mightiest and, in some circles, most despised economic force in the nation—this was no small accolade. Cassatt, a veteran engineer and executive of immense talent, had reluctantly emerged two years earlier, in 1899, from seventeen years of pleasant retirement to take charge of the Pennsylvania Railroad, thus becoming one of the most powerful men in the United States.

All about him was the luminous briny river air and ahead a wondrous sweep of sky and currents. Yet the very bodies of glistening water that encircled Manhattan and made the port city so rich were now starting to strangle her rambunctious growth. In 1901, only one major bridge, that marvel of grace and engineering, the Brooklyn Bridge, connected Manhattan to any other piece of land. Only one railway, the Vanderbilts' New York Central Railroad, came directly into Manhattan, and that from upstate. The New York Central ran down the east bank of the Hudson River, across the narrow Harlem River, and into the heart of Gotham. For many decades, sole ownership of this wonderful monopoly had made the Vanderbilts America's richest family, notorious for their churlish indifference to the well-being of their road's passengers. The late, large William H. Vanderbilt—his mausoleum still guarded by Pinkertons around the clock against grave robbers—had summed it up neatly with his infamously imperious, "Let the public be damned."

The other ten railroads serving New York, the world's greatest port as well as the nation's colossus of trade, finance, manufacturing, and culture, had had no choice but to build sprawling waterfront terminals on the industrialized New Jersey shore and to operate fleets of ferries across to Gotham. In typical corporate understatement, the PRR's official historians noted that "The Pennsylvania, as the Central's greatest rival, could not view this situation complacently."

Alexander Cassatt found these ferry rides a galling reminder that, unlike its nemesis, the Central, the Pennsylvania Railroad, which prided itself on being the nation's largest, richest, and best-operated road, still had no way to bring its trains into the commercial heart of the nation's busiest seaport. Easy access to Gotham was arguably as important in the twentieth century as had been the building of the transcontinental railroad in the 1860s or the great interoceanic canal now being proposed to cross the Isthmus of Panama. And yet, astonishingly, there was no definite plan. No bridge or tunnel of the magnitude needed to span the Hudson River had ever been built. But Cassatt could now console himself that he and his great corporation were actively considering building the gargantuan North River Bridge, the long-promoted solution of engineer Gustav Lindenthal and what would be the biggest bridge in the world. As Cassatt had confided to General William J. Sewell the previous spring, "We are now taking up the question of the construction of the bridge seriously."

British politician James Bryce had been stunned by the princely power and influence of American railroads and the men—"potentates"—who ran them, writing in 1888, "These railway kings are among the greatest men, perhaps I may say are the greatest men, in America . . . They have power, more power—that is, more opportunity of making their personal will prevail—than perhaps any one in political life, except the President and the Speaker." By 1900, the 185,000 miles of American rails equaled those of the whole rest of the world combined.

Alexander Cassatt, as the seventh president in the history of the Pennsylvania Railroad, intended to wield his corporate power to accomplish what no other man had yet done: He would somehow send the Pennsylvania Railroad across the mile-wide Hudson River and bring its elegant gleaming passenger trains triumphantly into the heart of Manhattan. "We stand on our last railroad tie within view of [Gotham] and cannot reach it," he said in frustration. "We must find a way to cross." He also intended to redress, some might say avenge, some long-festering corporate wrongs.

The ferry whistle shrieked, the powerful engines rumbled, and the behemoth ferry bearing Cassatt, his officers, and a thousand passengers began threading its way across the mile-wide Hudson, long known to sailors as the North River. Ahead, the sky enveloped the gray-green river, a wide panorama alive with maritime hustle. To starboard, an ocean liner attended by tugs steamed in from its Atlantic voyage, while all about sailed shabby workhorse sloops and huge six- and seven-masted schooners carrying loads of sand, bricks, granite blocks, and crushed stone.

Busy maritime traffic on the North River in 1898.

The Hudson River was vivid testimony to New York's extraordinary economic boom. Coming downriver from Albany were palatial sidewheelers as well as tugs towing three, six, eight, even ten blue Erie Canal barges laden with ice, coal, and lowing cattle. Later in the summer these barges would bear the bumper harvests of Midwest wheat and corn to be stored in the city's big dockside grain elevators before export overseas. The red, green, and olive passenger ferries lumbered back and forth, day and night, from shore to shore, as did the railroads' "floaters" and "lighters," huge wooden platformlike vessels (often complete with shed and rails) ferrying freight cars to rail yards for unloading in New York or continuation to New England. Some people never became accustomed to the odd sight of trains traveling slowly along atop the water.

On such a glistening spring day out upon the Hudson River, when the shore receded, and the primal feel of river and nature asserted themselves, a determined dreamer aboard the ferry could conjure up the ancient Ice Age whose brute geologic forces had gouged out Gotham's incomparable harbor. That very New Jersey riverbank, that grimy jumble of rail yards, terminals, ferry berths, and ocean liner docks, backed by high palisades, had all been encased by a massive thousand-foot-high glacier, as had much of North America. The glacier's pulverizing weight, edging gradually south, had crushed the land, heaving up hills and cliffs, its glacial advance down through the Hudson River valley scraping out an ever-deeper estuary that swept a hundred miles beyond present New York to the then Atlantic shoreline and an ocean ten thousand feet shallower than that of today.

When the world began to warm an imponderable seventeen thousand years ago and ice sheets gradually melted and retreated, the oceans rose precipitously. What would become New York City was left encircled by marvelously deep, broad waters, and the glacially carved Hudson River ebbed and flowed for 170 miles with the ocean's tides, its dark rippling currents separating the island of Manhattan from the wilderness of the mainland.

On the ferry, Alexander Cassatt and his fellow passengers could feel the languorous river breezes freshening as the New York skyline grew steadily larger. On the bluest and calmest of days, Manhattan seemed but a stone's throw away, and the ferry ride was a fifteen-minute interlude of nautical pleasure. Cassatt could now easily spot the shimmering gold dome of Joseph Pulitzer's World Building alongside six of the new twenty-story skyscrapers that dwarfed such familiar landmarks as the steeple of Wall Street's Trinity Church.

Cassatt was painfully aware that while the lumbering ferries seemed wonderfully stolid they were not. The previous fall, right off this very Cortlandt Street slip, the PRR's *Chicago* had been rammed by the crowded coastline steamer *City of Augusta* just after midnight and had sunk in minutes. Several passengers, a bootblack, and half a dozen teams of milk wagon horses had drowned.

Today all went smoothly, the ferry engines slowing as the vessel nestled expertly into the railroad's dock, where the oily river, full of refuse, "bits of wood, straw from barges, bottles, boxes, paper, occasionally a dead cat or dog, hideously bladder-like, its four paws stiff and indignant towards heaven," lapped at the pier. The city's urchins, indifferent to the river's debris, could be seen cavorting and swimming, their yells and shouts blending in with the harbor noises.

West Street in Manhattan where the ferries arrived from New Jersey.

Alexander Cassatt and his fellow passengers streamed off the Pennsylvania Railroad ferry that morning, into the bedlam of West Street, which the *New-York Tribune* excoriated as "a whirlpool of slime, muck, wheels, hoofs, and destruction," a cobblestoned maelstrom jammed with

cabdrivers, express wagons, garbage carts, beer skids, and yelling teamsters steering their powerful horses around the clanging trolley cars.
Here was a "waterfront as squalid and dirty and ill smelling as that of any
Oriental port . . . [lined with] storage and cold-storage warehouses and
large commission houses . . . whose closed iron shutters . . . look gloomy
and forbidding." Low corner saloons, dives that catered to the longshore-
men and sailors from all over the world, were plentiful, and criminal
gangs plagued the docks at night.

Scruffy street vendors loudly hawked fresh coffee and roasted peanuts.
In colder months came the oyster carts, offering juicy bivalves the size
of your hand. Pedestrians were used to negotiating the towering piles of
shucked oyster shells, one of the less disagreeable aspects of the city's
legendary filth. The sour, ever-present smell of horse piss permeating the
air was tolerable at this time of year. What made all this intolerable
to Cassatt was that the PRR's perennial rival, the Vanderbilts' New York
Central, delivered *its* passengers straight into the city's northern heart
in its recently expanded Grand Central Station, uptown on East Forty-
second Street. The frustrating truth was that the Pennsylvania Railroad,
while rumored to control whole legislatures and certain U.S. senators,
had not yet managed to overcome nature in the form of the North River, a
fact rudely reaffirmed on every ferry journey to New York and thus a
perennial "bitter trial."

Cassatt and his officers followed the crowds of commuters up Cedar
Street, crowded with pushcart vendors and tea merchants, to the railroad's skyscraper offices in the American Bank Exchange Building at the
corner of Broadway. True, the *New York Times* had recently declared the
Vanderbilt's railroad terminal "one of the most inconvenient and unpleasant railroad stations in the whole country . . . the ugly structure has long
been a disgrace to the metropolis." But this was small consolation to
Cassatt and his railroad, repeatedly stymied in their relentless thirty-year
quest to reach Manhattan.

A beautiful ferry ride like today's could only briefly erase the vexatious
reality that on many days fog swirled in from the Atlantic Ocean to
shroud the Hudson River, bringing danger and delays. Then, recalled
lawyer and developer William G. McAdoo, "Through the fog came a bedlam of mournful sounds, the deep bellowing of ocean liners, the angry

screams of tugboats, the long, eerie cries of the ferry sirens that reminded one of sea gulls . . . It was picturesque, but most people . . . had
no time for marine adventures. They were on their way to their daily
jobs, or to catch trains, or to keep appointments." In brutally cold winters
the Hudson clotted up with thick ice and became almost impossible to
navigate.

With each passing decade, the situation became more untenable,
more disastrous. In Cassatt's lifetime, the metropolis of New York had become a marvel of the modern age. As the nineteenth century with all its
industrial wonders—the railroads, the telegraph, the Atlantic cable, electricity, the new automobiles—became the twentieth, every citizen of New
York saw that this water-locked city reigned supreme. Not only was it the
world's greatest port, Gotham's powerful banks and rapacious Wall Street
financiers—men like J. P. Morgan and August Belmont Jr.—were forces
to be courted and feared. The city's influential battling newspapers—the
World, the *Journal American*, the *Herald*, the *Sun*, the *New York Times*,
and the *Tribune*, to name but the biggest—were read across the land.
The city's infamous political bosses—the Republican Thomas Collier
Platt, the thuggish Tammany chieftain Richard Croker—were key to any
presidential election. Platt even temporarily rid himself of the reformer
governor Theodore Roosevelt by foisting him upon President William
McKinley as vice president. The city's main avenue, Broadway, was a
phenomenon in its own right, a phalanx of dazzling theaters, world-
famous hotels, and stylish restaurants. Nearby was the iniquitous Tenderloin, Manhattan's vice district. Book and magazine publishing, department
stores, and a myriad of other enterprises fueled the city's amazing prosperity and set the standard for the rest of America. This world-class poly-
glot city simply had to be reliably and conveniently connected to the
nation it now dominated.

Gotham's visceral commercial energy was embodied in its new Wall
Street skyscrapers, its jammed avenues and sidewalks, and above all, in
its port. One journalist wrote of New York's waterfront: "In daylight,
dusk, and darkness, [the city] never halts or falters. Cargoes from every
port from every nook and cranny of the world . . . are forever clearing

or discharging at the wharves . . . Here on the South Street front is a veritable forest of masts." Sicilian lemons, Brazilian coffee, Indian spices, fine West Indian wood poured forth from these holds. When the reporter looked northward on the Hudson River side of the port, he saw "the great Atlantic steamers beside long piers crowned with double storied sheds of corrugated iron . . . Rank after rank of castled stacks stretch away into perspective, each marked with the distinctive color bands of its company . . . The Bermuda docks end the ocean trade, and oyster and ice boats, tiny in comparison with the liners, crowd the docks and bulkheads."

All this power and prosperity acted as an irresistible magnet, and the population of the newly consolidated boroughs of New York City had swelled to three and a half million. Each day a tidal wave of workers, shoppers, and travelers poured in to Manhattan, flooding the Brooklyn Bridge and the fleets of ferries coming from New Jersey, Staten Island, the Bronx, and Queens, crowding the commercial districts and pushing Gotham's energetic cacophony to fever pitch. By 1901 Manhattan had become one of the most densely populated places on earth, a gilded city notorious for high-living millionaires, corrupt Tammany rule, thriving vice districts, and the fetid misery of the tenements and flophouses for the legions of the down and out.

The sheer daily difficulty of getting in and out of Manhattan was creating more of these scabrous slums and choking the economy. All the railroads, except for the Vanderbilts', came to an abrupt halt at the Hudson River. In Jersey City, there sprawled the terminals and ferry depots for the Pennsylvania and Erie railroads, as well as those of the New York, Ontario & Western Railroad, and the New York, Susquehanna & Western. The Central of New Jersey terminal sat slightly downriver in Communipaw and also served the Baltimore & Ohio, the Philadelphia & Reading, and the Lehigh Valley railroads. Upriver in Hoboken lay the terminus of the Delaware, Lackawanna & Western Railroad, while the New York, West Shore & Buffalo came into Weehawken. All told, twelve hundred trains a *day* steamed into the various New Jersey terminals. By 1901 the railroad ferries of six companies, carrying eighty million passengers a year, were part of the busy maritime traffic of the mile-wide Hudson River, negotiating its daily moods, shifting weather, tides, and currents.

And so, when Alexander Cassatt agreed to ascend to the presidency of the Pennsylvania Railroad, his greatest ambition was to span that last watery mile across the North River and into Gotham, to transport his trains, at long last, in proper glory into Manhattan. As Cassatt told a fellow engineer while the two studied a map of the PRR lines, "I have never been able to reconcile myself to the idea that a railroad system like the Pennsylvania should be prevented from entering the most important and populous city in the country by a river less than a mile wide."

TWO

HASKINS'S TUNNEL AND LINDENTHAL'S BRIDGE

For decades, men of ambition had stood upon Gotham's poorly maintained wooden piers to wonder how they might breach the beautiful and strategic Hudson River. Many nineteenth-century men had conjured up grandiose plans, but the first to act was a California capitalist named Colonel DeWitt Clinton Haskins. The colonel, having built railroads out west, dug mines in Utah, and studied caisson-built bridges, proposed an ingenious and promising approach: subaqueous tunnels.

In 1873, Colonel Haskins's vision, which called for digging two rail tunnels under the Hudson River from Jersey City to Morton Street, was sufficiently compelling to attract $10 million in capital. As soon as work began the next year, both the New York Central (determined to preserve its monopoly) and the Delaware, Lackawanna & Western Railroad (its Hoboken terminal sure to be eclipsed) sued. They were implacably opposed to the tunnels, but after five years of litigation, Haskins prevailed. As work began, the *New York Times* hailed the enterprise: "Of all the great improvements projected or dreamed of in and about this City, this is unquestionably the most important."

And so, on a cold, clear November day in 1879, Colonel Haskins's company returned to work on its pioneering tunnels, this time digging a great, circular thirty-foot-wide working shaft near Fifteenth Street in Jersey City, one hundred feet back from the bulkhead line of the river.

All through the fall, winter, and spring, gangs of men labored day and night, and had soon excavated the shaft straight down sixty feet. "It is built in the most substantial manner and is lined with a brick wall 4 feet thick," reported one visiting journalist in the summer of 1880. "The bottom of the shaft is the level of the roadway of the tunnel, but . . . its bottom is now used as an immense cistern to contain the water and silt which is forced out from the head of the tunnel . . . The shaft contains an air-lock and a pair of engines used in forcing air and water into the tunnel."

Colonel Haskins had devised a patented system of pumping compressed air at a pressure of twenty pounds per square inch into the advancing tunnel to keep the pressure of the river and silt from crushing his nascent enterprise during construction. "That we have gone 300 feet into the river," said Haskins to the skeptics, "demonstrates to my own satisfaction the practicability of the work and that the air will hold the earth." Even so, there were frequent tiny "blows" in the still-raw parts of the tunnel as the river's extraordinary pressure penetrated the highly porous silt overhead. The "blows" made a telltale hissing sound, and the amazingly simple solution was to quickly patch the oozing spot with silt and straw before water and slimy river muck burst through, bringing deluge and disaster.

The *New York Times* reporter who came in mid-July 1880 to view the tunnel digging was given a suit of blue overalls, rubber boots, and a floppy hat. The young journalist then warily descended the ladder halfway down the brick-lined shaft where a "slippery blue black mud covered everything." There loomed the air lock, an ominous boilerlike iron object, fifteen feet long and six feet tall, that was the sole entry to the tunnel works. With trepidation, the journalist and his guide stepped into the dungeonlike space of the air lock (lit only by a sputtering candle), and the heavy door with its thick bull's-eye window clanged shut.

For fifteen minutes, the men sat in the gloom as the air pressure gradually increased, a process the reporter likened to "torture." Then the air lock door on the tunnel side (also with a thick round window) slowly swung open. The tunnel was a clammy, stygian space, illuminated by calcium lamps, smelling of human sweat and rank mud. In almost nine months, Haskins's tunnel teams had burrowed deep under the river and had already advanced the north tunnel three hundred feet through the silt toward Manhattan. The sweating reporter and his guide advanced down a steep slope and slithered through a narrow opening into the north tunnel, where the air was cooler. Almost the entire length of the excavated twenty-foot-high tunnel was deliberately refilled halfway with dirt, intended "to furnish a brace to the brick-work, and allow the cement to thoroughly harden, until the tunnel is finished."

Far ahead, miners stood atop an earthen staircase picking and shoveling to create "a thin semi-circular opening at the top of the tunnel, only excavating enough at a time to admit of placing the top [round iron boiler] plates in position," that were then welded together. As the top half of

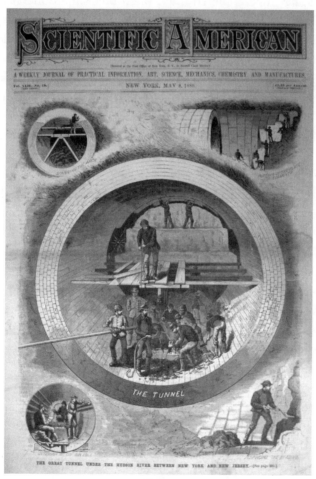

An 1880 illustration of Haskins's tunnel project
under the Hudson River.

the tunnel advanced, other miners steadily excavated the lower half. As soon as the welders attached the top and bottom iron cylinder, the brick masons lined the iron cylinders with cement and a two-foot-thick layer of bricks. Even as he was feeling miserable, the reporter admired this daring subaqueous enterprise, finding that "Everything about the tunnel appeared solid and substantial." He retraced his steps, endured the air lock, and returned gratefully to the fresh summer air, the sunshine, and river breezes. He sat for a while. The last visitor, in his haste to escape, had overexerted himself and fainted.

Three days later, in the dark predawn hour of 4:30 a.m., fourteen tunnel workers, having completed their lunch break up in the night air, acclimated in the air lock and stepped into the outer chamber of the tunnel where twelve men were waiting to head up for lunch. Suddenly, they heard the telltale hissing of a breach in the chamber. The blowout in the still-unbricked vault was too big and fast to be plugged, and with a sharp crack, the heavy joists snapped like bamboo. Timbers, iron, and mud began engulfing the tunnel. Eight men frantically clambered back into the air lock, then watched in horror when their fellow laborers were overwhelmed by oozing mud and debris, pinning one man half in the open air lock door.

" 'My God! The water is gaining on us," said one, 'what shall we do?'

" 'Keep cool, men; keep cool,' answered a voice from the river side of the tunnel." It was their supervisor. As the water rose relentlessly about him and the others, he calmly instructed the men in the lock to pull off their clothes and stuff them around the jammed-open door to keep out the water. The water slowed but still rose steadily in the tunnel and the air lock. Now their boss's voice, sounding far away, commanded, "Break open the bull's eye."

The men, naked in the air lock, the cold water rising toward their chests, hesitated, knowing if they broke the window on the shaft side, the others would almost certainly not escape.

Again, their boss ordered sternly, "Knock out the bull's eye; knock it out I say," and then faltered, "and do what you can for the rest of us."

At that they smashed away at the thick outer bull's-eye window, the cold water inching higher, lapping at their arm pits, then their necks. Then the air lock door burst open, pried open by rescuers. The eight men burst out into the shaft with the rush of water and waded helter-skelter toward the ladder. Up they stumbled to the surface, river water swirling just below and rising rapidly.

Once out and safe on solid ground, they stood naked and mud-smeared, heaving as rain drummed down all around in the dark. Beside them the whole shaft filled with roiled river water, becoming a muddy pool. Below its surface, twenty of their fellow workers were entombed. As the wet dawn lightened the sky, a thousand relatives and friends, eerily quiet but for occasional weeping, ignored the lashing rainstorm to press in around this flooded grave. As the *New York Herald* observed, "Engineering skill had set at defiance the laws of nature, and nature had avenged herself."

Eventually, Haskins, undaunted, pumped out the tunnel, recovered the corpses, and recommenced work. After all, he would explain, "This tunnel scheme is a bona fide operation. I put a fortune in it myself, and seven years of labor . . . If the scheme is successful it will pay me; if it fails, I shall lose."

Should it succeed, his tunnel would be *the* rail link into Gotham at a time when the *Commercial and Financial Chronicle* wrote, "The fact is that the railroad has revolutionized everything." All through the final decades of the nineteenth century, fast-expanding railroads were remaking the United States, whether Americans liked it or not, determining prosperity or obliteration with their routes and their rates. The raw power of the railroads was a marvel and a terror. "Many of these roads had a greater income than the States they served," wrote railroad historian John Moody; "their payrolls were much larger; their head officials received higher salaries than governors and presidents. The extent to which these roads controlled legislatures and, as it seemed at times, even the courts themselves, alarmed the people."

Starting on November 18, 1883 ("the day of two noons"), the telling of time itself, once set by the sun, had to be standardized to fit the new mechanical world of science and railroads. Within six months, seventy-eight of America's hundred biggest cities set their clocks and watches to Railway Standard Time. As an Indianapolis paper joked, "The sun is no longer to boss the job. People . . . must eat, sleep, and work . . . by railroad time . . . People will have to marry by railroad time."

Colonel Haskins, desperate to finish his trolley tunnels, pressed on. By late 1887, far behind schedule and digging only sporadically, he had completed 2,025 feet of the 6,000 feet under the river. He was running out of money and was unable to convince investors to ante up another penny. Two years later, the British-backed S. Pearson & Son excavated another 2,000 feet before another bad blowout scared off financing and forced them to abandon the tunnel in August 1891. The obstinate Hudson River waters flowed serenely on, and the railroads—save the Vanderbilts' New York Central—still came to an impatient halt at the many terminals on the Jersey riverfront.

Even as Colonel Haskins tunneled far below the Hudson River in fits and starts, the equally ambitious bridge engineer Gustav Lindenthal, a tall, elegant Austro-Hungarian immigrant with a Van Dyck beard, stood on Gotham's wharves. The year before, the Roeblings' Brooklyn Bridge had opened to universal acclaim. A triumph of engineering, the bridge was also a work of art, a noble structure whose wondrous web of cables, latticed girders, and masonry towers glistened poetically in the city's sun and shadow. Now, the erudite and charming Lindenthal, educated in Europe as a civil engineer and the preeminent bridge engineer in river-girt Pittsburgh, planned to make an even greater mark on New York. Hoping to build a great bridge to span the mile-wide Hudson, one almost twice the length of the Brooklyn Bridge with its span of 3,455 feet, he organized the North River Bridge Company in 1884, only to be stymied by the financial hard times of the late 1880s.

By 1890, the economy finally recovered, Lindenthal and his backers spent January and February haunting the underheated halls of Congress, emerging on April 11, 1890, with a valuable federal charter. The North River Bridge, asserted one witness, "is in national importance on a level with the Union and Central Pacific Railways or the Nicaragua Ship Canal." Prize in hand, Lindenthal came knocking on the Pennsylvania Railroad's monied doors.

Just as the PRR prepared to move, the Panic of 1893 struck. The booming economy spiraled into a slow-motion free fall. In these hardest of times, a third of the nation's railroads went belly-up. Wall Street titan J. P. Morgan, his girth and power ever expanding, scooped up so many of them, he gained control of a sixth of the nation's rails. For Lindenthal, however, one bright spot came in 1894, when the U.S. Supreme Court upheld his bridge charter.

Among all the visionary engineers and hard strivers dreaming of monumental New York bridges and tunnels, it might seem odd that the man who had dreamed longest about this great and vexing dilemma—how to connect the wealthy and influential island of Manhattan to the mainland and the rest of America—should be a Philadelphian. Yet it was Alexander J. Cassatt who had first extended the Pennsylvania Railroad lines up to Jersey City in 1871 and developed the whole system of New York ferries. Ten years later, even as New York was surpassing Philadelphia as the nation's leading port, Cassatt not only fended off a rival road's move to control the PRR's access to Jersey City but seized ownership of its rails.

The story of how Cassatt pulled off this coup—guaranteeing PRR access to New York City—came to be famous. In 1881, Cassatt was forty-two and the road's first vice president when John W. Garrett of the Baltimore & Ohio sashayed in to crow over securing complete control of the Philadelphia, Wilmington & Baltimore Railroad, a road whose tracks were used by the PRR to reach New York. The porcine Garrett, whose large sideburns compensated for his balding pate, assured the PRR's cautious president, George B. Roberts, "We are not disposed to disturb your relations with the property and you need not give yourself any uneasiness on that score."

" 'Well," replied Mr. Roberts, in his dry manner, "I did not know that you had progressed so far in your negotiations."

As soon as Garrett left, Roberts rushed out to tell Cassatt the bad news: "Garrett says they've got the PW&B."

"Oh no they haven't," countered Cassatt, who had hoped for the presidency and chafed under Roberts's too-prudent style. Cassatt had no intention of being dependent on the kindness of the B&O to get his company's trains to New Jersey. Cassatt raced to New York City, secured a big block of stock, and offered a better cash-on-the-line deal for the small road. That night, the PRR's board of directors authorized the purchase and the $14,999,999 check written on March 8, 1881, was then the largest single such deal in American business. The framed check hung for years in the offices in Philadelphia. It was this bold vision, decisiveness, and ability to execute the details that had always distinguished the apparently reserved Cassatt. And thus, the Pennsylvania gained "perpetual control of the traffic of the South and Southwest and brought into the family another rich feeder for its New York lines."

Unlike up-from-the-bottom Gilded Age titans like Andrew Carnegie and John D. Rockefeller, the tall, reserved Cassatt was a son of privilege. His father had made a fortune in banking and real estate first in Pittsburgh, then in Philadelphia before he retired to Europe for five years in the early 1850s with his wife and five children. When the family returned to the United States, Aleck (as his family called him), by now fluent in French and German, remained to complete his studies at a *gymnasium* in Darmstadt, Germany. He returned home to earn a B.S. degree in civil engineering in 1859 from the rigorous Rensselaer Polytechnic Institute in Troy, New York. His sister, Mary Cassatt, would eventually return to Paris and spend her life there as an expatriate artist.

After completing his degree at RPI, Cassatt worked briefly for a railroad in Georgia, where he toyed with the idea of starting a vineyard. With the outbreak of the Civil War, he headed north, not to enlist, but to join the Pennsylvania as a lowly rodman and surveyor's assistant for a dollar a day. The railroad played a pivotal role in the Union victory and was beginning its great expansion from Pittsburgh, where the mines and belching black mills and furnaces would soon be churning out stupendous tonnages of coal, iron, and steel. During the war, however, Cassatt was still an underling. For two years, "it was hard work tramping over hard places, struggles with underbrush, swamps, brambles, with heat, with cold, and with the hardships of camp life in desolate places." Young Cassatt discovered he had an enormous capacity for work, detail, and organization as well as a talent for getting along with men of all stations.

One day in April 1866, when Cassatt, then twenty-six, had been promoted to superintendent of motive power and machinery of a PRR subsidiary, the Philadelphia & Erie, Colonel Thomas A. Scott, Cassatt's dashing superior, paid him a visit. When he posed to Cassatt various bookkeeping questions, "Cassatt reeled off the figures," relates Cassatt's biographer. "Scott was amazed at his memory. 'How do you know that?'

Alexander J. Cassatt as a young man.

Scott asked the young manager. 'Oh,' said Cassatt in an off-hand way, 'I think it's a pretty good scheme to go through the books every few days, so that if anything happened to the bookkeeping department I might not be left in the lurch.' " And so young Cassatt's prodigious grasp of detail and his astonishing memory were revealed.

Another longtime manager, who had looked askance at Cassatt's elegant frock coat and silk top hat, was similarly amazed to find that this quiet new officer "seemed to grasp the whole situation in a few hours, and in a day or two after he had gone over the road, he knew more about that than we did who had been there for a year." Equally impressive, Cassatt showed "a natural talent for machinery and when riding over the road he would almost invariably be found handling the [locomotive], while the engineer rested. He was a good 'runner' and made good time."

The ambitious, charismatic Tom Scott was then the railroad's vice president and young Cassatt his foremost protégé. During his meteoric ascent at the Pennsylvania Railroad, Cassatt helped construct its much-envied network in "that important territory between Pittsburgh, the Great Lakes and the Mississippi and Ohio Rivers, while at the same time other leases and acquisitions had extended it into the Monongahela and Allegheny valleys and other coal fields of Pennsylvania." All the while Cassatt was seeking and delivering better, faster, safer, and more standardized rails, locomotives, and cars. A bold and original thinker, Cassatt persuaded his deeply skeptical superiors to adopt young George Westinghouse's air brake, a new and revolutionary invention that allowed the engineer to control the brakes on trains, rather than relying on numerous brakemen leaping from car to car, manually turning uncertain brake wheels. The air brake transformed the industry, allowing ever-longer, heavier trains to operate far more swiftly and safely, while eventually rendering the one-legged brakeman obsolete.

Promoted to a position in the company's manufacturing heart at Altoona, Cassatt now focused on standardizing the PRR's locomotives that were built and tested at the railroad's great shops and roundhouses. While there, Cassatt wooed Lois Buchanan, an Episcopal minister's daughter and the proud niece of former President James Buchanan. Showing his light-hearted side, Cassatt wrote his sweetheart, "You sing divinely, I adore music, you are fond of fried tomatoes, I dote on them! So you see we agree on all important points." Utterly smitten, Cassatt wrote Lois, "I see you now as you sat at the table yesterday evening—your face and hair illuminated into the most beautiful color—the roses in the bouquet could not vie with the beauty of your complexion, and your eyes—the brightest in the world—never was there a more engaging picture."

Cassatt approached his coming wedding and new home with characteristic enthusiasm and care. He made many trips to Philadelphia with Lois to consider home furnishings and wrote her, "I had to send back the paper we selected on Saturday. I found that the blue rubbed off so easily that your dresses would have been spoiled." He worried about where to place his parents' wedding present, an elaborate antique French clock once owned by Marie-Antoinette, and where they might best hang the beautiful mirror from President Buchanan's estate.

By 1873, Tom Scott was poised to become president of the Pennsylvania, and Cassatt had risen to general manager of the lines east of Pitts-

Thomas A. Scott, president of the Pennsylvania Railroad, 1874–1880.

burgh and Erie, the most important part of the sprawling system. In that post, among many other things, he imbued "the road's employees with the discipline and the politeness that have worked to make the road famous the world over. He equipped the track with the block signal system, and introduced the track [water] tank." As the PRR took to boasting in its advertising, "Speed, Comfort, and Safety Guaranteed by Steel Rails, Iron Bridges, Stone Ballast, Double Track, Westinghouse Air Brakes, and THE MOST IMPROVED EQUIPMENT."

The very size and complexity of the railroad corporations was completely new, hard to grasp. A mere twenty-five years earlier, in the 1850s,
one of the nation's greatest industrial enterprises was the Pepperell Manufacturing Company in Biddeford, Maine. These giant textile mills cost
about $300,000 a year to run and employed eight hundred hands. By
1859, those mills were already being dwarfed by nascent railroads, like
the PRR and the Erie, with their operating budgets of millions per year
and tens of thousands of employees. And while mill managers supervised
their eight hundred hands all in one place, "railroad managers had to
make decisions daily controlling the activities of men whom they rarely
talked to or even saw."

Railroads, which reduced the cost of transportation to a fraction of
what had been offered by horses, rivers, and canals, created a truly national and international marketplace, new industries, and a new industrialized world. "In all of the human past," writes historian Martin Albro,
"no event has so swiftly and profoundly changed the basic order of things
as had the coming of the railroad." In twenty-five years American railroads forced a bigger managerial revolution, points out historian Harold C. Livesay, "than had occurred in the previous five centuries. Before
the railroad . . . [it was] experience, instinct and information . . . No such
casual arrangement could obtain on the railroads . . . unreliable, incom-
petent, or insubordinate workers . . . could cause wrecks, damage property, and kill people." In fact, the carnage the railroads wreacked was
unprecedented. In 1897, almost 6,500 Americans died in train accidents, most from being hit while on the tracks, while another 36,731
were injured. Almost 1,700 railroad workers were killed that year, while
27,700 were injured.

By 1877, when the PRR controlled five thousand miles of track,
writes historian Robert V. Bruce, "No private enterprise in the nation's
experience had ever equaled the Pennsylvania's wealth and power . . .
From the Hudson to the Mississippi, from the Great Lakes to the Ohio
and the Potomac, from the prairies of Illinois to the marshes of the Jersey
coast, the rails of the Pennsylvania system stretched shining and unbro-
ken." In 1877, this great road was capitalized at $400 million, earned
profits of $25 million, and employed an army of twenty thousand men.
Lord Bryce had watched in wonder at the American railroad: "When the

master of one of the great Western lines travels towards the Pacific in his palace car, his journey is like a royal progress. Governors of States and Territories bow before him; legislatures receive him in solemn session; cities seek to propitiate him."

Nevertheless, PRR president Tom Scott, tall, elegant, with a distinctive white mane of hair and mutton-chop sideburns, was, by this point, seeking fresh revenues. He decided that the PRR, which carried two-thirds of the refined output flowing from John D. Rockefeller's up-and-coming Standard Oil Company, would itself take up refining the black gold. Scott fatally underestimated Rockefeller, who responded with fury, writing, "Why, it is nothing less than piracy!" Rockefeller retaliated with a boycott that cost the hard-pressed Pennsylvania $1 million. Colonel Scott further cut his workers' wages (as did other struggling roads in these hard times) in the middle of a sweltering July and doubled the length of each train. The PRR's firemen and brakemen in Pittsburgh struck.

Cassatt rushed to the scene, the sole PRR officer intrepid enough to enter the tense city. "I thought that my duty ought to be there, and I got on a train and went." As Cassatt rolled into Union Depot that muggy Friday afternoon of July 20, nine hundred of his road's loaded freight cars were blocked from leaving Pittsburgh by a fast-swelling crowd of PRR strikers, young rowdies, and the merely curious. When the sheriff failed to disperse the strikers, Cassatt, highly visible in a tall white hat and light suit, proposed bringing in militia from Philadelphia.

The next day, six hundred uniformed soldiers arrived. Cassatt, who wanted his freight trains freed, would later relate, "I went down with the troops as far as the western round-house, and went in there with the plan of starting the trains at once, as soon as the tracks were cleared . . . the foreman of the machine shop came to me, and said a riot was going on outside, and I got on the roof." There, only a hundred and fifty yards away in the oppressive afternoon heat, the belligerent mob was taunting the militia, tossing stones, pieces of iron, and other debris, jeering curses.

"They all seemed to be shouting and hallooing," said Cassatt. "There was quite a shower of stones." Cassatt suddenly heard a sickening sound: shots. The shots, he said, were "fired by the crowd, and then I saw the troops fire in return . . . It lasted a minute or two minutes, and I could

see the officers trying to stop the firing, after it commenced." Others said
the militia fired first. However the shooting began, when it was over,
Cassatt could see splayed bloody bodies all about. Twenty were dead,
twenty-nine wounded. The militia in their stained light blue uniforms retreated harum-scarum to the huge roundhouse.

Tom Scott's ill-starred battle with Standard Oil, and Cassatt's ill-
advised call for the militia had ignited Pittsburgh's Great Railroad Riot.
All that long night Cassatt and other leading citizens watched a Pittsburgh mob, now five thousand strong and many armed, commandeer
PRR coal cars, drench the anthracite with oil, toss in burning torches,
and shove these rolling bonfires down the tracks toward the Pennsylvania's Union Depot. Young men giddy on looted liquor donned hoop
skirts and took up the can-can. A great conflagration spread across the
sprawling PRR yards, engulfing the fine terminal and its attached hotel,
devouring both in towering flames. The Philadelphia militia soon faced a
Hobson's choice: emerge from the roundhouse whence they had retreated
or be roasted. By the time the militia escaped, twenty more Pittsburghers
were dead, many wounded, and several soldiers killed.

When the sun rose the next morning through the fire's filthy haze, the
PRR depot and yard had been reduced to a scorched tableau of smoldering ruins and train skeletons. All told, $5 million in prime PRR property
had been incinerated—39 buildings, 104 prized locomotives, 46 passenger cars, and about 1,000 looted freight cars of every kind.

The Great Strike of 1877 spread like wildfire to a hundred towns
coast to coast, unleashing anarchic violence as workers shut down the
nation's most vital rails, coal fields, and factories. The *New York World*
headline blared, "RIOT OR REVOLUTION?" Mobs clashed with militias and
police, leaving one hundred more dead. The *Pittsburgh Leader* declared,
"This may be the beginning of a great civil war in this country, between
labor and capital." Only when the railroads and coal mines grudgingly
made concessions that August did uneasy civil calm return.

When Cassatt wearily returned home to Haverford and his worried
wife and four children, he was covered from head to toe with prickly
heat. The contrast between the cool green fields and trees of his Main
Line estate, Cheswold, and the scorched destruction back in Pittsburgh
must have been grievous. These were nights that he would never forget

The torched Pittsburgh PRR yards after the 1877 Railroad Riot.

and would rarely speak of. He has seen firsthand the violence, the fury
sparked when powerful corporations pushed their men too far, and when
the workers of this new industrialism felt too aggrieved. Nor was that the
end of it.

So great were the PRR's losses that Colonel Scott had capitulated to
Standard Oil by mid-October. Not only did Scott give Standard Oil secret rebates on every barrel of oil the company shipped, he also gave
Rockefeller secret rebates—drawbacks—on every barrel Standard Oil's
competitors shipped. Scott and the PRR bestowed upon Standard Oil

the covert means of establishing a ruthless monopoly. "Through this secret arrangement," wrote *Pearson's Magazine*, Rockefeller "laid the foundation of the greatest fortune in the world, and crushed his competitors
in the oil business with no more pity than a Sioux warrior would show to
his enemy."

As much as Cassatt loved railroads, he saw this new and corrupt system of secret rebates and drawbacks as poisonously unfair. Why should
Standard Oil pay less per barrel than any other oil producer to ship its
product? Much less get a drawback for their rival's barrels? Nor could
Cassatt stand the rancorous and self-serving robber baron tactics that
undermined the proper running of many railroads, enterprises so critical
to the nation's well-being. Why were men like Jay Gould and his ilk allowed to fleece unsuspecting stockholders by manipulating roads?

Even the PRR's own president, the swashbuckling Colonel Scott, had
played fast and loose with certain slippery, self-serving deals. By mid-
1880, hopelessly tarnished by his reckless pursuit of a transcontinental
railroad empire and the disastrous Pittsburgh riots, Scott resigned. His
reputation, fortune, and health were in precipitous decline and he died
within the year. The conservative PRR board of directors, feeling burned
itself, elevated to president the cautious and prudent George B. Roberts. Roberts, an ardent Episcopalian, with such good works under his
belt as the creation of both the Young Men's Christian Association and
the Free Library, built the Church of St. Asaph in Bala near his mansion on the Main Line. Cassatt, only forty, but disappointed at being
passed over and uneasy with a world where powerful corporations bul-
lied and cheated, began to contemplate his departure from the Pennsylvania Railroad.

THREE

"THE ABLEST MAN THIS RAILWAY EVER PRODUCED"

O n December 7, 1881, Katharine Cassatt sat in the soft gray Paris light flooding the family's top-floor apartment near Place Pigalle at 13, avenue Trudaine, finishing up a letter to her older son. She wanted Aleck to retire. In an earlier letter she had inquired, "How do you manage with Roberts as chief? I think you didn't like the idea of serving under him." Her long dark hair elegantly twisted up, she adjusted her wire-rimmed pince-nez, then dipped her pen in the ink and finished her missive, "Don't put off resigning too long—remember the fate of your predecessor." In fact more than one top officer of the Pennsylvania Railroad had died from sheer overwork.

Robert and Katherine Cassatt, Alexander's parents, had settled in Belle Epoque Paris four years earlier to make a home for his younger sister, Mary, a serious artist, and his older sister, Lydia, invalided by Bright's disease. The Paris branch of the family encouraged Aleck to collect, buying him paintings by Monet, Pissarro, and Mary's friend Degas. "When you get these pictures you will probably be the only person in Philada. who owns specimens of either of the masters," crowed his father. "If exhibited at any of your Fine Art Shows they will be sure to attract attention."

When Cassatt, forty-two, retired in September of 1882, his bland resignation letter insisted he wanted only "to have more time at my disposal than anyone occupying so responsible a position in railroad management can command." Cassatt could well afford to retire for he was a self-made millionaire. Within weeks the Cassatts had boarded the *Servia* ("the worst old roller on the sea") and endured a storm-tossed passage en route to Paris. With their children in school, Cassatt and his wife, Lois, traveled down to Rome to see the Forum, the Colosseum, and the cavernous Baths of Caracalla. Back in Paris, Aleck enjoyed horse rides in the Bois de Boulogne and sat at great length for yet another portrait by his sister.

As ambitious and strong-willed as her engineer brother, Mary Cassatt had been a conventional painter of academic genre portraits when, in 1877, she saw the work of Edgar Degas. "It changed my life," she would write later. "I saw art then as I wanted to see it." Mary boldly aligned herself with the Impressionists, becoming the one American to exhibit with them. Lois Cassatt, a society figure, never warmed up to Mary, complaining in an 1880 letter, "The truth is I cannot abide Mary & never will—I can't tell why but there is something to me so utterly obnoxious about that girl . . . She is too self important, & I cannot put up with it."

By late spring the Cassatts were sailing home so Alexander could run his new stock farm, Chesterbrook, a six-hundred-acre pastoral universe in Berwyn of prize sheep, Berkshire pigs, Guernsey cattle, and above all, his championship racehorses. When asked why he had retired, Cassatt replied, "Had to do it. The farm needed me."

For two decades now Alexander Cassatt's life had straddled two very different worlds. In his work, he had been the master of the heavily mechanized, gritty, commerce-centered railroad industry. The state of Pennsylvania was an industrial powerhouse, while Philadelphia, the state's chief port, was home to the Baldwin Locomotive Company, world leader in locomotive and streetcar production, and William Cramp and Sons, dominant in steamships. But the city and the state's crowning industrial glory was the Pennsylvania Railroad.

In the warmer months, when Alexander Cassatt left this high-powered industrial world at the end of each workday, he commuted westward on his road's Main Line to Haverford. At his bucolic demesne, Cheswold, and at the far larger Chesterbrook (with its half-mile track), Cassatt was a passionate gentleman farmer and horse-besotted country squire, an avid breeder and trainer. President of the Radnor Hunt, handsome in riding jacket, jodhpurs, and tall shiny boots, Cassatt hurtled over the hedges atop his favorite steed, Fanny, a Percheron mix. At Cas-

Alexander Cassatt riding at Cheswold,
his Main Line Haverford estate.

satt's tongue-in-cheek Farmer's Club Dinners, the guests ate with tiny
hoes and shovels while chickens and ducks wandered about.

By mid-September of 1883, the Pennsylvania Railroad had lured
Alexander Cassatt back onto its board of directors, and it was from there,
as "director of roads," Cassatt first led his company's obsessive quest to
enter Manhattan. As one PRR officer said of that time, "We listened to
any scheme to get into New York." Otherwise, Cassatt satisfied his love
of railroads and technical challenges by building a small line to Virginia
known as the "Berry Express" to swiftly haul fresh fruits and vegetables
from southern farms to northern tables. In between lapped thirty-six
miles of choppy Chesapeake Bay. Cassatt surmounted this watery obstacle by designing powerful transfer tugs to whisk trains across the waves.

While Cassatt was a diligent member of the PRR board, by and large,
as one journalist wrote, "For seventeen years this big, brainy man endeav-
ored to find satisfaction in European travel, in books and in the organization of a great horse-breeding farm at Berwyn, Pennsylvania, where he
reared famous champions of the turf." Cassatt relished the scheming and
drama of horse racing. "Seagram's . . . only win at Brooklyn," he wrote in
early 1894, "was one of [the] most extraordinary flukes ever seen on a

race course, and he was an exceedingly nasty horse." Over in Paris, his family followed his exploits with high-spirited glee. Wrote Mary, "Mother seizes the paper the minute it arrives & wont give it up until she has read all about your horses," and then later, "On Tuesday evening the paper containing the news of the 'Bard's' victories reached us . . . we all congratulate you." When the New Jersey racing scene went crooked, Cassatt took to breeding hackney carriage horses with the same passion.

In 1888, Alexander Cassatt had purchased a handsome townhouse-mansion at 202 West Rittenhouse Square with a picture gallery in the rear, so his wife and daughters could better lead Philadelphia society. One winter the family toured Egypt, awed by ancient wonders. Cassatt bought a yacht, the *Enterprise* (reportedly for more than $500,000), "elaborately fitted," its salon "furnished in bird's eye maple and walnut with a frescoed ceiling." The years slipped pleasantly past for this devoted paterfamilias, though his health, despite his outdoor life and athleticism, was not perfect as he ended his fifth decade. He suffered a mild heart attack in 1897. By Christmas, Lois wrote one of their daughters, "I am glad to say he seems on the mend now. He has just walked around the square once. Dr. Sinkler gave him some capsules which seem to act like a charm."

When PRR President George Roberts died of a heart attack in his Bala Cynwyd estate in 1897, his greatest accomplishment was the completion of Philadelphia's Broad Street Station, a red-brick and terra-cotta Moorish-Gothic castle. The station brought sixteen tracks right into the city's heart, a feat made possible only by building a "massive elevated stone causeway . . . cutting the city in two between Market and Arch." It was called the "Chinese Wall." The PRR's corporate offices occupied the station's second floor and looked out at Philadelphia's rococo City Hall, a French Second Empire granite and marble pile thirty years (and many corrupt contracts) in the making. On the other side of City Hall was the terminal of the Reading Railroad, a major coal road seemingly always in receivership.

In the wake of Roberts's death, vice president Frank Thomson, a friend of Cassatt, took over. He was a solid choice, but as the *New York Journal American*, not known to mince words, commented, "He is by no means a genius." And indeed, Thomson found the railroad's

The PRR's Philadelphia Broad Street Station. Note half-built City Hall tower.

problems crushing. The American economy had finally recovered and now the fast-rising tide of Pennsylvania's industrial output—whether Carnegie steel, Frick coke, or Westinghouse products—swamped the PRR. Pittsburgh was a filthy Vesuvius of roaring capitalism, its putrid black sky proof of its "first place in the world's production of iron, steel, tin-plate, iron and steel pipes, steel cars, air-brakes, electrical machinery, brass, coal and coke, fire-brick, plate-glass, window-glass, tumblers, tableware, petroleum, pickles, white lead, and cork . . . It originates a tonnage of freight nearly five times as great as that of either New York or London; and greater than that of New York, Chicago, and Philadelphia combined."

The Pennsylvania Railroad was overwhelmed. And yet even as it suffered from a shortage of cars and congested tracks, it was finding itself blackmailed into giving secret and illegal rebates to its most important customers. These extorted discounts enfeebled all the nation's railroads and left smaller merchants, shippers, and farmers paying unfair higher rates for freight. The Pennsylvania's conservative board of directors (of which Cassatt had long been a restless member) bemoaned that "disaster was imminent . . . none but the strongest and best equipped lines could earn a profit." The PRR was earning, to its deep dismay, the lowest ton-mile rate in its history.

Between the avalanche of industrial wealth and the intractable evil of secret rebates, Thomson lasted but two years, dying suddenly in mid-1899 at age fifty-eight. Yet another PRR president had died in office.

And so on a lovely day, June 8, 1899, shortly after Thomson's death, a sober-suited delegation from the railroad's board journeyed out on their Main Line to Haverford. Under a glorious bowl of blue sky they drove past the clipped emerald greensward of the Merion Cricket Club (of which Cassatt was president), and onto a meandering drive past a flock

Frank Thomson (middle), president of the Pennsylvania Railroad, 1897–1899, died in office.

of Shropshire sheep cropping buttercups. Nestled among the trees stood Cheswold, Cassatt's charmingly gabled fieldstone mansion, now completely ivy-covered with gaily striped awnings at all the windows. Cassatt, the master of this country paradise, was out in the fields exercising one of his beloved horses. The men redirected their carriages down another road and spied him.

Cassatt stood in the June sunshine, perhaps thinking of his very good life as a country gentleman, knowing as well as anyone present the almost insuperable problems bedeviling the railroad. His fellow board members got down from their carriages, and offered him their greatest honor, the presidency of the Pennsylvania Railroad. He paused and then responded quietly that yes, he would be very interested. But, Cassatt warned them, if he became president, he would pursue a swift and monumental expansion. He would require a completely free, almost dictatorial, hand to proceed as boldly as he felt necessary. The conservative board, attired in their dark frock coats, heard his hard-edged determination to do big things and murmured uncertainly as they departed. Agnes Repplier, a Philadelphia essayist of that time, deemed her hometown "a droll city . . . And tepid. Oh, so tepid." The board was not certain about such boldness.

But ultimately, the board of directors capitulated, for no other man could possibly match Cassatt's engineering experience and prodigious knowledge of the complex PRR system or his steely nerve. One railroad president declared at the time, "No person understands better than he the financial conditions and policy of the Pennsylvania Railroad, and no man is more familiar with the details of the management. Why there is scarcely a man of any consequence in the employ of the company that Cassatt does not know personally." Within the PRR, he was widely regarded as "the ablest man this Railway ever produced," a compliment of the highest order, for no railroad was near the equal of the fabled Pennsylvania (even in its current distress), hailed by *American Architect* as "the most intelligent and thoughtful railway corporation in the world."

And so it was in late spring 1899 that Cassatt found himself president of the Pennsylvania Railroad. And, after all these decades, he was dreaming seriously of spanning the Hudson River.

FOUR

"THE NORTH RIVER
BRIDGE MATTER"

Within months of Alexander Cassatt's ascension to the PRR presidency, Gustav Lindenthal, who had moved to New York and established an office downtown at 45 Cedar Street, was hoping to entice this corporate Caesar into building his long-aborning North River Bridge. "Permit me to suggest again," wrote Lindenthal to Cassatt in late November 1899, "that the Pa. R. R. Co. should control the North River Bridge Co. . . . It is certain that another charter of equal potentiality will never be granted by the Congress of the United States." A colossal yet graceful all-steel railroad arch suspension bridge, Lindenthal's proposed masterpiece would vault airily across the mile-wide Hudson from Hoboken to West Twenty-third Street, its three decks of trains and carriages traveling high above the river's powerful tidal waters, allowing easy passage of towering warships and oceangoing liners.

When Cassatt expressed very serious interest, Lindenthal was delighted, but after all these years, understandably impatient. By the following summer, he began pressing for definitive action. Knowing that Cassatt was about to sail for Europe, Lindenthal had written him on July 11, 1900: "Your decision as to the position of the Penna. R.R. Co. in the North River Bridge matter is of great and immediate importance in the negotiations with the other railroads, and I fear that if more time is lost difficulties will arise with the charter." If built as Lindenthal intended, the behemoth North River Bridge would dwarf and eclipse every other bridge extant or in the works. It would reign as one of the supreme wonders of the industrial world.

Scientific American marveled at its sheer enormity: "The anchorages would be half as large as the capitol at Washington, and each would contain fifty per cent more masonry than the largest of the Egyptian pyramids. The cables would be four feet in diameter (the Brooklyn Bridge cables are fifteen inches), and the towers would be 500 feet high." *Engineering News* opined, "The grandeur of the project is almost appalling, creating at first sight a natural feeling that the chance for its construction must be small. But this is an age of great enterprises and superabundant capital."

By 1900, the North River Bridge project had a long and convoluted history of redesigns and resitings, dating back to 1884 when Gustav Lindenthal had first met PRR engineer Samuel Rea, a tall, stolid man with a thick brush of brown hair and a matching bristling mustache. From the start, Rea championed Lindenthal's bridge, seeing Lindenthal as a kindred spirit, a self-made man and engineer yearning to make a big mark on the world. "To propose a bridge with a span almost twice that of the Brooklyn Bridge was so unprecedented," Rea wrote, "and would have involved so much money." He and a number of prominent financiers joined the board of the North River Bridge Company as directors. While Rea had been steadily advancing up the PRR's corporate ladder as an engineer, he and his brother Thomas had established Rea Brothers & Company, a Pittsburgh banking and brokerage firm.

Having lost his father at age thirteen, Rea labored in local farms around Hollidaysburg, Pennsylvania, before joining the great enterprise of his day—the railroads—at age sixteen. Like the far better educated Cassatt, Rea launched his Pennsylvania Railroad career at the bottom as a rodman and chainman, slogging across hill and dale for seasoned engineers surveying new routes. However, lacking a powerful mentor, Rea was twice laid off in the 1870s, and rose slowly as an engineer and manager. Though Rea had finally achieved the hallowed precincts of PRR corporate headquarters in 1888, he resigned in frustration in 1889 and accepted the more exalted positions of vice president of the Baltimore & Ohio's Maryland Central Railway and chief engineer of the Baltimore Belt Railroad. There he helped plan complex urban subaqueous railroad tunnels and their necessary adjunct—powerful electric locomotives. The asphyxiating smoke and fumes from coal-burning locomotives made them impracticable for travel through long, unventilated tunnels.

"In 1891," Rea later wrote, "I resigned my position in Baltimore on account of ill health, and on the same day I had a message from Mr. [George] Roberts asking me to refrain from committing myself to any professional engagement until he could see me. This was exceedingly gratifying to me, as well as a surprise, for when I left the Pennsylvania Railroad I felt it unlikely that I would ever be invited to return to the service." Having lost him to a rival road, Rea's old superiors wanted him back, a signal tribute to his stellar qualities—his brains, his quiet thoroughness, his easy way with his men, his voracious intellectual curiosity

Samuel Rea as a young PRR employee.

and technical brilliance. What Cassatt particularly liked was Rea's hustle. Rea did big things right, without fuss or folderol. And like Cassatt, Samuel Rea was a reader, a curious man who wanted to know what went on in the world beyond engineering. They were both also, unusual for their kind, Democrats.

On May 25, 1892, Rea, now rested and recovered from his health problems, met with PRR president George Roberts at the Broad Street Station offices, where one could hear and feel the hiss and rumble of the powerful steam locomotives in the gigantic train shed below. Rea would work for Roberts himself. His new bailiwick was equally flattering: the study of various large and vexing engineering problems, above all that perennial "bitter trial"—how best to enter New York. As Rea was about to sail to England on vacation, President Roberts asked him to study London's rapid transit tunnels, especially those under the Thames River.

Soon after Rea returned from England in the fall of 1892, Roberts told him, "I would be glad to have you see Mr. Cassatt, who has had more or less to do with the question of reaching New York, and take up this subject in its broadest sense." He, President Roberts, and Cassatt began spending hours around the big wooden conference table discussing five possible solutions. "The railroad situation at New York is unique: a parallel does not exist," Samuel Rea once explained. "Here is a great seaport . . . of commercial importance second to none in the world, separated by navigable waters of a river from all the rail transportation systems of its country, with but a single exception, namely the New York Central system." Moreover, Rea had warned Roberts back then, "This is not a simple task." Entering Gotham would be "one of the World's great undertakings—on a parity with such works as the Suez and Manchester Ship Canals, and of equal, if not greater importance."

Roberts, ever one for the tried and true, favored a plan already in use for New England-bound trains, which were floated across the harbor to be put on the tracks of the New Haven line. He envisioned a "floating service for trains" that would run hundreds of daily passenger trains arriving at Exchange Place straight onto swift steamships that would ferry them across the Hudson to the "foot of West Thirty-fourth Street, where, with transfer bridges, the cars would be placed on tracks that would run in a tunnel under Thirty-fourth Street to a point near Ninth Avenue and turn in under the Blind Asylum property . . . where a suitable station was to be located." Roberts could persuade no others to like this plan.

George B. Roberts, president of the Pennsylvania Railroad, 1880–1897, died in office.

A second option: resurrecting and finishing Haskins's moribund tunnel, intending to operate cable-drawn trolleys from Jersey City into a lower Manhattan terminal and elevated stop. Opinion here was also lukewarm. If the tunnel could be finished—a big if—it was still inadequate to the problem. The third option also involved trolley tunnels, but new ones from Jersey City to Cortlandt Street and Maiden Lane, and under the East River to Flatbush Avenue. These evoked more enthusiasm. Rea and Charles Jacobs, a British engineer, even made surveys, studies, and estimates, "but only for small-sized cars doing a local suburban business." Cassatt was opposed, for weary train passengers still had to drag themselves and their luggage to the trolley.

Cassatt had championed a fourth solution, a convoluted "back door" entry into Manhattan via "a tunnel under the 'Narrows' and thence across Brooklyn via the Bay Ridge route, and by bridge across the East River to a terminus at Thirty-eighth Street and Madison Avenue." But the plan's advantages were offset by three serious flaws: it required steam locomotives to get through the tunnel, it would not serve the PRR's many New Jersey commuters, and it added ten miles to the trip. Only Cassatt was enthused.

The fifth possibility was, of course, Gustav Lindenthal's North River Bridge. Rea argued in favor, asserting, "This . . . solves the problem. It would furnish an ideal terminus in the heart of our greatest city for passenger traffic, and in addition would develop freight facilities of inestimable value." Rea had calculated that the North River Bridge itself would cost $27 million, and the station, hotel, and warehouses another $15.5 million. With right-of-ways and other necessary real estate, the full tab was a breathtaking $100 million. Of course, the federally chartered bridge would be (in fact, had to be) shared with all other lines, and they in turn would certainly help finance it and pay to use it. But the Pennsy, the "Standard Railroad of America," would have to lead.

Now, Rea exhorted his colleagues, "No half-way solution should be attempted by the Pennsylvania Railroad Company. It should ultimately go into New York in such a manner as to answer the needs of the Company for the next half century at least, and on an equality with, if not on a more elaborate scale, than the New York Central & Hudson River Railroad." Samuel Rea was making an impassioned call to corporate arms. Were they to continue letting the Vanderbilts best them? Were they to shy away from this monumental challenge? Before they could act, the Panic of 1893 struck and industrial depression ended all such ambitious enterprises.

And so in mid-1899, when Cassatt dutifully emerged from his early retirement to take charge of the beleaguered Pennsylvania Railroad, Lindenthal's vast suspension bridge still seemed the best answer to the PRR's long quest to enter Gotham. Not only was the bridge federally chartered, a status confirmed by the U.S. Supreme Court, the Army Corps of Engineers had bestowed its blessing and Lindenthal had redesigned it yet further to handle the ever-increasing volumes of traffic. The design for the North River Bridge now featured fourteen train and trolley tracks as well as numerous pedestrian and carriage lanes soaring high above the mile-wide North River. It would touch down in Manhattan and wend its way to a gigantic and glorious Union Station at Thirty-fifth Street and Seventh Avenue, there to intersect with the lines of the elevated and trolleys. And the era's powerful steam locomotives with all their belching coal smoke and cinders could easily enter Manhattan via the large open-air bridge. On October 24, 1899, Samuel Rea, who was actively working with Lindenthal on financing the bridge, wrote Cassatt wondering, "Did you make an engagement in New York this week with Mr. J. P. Morgan?"

For almost three irksome decades, day and night, through rain, shine, sleet, and snow, the Pennsylvania Railroad's ferryboats had plied the Hudson. To handle the ever-growing multitudes coming and going between Manhattan and the rest of the world, the PRR had added in 1897 another ferry stop at West Twenty-third Street, while an entirely separate PRR fleet known as The Annex boats served downtown Brooklyn. Now, when Cassatt boarded his ferries, and they chugged forth into the luminous space of river and sky, he could look north and envision Lindenthal's North River Bridge, imagining a few years hence his beautiful PRR trains steaming elegantly into Manhattan at last.

Ferryboat plying the North River between New Jersey and Manhattan.

On September 12, 1900, the PRR's directors formally committed their railroad to this monumental project. The PRR made no public announcement, but guaranteed Lindenthal in writing that 200,000 of their passenger cars (at four dollars each) would roll across the Hudson each year on his bridge. This had been a hard-won triumph, but would not be enough revenue. Lindenthal calculated that when his North River Bridge first opened, it could handle 900,000 "passenger coaches, baggage and express cars, dining, parlor and sleeping cars, but not counting mail cars."

To obtain financing, Lindenthal required firm commitments from each railroad, especially the major trunk lines. Even the Vanderbilts would come in as partners, for the Grand Central Terminal was close to its capacity, and a second Manhattan depot could well serve their West Shore line. And so, Alexander Cassatt and the PRR finally had at hand a definite plan for entry into Gotham. They had only to convince the other roads that it was in their best collective interest to back the bridge and enable all to steam into Manhattan in monumental style.

But before Alexander Cassatt could help build the North River Bridge, he had to stave up the tottering finances of his powerful road. This meant doing what no other American railroad monarch had ever yet managed: killing illegal railroad rebates, for decades the bane of the business world, "a thing whose existence was half admitted, half denied, a kind of ghostly economic terror." Moaned the PRR's board, "The struggle for competitive traffic had forced down the actual rates paid by shippers to a point where none but the strongest and best equipped lines could earn a living profit . . . Agreements to maintain rates were not worth the paper upon which they were written."

The railroad rebate had distorted the whole economy to the benefit of the big, the strong, and the bullying. Consequently, reported one associate, "Cassatt had not occupied the President's chair an hour," back in June of 1899, when "he startled the railroad and financial world by his unheralded call on Mr. [William K.] Vanderbilt at the Grand Central Station, and in a short conference evolved his 'community of interest' plan." It was a hugely audacious and expensive strategy, involving a concerted alliance with the Vanderbilts, the PRR's biggest rival, and their New York

Central, equally beleaguered by secret rebates. To stop the weaker roads and their pusillanimous yielding on rebates, declared Cassatt, "Why, simply buy a dominating interest in them."

And so the Vanderbilts and the PRR each spent staggering sums—the PRR's part was $110 million at a time when its net profits were $333 million—to secure dominance in the Baltimore & Ohio Railroad, as well as a handful of smaller lines. With their own newly appointed men instilling backbone on these boards, in the spring of 1900 Cassatt announced in his low-key manner, but with great relish and surprising certainty, that the Pennsylvania Railroad's published public rates were the now real rates. For everyone. The question was, could Cassatt and the PRR outlaw rebates when for two decades all others had failed?

The PRR's biggest and most difficult customer *and* its most persistent and entitled rebater was none other than Andrew Carnegie, the brilliant, diminutive Steel King. Carnegie always cast himself as a public-spirited man superior to other run-of-the-mill millionaires. Yet this cutthroat genius of capitalism had for years ruthlessly (and illegally) played one road against the other for sub rosa rock-bottom rates and rebates. One of Carnegie's old employees jeeringly reminded his longtime boss of this darker, predatory side, for "through the great volume of your business, you were able to take railroads by the throat and to compel them to secretly violate state and federal laws—to *steal* vast millions of money from their stockholders and dump them into your Carnegie Steel Co. Ltd. . . . you were the 'chiefest rebater' of the Penna. R.R. Co. . . . [Why don't you] frankly acknowledge that you have been the Prince of Grafters and the King of Rebaters as well as the Steel King and the Emperor of Libraries?"

By 1900 Carnegie, whose state-of-the-art mills spread across Pennsylvania's grimy riverfronts produced more steel than all of England, was ostensibly retired to Skibo, his Scottish Highlands estate, and a life of golf and salmon fishing. Nonetheless he was in a choleric state about Cassatt's new No Rebate policy. On October 9, Carnegie dictated a letter to young Charles Schwab, his hand-chosen successor as president of Carnegie Steel: "Mr. Cassat's [sic] action is the most serious blow we have ever received, and it is a life and death struggle . . . He is a clever, able man, has a versatile brain. He has hastily assumed that he could

Gustav Lindenthal's North River Bridge design in 1890.

make what rates he pleased through combination with competing lines. That the public will not stand." And so the battle was joined.

Alexander Cassatt was determined to destroy the entrenched system of spectral rebates. Above all, the PRR desperately needed that lost revenue and more to begin the monumental revamping, rebuilding, and expanding of its gridlocked system. Until then on his proud but beset road, "Overworked engines failed every day by dozens on the lines. Yards were piled with freight that should be moving to its destination. The main tracks were not sufficient to accommodate the traffic, and the equipment not enough to carry it. Shippers were raising angry voices from one end of the system to another." Only when the lost revenues were recovered could Cassatt make real his longtime dream, the building of the New York extension via the North River Bridge.

But some of Cassatt's motivation was more personal. As the twentieth century dawned, Cassatt possessed the prize of power that had eluded him as a younger man. He had that rare opportunity—a second chance in life to rectify a terrible wrong. After those searing days of the Pittsburgh Railroad Riots of 1877 and the PRR's subsequent capitulation to John D. Rockefeller, Cassatt had come to appreciate how terrible corporate power could be when carelessly or wrongly wielded. Afterwards, he had been the only railroad official to willingly testify at government inquiries into Standard Oil's predatory chicaneries. At a time when more and more of the middle class feared the rising power of the trusts and monopolies, Cassatt felt it his duty to use his newfound power to conduct business honorably. Though he generally shunned the press, he had helped the star journalist of *McClure's Magazine*, Ida Tarbell, understand how Standard Oil unfairly destroyed its early rivals. The conflict between labor and capital was as bitter as ever, but Cassatt, whose impatience in Pittsburgh had contributed to the deadly riots, now tried to be fair to his own employees, sharing the road's wealth by establishing a pension plan for workers retiring at age seventy, and a Relief Fund. All employees making less than two hundred dollars a month were given two 10 percent raises.

None of this interested Andrew Carnegie, who was hell-bent on retrieving his rebates. On the last day of 1900, the Steel King sat in his Fifth Avenue townhouse at West Fifty-first Street (a wedding present to his much younger wife) writing Cassatt a hectoring letter: "You have returned to harness after years of recreation and rushed into a policy which, being unsound, as I believe, you will soon abandon . . . there will be a return to the rates which your predecessors thought it wise to give us East and West." Carnegie, who always adored the limelight (he had a special drawer in his rolltop desk where his secretary slipped in favorable articles about him), attacked Cassatt in the most high-profile way in the New York and Pittsburgh papers: "Carnegie Says Railroad Rates Are Outrageous," and the triumphant but untrue, "Carnegie Forces Pennsylvania to Reduce Rates."

Fortunately for Cassatt, Andrew Carnegie was not only engaged in a high-profile war with the PRR, he was also—in between games of golf, his latest passion—mobilizing against Wall Street financier J. P. Morgan over steel. The ferocious Morgan, with his plutocrat's large belly and his nose permanently inflamed by acne rosacea, had angered Carnegie by cobbling together a small steel tube trust. No one doubted that Carnegie could obliterate Morgan's firms with better, cheaper tubes. Morgan chomped on his Cuban cigar and complained, "Carnegie is going to demoralize railroads just as he demoralized steel."

Nor did Charles Schwab, thirty-eight, the handsome strapping president of Carnegie Steel, harbor much zest for Carnegie's warlike machinations. He was ready to enjoy his millions. As 1901 dawned, he and Morgan combined most of the nation's iron ore deposits and steelmakers into one giant trust, U.S. Steel, the world's first billion-dollar corporation. J. P. Morgan bought out Carnegie for $480 million in a deal that stunned and unsettled the nation. Morgan's billion dollars "represented a twenty-fifth of the whole national wealth, more than the combined dividends from the railroads for eight years, and more than the value of all the wheat and barley and cheese and gold and silver and coal produced in 1900 in America." Few had dreamed that even J. P. Morgan had the wherewithal to pull off such a coup. The historian Henry Adams quipped to his friends, "Pierpont Morgan is apparently trying to swallow the sun."

Morgan's pact with Carnegie delivered Cassatt and the PRR a most felicitous peace, for in dispatching the Steel King to golf and good works, Morgan had ended Carnegie's war to retain his illegal railroad rebates.

With great pride President Cassatt would tell a reporter, "We have trampled out the secret rate and rebate system, which was not only ruining the railroads, but also made for unequal and unfair conditions of business in America." And so, with the combative Andrew Carnegie bought out, the rebates "trampled," and the PRR's coffers filling nicely, in the early summer of 1901 Alexander Cassatt was firmly focused on building Gustav Lindenthal's gargantuan North River Bridge.

FIVE

"A SEVERE DISAPPOINTMENT"

A s Gotham suffered through the miserable days of a "hot wave" in late June 1901, Alexander Cassatt busied himself with financiers and railroad officers, pushing forward the North River Bridge project. "The Pennsylvania Railroad," confided one anonymous financier to the *New York Times*, "is bound to have this bridge built. It has decided that it needs an entrance, and it is going to have it. It is not satisfied with its terminals in Jersey, and it is not going to stay there. It has made up its mind to this effect, and when the Pennsylvania undertakes to do a thing it always does it." Cassatt believed that persuading the other roads would not be too difficult. In the previous year, ninety million passengers crossed from New Jersey on ferries, almost forty million of those on the PRR's boats. And the city and nation were still growing like Topsy. President William McKinley had been handily reelected and the country was riding a wave of unprecedented prosperity.

By Monday July 1, the "hot wave" had become so scorching and relentless it had vanquished Manhattan's legendary energy. At dawn in the tenement districts, entire families slept inert on every fire escape and sidewalk. The greensward of the Battery, with its tiny harbor breezes, was solid with splayed, prostrate figures, reminiscent of a Civil War battlefield. By two o'clock that afternoon the thermometer in Herald Square hit a record-breaking 108 degrees, and heat "devils" shimmered

up from the broiling cobblestones. By Monday night, eighty-seven people had died from the heat. On the streets, dead horses gathered flies.
By Tuesday morning, the "heat was so intense," reported the *New York
Times*, "that the entire city was as if paralyzed. Many big companies and
wholesale houses closed their doors as early as noon." That night another
two hundred souls died. Finally, the next day, violent thunderstorms
swept through Gotham, refreshing the spent city with its torrents, followed by a steady drizzle that cooled the night.

Cassatt and Gustav Lindenthal resumed their meetings and by early
July 1901, the *Wall Street Journal* was reporting that "all the trunk lines
terminating in New Jersey, opposite New York City" were considering
the North River Bridge into Manhattan. It was a complete surprise to
the public that the Vanderbilts would participate. In fact, the sums to be
raised were so gigantic the wealthy Vanderbilts were critical. Lindenthal
wrote Cassatt in one memo that "the financial syndicate [would include]
the names of Vanderbilt and his followers. Your Company and the New
York Central taking the lead, it was expected that all the other railroads
in New Jersey would willingly come in with their quota of cars under the
proposed agreement."

As was its conservative wont, the PRR had as yet made no formal
public announcement that it was committed to Gustav Lindenthal's
bridge, but all kinds of rumors bubbled up as Alexander Cassatt pressed
forward at full speed. The North River Bridge into Gotham was shaping
up to be the nation's largest and most important civil engineering project
since the building of the transcontinental railroads. Moreover, Alexander
Cassatt's vision had grown even more ambitious. The previous May, the
PRR had beaten out the Vanderbilts to acquire the Long Island Rail
Road, a small commuter road active mainly in the summer. Cassatt coveted its large rail yards on the New York waterfront and viewed the LIRR
as a key link in the PRR's eventual all-important access to New England.
Cassatt also intended to bring the LIRR lines physically into Manhattan
and the LIRR's previous president, Austin Corbin, had had plans underway for tunnels under the East River, until his sudden death in mid-1896
in a carriage accident at Newport.

His successor, the handsome, young William H. Baldwin Jr., was
equally ambitious. President Charles Francis Adams had hired Baldwin
straight out of Harvard in 1886 to work with him at the Union Pacific,

a railroad which was then "in bad repute, loaded with obligations, [and] odious in the territory it served." In a business peopled largely by what Adams called "a coarse, realistic, bargaining crowd," Baldwin stood out. Not only was he a "practical" businessman who loved to make money, "he was the soul of chivalry, of honor, and of moral courage." He looked the part, with a clear mien, a high-domed forehead, deep-set, intense dark eyes, a thick moustache, and dimpled chin. Men marveled at Baldwin's combination of manly charm and warmth, railroad savvy, and sterling personal qualities.

So swift was Baldwin's rise in the rough-and-tumble railway profession that he became president of the Long Island Rail Road when just thirty-three. Already, in his brief tenure he had sufficiently improved the road that the trip into Manhattan (or to the road's ferry terminal into Manhattan) had been shortened by a half hour. Baldwin was also pushing forward the plans to build tunnels under the East River from the LIRR's Flatbush station in Brooklyn to New York's East Side. He was more than delighted to find that the mighty PRR coveted the LIRR and its extensive holdings along the East River, where "freight depots, yards for carload deliveries, and coal and lumber yards can be conveniently located." Yet even under Baldwin, the LIRR still lagged far behind PRR standards.

When the PRR added the LIRR to its empire in May 1900, Cassatt gained in Baldwin an invaluable and well-connected ally. Adams once observed that Baldwin had "quite a remarkable faculty for getting on with men." So much so that Baldwin was already a Gotham insider, well versed in the complexities of New York's local power brokers, its grafting bosses, and politicos. But he was also that most curious of beings—an influential railroad executive who was also a passionate reformer. His few years running roads in the Jim Crow South opened his sympathetic eyes to the wretched plight of American blacks. In 1895, just before coming to the LIRR, Baldwin had joined the board of Booker T. Washington's Tuskegee Institute, which offered Negroes a practical college education. Since then, Baldwin and Washington had become quite close as Baldwin dedicated himself to this difficult and wrenching cause. A typical Baldwin missive to the black leader in the fall of 1899 declared, "I just want to write a line to tell you that my mind and my heart are constantly on you and your work."

Thus, it was hardly surprising that William Baldwin had also become swept up in 1900 in the great Gotham reform movement to somehow root out the worst excesses of a vast and proliferating web of Tammany-protected prostitution (the "social evil" as it was genteelly termed). Harlotry was as old as the hills, but Tammany Hall's tightly controlled police force was so actively promoting and protecting the oldest profession that prostitutes were infesting and corrupting new neighborhoods with impunity. "That an army of strumpets," complained one reformer, "should be allowed to carry on the calling in the midst of a defense-less home-life thronged with children, was a thing too odious for any community to tolerate."

By November 1900, Baldwin had emerged as the activist head of the Committee of Fifteen, a high-profile group of influential men determined to force some kind of exposé and action. Many people admired Baldwin, who showed no "fear of ridicule, no dread of interference with his own business interests, no thought of possible adverse criticism . . . He knew not only how to initiate and to decide, but how to listen, to compare, and to conclude." Predictably, there was far more press in 1901 about Baldwin, the doings of the Committee of Fifteen, and its pursuit of vice than there was about the Pennsylvania Railroad and its intended entry into Gotham.

What Cassatt, Samuel Rea, and Lindenthal now began to learn—to their deepest dismay—was that the other railroads were *not* willingly signing on to their grand plan. George F. Baer, president of the Central Railroad of New Jersey, pointed out that his road's net annual profit was only $214,000. "You see how impossible it is for the Central to undertake to pay $800,000 a year [its share], or even one-third that sum, to the Bridge Company . . . Whatever advantage this bridge might be to companies having a long haul, it is absolutely impracticable for this company." As for the other companies, while the Erie and the Baltimore & Ohio "appear willing to use the bridge on some terms," it turned out that it would not bother them so very much if their passengers still had to herd on to ferries to reach New York. After all, had they not done this for years to no great ill effect?

The Vanderbilts, who had been inclined to join in when universal participation looked like a sure thing, now balked. Indeed, why should the Vanderbilts put up tens of millions of precious capital to help their greatest rival steam right into the heart of Gotham and all its riches? It made more sense to sabotage the enterprise to their own lasting advantage, and they duly informed Cassatt of their opposition. As for the other major lines marooned on the Jersey shore across from Manhattan—the Erie, the Delaware, Lackawanna & Western, the Lehigh Valley, the New Jersey Central, the New York, Susquehanna & Western—they seemed convinced that Cassatt and the PRR might well build the federally chartered bridge, that by law had to be open to all roads, with them or without them, so why should they pay a penny in advance? As a highly irate Samuel Rea explained, "If the Pennsylvania R.R. desired to secure such a terminus it would alone have to stand behind it financially, and, when consummated, admit others to its advantages who had not aided in its promotion. This was unfair."

In early July 1901, Cassatt, soon to sail for Europe, once more wired the president of the New Haven line, "I should very much like to know before leaving whether you have come to any conclusion as to joining us in the building of the bridge lines, so that instruction may be given to acquire the charter." The New Haven was no more inclined to help the PRR than was the New York Central. "Matters were, therefore, at a standstill," wrote Rea. "The inability to carry out the bridge scheme was a severe disappointment." To say the least.

SIX

"IT MIGHT OFFER
THE SOLUTION"

O n Wednesday July 10, 1901, the heat was already building when Alexander Cassatt, his wife, Lois, and granddaughter, young Lois, made their way through yelling teamsters and newsboys to board the S.S. *Cymric* at the White Star Line's West Side Pier 48, departing Gotham at noon for Liverpool. Once again, Cassatt found the PRR stymied, its North River Bridge project blocked. The ragged newsboys were hollering about the latest Tammany imbroglio, the "Park Pay Chair Riots." The day before, Tammany's park commissioner had tried to impose the longtime European custom of making people pay for the right to sit in park chairs. But this was democratic Gotham in the grip of yet another "hot wave" and when the fee collectors fanned out amidst the cool sylvan lawns and towering shade trees of Madison Square Park, they were met by vehement resistance, fisticuffs, and violent melees.

Explained the *New York Times*, "To the great majority of visitors to the parks, and not merely to the hoodlums and the tramps, it was intolerable that a distinction should be made . . . between 'first-class' and 'second-class.' " Worse was the dark suspicion that it was yet another outrageous Tammany rake-off, charging weary citizens to sit down in their own parks! In the name of democracy and civic peace, the pay chairs became free to all that very day.

When the Cassatts steamed gratefully out of New York harbor and the heat to "cross the pond," they were sophisticated veterans of what had become a great Gilded Age ritual, the mass migration of Americans to the cultured precincts of England and Europe for leisurely tours. The Cassatts lingered for a week at Claridge's in London, and then crossed the Channel to Paris to visit Mary, now an established artist with a talent for capturing quiet domestic moments. Both their parents and Lydia were dead, and Mary spent her summers at her château, Beaufresne, in Mesnil-Theribus, fifty miles northwest of Paris. She gardened and painted, attended by her maid, her little Belgian Griffon, and occasional guests.

Alexander and Lois Cassatt stayed as usual at the luxurious Hôtel Castiglione in the elegant *quartier* just south of the Place Vendôme. Years earlier, there had been an unfortunate episode of a James Whistler portrait of Lois. Mary liked it, writing at the time, "After all it is a work of Art, & as young [John Singer] Sargent said to Mother this afternoon, it is a good thing to have a portrait by Whistler in the family." Moreover, she reminded, "I recommended Renoir, but neither you nor Aleck liked what

The Gare du Quai d'Orsay.

you saw of his; I think Whistler's portrait very fine." Lois did not, and this disagreement was yet another strain in their relationship.

For Alexander, this European trip was both business and pleasure, for he was meeting with bankers in France and Germany to discuss raising the many tens of millions in loans the Pennsylvania Railroad needed for its vast expansion. After a sojourn to Hamburg, the Cassatts returned on Tuesday August 20 to Paris and the Hôtel Castiglione. Each day, Cassatt's assistant, William Patton, dispatched a brief cable from Broad Street Station, advising his boss of conditions back home. In early August, Patton wired a perfunctory, "Business very good on road." In mid-August, he reported a steel strike had started in Pittsburgh, but reassured, "No disorder; strike not spreading."

In that third week of August, the PRR president heard a knock at the door of his Paris hotel suite. He was handed a cable from Samuel Rea, who was as frustrated as Cassatt over the North River Bridge project. "The inability to carry out the bridge scheme was a severe disappointment to me as well as to its other advocates," Rea would recall many years later, "because at that time I believed it was the best proposition, but I realized that if we were ever to build into New York we must do it alone, as we could not get a bridge scheme authorized for any one company." Rea had had a new idea. In his telegram, he urged Cassatt to inspect the new Quai d'Orsay Station on the Seine across the river from the Tuileries and the Louvre. This railway terminal, opened in time for the great Paris Exposition of 1900, was a glorious Beaux Arts palace with the actual train station discreetly below ground. Built by the Orleans Line, it served all the trains coming up from the fertile environs of Bordeaux, Poitiers, and Toulouse. Now Rea was starting to think tunnels and wanted Cassatt to think about them, too.

And so on a breezy August day, with clouds sailing across the Paris sky, Cassatt headed over toward the Left Bank to examine the white limestone Gare du Quai d'Orsay, widely acclaimed as a triumph of public architecture. Designed by Victor Laloux, monumental in size, its seven giant arched entry arcades were splendidly framed on each end by a handsome pavilion and clock tower. A tall, sloped mansard roof acknowledged the Louvre just across the river. The facade was profusely ornamented with sculptures and embellishments—lion's heads, oak branches, laurel leaves.

Here was a depot truly worthy of its prominent location in the historic heart of (once) royal Paris. This industrial palace that elegantly integrated the all-important railway into the city's fabric, was only possible because the trains operated on electricity and so could use long riverside tunnels. Consequently this magnificent and useful monument to the new century was a distinct break with the familiar domed glass train shed terminal, semi-open, permeated by coal smoke and echoing with noise. The Gare du Quai d'Orsay was a striking marriage of art and industry, the first modern station designed for electric traction. Voyagers descended downstairs to one of fifteen train track platforms, first putting their baggage on moving ramps. "The station is superb," wrote one artist. Attached to the terminal was a luxurious 370-room hotel.

Cassatt watched powerful electrified forty-five-ton locomotives— oddly shaped engines called "salt boxes"—pull three-hundred-ton passenger cars through a long tunnel paralleling the Seine River and into the train terminal. Could this be the solution? With such powerful electric locomotives the PRR could enter Manhattan *under* the Hudson River with multiple tunnels solely for its own use. Likewise, the Pennsylvania could build its own magnificent terminal, just for its passengers and those of the Long Island Rail Road, whose tunnels would come under the East River and Manhattan.

Cassatt, the trained engineer and lifelong railroad man, methodically inspected every aspect of the Gare du Quai D'Orsay system, his excitement rising. If there could not be a North River Bridge, there perhaps could be tunnels. Cassatt immediately cabled Rea back that "he was much impressed with it, and he believed it might offer the solution to our problem." The fundamental engineering question was, Could tunnels be built under the Hudson River that could stand up to the gigantic tonnage of PRR passenger trains? If so, Cassatt's road could certainly build its own terminal. Let the others cling to their New Jersey depots and ferry fleets and be damned!

Why had it taken Rea and Cassatt more than a year to discover this important French advance in electric traction? After all, the Quai d'Orsay terminal had opened for business in May 1900 to serve the marvelous Exposition Universelle. Cassatt had even been in Paris the previous summer, for one of his sons had been an American commissioner at the exposition. Now the fairgrounds were closed, the huge exhibition halls empty and forlorn, and Cassatt was suddenly discovering the electrified tunnels. One can only speculate that Cassatt and Rea had been so certain about the North River Bridge and so committed to that imposing vision that they didn't consider other solutions. As Rea himself, long an officer of the bridge company, would later say of the North River Bridge, "I believed it was the best proposition." But with the bridge at a stalemate, Rea explained, "It was my duty to support the tunnel scheme provided it was feasible."

As ever, Cassatt wasted no time. He already knew just whom he needed if he was on to tunnels—Charles Jacobs, the dashing Englishman and tunnel mastermind. And Cassatt also knew that Jacobs was right then over in London. By August 27 Cassatt had crossed the Channel in rainy weather, checked into Claridge's, and located Jacobs, already under a PRR contract for the proposed LIRR tunnels from Brooklyn to Manhattan. Jacobs, fifty-one, was a powerful and charismatic marine engineer, a distinctive and authoritative figure with a large bald head, brilliant blue eyes, and a luxuriant white handlebar mustache. A native of Wales, he had really made his name in tunnels while working in the United States.

Back in 1893, LIRR president Austin Corbin had hired Jacobs to build two big natural gas tunnels from Ravenswood, Queens, to Manhattan under the East River. Surveys showed the riverbed to be solid rock, and so it was quite a shock when the shaft was sunk to find thick fissures of soft, oozy mud. Then, not just river water but an army of crabs invaded one tunnel, causing the laborers to flee in panic. The contractors demanded the shaft be sunk fifty feet deeper. Jacobs, the engineer, disagreed. The natural gas company dismissed the contractors, and Jacobs took over the job, saying, "Give me a plant and workmen and I'll put it through myself." The outraged contractors went to court, calling experts to testify the tunnels were not feasible. When Jacobs came to the witness stand in 1894, he suggested the judge see the now completed tunnels for himself.

In Paris, at the splendid Gare du Quai d'Orsay, Cassatt saw that technology had advanced to the stage that the PRR might propel heavy trains electrically under the Hudson River in mile-long tunnels. But the building of these subaqueous tunnels under the swift-flowing North River was still fraught with perilous uncertainty.

The world's first attempt at a subaqueous tunnel—a trolley tunnel under the Thames at London—had been launched with great fanfare in 1825 by the engineer Marc Isambard Brunel. "Seldom has a construction development attracted such attention, national and international, as the Thames tunnel. It was being discussed the world over, and ambassadors to the Court of St. James were ordered to keep reporting on its progress." Such was the fascination (and the need to offset the huge costs) that the Thames tunnel builders admitted hundreds of paying tourists every day to the slowly advancing construction site. But gushing leaks followed by many other catastrophes soon struck. It would be sixteen years before the twelve-hundred-foot Thames tunnel was finally complete, a financial disaster that had cost seven lives and destroyed the health of hundreds who worked on it.

The next major underwater tunnel project was far more ambitious. This time, the Great Western Railway proposed to lop an hour off its London to Cardiff route by tunneling under the Severn River. Work began in March 1873 on the twelve-thousand-foot-long tunnel, through which cables were to pull the trains. Year after year, the tunnel advanced without incident. Then in October 1879, when the two sides of the tunnel were within 130 tantalizing yards of one another, an underwater spring inundated one tunnel half. Such were the travails that the tunnel wasn't ready for regular service for seven more years. The contractor vowed never to work on a tunnel again.

And, if one needed a spectacular tunnel failure closer to home, in the United States, there was DeWitt Haskins's moribund tunnel lying right under the very Hudson River in question. The general opinion was that the Hudson River bed was simply not a place where one could successfully build an underwater tunnel. True, a handful of other less ambitious subaqueous railroad tunnels had been completed without such drama and disaster, but the Thames, Severn, and Haskins tunnels were brooding reminders of the unknowns lurking beneath riverbeds.

Neither Alexander Cassatt nor Charles Jacobs were the sort to play it safe. Within days, the Cassatts and Jacobs had quietly boarded the

White Star's S.S. *Celtic* to sail back to New York. This was a most fitting vessel for two engineers dreaming of monumental projects, for the recently launched *Celtic* was the largest steamship in the world, an astonishing paean to majestic size and the possibilities of modern daring. On its maiden voyage to the United States several weeks earlier, the New York papers had been awestruck by the steamship's combination of enormity and elegance. "She Seems To Dwarf Everything In Sight, Even Her Pier," ran one headline in the *New-York Tribune*, observing that the tugboats bringing it into shore were like "pygmies."

As Cassatt and Jacobs sailed across the Atlantic, they walked miles of pristine deck as the ocean spread out infinitely before them. Jacobs, his intense blue eyes alight, Cassatt, tall and commanding, strolled and talked, and strolled and talked some more, lingering in the skylit Smoking Room with its brilliant colors, embossed leather walls, and marble-topped tables, and pausing in the oak-paneled library. But always, always they were talking tunnels, afire with purpose. The advantages were indisputable. With tunnels under the North River, the PRR would have exclusive access from New Jersey to Manhattan, its own magnificent new Manhattan terminal, *and* if the tunnels were bored straight onward under Manhattan and below the East River, the Pennsylvania would eventually have a continuous and convenient direct route via the proposed New York Connecting Railroad to New England. It would not only transform and open up the whole of Gotham and its surrounding environs, guaranteeing the city and port would remain the nation's most important, it would knit together the eastern part of the United States. And it would ensure the continued dominance of the PRR itself. After all these years, here was a real solution, wrote one PRR executive, to "this object [that] has obsessed our officers by day and haunted their slumbers by night."

Time and secrecy were now of the essence. Of course, what Cassatt, Rea, and Jacobs all burned to know was, Could they build tunnels large enough, strong enough, and stable enough eighty feet below the surface of the North River to handle big Pennsylvania passenger trains pulled by locomotives operated electrically? And, if they could, what of the all-important state and city franchises they would need? Gustav Lindenthal had spent years securing the necessary federal charter and then state permits, overcoming one objection after another. The political and practical waters swirling round New York were corrupt and treacherous. It was one thing to propose the North River Bridge, a giant work open to all the roads, benefiting them all. It was quite another for the PRR to build its own tunnels and terminal. In that case, the politically powerful Vanderbilts and others were not likely to sit idly by while their greatest rival invaded their profitable territory.

SEVEN

"GET A LITTLE OF
THE TENDERLOIN"

The golden September sunshine gleamed off the Manhattan skyline as the S.S. *Celtic* glided majestically amongst the ferries and coal barges to dock at the White Star pier on the afternoon of Saturday September 7. Charles Jacobs and the Cassatts debarked amidst the hubbub, already knowing what the gaggles of newsboys were loudly ululating outside the customs shed. "EXTRA! EXTRA!" the boys wailed, each waving his stack of the *Tribune, Herald, World, Sun, Times,* or *Journal American*, all sporting the same calamitous headlines: "President Shot at Buffalo Fair," "IN GREAT PERIL, President McKinley's Wound Very Serious—The Stomach Perforated," "PRESIDENT McKINLEY SHOT: Assassination Attempted by an Anarchist at the Pan-American Exposition."

The president was still alive. Physicians spoke optimistically of recovery for the popular McKinley, yet acknowledged that surgeons could not locate the second bullet lodged in his stomach. The somber mood gripping Manhattan belied much real hope. The bells of the tramcars still rang out unendingly, iron horseshoes clanged on the cobblestones, there was the deep rumble of the overhead elevated trains and the whoosh of too-fast automobiles, but the city's throbbing energy was muted as anxious crowds gathered to scan the latest bulletins posted outside the great newspaper offices. This marked the third time in Cassatt's adult life that an American president had been shot. Abraham Lincoln's assassin had been sympathetic to the defeated South, James Garfield's a deranged and disappointed seeker of a patronage job. William McKinley had been attacked by a baby-faced citizen named Leon Czogosz, who declared, "I am an Anarchist. I am a disciple of Emma Goldman. Her words set me on fire." In an era of such simmering raw antagonism between labor and capital, few were shocked.

McKinley was dead a week later, and Cassatt had to arrange the elaborate PRR funeral train that traveled slowly south to Washington, D.C., bearing the president's body in a black casket under a sheaf of ripened wheat. Republican kingmaker Senator Mark Hanna slumped in gloom and poor health in one of those sumptuous Pullman cars, cursing the day that New York Republican boss Senator Thomas Collier Platt— outraged at Theodore Roosevelt's "various altruistic ideas"—had forcibly exiled Teddy to vice presidential oblivion after a mere two years as governor in Albany. Exploded Hanna, "Now look—that damned cowboy is President of the United States."

Roosevelt pledged to hew to McKinley's cautious, pro-corporate rule, but who could imagine the exuberant, pugilistic Teddy long eschewing his vociferous political style or his powerful need to speak blunt, honorable, and colorful truths? Staunch GOP men knew it was a new and perilous day when New York's other Republican senator, New York Central chairman Chauncey Depew, entered Teddy's White House office just as another man was departing. Teddy asked Depew, " 'Do you know that man?' Depew replied, 'Yes, he is a colleague of mine in the Senate.' Roosevelt said, 'Well, he's a crook.' "

Even as the *Sturm und Drang* of William McKinley's valiant but losing battle with death unfolded, Alexander Cassatt pressed quietly forward with the tunnel plan. Gotham was in mourning: all up and down the avenues flags flew at half mast and buildings were draped in black crepe. But this was the Empire City and business pulsed on. "We immediately started on surveys and estimates for a tunnel extension into New York," recalls Samuel Rea. Gustav Lindenthal, learning of this latest dispiriting threat to his stalled North River Bridge plan, wrote Alexander Cassatt on September 21, "Last week Mr. Samuel Rea informed me that you have under examination a tunnel route from the New Jersey side into New York for the exclusive use of your Company, in connection with and in continuation of the tunnel to the Long Island Railroad." It was indeed true, though the PRR did not want so much as a whisper known beyond its inner circles.

During these fresh September evenings, Charles Jacobs ventured out each night onto the Hudson River in a sturdy tugboat to perform tests on the riverbed to determine if the tunnels were feasible. While Jacobs's mission was utterly practical and of deepest consequence, a man would have to be made of stone not to savor the romance of the nocturnal river. All around him the glistening waters of the harbor were alive with other vessels, including the brilliantly lit palacelike pleasure steamers trailing music and laughter. Over in Manhattan, the new skyscrapers loomed against the heavens, and there was a kind of radiant electric aura above the broad and lustrous avenues. Out on the water, Jacobs quietly made fourteen borings, some going 250 feet down, in a straight line from shore to shore.

Gustav Lindenthal did his damnedest to save his bridge. He raised very tough and legitimate questions about running subaqueous tunnels through the Hudson River's deep glacial silt. Paramount was the possible disaster of the tunnels' settling as trains weighing hundreds of tons rumbled through day in and day out: "Even a slight settlement under passing loads may rupture the iron lining, resulting in leaks under a great head of water," he argued. Equally worrying was corrosion. When one considered, wrote Lindenthal, "the iron tunnel lining in contact with the silt, charged with salt water and sewage, [this] is not a fanciful objection . . . As the corrosion would take place outside of the shell, it could neither be discovered nor prevented." And then there was the terrible prospect of harm from the river itself and the immense flotilla of ships plying its waters. Tunnels would be "exposed to the danger of scour, dragging anchors, or vessels happening to sink on them and breaking them in two. It is always the unexpected that happens."

For Lindenthal, these were the most dire and obvious negatives. But there was also the question of pure aesthetics. "A bridge is more attractive to the public for crossing a wide river than a submarine tunnel, which has a bearing on its business future and on the revenues." Even Samuel Rea had argued (in the days when the North River Bridge looked to be the best prospect) that tunnels are "expensive to maintain and disagreeable to the passengers who would probably prefer crossing on the ferries to trusting themselves on slow trains running through damp and chilly submarine tunnels."

Perhaps on a note of some desperation, Lindenthal proposed that the lines carried on the bridge could be connected with the deeper underground LIRR line via huge elevators that would transfer through trains from one level to another in the new station. He believed that once all this was built, the "unwilling roads" would want in. "The bridge is specially designed for an expanding capacity to 12 or 14 tracks at comparatively small additional cost." Lindenthal signed off, asking to meet, saying it was a matter of "so much personal importance to me." Cassatt promised him that when more was known about the tunnel plan, he would compare the merits of the two plans.

Cassatt, meanwhile, was anxiously awaiting word from Charles Jacobs on the feasibility of tunnels. Cassatt had returned from Europe "with the complete plan of the Pennsylvania Railroad tunnel entrance to New York fully developed in his mind," recalled Jacobs's American partner, engineer J. Vipond Davies, who was at the first conference where Cassatt "propounded his complete scheme. At that time he contemplated a location for the station on the east side of Fourth Avenue." Davies had to inform Cassatt that "the grades for the approaches, eastward and westward, would not permit location otherwise than west of Broadway. This was a disappointment." That being the case, Cassatt then envisioned his palatial Manhattan depot rising upon the derelict yards of the New York & Harlem Railroad Company at West Thirty-third Street on the river.

Once Jacobs had a chance to look into this plan, he told Cassatt the unexpected and highly unsettling news that this site also would not do. A train station in this location would force the tunnels to be tilted at too steep a grade for a railroad to operate efficiently. The Pennsylvania Railroad's terminal, which would also serve the Long Island Rail Road, coming in on tunnels under the East River and then under Manhattan, would have to be sited further in toward Seventh Avenue, a rundown area described by one chronicler as "given up to the French and negro colonies, to much manufacturing and to buildings that grow more and more shabby as they approach the river, finally degenerating into a slum . . . This section is today one of the most troublesome in New York."

And so, a significant new hurdle was added to the project. The PRR would have to secretly acquire four contiguous square blocks of Manhattan real estate bounded by West Thirty-first and Thirty-third streets between Seventh and Ninth avenues. Speed and subterfuge were paramount, and the PRR now had to act *before* it could be absolutely sure about the feasibility and long-term safety of the tunnels. Wrote Rea, "As much property as possible had to be bought before plans were divulged, and the risk taken of afterwards securing the franchises. If the worst came and they were not granted, then a compact body of land would be secured . . . and the loss upon reselling would not be great."

Cassatt also felt the PRR had little choice but to surreptitiously capture as much of the necessary territory as possible. In early October 1901 the company quietly retained Douglas Robinson, "a real estate agent of high character and standing." A rich, bullying Scotsman, Robinson not only managed the vast New York holdings of the Astor family, he had, in the twenty years since marrying a deeply reluctant Corinne Roosevelt, served as a key financial and political advisor to his famous brother-in-law, Theodore Roosevelt, delighted new polymath president of the United States. Now Robinson and his men assembled the assessed values on every single property—ranging from $5,000 for dilapidated wooden shanties to as high as $85,000 for big corner commercial buildings. By the second week of October, Robinson had determined the names of the almost two hundred owners and projected the total cost for the four full blocks at about $5 million.

Soon thereafter, on an overcast fall day, LIRR president William Baldwin took the elevated uptown from his Wall Street office to see the four square blocks they needed to buy, so he could relay his impressions to Cassatt. As Baldwin well knew, the great Pennsylvania Depot—if it ever came to be—would be rising not just in a rundown, marginal neighborhood, but in one of Gotham's most notorious vice districts. Their four blocks were part of an area infamous far and wide: the Tenderloin, an area bounded by Fifth Avenue, West Twenty-third Street, Forty-second Street, and Ninth Avenue.

Many respectable and hard-working folk lived and toiled here, as the recent census recorded, and by day it appeared to be just another shabby city enclave. Yet Baldwin's Committee of Fifteen's own inquiries had pinpointed more than a hundred known whorehouses in the blocks due

north and dozens more in the blocks toward Fifth Avenue. When night
enveloped Gotham, and Manhattan's skyscrapers and grand hotels glowed
with the wondrous electric light, the streets here became a hotbed of
vice. Conveniently close to the Broadway theaters and the better hotels
and restaurants, the Tenderloin catered not just to the rougher elements,
but also to slumming (married) middle-class men and daring out-of-
towners. Nighttime Sixth Avenue, with the brightly lit elevated trains
rumbling overhead, was often jammed with pleasure seekers. The Tenderloin was, odd to say, a neighborhood that the well-to-do Baldwin knew
far better than most, for he had reviewed hundreds of the committee's
private detailed vice reports for his reform work.

The Tenderloin's fittingly fleshy moniker was coined in 1876 by the
infamous police captain Alexander "Clubber" Williams when he was
transferred uptown to the Nineteenth Precinct's West Thirtieth Street
station house. "I've been living on chuck steak for a long time, and now
I'm going to get a little of the Tenderloin," chortled Williams, a huge
brute of a "blue coat," proud of dispensing instant "justice" with his night-
stick. Williams was just one of the more enterprising and cocky "servants" of Tammany Hall, the city's long-entrenched, proudly corrupt
Democratic machine, its symbol the Tammany Tiger. As William Baldwin walked toward the river along West Thirty-second from Seventh Avenue with its dingy old frame storefronts that autumn day, he found a
dirty, busy street lined with small shops, a Chinese laundry, "cheap, low-
class Italian tenements . . . and the Industrial School of the Children's
Aid Society on the corner, which is the only building of any consequence." When the federal census taker had come through a year earlier
he had recorded many Italian families with lodgers, as well as Jews and
Irish, working as waiters and tailors.

On one block small boys in knickers and girls in pinafores gathered
round the itinerant knife sharpeners. The next block north was heavily
black, families from Georgia and Virginia escaping the Jim Crow South.
It was all a bit rough and there were clumps of young men standing
about, their derbies at a rakish angle. They toiled as railroad porters, hotel porters, waiters, launderers, stable hands, and cooks. Just over a year
before, on a hot August night, this stretch of Eighth Avenue had been the
scene of a short-lived race riot set off by a drunken black man stabbing a
white policeman to death in a saloon a bit uptown. Long-smoldering

"hard feelings" had erupted and mobs of white locals rampaged, randomly attacking Negroes, dragging men off passing streetcars and beating them. The blacks gave as good as they got. By midnight, Tammany police, having at times joined in the attack against the Negroes, finally imposed peace.

When Baldwin crossed the filthy cobblestones of Eighth Avenue, the stench of the stockyards was just discernible when the wind blew off the Hudson. Continuing on toward the river, he found on both sides "decent, respectable but cheap grade apartment and boarding houses, the entire block." Invariably the old-clothes men plied their trade here, looking for worn but serviceable garments. The 1900 census had listed many Americans of German and Irish extraction employed as ice men, actors, musicians, bartenders, detectives, and milliners. Possibly some worked at the block's numerous modest Italian restaurants.

New York saloon at the turn of the century.

At Ninth Avenue, the IRT's elevated tracks cast the street in a permanent state of shadow while the jammed electric trolley cars clanged along, vying with the many teams of horses and ever more common motorcars, status symbols of the rich and daring. Here Baldwin noted the many small stores, the ubiquitous corner saloons, and a very tall, weathered brick wall that enclosed the whole blockfront on the far side of West Thirty-third Street. Behind that wall loomed the venerable Institution for the Blind.

Down several blocks on West Twenty-eighth and Twenty-ninth streets were many bars: "drinking places are fitted up in the most lavish Oriental style and are known by such names as the Cairo Smoking Room, Bohemian Palm Garden, and similar names designed to attract the patronage of the Tenderloin all-nighters." The Tenderloin was not surprisingly, according to the police, "the center for the criminal classes. No one interfered with them . . . Even if outrages occurred they [the police] knew they were not to interfere as the [whore]houses had paid the captain for protection . . . I heard once of an [police] officer of the name of Coleman, who was killed in a disorderly house, and there never has been an inquest or an arrest." Clearly, building a huge new railroad station here could—if the surrounding neighborhood remained unchanged—present certain predictable problems.

Heading back on Thirty-third Street, Baldwin passed a "good class of apartment houses, with respectable boarding houses. There is a Baptist Church in the center of the block." The huge brick Haeger Storage Warehouse fronted on Eighth Avenue. In the next block of Thirty-third Street, Baldwin saw mainly "boarding houses and tenements of a cheap class. There are a couple of stables, Chinese Laundries and insignificant small stores." Over on Sixth Avenue, yet another elevated line rumbled north and south. Every single building and institution Baldwin had just seen would have to be bought. It was a gigantic and complex undertaking, fraught with possibilities for failure.

Some of the roughest Tenderloin joints, wild dance halls like the Tivoli, the Sans Souci, and the Egyptian Hall, were closer to Fifth Avenue but would still set a low tone for the neighborhood. The most famous was Eddie Grey's huge, raucous Haymarket at West Thirtieth and Sixth Avenue, in the shadows of the El. Painted bilious yellow and ablaze with outside lights, the Haymarket's prominent hanging sign promised *Grand Soiree Dansant!* Inside, past the chief bouncer, Weeping Willie, smoky chaos prevailed every night, with blaring music, overpriced champagne ("wealthy water"), swirling crowds of men dancing the waltz and

the two-step with pretty and willing women, frequent fights, and cur-
tained cubicles upstairs in the galleries for lascivious private shows or
sexual encounters. One longtime habitué recalled that for female patrons "Rule No. 1 was that no man who fell for them was to be robbed on
the premises."

Anyone abroad in the Tenderloin late at night had to beware. In the
tenebrous side streets the hardened criminal classes held sway, and
brazen streetwalkers lured unwary rubes to panel houses where sliding
bedroom walls made stealing watches and wallets easy. Murder was not
unknown either. Just as Wall Street gloried in its fearful financial power,
so the Tenderloin gloried in its lurid menu of vice and corruption—
luxurious French brothels with "cinema nights," high-stakes gaming
halls, "badger" games, and opulent opium joints. Every professional gam-
bler, saloonkeeper, white slaver, and madame in the Tenderloin dutifully
bribed the police and worked to fleece the unwary. The Democrats of
Tammany Hall turned a blind eye to what reformers had long denounced
as Satan's Circus. And just as many a tourist had to see Wall Street, so
many of the men among them had to see the Tenderloin.

New York night life in the Gilded Age.

By the time Alexander Cassatt set his heart on his Manhattan tunnels and terminal, the Tenderloin and its flourishing culture of Tammany police-protected vice had been thoroughly investigated and exposed (to little avail) by two state legislative committees. The first, the Lexow Committee, had deposed (among many others) the infamous "Clubber" Williams, who admitted, noted the *New York Times* in 1894, that "on a salary of $2,750 a year, [he] has a country place, a steam yacht, a considerable number of bank accounts, and some real estate in the city," leading the newspaper to perorate: "That he is the most outrageous ruffian on the police force is . . . a matter of common knowledge. That he is one of the richest men on the police force has been . . . a matter of common belief." "I'm so well known in this city," Captain Williams boasted, "that the car horses nod to me in the morning." Williams claimed to have made his vast sums investing in real estate in Japan. Still, he decided it best to retire when summoned by then reform police commissioner Theodore Roosevelt.

William Baldwin could only hope as he concluded his inspection of these rundown blocks that the building of a great railroad terminal in the heart of the Tenderloin would dramatically cleanse it of vice and crime.

EIGHT

"CROOKED AND GREEDY"

Just as policeman Clubber Williams thought it wise to resign after his grilling by Lexow, Tammany Democratic chieftain Richard Croker, the epitome of disciplined corruption, thought it best to decamp to England for self-imposed exile lest *he* be called to testify. "Like many other millionaires, Croker had come up the hard way," writes historian Lloyd Morris. "Stern-visaged, cold-eyed, with the heavy body of a bruiser, he was a study in iron grey—hair, beard, handsome suit, and overcoat were all of the same dark hue. Croker, the child of poor Irish immigrants, had landed in New York in 1846, at the age of three. He had little schooling, a rough youth as a member of the Fourth Avenue Tunnel Gang, got on the city payroll in his early twenties, served as alderman in the regime of Boss Tweed, was tried for murder after an Election Day battle and set free because the jury disagreed. But all this was now far in the past." Still that past cast a powerful shadow and few dared to cross Boss Croker.

In England, the thuggish Croker moulted into an approximation of British gentry, sporting the proper (if unconvincing) plumage of formal suit, gleaming top hat, and expensive cane. He acquired the requisite London town house, stables near Newmarket racecourse, and a moated country estate in Wantage, Berkshire. There Croker indulged his every whim and his passion for expensive horses, cutting an unlikely figure

New York Democratic boss William Croker at
the race track.

on the English turf and racing circuit with his trademark black cigar
clenched in his mouth.

The less polite New York press quickly dubbed Croker the "Baron of
Wantage," and gleefully reported the Tammany boss's new hobby of raising world champion bulldogs, with one famous puppy rumored to cost
ten thousand dollars. But, wrote one biographer, "Croker's greatest fun
was feeding the pigs. These he had named after New York politicians
whom he knew to be crooked and greedy." Thanks to the miracle of the
telegraph, Croker could play the English squire even as he ran the Tammany Wigwam with an autocratic iron fist. He deigned to return to Manhattan (he had another horse farm in New Jersey) in formal sartorial
glory only to manage crises and direct strategic elections.

With his simian air of ferocious, sullen reserve, he exuded an intensely intimidating power dedicated to horses, graft, and politics. For decades, Tammany Hall had ruled through a very simple formula, explained by Croker in a rare interview: "Think of the hundreds of foreigners dumped into our city. They are too old to go to school. There is not a mugwump [reformer] who would shake hands with them . . . Tammany looks after them for the sake of their vote, grafts them upon the Republic, makes them citizens in short; and although you may not like our motives or our methods, what other agency is there . . . If we go down into the gutter, it is because there are men in the gutter."

It was really quite elementary, wrote muckraker Lincoln Steffens: Tammany owned the "plain people" because in the absence of government services, Tammany provided a helping hand. "They speak pleasant words, smile friendly smiles, notice the baby, give picnics up the River or the Sound, or a slap on the back; find jobs, most of them at city expense, but they also have news-stands, peddling privileges, railroad and other business places to dispense." And with those votes, Tammany ruled city government and its tens of thousands of jobs and the vast ocean of boodle harvested from controlling the docks, the police, the health department, and the courts. It was a reliably rich take. The Pennsylvania Railroad could make it even richer.

Along with Croker the other virtual political dictator of New York was U.S. Senator Thomas Collier Platt, fifteen-year absolute monarch of the state Republican machine and legislature. Platt had the look of a pallid haberdasher's clerk and cared only for the minutiae and power of politics. Unlike the men of Tammany, whose "offices" were generally located in neighborhood saloons (though few top leaders ever touched a drop of liquor), the "Easy Boss" (as he was known) held court each Sunday in the "Amen Corner" of the plush Fifth Avenue Hotel. There he had long lived with his wife (though now he was a widower), and endlessly parsed elections and appointments and made deals with loyal leaders who came on pilgrimage from all over the Empire State. In his first stint in the U.S. Senate, Platt was derided by journalist William Allen White as a political "dwarf." When Platt entered the U.S. Senate for the second time in 1897, White described him as cutting "a small figure. He was a negligible man . . . He took no active interest in the large trend of national events . . . he was miserable until the tedious business of a session was done. Then back at his express office, or sitting at his desk in the Fifth Avenue, he could gloat over his power."

New York Republican boss Thomas Platt.

Unlike Richard Croker and others of the Gilded Age bossocracy, Senator Platt did not steal, nor did he, wrote even his nemesis Theodore Roosevelt, "use his political position to advance his private fortunes . . . He lived in hotels and had few extravagant tastes." In contrast to Tammany and its legions of poor, immigrant voters, Platt's supreme power came from catering to the great trusts and corporations doing business in Albany. Their grateful largesse flowed into Platt's formidable Republican campaign chest. Platt distributed these dollars with strategic care to his chosen candidates and district leaders during elections. Total fealty ensued. Platt's word had long been the law up in Albany at the state legislature.

William Baldwin and Alexander Cassatt would soon have to navigate the political waters where these two very different men had long reigned supreme. A construction project of the magnitude they planned—sixteen miles of tunnels, a monumental terminal, and a huge rail yard—could not move forward without all manner of franchises and legislation at every level of government.

Theodore Roosevelt had, of course, been a great and unhappy exception to Platt's usual ways; Platt had backed him for governor only under severe duress. As hero of San Juan Hill and famous for his probity and honesty, Teddy seemed the only Republican candidate likely to win the governorship in the wake of a particularly rank embezzling scandal. Due to the assassination of President McKinley, the obstreperous and unreliable Teddy had triumphed, joyfully ascending to the Bully Pulpit of the presidency. Alas, Senator Platt had also miscalculated when he rammed through legislation creating Greater New York City, in the hopeful (but deluded) belief that the new outer boroughs would furnish more Republicans than Democrats, and thus a juicy plum for his party. Instead, it had created more boodle for Croker and the Democrats, who in 1897 had installed Robert Van Wyck as first mayor of consolidated Greater New York.

In truth, Croker and Platt often coexisted peacefully, divvying up Gotham's plentiful spoils. But in 1899, the Easy Boss could not resist twisting the Tammany Tiger's tail by unleashing the second state investigation (known as the Mazet Committee) into Gotham's lubricious graft and corruption. This time the brooding Richard Croker himself was forced to take the stand and testily admit to pocketing Tammany rake-offs from judges (at $10,000 per) and others. The prosecutor asked, "Then you are working for your pocket, are you not?" Croker snapped back with words that acquired instant infamy and immortality, "All the time; the same as you." The drawn-out hearings, filling five fat volumes worth of testimony, revealed the long-entrenched system of vice and police protection to be more flagrant than ever, a fact of little moment to the great mass of Tammany voters. What Mazet confirmed about the ice business was altogether another matter.

In May 1900, as the weather warmed, New Yorkers buying ice—an absolute necessity for keeping milk and meat from spoiling—had been stunned to hear the price had inexplicably doubled from thirty cents a hundred pounds to sixty cents. In the tenement districts, the poor wanting to buy the cheap five-cent pieces were turned away. Ice was for sale only in one hundred-pound blocks. Young William Randolph Hearst's crusading *Journal American* unleashed its best lawyers and reporters, demanding in giant headlines "PUT AN END TO THE CRIMINAL EXTORTION OF THE ICE TRUST." Day after day, Hearst pounded away, splashing heartrending cartoons across the *American*'s front page to drive home the infamy of it all. In "The Ice Trust and the Poor" a weeping young waif clad in rags stood by her feverish, bedridden mother, murmuring, "Can't get any ice, mamma; the trust man says they won't sell any more small pieces to poor people."

Hearst eventually dug up the scandalous and Augean truth: the Ice Trust was the creation of Tammany officials, including Gotham's own mayor, Robert Van Wyck. The scheme was simple: Only their company's ice barges could unload on city-owned piers. Over in Wantage, Richard Croker was sufficiently displeased to prepare to return to Gotham. Grafting off the poor (and getting caught red-handed) was bad Tammany politics.

The Mazet hearings roiled up all kinds of vile murk. Hundreds of witnesses detailed a debauched underworld—brothels, "panel" houses where thieves stole wallets from unsuspecting men engaged in sex, "cinema nights" where voyeurs paid to secretly peep into rooms where whores were plying their trade, new legions of prostitutes operating out of tenement houses full of young children, and, most horrifying, the rise of white slavery. The respectable newspapers found it hard to cover the story. Tammany police had become so greedy that denizens of the underworld were pleased to expose them. One witness, proprietor of the White Elephant in the Tenderloin, complained about the outsized bribes police now demanded. He also testified, "There are more gambling houses and more disorderly [whore]houses open, running business openly, a great many more." Police chief Richard Devery, a bloated buffoon grown immensely rich on graft, denied all, saying with his trademark smirk, "Touchin' on the question of gambling, I'll say that when the department gets evidence it will act . . . We will act any time on the complaint of reputable citizens."

Certain reform-minded middle-class citizens, infuriated by the Mazet dirt, had decided to call the insufferable Chief Devery's bluff. He wanted evidence of crime and corruption? They would bombard Tammany with all the evidence Big Bill Devery could ask for. Their leader was the charismatic William Baldwin, president of the Long Island Rail Road. At rallies and meetings, the handsome young Baldwin exhorted his listeners to action: "Last fall there arose in this city a cry, an agonized cry, from fathers, mothers, and daughters, that vice was rampant in the city. It was a cry for help that scarcely anybody could endure. It was out of this . . . that the Committee of Fifteen was born." The committee raised money, hired private detectives, and sent them forth to methodically gather evidence and force prosecutions. There were some who saw in the activist young Baldwin a potential future mayor. After all, he was young, smart, good-looking, a hard worker, a respected businessman, and a very winning personality. And he got results. The reformers, true to their word, month after month stacked up ample proof of gambling, graft, and prostitution.

All the hue and cry led one Tammany district leader, the redoubtable George Washington Plunkitt, to daintily explicate about "honest graft and dishonest graft." The latter, which he did not care for, relied on "blackmailin' gamblers, saloonkeepers, disorderly people, etc. . . . [Then] there's an honest graft . . . say, they're going to lay a new park at a certain place. I see my opportunity and I take it . . . I buy up all the land I can . . . Ain't it perfectly honest to charge a good price and make a profit . . . Well, that's honest graft." These were exactly the sort of sentiments that made the Pennsylvania Railroad chary as it contemplated embarking on the nation's largest civil engineering project in the heart of Gotham.

Meanwhile, letters and phone calls poured in to Baldwin's reform group from New Yorkers angry about local riffraff and criminals. Between those and the Fifteen's own private inquiries, the president of the LIRR had come to obtain his firsthand education about many of the very blocks in the Tenderloin that the PRR now needed to buy. On West Thirty-first Street, warned one caller, right behind the Nineteenth Precinct police station house, "four or five houses are regular houses of ill-fame. Soliciting is going on from the windows." Another wrote furiously about a saloon on the ground floor of his Seventh Avenue apartment building, "a dive of the worst character . . . The most vile and filthiest streetwalkers in the neighborhood, white and colored, are harbored in this place all day from sunrise till long after midnight, much to the disgust and annoyance of the tenants, all respectable people."

While many Gothamites felt little ire over gambling, Sunday drinking, or hardened streetwalkers, almost all recoiled at white slavery. The new Republican justice William Travers Jerome (a last-minute gubernatorial appointment before Teddy headed to D.C.) barnstormed the city bluntly describing how squads of smooth-talking Lotharios called "cadets" (protected by Tammany) now worked the immigrant tenement districts, luring naive young women into "romances." Promised respectable matrimony, these innocents instead found themselves imprisoned in brothels and "ruined." "The girl in there [the whorehouse] has no means by which she can escape," explained Jerome, a most unlikely looking firebrand with his rimless glasses and bow ties. "Her clothes have been taken from her: she has perhaps a wrapper, a pair of stockings, and slippers . . . Literally, screams issuing from the upper windows of such a house, and heard by men in the street, are by policemen in the street not heard or investigated. They do not dare hear; they do not dare investigate; the keeper of the house pays protection. You hear talk about the horrors of white slavery . . . like hearing evil fairy tales . . . of far-off lands." But it was a chilling and growing reality in the Manhattan of 1901.

As other reform groups mobilized and pressure built, Richard Croker returned home, gathered his leaders, and tersely instructed them to rein in the worst of their excesses. When one Tammany brave objected, the grizzled Croker bounded up in fury, hissing, "If the people find anything is wrong, you can be sure that the people can put a stop to it, and will!" When Croker sailed back to England, however, his minions were in sullen revolt, determined to keep raking in the lucre of vice, said to be $3 million a year for the police department alone.

Tammany predictably began subterranean whisper campaigns, warning Baldwin that if he persisted in his investigations he "would find his business responsibilities interfered with, that means would be devised for hampering the operations of the railroad corporation of which he was head." As the rumors and threats swirled about, Baldwin declared, "I have taken up this work for the city and I propose to go on with it. If there is any dread lest my responsibilities in the management of the railroad may be interfered with, my resignation as President is ready. This work of the Fifteen I have promised the community to do, and I shall do it to the best of my ability."

It was not hard to imagine the PRR's directors rather taken aback to find the president of one of their new subsidiaries engaged in such lurid rabble-rousing. Negro uplift was all very well, but rousting out prostitutes? Even as Alexander Cassatt was inspecting the Quai d'Orsay Station and then seeking out Jacobs in London in August 1901, Committee of Fifteen investigators pressed on, engaged in their own unusual inspections, again and again documenting that prostitution continued to be open and rampant. During a typical encounter in the Tenderloin on the warm midnight of August 30, a dark-haired French woman at 128 West Thirty-first Street solicited the two detectives engaged in this odd form of civic betterment.

Once inside with the men, she disrobed, reported John Earl, "She got on the bed, exposed her parts to me and wanted me to have sexual intercourse with her which I declined to do." Instead, he dutifully filed his report, one of hundreds showing what police routinely ignored. Little did William Baldwin dream the previous summer that his antivice crusading and the PRR's most fundamental interests were soon to intersect in this seamy neighborhood. And yet within months this benighted piece of real estate had come to be absolutely essential to the PRR's decades-old dream of conquering Gotham.

NINE

"SOMEONE IN THE PENN
IS LEAKING"

The day after President McKinley's death, Richard Croker, grayer and grimmer than ever, stepped off the S.S. *Lucania* ready to wage political war. Escorted by several top lieutenants as he walked off the pier, Croker's face was its usual stoic mask. He brushed aside the reporters with a "Nothing to say, boys." Nothing was more important to Tammany than the imminent mayoral election, for City Hall was the key to everything that nourished the voracious Tammany Tiger—above all the jobs, the permits, the franchises, and all the gears of government-generated boodle. The city was in a quickly escalating state of high political agitation and excitement. Indeed, the whole nation was watching this election.

As drama it did not disappoint. Seth Low, scion of a silk merchant, wealthy ex-mayor of Brooklyn, just-resigned president of Columbia University, led the reform Fusion ticket, running for mayor. Rotund, with sandy, wavy hair and a matching bristle mustache, Low was "very competent, very dignified, and rather dull." It was an unfortunate fact that people respected Low but did not like him. He was a cold fish. Tammany's rambunctious chief of police Richard Devery stroked his luxuriant whiskers and bestowed upon Low the jeering nickname of "Little Eva."

The canny Croker, in a move denounced as "audacious and desperately skillful," put up for mayor the excellent Edward M. Shepard, a Brooklyn attorney of sterling character, most admired for prosecuting

Tammany vote fraud. The reform firebrand Justice William Travers Jerome ran for district attorney, whipping up his tenement audiences to collective outrage over the Ice Trust and the reviled "cadets." As the raucous election season careened along, Croker holed up in his elegant Democratic Club way up Fifth Avenue. "From early morning until far into the night, the Boss was at work, pouring men and money into crucial districts; driving his lieutenants to their uttermost; tapping every channel of influence and power."

Election Day—Tuesday November 5—dawned gray and wet, to Tammany's delight. Many a well-dressed New Yorker, the kind who favored reform, would not want to venture forth in inclement weather. Nonetheless, from the minute the polls opened at 6:00 a.m., the men of Greater New York poured forth to vote. The camera "experts" from newspapers like Joseph Pulitzer's *World* and Hearst's *American* snapped photographs as the candidates voted. By evening, wide rivers of excited New Yorkers flowed into the main avenues looking for news. Those heading to the big plaza at City Hall and newspaper row were unable to advance because the whole place was a great construction pit for August Belmont Jr.'s new subway. Uptown, the huge sea of citizens forced the closing of Broadway as they watched returns on a big sheet on the New York Times Building. Everyone knew it was over as the returns came in from the Lower East Side tenement districts. The crowds gasped. Low, the Silk Stocking reformer, was winning! Tammany was out.

Three days later, on Friday morning at 10:46, Alexander Cassatt telephoned Samuel Rea at the PRR's sixteenth-floor Manhattan office and left a message, "The purchase of that property ought to be started at once, and I will be glad if you will take up the matter with Mr. B[aldwin] and agree upon a line of action. Call me on the telephone if you want to say anything." Low's victory was a most felicitous development for the Pennsylvania Railroad, a triumph engineered in part by William Baldwin and his Committee of Fifteen. The secret buying of the Tenderloin would now begin.

On this very same day, November 8, Cassatt received the definitive answer he had so fervently hoped for—Charles Jacobs reported that he believed the subaqueous railroad tunnels could be safely built and operated, thus making possible the whole gargantuan enterprise. Beginning with a double-track line across New Jersey's marshy Hackensack Meadows, they would dig two tunnels through the Bergen Cliffs, continue down under the mile-wide Hudson, emerging deep underneath a great terminal. From there two tunnels, each with two tracks, would continue on under and through Manhattan, becoming four separate tunnels under the East River. Two would be for the LIRR, and would thus create a through ride all the way from the mainland to Long Island. The two other tunnels would serve the PRR, whose empty trains would terminate in Sunnyside, Queens. There would be built the largest passenger-car yard in the world. Better yet, in a nine-page preliminary estimate, Jacobs projected a $40 million cost for the whole monumental project, including their own Grand Depot. This was far less than the original $100 million price for the colossal North River Bridge or even Lindenthal's scaled-back version for $46.5 million. And so the PRR could launch its opening moves in the Tenderloin with confidence.

Within the week, real estate man Douglas Robinson wrote Cassatt, "We have gone systematically to work since Friday to get the prices at which the owners will sell the various plots, and have succeeded in getting prices on several. We think in a couple of weeks we will be able to know pretty well at what price the full plot of land can be bought." At the same time, Samuel Rea wrote Cassatt warning him, "There has been so much talk about—bridges tunnels subways etc—that property owners on west side in vicinity of our location are skeptical." The PRR's opponents especially were already on guard as the railroad studied the real estate chessboard of these strategic blocks. Rea proposed they capture selected properties throughout their site to "establish prices." Wondered Rea, "Do you not think if we invest say $200,000 now judiciously, and promptly, that we could then ease and go at it leisurely, so as not to excite suspicion?"

And so the great high-stakes real estate acquisition began. As Douglas Robinson would later relate, "The actual work of purchasing was done by three men, the blocks being more or less evenly divided between them, and when they were sent out to make the purchases they, themselves, did not know who was the actual buyer of the property." Robinson's three buyers, unaware of one another, but blessed with a string of crisp fall days, fanned out across the Tenderloin carrying big wads of cash in their pockets and option contracts provided by the Title Guarantee & Trust Company. On any given block, they aimed to buy a range of building types to determine, and then set, local values.

During those autumn days, the three men discreetly inquired and sought out those who controlled certain buildings. "The owners," Robinson would later explain, "being of moderate means and mostly workmen, had to be traced to all parts of the city, and out of the city, but as quickly as it was possible." And so, the men hopped on the elevated trains, rode the ferries to the other boroughs, quietly tracking down Tiernans, Conklings, Ackermans, and Werckeles. "If his [or her] price corresponded with our appraisal of the lot in question, a copy of the option was drawn and he was induced, if possible, to sign it (and it may be said that the first sellers signed with perfect willingness). Five hundred ($500) dollars was given to the seller and the signature on the option was witnessed, so that it became a binding document." With speed and secrecy critical, Robinson quickly drew up sales contracts, wrote checks, and dispatched each man to retrace his steps and seal yet another deal.

Despite this caution, rumors were rampant within a week. Robinson scrawled a note to Baldwin, "I'm afraid someone in the Penn is leaking. We tried to buy a piece of property and were told by the owner that she knew what was up . . . that someone in the employ of Penn told her the RR had decided to buy all the block. I tell you this for what it is worth. A man we bought from last night backed out today said he had heard it definitely and wants a higher price and told him I wouldn't buy and did so to bluff him." Undaunted, the PRR scooped up shabby houses and stores and warehouses, for $6,000 here, $40,000 there. Wrote Robinson, "Within two weeks, we had secured a great many lots . . . thereby establishing . . . the value of the adjoining parcels . . . At that time the buildings in the Terminal zone were occupied by many negroes, saloons, dance halls, gambling joints, and for many other purposes which made the work of those who did the buying not only difficult, but also often dangerous; although it is fair to admit that of the large sums carried in cash never one cent was lost through encounters with the owners or their tenants." Robinson and Rea moved swiftly but carefully, for they needed a good sampling of prices, their biggest future weapon if condemnation became a necessary tactic against owners holding out for big sums. Baldwin sent Robinson's note about "someone in the Penn leaking" on to Cassatt that same Thursday, suggesting, "It may be well to call off the buying for a few days."

Then, on December 1 as the weather turned wintry, the *New-York Tribune* broke the story that it was rumored to be none other than the PRR buying land as fast as it could amidst the brothels and saloons. However, "real estate dealers in the neighborhood of the reported terminal said . . . they had no definite knowledge." Baldwin, Cassatt's point man in Manhattan, was not about to confirm such rumors, saying ingenuously, "I think the story must have arisen from the rumor that a bridge was to be built across the North River." The paper, in turn, noted that the site was "only a few blocks away from the terminus of the [proposed] North River Bridge." Baldwin, the executive who knew best how the whole complex political scene operated, wrote Cassatt the next day to commiserate. "The reports about land purchases are very exasperating . . . Nobody in my office or in the L.I.R.R. knows a thing about the purchases of the Stuyvesant Land Co. There has not been the scratch of a pen. I think that observing people *expect* you to build a tunnel." In that first month, the PRR had bought sixty-eight parcels for $2,398,750.

The PRR had tried to further disguise its identity and distract its opponents by creating the Stuyvesant Real Estate Company. But to no avail. The speculators began to circle, scenting easy pickings and profits. For years, said one real estate man, Seventh Avenue had been "like a chinese wall . . . beyond which no respectable man or woman could safely go. It is known to be filled with thugs, bums, and wicked negroes." Now, all that would be changing. Sensing his corporate enemies gathering, Cassatt felt forced to press forward before he was truly ready.

TEN

"THE TOWN IS ON FIRE"

A s the thin winter light dawned on Wednesday December 11, 1901, the wealthier classes of Gotham opened that day's *New York Times* to read on the front page that the night before a gigantic broken water main at Madison and Fifty-fifth Street had created an explosive gusher, causing a mighty flood for blocks all around. "Rich Homes Are Wrecked" read one subhead. Down on Thirty-first and Broadway, yet more disaster—crackling sheets of flames had engulfed a building, scorching a dance academy, a boxing studio, a pool hall, and threatening the Bijou Theater. A team of horses had bolted, injuring the driver. Back in the sports pages, the six-day cycle race at Madison Square Garden was in its third day before roaring crowds, while a small item reported that the streetcar strike in Scranton had become violent.

But for certain readers, men of affairs whose holdings included railroad stocks and bonds, the story that mattered most sat squarely in the center of that plain gray front page (eschewing the new-style blaring headlines and photographs of Pulitzer and Hearst). A small double-decker headline read, "May Build a Tunnel under North River" "The Pennsylvania Road Having Plans for It Prepared." The source of this calamitous breach in secrecy was plainly identified as the Pennsy's own financiers, Kuhn, Loeb & Co.

Worse than this front-page revelation, Alexander Cassatt feared that unnamed forces hostile to the PRR were mobilizing a rearguard real estate action to checkmate its entry to Gotham. "It was hoped," Alexander Cassatt explained to his board soon thereafter, "that [our] plan might be kept from the knowledge of the public until it was more matured and until further purchases of real estate had been made. [But] information was received which caused it to be feared that rival interests might acquire—and were perhaps actually about to acquire—property in the area selected for the station site, which might have blocked the whole plan." The PRR's enemies were preparing to pounce.

The *New York Times* article admitted that "the exact location for this tunnel could not be learned," but then guessed it would be "near the terminal of the Long Island Railroad tunnel at Thirty-second Street and Seventh Avenue." Newspaper stories were a deep worry, but it was the specter of shadowy opposition—almost certainly the Vanderbilts, perhaps also subway magnate August Belmont—coalescing to strike, that forced the Pennsylvania into preemptive action.

That very same morning, Wednesday December 11, 1901, even as households were opening their morning newspapers, LIRR lawyer William J. Kelly was rushing to board the New York Central line to ride upriver along the Hudson to Albany. There in the state capitol he formally incorporated an entity known as the Pennsylvania & New York Extension Railroad Company. "It was deemed necessary to at once take out a charter," explained Cassatt, "and cover the route and station property by filing a plan . . . in accordance with the law . . . so that we are now protected against the taking of the station site or the occupancy of the proposed route by any adverse interests."

That afternoon in Manhattan, after the stock market closed, Alexander Cassatt had the great satisfaction of issuing an announcement: At long last the Pennsylvania Railroad was coming into Gotham in grand, utterly modern style. Not, as surprised New Yorkers had heard rumored, over a shared North River Bridge, but via underwater tunnels buried deep below the Hudson River. Even Joseph Pulitzer's ever-savvy *World* reported, "Until the announcement . . . yesterday everybody but the initiated believed that the Pennsylvania was buying land for a bridge approach."

Cassatt's quietly triumphant statement released that Wednesday afternoon was all of six paragraphs long and conveyed only the barest details: "The line as adopted will traverse the City of New York from the

Hudson River to the East River and be underground throughout and at such depth as not to interfere with future construction of subways by the city on all its avenues." Not until the next day when the PRR's plans— still rather sketchy—were filed downtown in the Office of the County Clerk, did the magnitude and daring of Cassatt's tunnels and terminal enterprise became apparent. The new tracks into the tunnels would cross the meadowlands of New Jersey on a high fill, pass through two tunnels blasted through the solid rock of the Bergen Portal, and then plunge steadily down, far below the glacial muck of the mile-wide Hudson, to emerge in Gotham fifty feet below street level into what promised to be a magnificent Pennsylvania Terminal in Manhattan at Thirty-second Street and Eighth Avenue. There the rails would fan out to accommodate twenty-eight tracks. The station itself would be one of the biggest structures in the world and modeled on the superb Gare du Quai D'Orsay. But the two tunnels would not stop at the station. They would continue on deep under the streets of Gotham, each tunnel now wide enough to hold two tracks as they traversed below West Thirty-first and Thirty-second streets. Nearing the East River they would plunge down again, becoming four separate tunnels, finally surfacing at Long Island City. By opening up rural New Jersey and Long Island, these tunnels would do more than any legislation to alleviate Gotham's crowding and slums.

The Pennsylvania Railroad's New York Tunnels and Terminal Extension, as it was officially known, now became the nation's biggest, most difficult, and most important civil engineering project. And, unlike that celebrated and much-ballyhooed enterprise, the transcontinental railroad, it would be privately financed. Presumably to avoid alarming the skittish financiers and stockholders they would rely upon in the coming years, they were strikingly reserved about the sheer Pharaonic scale and difficulty of their historic enterprise. Tunnel master Charles Jacobs would describe it privately as "one of the greatest engineering works undertaken in this day and generation." But such expensive-sounding and extravagant phrases were never uttered in public discussion.

The New York Extension was, as Cassatt had anticipated, a controversial enterprise. All told, the engineers of the PRR would be building 16 miles of tunnels, more than any other civil engineering project to date. The two famous Alpine mountain tunnels, the Simplon and St. Gothard, were 12½ and 9½ miles respectively. The longest underwater tunnel, the Severn in England, was 4½ miles. The truth was, as one PRR engineer would later write, "Tunnels of the kind contemplated, to be used for heavy and rapid railroad traffic, had never been constructed through materials similar to those forming the beds of the North and East Rivers." And it was this uncertainty, this prospect of risk, that caused legions of the PRR's vast army of shareholders to hate the whole enterprise. The stock price began to drop. Some engineers, said Samuel Rea, "believed there was a drift, or tendency of the silt to moved southward with the flow of the [Hudson] river and that this drift might shift any tunnels built through it unless they were anchored in some extremely secure manner." The *Wall Street Journal* marveled at the largeness of Cassatt's "sublime exhibition of faith" in the face of "all the croakings of pessimism."

To counter the possibility of drifting and insubstantial silt, explained LIRR president Baldwin, the tunnels under the Hudson River would actually be "an underground bridge. That may sound like an absurdity, but that, nevertheless, is just what this scientifically planned paradox is intended to be—a tunnel burrowed through the soft mud of the river's bottom and supported at short intervals by piles driven deep enough for their ends to rest on rock bottom." In addition to these complicated tunnels and monumental station, a huge 192-acre train yard was to be built in Sunnyside, Queens. Nor was that the end of it. Cassatt wanted his road to link up to the lucrative New England markets. In July 1901 the PRR had purchased a company known as the New York Connecting Railroad, which held a federal franchise to build a gigantic railway bridge across the Hell Gate on the East River. Here at last would be the PRR's rail connection to New England.

"Electricity and modern science have made it possible for us to do this thing," Baldwin proclaimed as the reporters pored over the PRR's hastily filed plans. In marked contrast to all the Vanderbilt trains steaming into the city, showering sparks, cinders and soot as they made their way along Park Avenue to Forty-second Street, Cassatt painted a vision of elegant Pennsylvania passenger trains rolling electrically into Gotham: "There will not be any smoke, dirt or noise, and as all the surface property may be built upon after being utilized underneath for railroad purposes, the neighborhood of the station will be improved instead of marred, as is so often the case when railroad lines are constructed."

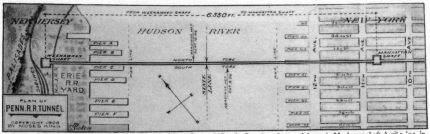

PENNSYLVANIA TUNNEL PLAN; contract let May 2, '04, to O'Rourke Eng. Con. Co.; work begun in Manhattan shaft April 1, '04, in Weehawken shaft Sept. 1; shields of north tube met 168 ft. west of state line Sept. 12, '06, south tube, 370 ft. east of state line, Oct. 9, '06.

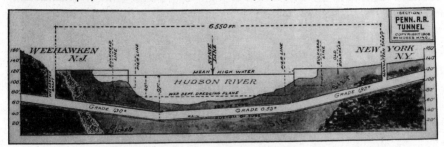

The route of the PRR's North River tunnels.

As details emerged, the New York newspapers engaged in all manner of erroneous speculation—the PRR planned a new port for ocean liners and freighters out on the tip of Long Island at Montauk, its headquarters would soon be relocated to Manhattan, other roads like the Erie or the Lackawanna would be given use of the tunnels. What the papers and the public quickly realized (on the same day that heavy morning fog caused the wreck of a ferry and the evacuation of all its passengers by lifeboats) was that the PRR's grandiose tunnels and terminal project dwarfed even the earlier hugely ambitious plans for a North River Bridge. When it was all finally completed—and Baldwin spoke of three years—this vast and ambitious project would forever alter the physical and mental geography of the nation's most important city, New York, and its environs, New Jersey and Long Island.

On Saturday evening December 14, 1901, William Baldwin sat at his desk in his handsome Willow Street house in Brooklyn as the rain pattered down outside. He was elated but fatigued. He had spent much of the previous day enthusing to journalists in Manhattan about the glories of the New York Extension before returning early in the evening to confer with mayor-elect Seth Low at his Brooklyn mansion about strategy. Baldwin wrote Cassatt in a jubilant mood, "The town is on fire. The universal sentiment, with high and low, is one of approval and anticipation. The more we stir them up, the cheaper will be the terms . . . The editorials all seem to demand prompt and reasonable conditions on the part of the city." The "conditions" Baldwin was alluding to encompassed the still uncertain legislative hurdles and the dollar cost of the franchises. After all, much of this was fresh legal terrain. For starters, Baldwin proposed, "I suggest that we try to secure the approval of the Rapid Transit Commission to an amendment to the charter in relation to terms of franchise of steam railroads etc."

While ultimately the vast tunnel system and monumental terminal were to be an extraordinary and herculean engineering feat, Cassatt, Baldwin, Rea, and the Pennsylvania Railroad first had to successfully maneuver through New York's complicated and perfidious local politics. Naturally, they anticipated good-faith negotiations to satisfy the city's publicly stated conditions. But even more important might be the unspoken illegal "terms," that is, the bribes and inside deals certain to be expected by Tammany Hall. It was Cassatt's extraordinary good fortune that tenement voters—angry over Tammany's ill-timed rigging of ice prices and excessive promotion of vice—had punished the Wigwam by electing Silk Stocking reformer Seth Low as mayor.

Baldwin had already reported that Low "realizes the importance of the enterprise." The new mayor was a trained attorney who had given up the management of the family silk trade to first enter politics in the (then) city of Brooklyn, serving twice as a crusading mayor, and then accepting the presidency of Columbia University. There he had orchestrated the move uptown to the Morningside Heights campus designed by master architect Charles McKim of McKim, Mead & White. But Tammany still controlled key governing bodies—notably the Board of Aldermen—and the Pennsylvania Railroad could not so much as stick a shovel in the earth until it secured their consent.

For all the decades that Tammany had ruled Manhattan (interrupted by occasional short-lived reform governments) every city employee, including policemen and judges, duly paid Tammany large set sums (the rate then was $5,000 to $15,000) for the privilege of obtaining (and keeping) their jobs. By the same token, many who conducted private businesses in Manhattan were expected to fork over to Tammany when so instructed.

In one recent instance, Tammany boss Richard Croker had appeared in 1898 to ask a "favor" of George Gould, the gregarious son and crown prince of the late unlamented Jay Gould. The young Gould presided over the family's corporate empire, the ill-run Wabash Railroad, the mighty Western Union Telegraph Company, and the Manhattan Elevated Railway. Unlike his dour, secretive, funereal father, writes historian Maury Klein, "George wore fine clothes, sported a well-trimmed moustache, and strutted like a dandy. Small and lithe, he loved fast horses, hunting, fishing . . . He became an excellent polo player and did much to establish the game in the United States. His tastes ran to clubs, parties, and the theater." He had first spied his lovely wife on the stage. Nonetheless, Gould fancied himself a serious businessman.

In late 1898, Croker, glossily resplendent in gray English tailoring, strolled into Gould's large office at the Western Union Telegraph Building. Gould greeted him cordially. The Tammany boss got right to the point—a certain company wished its compressed-air pipes to be mounted on Gould's Elevated structure. Gould demurred, saying he would have to consult his engineers and lawyers. Croker snapped "Oh, hell! I want those pipes put on, and I don't want any circumlocution." Gould again resisted. Croker glowered and decreed, "We want those pipes put on, and we don't want any fuss about it." George Gould, a gentleman of privilege and proud owner of one of Fifth Avenue's finest turreted mansions, rose imperiously, outraged at such thuggish effrontery. "Under the circumstances, Mr. Croker, I will settle the question now, without referring it to my officials. We will not permit you to attach your pipes to the Elevated structures."

From that moment on, recounts Croker's biographer, "almost every branch of city government took part in [a] concerted assault [on Gould's business]. The Health Department declared several hundred points on the Elevated structure to be unsafe, and served notice that repairs must be made forthwith. The Park Department ordered the company to remove its tracks from Battery Park immediately, citing an obscure clause in the original franchise. The Board of Aldermen threatened to pass a series of ordinances that would cost the company millions of dollars." Though young Gould might be a bit of a fool, he was a powerful plutocrat. And yet Croker had not thought twice about savagely attacking Gould's corporate interests—and even crippling a critical part of the city's transit system—when Gould balked at lining Tammany's pockets.

Even such a necessary and important civil enterprise as the Roeblings' Brooklyn Bridge had been forced to pay illegal tribute. Back in the 1870s, Tammany had exacted sixty-five thousand dollars in bribes and placed the soon-to-be-infamous boss William Marcy Tweed on the bridge's board. As the building of the great bridge dragged on year after year and the costs steadily mounted, a hue and cry arose. Inveighed one newspaper, "Had Mr. Roebling done his duty instead of becoming the cat's paw of the [Tammany] Bridge Ring, he might have saved millions of dollars to the two cities."

Numerous inconclusive investigations never quieted public suspicions about the bridge project, and so, writes historian David McCullough, "A good part of the public would remain convinced that every day the work continued some crooked somebody behind the scenes was getting rich on it." Considering what their predecessors decades earlier had extorted

Board of Directors of the Pennsylvania Railroad Company, July 1905.

from the Brooklyn Bridge builders, the Board of Aldermen must have licked their venal chops indeed when they learned that the mighty PRR needed a franchise to bring its tunnels into Manhattan and build its palatial temple to electrified railroading.

Though never directly stated, Tammany men saw this looming opportunity and intended to be well paid for their votes and efforts. The Pennsylvania Railroad was, after Morgan's recently organized U.S. Steel, the nation's biggest, wealthiest, and most powerful corporation. *Cosmopolitan* magazine reported that very year that the PRR operated "more than ten thousand miles of road, using over three thousand locomotives and fifty thousand cars. It carried more than sixty-one million passengers . . . It moved over eighteen billion tons of freight one mile." It employed a vast army of 150,000 men and was worth more than $300 million. The Pennsy was also famously politically savvy, possessing inordinate sway over the Pennsylvania state legislature and its two influential U.S. senators. Tammany might have been forgiven for assuming the PRR would simply view Gotham bribery and boodle as the usual cost of doing business.

Back at the road's corporate offices above Philadelphia's busy Broad Street Station, the sixteen members of the PRR board of directors gathered in the sumptuous wood-paneled meeting room and arrayed themselves around the unusual doughnut-shaped table, polished to a high gleam. The floor was covered with a huge oriental carpet. On the walls hung large gilt-framed oil portraits of the road's previous six presidents. Cassatt had served under four of these eminent executives and it was fitting that they (all deceased) could now bear witness to discussions of their road's impending conquest of Gotham. The road's directors, attired in the formal somber suits of their class, required by law to be residents of Pennsylvania, and paid only in prestige, were to learn just how many hoops their company would have to leap through.

Cassatt looked about at these men he had known for many years, and began, "The New York law names the Rapid Transit Commission as the body which is to issue a franchise for building and operating the line within the City of New York, and it is proposed to at once enter into negotiations with the Commission . . . The franchise, when granted by the Commission, will require the approval of the Board of Aldermen, the Board of Estimate and Apportionment, and of the Mayor. The New York law also requires that the route be approved by the Board of Railroad Commissioners, and that the assents of the owners of a majority in interest of the property fronting any streets occupied be obtained, or failing to obtain such assents, that the Supreme Court shall adjudge the construction of the road necessary to the public interest."

In short, the PRR would soon be wading deeply into the muck of New York politics, thus confronting Tammany. The most important (and precarious) encounter, however, would almost certainly be with the Tammany Board of Aldermen, described by English socialist Beatrice Webb as an "inconceivably low looking set of men." Another favorite sobriquet was "The Forty Thieves," though in fact, since the consolidation and creation of Greater New York, there were now the almost ludicrous number of seventy-nine aldermen.

The whirl of Christmas and New Year's festivities placed such purely political matters briefly on hold, but the PRR put the time to good use by buying up more Tenderloin properties for their terminal, even as all around the police were suddenly raiding gambling "resorts" and pool halls. On Christmas Eve, Rea telephoned Cassatt just before lunch from the firm's New York offices at 85 Cedar Street (on the corner of Broadway) to discuss real estate. Every property they needed to buy had been mapped out and listed by address. Cassatt was out and Rea left this message: "I have been all over the property with Mr. Robinson this morning, and when convenient I think you should also look over it, because we have reached a point where we ought to determine on some more purchases before entering our condemnation proceedings . . . #213 is a four story new building, the first floor is used as a stable and the other floors as lofts. Mr. Robinson still thinks he can buy it for $40,000, and recommends its purchase. I would like to have you review this again and say whether he shall take it. #217 we cannot get now."

And so it went, day in and day out throughout the holiday season, with Rea, Robinson, and Cassatt constantly surveying the complex real estate chessboard, contemplating this building and that block, buying a corner here, a factory there. By January 2, they had purchased 40 percent of one block, almost 70 percent of another, and just over half of a third at a total cost of $3,250,401. But they would need every single structure.

On January 7, Samuel Rea lunched with William Baldwin to plot strategy for the franchise. Afterwards at 3:22 p.m. Rea called Cassatt to tell him, "Before you decide definitely what action we shall take, relative to amending the law, it is imperative for you to see the Mayor." Cassatt quickly telegraphed New York and secured an appointment. As the general of the PRR's mammoth campaign to enter Gotham, Cassatt was, albeit reluctantly, now truly a public figure. The *New York Times* described him "coming up Cortlandt Street [from the ferry] several times each week, making his way with great strides to the offices of the Pennsylvania Railroad Company at Broadway and Cedar . . . [He is] a man of large stature, who gives instantly the impression that he is a man of affairs and of power, that he is occupied with great problems, and yet is alert and observant."

Cassatt had over the decades acquired the reputation of being almost reckless in his audacity and yet, oddly, wrote veteran business writer

New York mayor Seth Low on November 5, 1901, soon after his election.

Frank H. Spearman, "In his presence no atmosphere of 'drive,' hasty action, or confused thought suggests itself. This is a very safe man, one reflects instinctively, deliberate in considering, slow of judgment, patient in decision, but capable—when action must come—of a tremendous initiative and follow-through. The source of such strength is apparent in the man's manner; Mr. Cassatt has the simplicity of Lincoln."

Cassatt, like anyone walking the jammed canyons of lower Manhattan bedecked with American flags, with new skyscrapers shooting up on all sides, could feel just how desperately hemmed in and crowded the world's greatest port had become. The sidewalks were thronged and teeming with purposeful men, women, and youngsters, all moving fast. "The very dogs had apparently no time to loiter," wrote one bemused visiting Englishman, "but scurried about, as though late for their engagements." The air pulsed with mechanical urban energy: "The dull roar of traffic and the sharp alarm of the cable gong never ceases here, and grows more ominous when about five o'clock the toiling day-dwellers of lower Broadway throw work aside to turn homeward."

All along the cobblestoned streets, vendors braved the winter cold to tempt the passing crowds with trinkets, jewelry, and fruit. The rivers of people surged to a floodtide just below City Hall as they flowed toward the Fulton Street ferries and onto the Brooklyn Bridge, great armies of office commuters battling to get home. That scorned architectural hybrid of multitiered columns, the General Post Office, dominated the south side of City Hall Park. Normally the park was a rare oasis of peace with tall trees and soothing ornate fountains, its curved park benches filled with idle waifs and newsboys from Park Row straggling over from the newspaper offices overlooking City Hall. But where the park should be there yawned a great cut-and-cover maw, where the very rich and arrogant August Belmont was building his Interborough Rapid Transit Company subway stretching from Brooklyn to Harlem. As the Pennsylvania Railroad prepared to enter Gotham, it was still unclear if he was friend or foe.

ELEVEN

"WE SHALL MAKE
OUR FIGHT ABOVEBOARD"

On January 9, 1902, Alexander Cassatt formally initiated the PRR's political campaign for its New York franchise by calling on His Honor Seth Low at Gotham's white marble Italianate City Hall. The small, crowded antechambers reeked of stale cigar smoke and bustled with aides, job seekers, and well-wishers. Mayor Low and Cassatt closeted themselves and got right down to business, a frank discussion about strategy, legislation, franchises, and, of course, bribes. Tammany, payoffs, and boodle were something Seth Low knew all too well.

As the young Republican reform mayor of Brooklyn in the early 1880s, Low had served on the board of the much-delayed Brooklyn Bridge and gained a firsthand education in the pitfalls of "doing business" with Tammany. Bribes were not enough. These venal men wanted rigged bidding, padded payrolls, and whatever else could line their pockets. Greed trumped any consideration of proper engineering, public safety, or swift completion. As Tammany boss Richard Croker had so candidly said, "I'm always looking out for my own pocket."

Consequently, His Honor needed to know exactly where Cassatt stood on bribes. Alexander Cassatt had just expended vast sums on his "community of interest" stamping out secret rebates. He harbored nothing but contempt for scalawags who ran their roads into the ground for personal gain and the ruination of their gullible investors. He was working hard to legislate (without success) against the squandering of $1 million a year in PRR stockholder's money on the pernicious tradition of free rail passes to every politician and self-important journalist.

Predictably, Cassatt was against paying bribes or sealing secret deals with Tammany. Why should his magnificent company grease any palms for the privilege of expending $40 million to build a monumental public work? Not only would the PRR provide construction jobs for thousands of New Yorkers for many years, but the completed terminal would be a crown jewel in the nation's greatest city as well as an important economic asset, while the tunnels would at last connect Gotham with the rest of the nation. In short, the Pennsylvania Railroad under the presidency of Alexander Cassatt was *not* inclined to see boodle as business as usual.

" 'If I help you,' said Mr. Low, 'You must give me your word that you will not attempt to get by secret means what you cannot get in an open way.'

" 'Nothing could suit me better than that,' said Mr. Cassatt heartily. 'I give you my word and the word of my company. We shall make our fight aboveboard, and our plans must go through on their merits, or not at all.' "

Alexander Cassatt now had a crucial ally. Low's initial advice was to secure legislation up in Albany that would give the city's Rapid Transit Commission (presided over by Low) first crack at granting the tunnel franchise. Those hearings would draw out friend and foe and reveal their strengths and weaknesses. The two men agreed to have their respective corporation counsels meet to consider the framing of the initial bill.

A week after his City Hall colloquy with Mayor Low, Cassatt waded deeper into the political fray, writing Pennsylvania's Republican senator Matthew S. Quay in Washington, D.C. "We shall require some legislation at Albany, as well as in New York City, to enable us to make our extension by tunnel into New York. As Mr. Edward M. Shepard [the Tammany mayoral candidate who lost to Low] has had large experience in this class of legislation, we had proposed to retain him as Counsel in this connection, but it had occurred to us that perhaps, for political reasons, his appointment would be inexpedient. Could you do me the favor of ascertaining how Mr. Platt would feel about this?" Senator Quay, the Keystone State's all-powerful Republican boss, was a famously reticent and erudite politician, a saturnine scholar of Horace and Pliny renowned for keeping "silent in sixteen different languages." Short, droop-eyed, and secretive, he was a longtime ally of Senator Platt's and thus well placed to assist Cassatt. And, as it turned out, the Republican "Easy Boss" felt that Shepard was not nearly as qualified to represent the PRR as his own lawyer son, Frank Platt.

In a confidential letter William Baldwin, with his insider's knowledge of New York's byzantine politics, strongly counseled Cassatt against any such political hiring: "Mr. Frank Platt is a lobbyist, and his name connected with this work would suggest at once that there was money in it. If he gets his hands on the handling of the matter in any way, difficulties will appear, and it will have the wrong atmosphere. As I have said to you from the first, this whole enterprise is so big and so important, that there is absolutely no need of your making any move that would embarrass you in any way."

Boss Platt and his son were on poor terms with New York governor Odell, but as the reliable dispenser of largesse from the giant corporations and trusts, the "Easy Boss" could still command the legislature on many a vote. Cassatt duly contacted Senator Platt in Washington, who provided gratifyingly "prompt attention to our business." But Cassatt also let Platt know that "On further reflection, we did not consider it necessary to employ special counsel . . . If you should consider it necessary that anyone should go to Albany to explain our purposes, I can arrange to have one of our executive officers go there at any time." Platt did not let this interfere with zealous service, and moved quickly to pass the PRR's New York State bill. Cassatt wrote Platt, saying, "You have placed us under an obligation which it will be a pleasure to acknowledge when an opportunity offers." Little did Cassatt dream of the struggles that still lay ahead.

It would be hard to conjure up two more opposing worldviews than those of the Pennsylvania Railroad Company and Gotham's boss-dominated politics. The PRR of Alexander Cassatt prided itself on being a modern twentieth-century corporation, a huge and complex organization where efficiency and a hierarchical meritocracy reigned supreme. It was the "Standard Railroad of America," admired and respected for its methodical pursuit of technical excellence and an almost fanatical dedication to better service and safety. Management worked every day to improve the railroad that they proudly viewed as the centerpiece of an increasingly urbanized, industrialized America. They did not earn their steady profits by manipulating or watering their stock but by providing outstanding service. In an industrialized world of larger and larger modern entities— whether vast railroad, telegraph and electrical systems, big steel, bigger government, cities with their mushrooming populations and twenty-story skyscrapers, new universities dedicated to science and technology—all of these modern enterprises in the new and unfolding century now demanded proper organization and forward-looking management. This the Pennsylvania Railroad had in spades.

But old-style nineteenth-century political bosses like Richard Croker evinced little interest in the complexities of the modern age. Even as President Teddy Roosevelt wrestled with just how activist and progressive government had to be in this new era of cosmopolitanism and corporate giantism, Croker clung to an almost feudal worldview that concerned itself purely with raw power and the proper rewarding of armies of political vassals. New York was the nation's largest city and the world's most important port, growing at an unprecedented rate but beset with wrenching woes: impoverished immigrants, disease-ridden tenements, overwhelmed transit systems, poorly maintained piers and docks, and inadequate sanitation.

Croker, who had ruled Tammany and New York with an iron fist for almost two decades, "did not comprehend the issues of his day even remotely," opined editor William Allen White. Tammany's worldview was, in fact, dangerously parochial. To give just one small example: Tammany regarded the New York Health Department as little more than a handy political clubhouse, with employees "sitting around the corridors smoking and gossiping, . . . others [being] in a state of intoxication," a dangerously ignorant attitude that had had devastating consequences in 1901 when smallpox struck New York's slums. A near epidemic swiftly erupted, with almost 2,000 cases and 410 deaths, before the department bestirred itself to inadequate action.

Thomas Collier Platt played a somewhat different game, catering as he did to the great trusts and corporations of the day, but the "Easy Boss" despised reformers as heartily as did Croker. The pallid Platt had only loathing for troublesome Republicans like Seth Low and Teddy Roosevelt who engaged in the mysterious "altruism," that is, reformist impulses to serve the people. Platt, from his gilded horsehair settee in the "Amen Corner" of the Fifth Avenue Hotel, had actively sabotaged both men's political careers, but the sheer size and power of these new modern entities—whether corporate trusts or skyscraper cities—cried out for the stronger and more imaginative governance the reformers espoused.

Americans no longer lived in the ideal yeoman farmer world of Thomas Jefferson, where each man, each family forged its own way. This was the Gilded Age of J. P. Morgan, Andrew Carnegie, and John D. Rockefeller, men whose giant corporations and industrial trusts held the fates of millions of citizens in their hands. Nearly seven-eighths of American wealth was now owned by 1 percent of its families. The sheer size of the workplace and the booming metropolises created complexities and demanded all manner of new laws and regulations. Reformers had fought hard to restrict child labor, for a ten-hour workday, to protect those injured in industrial accidents, to ensure that those living in city tenements had light and air, and that cities had clean water. Yet both Croker and Platt disdained the "constructive" side of politics and government, except as it might augment influence, patronage, or boodle.

And so New York's powerful newspapers watched in almost morbid fascination as the redoubtable Alexander Cassatt, who led the nation's largest, most profitable, and most admired railroad, strode into the city's rough-and-tumble political arena utterly determined to proceed honorably, actually presuming to prevail because of the sheer magnificence and scale of his railroad's proposed enterprise. This was such a radical approach that it elicited praise from the New-York Tribune: "There was no secrecy about the matter [of the franchise] at Albany or elsewhere, and no sharp practices . . . employed to gain support in any quarter." Of course, it would be great sport to watch Cassatt as he proceeded gamely forward.

On Friday morning March 21, 1902, Alexander Cassatt and a phalanx of top PRR officers arrived at City Hall at eleven o'clock for the first formal hearing on their tunnel bill. All about the grandiose structure, trees were budding a fresh green, while across in City Hall Park pounding construction deep down in the IRT subway site joined the blaring clang and roar of the incessant traffic.

When Mayor Low opened the Rapid Transit Commission's hearing, even those officials "heartily in favor" of the tunnels and terminal complained about the prospect of a *perpetual* franchise. The Citizens Union denounced the bill for that reason, as did the Merchants Association. The PRR counsel remained adamant on this point, saying, "To get a perpetual charter is absolutely necessary, and if that cannot be had the plan is useless." If their franchise was beholden and wobbly, the PRR explained, no financier would lend the huge sums needed for construction.

Banker August Belmont, supercilious and ill-tempered, was present to register his suspicions that somehow, somewhere the PRR franchise would interfere with his nascent subway empire. And so it went, mistrust evident in every utterance. After all, corporate encounters in recent years had left the cynical citizenry of Gotham feeling badly snookered. In a press release, Cassatt quickly asserted that the PRR was "perfectly willing to pay the city proper compensation for any privileges granted and to have this compensation readjusted every twenty-five years." As the PRR men headed back to the ferry and home, it seemed a most inauspicious start. The Saturday headlines the next day said it all: "Tunnel Bill Opposed."

On Monday, Cassatt, determined to salvage the situation, raced back to Gotham from Philadelphia, showing off a bit and indulging his love of speed. One of the PRR's swiftest engines, pulling only the president's deluxe Pullman car, sped the ninety miles north on that bright and sunny morning in a record-breaking seventy-nine minutes, thus clipping four minutes "from the record made by J. P. Morgan's special train on February 7." Of course, after this exhilarating sprint, Cassatt and his party still had to slog across on the ferry. Cassatt made one point clear to the inquiring *Tribune* reporter: "There will be no room for anything besides our own passenger traffic. The best thing for our neighbors to do is to build a tunnel or tunnels for themselves as we propose to do."

At City Hall, Cassatt and his men huddled with Mayor Low. As many politicos and newspapers—filled with ads for Easter hats and gloves—had reminded His Honor, he had once solemnly vowed never to grant a perpetual franchise. This was true, the mayor acknowledged that day to the press, explaining, "No one in this community is more averse to the

perpetual franchise than am I." The city reserved the right to future ownership of the still-to-be-built subways, "but in the case of the Pennsylvania Railroad tunnel, on the other hand . . . the city would acquire what
would be of comparatively little value without the outside railroad systems connected therewith." That said, to universal surprise, Mayor Low
ignored the naysayers, and signed the tunnel bill. Yet even as Mayor
Low signed, he announced the bill would return to the state legislature
for certain changes before going over to the Board of Aldermen. A cautiously jubilant Cassatt said, "We do not know just what course things
will take . . . If nothing unforeseen happens we will begin construction
work by early summer."

TWELVE

"UGLY RUMORS OF BOODLE"

Young William Randolph Hearst's populist, powerful, and widely read *Journal American* immediately attacked Mayor Seth Low for signing the tunnel bill, trumpeting "A Colossal Robbery of the People of New York in Progress." This was a disturbing development for the Pennsylvania Railroad, for Hearst was a dangerous enemy, as Tammany had discovered during the Ice Trust scandal. His editorial particularly objected to the perpetual franchise, asserting, "It is infamous that the rights of the people in these franchises, worth hundreds of millions to the Pennsylvania Company, should be given away forever . . . IT IS A JOB. A GIGANTIC JOB."

Oddly, Hearst, himself a rampaging reformer, had taken a vociferous dislike to the new mayor. In early March, William Baldwin had made sure the PRR's Philadelphia office saw a Hearst editorial attacking Low as a "snob," leading "an administration of men who look upon the ordinary voter exactly as they look upon one of their servants downstairs in the kitchen." Moreover, the Hearst paper portrayed Low as a yacht-owning elitist in cahoots with the Pennsylvania Railroad, evidenced by his appointment of Gustav Lindenthal as bridge commissioner. (While Lindenthal was more than qualified for such a position, one suspects it served as consolation for Lindenthal's beloved North River Bridge losing out to the tunnels.) "[Low] does know very well and intimately the

Pennsylvania millionaires . . . and he plans to give them a perpetual franchise in New York City in defiance of existing laws."

Newspaper publisher William Randolph Hearst in 1904.

Young Hearst had confounded Gotham with his lightning rise to power. Armed with his family's glittering mining fortune, he had stormed the New York newspaper world in the fall of 1895, hell-bent on trouncing publisher Joseph Pulitzer and displacing the *World* as Gotham's and the nation's leading Democratic newspaper and champion of the working people. At first, few took Hearst or his newspaper seriously. Plenty of better men had expended vast sums and failed to make a mark among New York's crowded field of powerful newspapers. "Though he continued to dress like a dandy and live the life of a playboy, Will Hearst was, or believed himself to be, as authentic an advocate of the workingman as his rival," writes biographer David Nasaw. "There was no blue blood in the Hearst family. While Will had been raised with a silver spoon in his mouth and gone to Harvard, he had never forgotten where his father came from . . . In New York, as in San Francisco, he ran a paper that was pro-labor, pro-immigrant, and anti-Republican."

The paterfamilias, George Hearst, had been a barely literate scraggle-bearded miner savant, a self-taught geologist who roamed the West for years and struck one fabulous bonanza after another. His holdings were legendary: the Homestake gold mine, the Ontario silver mine, and the Anaconda copper mine, among others. The elder Hearst bought himself a U.S. Senate seat from the California legislature, served with no distinction in Washington, D.C., and died there in early 1890. Now his formidable widow, Phoebe Apperson Hearst, reluctantly doled out millions to her ambitious only child.

William Randolph Hearst swiftly showed he was very much a force to be reckoned with, a genius at journalism, promotion, and ballyhoo. From the start, the *Journal American*'s illustrations were extraordinary, while the news was always played to be as sensational as possible—blaring, eye-catching, a titillating mix of crimes and accidents, dirty politics, scandals, and his trademark crusading investigative reports. Hearst was fearless in taking on all the powers that be. With his daily paper (price: one cheap penny) gaining readers fast, Hearst next raided his targeted rival, the *Sunday World*, with its circulation of 450,000, dangling an irresistible salary before editor Morrill Goddard, a seasoned and brilliant newspaperman. Goddard was sorely tempted, but couldn't bear to leave behind his carefully cultivated staff. Master of the grand gesture, Hearst expanded his offer to include them as well. Pulitzer, learning that Goddard had jumped ship, responded with a better offer. Goddard returned to the gold-domed Pulitzer Building. Hearst bid higher and "Pulitzer was left with an empty office and one stenographer," writes Hearst biographer Nasaw. "Even the office cat, it was reported, had defected to Hearst."

Nor was it simply a matter of money, though the ink-stained wretches of Park Row found man-about-town Hearst wondrously generous, a boss like no other, heaping bonuses on top of handsome salaries. Explains Nasaw, "Pulitzer had become an impossible man to work for, a nasty, vituperative, foul-mouthed martinet. [Now] Blind, and so sensitive to sound he had to eat alone lest he be disturbed by a dinner companion's biting on silverware, Pulitzer had abandoned New York but had been unable to settle down anywhere else . . . Incapable of managing his papers at close hand, but unwilling to let go, he interfered at a distance." Despite the mass defections and Pulitzer's wretched health, the *World* remained a great populist paper, widely read and much admired. Now it was joined by Hearst's even more fiery, far less admired, highly partisan and increasingly influential *Journal American*.

It would be almost a month before the PRR officials extricated the new improved tunnel bill from the state legislature, a bill specific enough in its detail to placate many of its critics on the Rapid Transit Commission. In this first round, Mayor Low had also quietly scored a crafty coup. Reported the *New-York Tribune*, "The Board of Aldermen will have no power to modify the grant or contract made to the Pennsylvania Railroad, but can either approve or disapprove the grant or contract, as they please." With the franchise back on track, a manager from the PRR's New York office ventured over to speak with S. S. Carvalho, managing editor of Hearst's *Journal American* (and another Pulitzer alum). He reported back to Philadelphia with delight, "Mr. Carvalho assured me that he has great personal admiration for our Management, and asked me to say to Mr. Cassatt that no paper in the country is more friendly to the Pennsylvania Management than is the New York Journal. I have the assurance of Mr. Carvalho that . . . the Journal would not go out of its way to criticize or complain of matters in which our Company may be, hereafter, interested." Whatever the reason for this abrupt change of heart, it was welcome news indeed.

It would take another two months of closed-door negotiations, but as summer neared, Mayor Low and the Rapid Transit Commissioners finally voted on June 15, 1902, in favor of the franchise, which would be perpetual. (It was perhaps not irrelevant that five weeks earlier Cassatt had decided the PRR did after all need the legal services of Platt's lawyer son at $10,000 a year.) The franchise would also allow the PRR the all-important privilege of buying and closing the part of West Thirty-second Street that otherwise would run right through the proposed terminal. For these privileges, the PRR would pay $75,535 annually for a decade and then $114,871 each year for the next fifteen years, for a total of almost $2.5 million. Thereafter, the franchise fees would be renegotiated. The *New-York Tribune* marveled at "the almost boundless confidence of President Cassatt and his advisers in the future of this city, for the Pennsylvania is preparing to pour out money like water for the privilege of placing a station in the heart of the nation's metropolis."

In truth, Cassatt was miffed. In no other city in the world would a corporation pay to build a tunnel. In any case, the battle had taken more than three months. But Cassatt and his tunnel franchise had survived the first great test. At the end of the meeting, Cassatt rose, grinned happily, and shook hands with each and every one of the commissioners at the long wooden meeting table. Mayor Low deemed the agreement historic, being the first time that the "city has received such a large sum for a franchise." Now came Tammany.

On Tuesday July 1 as the rain was clearing outside, the clerk serving the Board of Aldermen stood up in the pungent City Hall chamber with the PRR franchise in his hands and began to read it aloud, signaling its formal introduction. Many of the seventy-nine members were not present and those who were paid little attention, loafing about in their wooden swivel chairs, chattering and smoking instead among themselves. The suffragette Beatrice Webb had visited these very chambers several years earlier and been appalled by the aldermen, finding "one face more repulsive than another in its cynicism, sensuality or greed . . . The type combined the characteristics of a loose liver, a stump orator and intriguer with the vacant stare of the habitual lounger." The reading clerk was only a sentence into his dronelike recitation of the PRR franchise when Alderman John Diemer, a clean-shaven gangly fellow, motioned him to stop and quickly consigned the document unread to the Committee on Railroads that he chaired. Ten days passed of what was turning into a rainy, cool summer, and there the tunnel bill languished.

New Yorkers watched with a sort of perverse pride as rumors wafted languidly forth from that ungracious civic body of aldermen indicating no hurry to proceed or likelihood of action. There were rumblings of unnamed "lobbyists" lining up to defeat the measure, of Tenderloin aldermen Reginald Doull and William Whittaker waxing obdurate because the terminal would displace vast numbers of their constituents. Most assumed that the Tammany aldermen were simply settling comfortably into their accustomed expectant posture, waiting to be "seen" (i.e., paid off), with the figure $300,000 whispered about. Alexander Cassatt, president of the wealthy Pennsylvania Railroad, could assert all he pleased, as the *New-York Tribune* reported, "that the company would not pay one dollar in order to get the franchise through the Board of Aldermen." But why did that high-handed gentleman feel he or his project were any better than the rich and disdainful August Belmont and his Lenox Avenue IRT extension? Belmont had "seen" the aldermen to the tune of $20,000, according to the *Trib* and City Hall scuttlebutt. Gotham and Tammany had their own long-entrenched political folkways and there was no persuasive reason this corporate titan from Philadelphia should not honor them.

Repeatedly prodded by Mayor Low, the aldermen on the Railroad Committee finally bestirred themselves to consider the PRR franchise. And when they did, they found little to like. Proclaimed Republican alderman William Whittaker, "No vote of mine shall ever bestow a perpetual franchise of the city's property above or below the streets and I warn the honorable Mayor and Rapid Transit Commissioners to flee from the wrath to come."

Several demanded the franchise be recast to oblige the PRR to hew to the municipality's own eight-hour labor and wage rules, despite court verdicts against such rules for private companies. Otherwise, prophesied Alderman Doull, "scab labor would be brought from Pennsylvania to build the tunnel under charge of padrones." They also complained that the franchise compensation was mingy; the city should have some control of the actual tunnel; it was all a plot to divert the city's immense freight business out to Montauk. One alderman idly wondered why the city didn't build the tunnels itself? When the franchise was sent out to the full chamber on Monday July 21, the aldermen vented their ire by voting it down 56 to 10 and scornfully tossing the whole matter back to the Rapid Transit Commission.

The conservative press howled, denouncing "The Short-Sighted Aldermen" and wondering "What Are Their Reasons?" The *Commercial Advertiser* assumed "blackmail" and lamented the defeat of a "Great public improvement . . . of vast and enduring benefit to the whole city." Even Joseph Pulitzer's staunchly Democratic *World* heaped contumely. The purported objections—franchise terms, labor issues—were "Worse Than Silly." "It is a veiled 'hold up,' and the veil is thin." Hearst, who was now hoping for Tammany's backing for a congressional bid, took a tempered stance: "Let us give credit for common honesty to the men we elected, until they are shown to be unworthy, anyhow." Mayor Low assumed a statesmanlike tone, reassuring the public that the aldermen's action was "straightforward and manly" and that the Rapid Transit Board would "try to meet the criticisms of the Aldermen as far as practicable." Low gathered a handful of the more important irate aldermen on his yacht *Surprise* the following warm Saturday to cruise about the harbor and soothe their ruffled feathers and talk some sense. Perhaps he thought the sight of all those jammed ferryboats crisscrossing the busy waters might instill some small feeling of civic obligation.

As August rolled around, anyone who could escape to a resort had fled. President Roosevelt was out at Oyster Bay, Long Island, mixing his vigorous idea of relaxing with politics. Brother-in-law Douglas Robinson summed up "the true Roosevelt style" as "going it with a vengeance . . . not a minute unemployed eating, talking." But despite the president's busy frolics and fun with his brood of children, he was growing increasingly worried about a spreading coal strike. Alexander Cassatt had headed north with his family to the cool days and evenings of Bar Harbor, Maine. Mayor Low remained dutifully in Gotham, doggedly persevering on the PRR's behalf. In the muggy heat, even the trees looked exhausted, while the baking streets exhaled a sour stench. Men wore their straw boaters and cooler linen suits, while women in the popular white Gibson Girl dresses used parasols against the sun. On Sundays, hordes of cyclists clogged the avenues heading out of town. The city's frenetic pace slowed. The street vendors offered ice cream and lemonade.

At City Hall, Mayor Low presided over a joint meeting of the Rapid Transit Commission, the Board of Aldermen, and the PRR. Everyone shifted about uncomfortably in the stifling meeting room, and the same aldermen stood up to complain once again about labor, the perpetual franchise, and the railroad's intentions. Hot and bored, the PRR's elegant vice president and attorney Captain John Green, a veteran of Sherman's March, finally lost all patience. A slight, wiry man with a bushy gray beard, he had a prickly temper. When one alderman spun a dark vision of the PRR making Montauk a great port at New York's expense, Green ex-ploded, "No sane man ever thought or dreamed of taking commerce out to Montauk Point. You could no more take commerce away from New York than you could take blood out of your body and live. Montauk Point will never be a terminus. It is absurd even to discuss it . . . There is no more chance of the Pennsylvania Railroad doing that than there is of my flying over a house."

And, reiterated Captain Green for the umpteenth time, various court rulings forbid requiring eight-hour labor and prevailing wage clauses in such a franchise. Moreover, the PRR prided itself on good relations with its workers. "We always pay him well." At the end of the session, Green wearily repeated, "We have come here with clean hands and asked for a franchise which it will be to your advantage to grant . . . We propose to spend $40,000,000 to $50,000,000 and propose to observe the law." Translation: No boodle. To Cassatt, he complained, "Had to listen to two hours of blatherskiting."

And so summer drifted into a lovely autumn, and week after week there was a franchise parley here, a minor concession there, but no sign of prog-ress. It was, it seemed, a season for standoffs. Down in Washington, D.C., President Roosevelt was yearning to somehow end what had become a rancorous and potentially devastating Pennsylvania coal miners strike. The 147,000 striking anthracite miners—mainly Slav immigrants—displayed an evangelical fervor, swearing off liquor, smoldering in their determina-tion to wrest better pay and union recognition. The cartel of coal mine and railroad operators who controlled this all-important industrial and domestic fuel were equally adamant, refusing to so much as meet the miners or United Mine Workers president, John Mitchell. Mine owner and railroad president George Baer pontificated, "The rights and inter-ests of the laboring men will be protected and cared for—not by the la-bor agitators, but by the Christian men to whom God in His infinite wisdom has given the control of the property interests of the country." This produced great brays of derision in even the most conservative of journals.

But the coal strike was no joke. If the two sides did not come to terms soon, how would the great cities heat themselves? Or the nation's steam engines run? Even were the strike to end instantly, the nation was already ten million tons short. Now the eighteen thousand bituminous miners had joined in, thus forcing the layoffs of the fifty thousand men running the labyrinthine system of coal railroads. Moreover, what was now the biggest organized strike in the nation's history was flaring into violence just as the nights were growing noticeably colder. Lacking any real authority to intervene, Roosevelt wrote Senator Henry Cabot Lodge, "I am at my wits' end how to proceed." When fall frosts shimmered on chill mornings with their intimations of winter, the president became desperate and summoned the two stalemated sides to meet October 3 in Washington. The mine owners came but arrogantly spurned all compromise.

In Manhattan, the PRR tunnel franchise languished at the Rapid Transit Commission while Mayor Low valiantly sought allies among the aldermen. Complicating the entire bogged-down process was Tammany's own summer of turmoil. Boss Richard Croker had, after two decades of corrupt power, partially ceded his tarnished throne. In these months, many vied for that prize, including Alderman Timothy P. Sullivan, a burly saloonkeeper who declared himself staunchly against the franchise unless there was a labor clause. In response, the PRR again cited Court of Appeals rulings that declared such a clause illegal. Week in and week out the PRR engaged in franchise parleys, making minor concessions here and there. Yes, the city could put police and fire phone and telegraph wires in the tunnel, yes it would be under the city's police laws, and so forth. Meanwhile, the public charges of "hold up" grew clamorous.

Determined to move things forward, Mayor Low turned up the pressure and placated critics by holding another public hearing on the afternoon of Thursday October 2 at the commission offices at 320 Broadway. As soon as he learned of it, Cassatt sat down at his desk at Cheswold, where the meadows were full of autumn wildflowers, to quickly write for help from one of the grand old men of New York public life, former mayor Abram S. Hewitt. Would he testify for the PRR? "It is asking very much, I know, but your publicly expressed approval of the terms of the franchise would be of the greatest service at this juncture."

Hewitt, a Democrat and self-made man who had also wisely married a wealthy heiress, was a known antagonist of Tammany. His unlikely 1886 mayoral candidacy had been a desperate and successful ploy to defeat the popular radical reformer Henry George. But once in office, Hewitt dropped Tammany and refused to have any truck with the Tiger, culminating in his refusal to fly the Irish flag at City Hall on St. Patrick's Day. Hewitt, who had gone on to serve five terms in Congress, was also much admired for being the original and visionary proponent of underground rapid transit subways, now finally under construction.

By the fall afternoon of Low's public hearing, the Pennsylvania Railroad's long-stalled tunnel franchise had become a cause célèbre. Crowds of property owners, aldermen, politicians, lawyers, and labor leaders jammed into City Hall's elegant wood-paneled meeting room, spilling noisily out into the hall and filling the curved upstairs gallery. In the tortuous eight months since Cassatt's initial meeting with the mayor, the whole city had had ample opportunity to take sides. Soon, the cigar smoke grew thick, the room warm with too many bodies. The venerable Hewitt appeared for the Chamber of Commerce to laud the PRR, exclaiming over the "miracle . . . of connecting our shores with New Jersey. I myself never expected to see the day of the problem's solution." Restive labor elements in the audience heckled and jeered: "Listen to him!" "Let him sell the city!" "Let 'em build by divine right!" Tammany had cast itself as the great champion of labor in yet another chapter of the acrimonious battle between capital and labor. In Pennsylvania, the coal strike was growing ever more tense. Here in Gotham, thirty-five labor unions—having failed to secure the eight-hour wage clause—remained staunchly antitunnel.

As the light outside waned, William Baldwin, ever the reformer, presented the PRR as that rare benevolent and honest road: "It has made its proposition with the higher sense of duty to the public. The Pennsylvania Railroad does not object to union labor . . . This corporation is offering to build the tunnel not simply to make money for itself, but because the people want the tunnel. And the people will have it!" Mayor Low hoped all this hostile venting, plus the ardent endorsements by merchants, business interests, and the press would do the trick. And indeed, within the following week, the Rapid Transit Commission had once more passed the revised franchise and sent it over to the aldermen. Growled the *New York Times*, "Public opinion . . . will not patiently tolerate any trifling with the matter." Meanwhile, the PRR had bought so much of the needed real estate that the interest alone was now a thousand dollars a day, making the foot dragging rather pricey.

As October passed, the Tammany aldermen professed to be far too busy with upcoming November elections to take up the franchise bill. Great trainloads of Tammany men had headed north to their nominating convention, where William Randolph Hearst was backed as a Democratic candidate for Congress from an east side district.

In Washington, President Theodore Roosevelt was grimly contemplating the worsening debacle of the United Mine Workers' coal strike. Seven men were dead in angry clashes. Winter was looming, anthracite had skyrocketed to thirty dollars a ton, and anxious memories hovered of the anarchic Great Railroad Strike of 1877. If the pigheaded operators did not come around soon, Roosevelt intended to order the army reserve to seize and reopen the Pennsylvania mines. To forestall such an unheard-of federal assault against capital, J. Pierpont Morgan stepped in. As a major coal road stockholder, a glowering Morgan managed to cajole the haughty mine owners into submission. By October 15 they had agreed to a face-saving commission to accompany the reopening of the mines. The Coal Commission hearings shocked the nation, with revelations of child labor working night shifts in the mines. The Hearst papers dubbed the mine owners, "The Dollar-Rooting Swine of the Anthracite Fields." The miners won most of their not-unreasonable demands. The president was jubilant at the settlement, declaring he felt "like throwing up my hands and going to the circus." For the first time, an American president had given equal weight to both sides when he intervened in a bitter labor struggle. Like Cassatt, Roosevelt feared the consequences of corporations refusing to fairly reward the working man.

Mayor Low lacked the president's power and only the incessant clamoring of the New York press caused the Board of Aldermen's Railroad Committee to set a hearing date on the tunnel franchise. On Wednesday November 26, five hundred people mobbed the wood-paneled City

Hall hearing room. Reform and Tammany politicos traded bitter and passionate jibes with the silk-hatted merchants, while the ranks of labor engaged in such loud booing and hissing that Chairman Diemer had to pound his gavel violently to bring order. Hour after tumultuous hour, one side—"the railroad interests, the Rapid Transit Commissioners and the great commercial associations"—sang the praises of the great tunnels and terminal, while foes—"united labor"—hectored on about the lack of a labor clause ("If this rich corporation wants the tunnel, let them agree to pay . . . $2 a day for eight hours work"), insufficient payment for the franchise privilege, and the general chicanery of the corporations. Alderman Reginald Doull alone occupied thirty minutes ranting, as was now his wont, about the PRR's "trickery and bribery" in buying up so much of his district. When the session finally dragged to an end after five dispiriting hours, lower Manhattan was dark and oddly quiet, for the working world had long gone home to prepare for Thanksgiving the next day. The PRR's fourth vice president Samuel Rea told a reporter, "I am sure that the pride of this community and the enterprise of its citizens will not allow us to abandon the tunnel."

The PRR was growing weary of this stalling and John Green, third vice president, told one reporter as he departed, "If we don't get permission within the next twelve months to build the tunnel we will abandon the whole enterprise and sell the real estate we have already bought. We can do that without any trouble. We have received offers for it." Once again, the *Tribune* boldly warned of a "clique . . . determined to extort from the Pennsylvania company a round sum for the tunnel franchise," hiding behind a sudden "love for the cause of labor." The figure of $300,000 remained the purported sum. Alexander Cassatt reiterated, "We have come to New York for this franchise with clean hands, and we are going to keep our hands clean. We will not pay one cent for the granting of this franchise beyond the terms stated in the proposed contract."

With the bill still mired in the Railroad Committee more than a week later, the *World* ran a big front-page cartoon on Thursday December 4 featuring a hungry Tammany Tiger holding an empty, open "dough bag," its large paws pinning down the PRR franchise legislation. Lounging about were a handful of cigar-smoking politicians complaining, "Nawthin' in it for us!" The accompanying story, titled "Ugly Rumors of Boodle," spoke darkly not just of the usual bribery but of "powerful interests" out to thwart the PRR's entry into Manhattan. The talk of defeat intensified. The next day Manhattan had its first snowfall and the temperatures began to plummet. Within days it was so bitterly cold, the aldermen voted $100,000 in free coal for the poor in their frigid tenements. The harbor began to clog with ice, forcing the ferries to struggle across, a potent reminder of the dire need for tunnels.

Every important Gotham newspaper and magazine (save Hearst, who had just won a congressional seat with Tammany backing) had joined in a prolonged and collective howl of high dudgeon and outrage. The *New York Times* denounced the aldermen as crooks: "There is not an honest hair in the head of one of them." *Scientific American* excoriated the aldermen for "one of the most shamefaced exhibitions of political tyranny that ever disgraced the city of New York." Letter writers hurled contempt, lamenting "the shameful spectacle" and castigating the aldermen as "a perpetual menace to good government." By December 9, the much-abused Railroad Committee at last disgorged the franchise bill to the Board of Aldermen.

Now the serious arm-twisting and vote counting began, with every paper running detailed lists of which aldermen were For, which Against, and which In Doubt. The "Easy Boss" declared from the fastness of the Amen Corner that every one of the fourteen Republican aldermen would faithfully vote for the franchise, as his party did not want any responsibility for "defeat of a measure of such vast importance to the city." Senator Platt and others further warned that should Tammany fail to do right, they intended to sidestep them via legislation in Albany. Governor Odell, ever hostile to Platt, disputed this claim. Charles F. Murphy, the wealthy owner of four saloons who had beaten out Tim Sullivan for the Tammany leadership, claimed neutrality, but few believed him.

In its December 12 issue, the *Railroad Gazette* marveled that "every daily newspaper in New York" endorsed the franchise. "Public opinion is overwhelmingly in favor of what is unquestionably one of the most valuable public improvements ever devised for the city. This nobody questions, but the franchise is held up by a band of political buccaneers . . . It is hoped that . . . a few of those who now oppose the franchise will come to their senses." The early perverse civic amusement at Tammany's greedy antics had given way to sober concern that the PRR's marvelous enterprise, this $50 million private solution to water-locked Gotham with its forty-one ferry routes, might actually be rejected. And so petitions in the tunnel's favor began inundating the aldermen. Great department stores like R. H. Macy & Co. and Saks & Co., leading hoteliers from the Waldorf-Astoria, the Delavan, and the Navarre, real estate companies with major holdings, even fifty-two labor unions beseeched the dilatory aldermen "not to deprive New York City of this great project." But Tammany's "Little Tim" Sullivan insisted that he and forty-three of his political Myrmidons intended to do just that. They had the votes and they would vote nay. "No power on earth can deliver me into the hands of the Pennsylvania Railroad," he vowed.

On Tuesday December 16, Gotham was swathed in light snow from a furious weekend nor'easter. Now, the skies were an iridescent blue, but a bone-chilling damp encased the city. Coal shortages plagued the slums. The city's bedraggled, bundled-up shovel brigades shuffled and scraped as they cleared the streets and sidewalks, dumping the snow into horse-drawn carts for disposal in the river. It had been an exasperating year since Alexander Cassatt had first announced the PRR's tunnels and terminal project.

Finally, on this freezing wintry day the full Board of Aldermen would determine the PRR's fate. All Gotham was abuzz over this high-stakes cliff-hanger, the final act in the rare spectacle pitting Alexander Cassatt and his unusual ethos of corporate honesty versus the entrenched grafters of Tammany Hall, holding out for their $300,000. The *Journal American* had reported a week before "the presence of Mr. Patton, President Cassatt's right-hand man in this city for a few hours . . . His movements could not be traced, but it was understood that he had given assurances [to key aldermen], in nowise connected with the payment of money." In an era of flagrant bribery and boodle, the *Railroad Gazette* praised the PRR simply for being honest and thus "an example to other corporations . . . And there has been no retreat, no dickering and no serious concession." The tunnel bill needed 40 votes to pass. The newspapers listed only 22 aldermen willing to go on record thus far as yeas.

This was certainly an improvement over the board's original dismissive vote of 10 yeas and 56 nays, but it was no winning number.

And so, once again, the aldermanic chambers and galleries were jammed with spectators, a shifting sea of black derbies and silk top hats, all anxious to witness and influence this historic clash. At 2:07 p.m. on December 16, the session was gaveled open. Mayor Low had dispatched to every member of the "honorable board" (and the city press) a heartfelt letter, pleading with them to consider the monumental importance of the tunnels. "It means, if accepted, more work for the laboring man of New-York, not only during the process of construction, but also through the centuries of the railroad's operation; it means more business for our shops, more employment for our factories, and more commerce for our port; and it means cheaper and better homes within the borders of our city for multitudes of our population. It will go far to make sure of the permanent pre-eminence of New-York among the cities of the world."

The first order of business was a full reading of the Railroad Committee's favorable report. Then two antis stood up to deliver cantankerous reports against the tunnels and the PRR. Alderman Moses Wafer proposed consigning the franchise once again to the Railroad Committee. The first moment of truth had arrived, causing a ripple of excitement in the galleries. A dozen aldermen scurried out of the chambers to avoid casting votes, while those remaining strutted and speechified at length before voting yea or nay. It was perilously close, but the PRR won 35 to 32 on this issue of consignment. The franchise *would* be voted on this afternoon. Such was the importance of this vote, that all but one (out ill) of the seventy-nine aldermen were present.

For four tense hours discussion dragged on, "during every minute of which there was constant effort being made by the opponents and friends of the franchise to win votes." There were small surprises, as when a Tammany man, Frank Dowling, stood up to say, "If you pass this tunnel franchise, it is in the interest of labor . . . If it is a crime to give people work, than I am going to commit that crime." Finally, as six o'clock approached, the roll call began. Again, numerous aldermen exited. Of those present, only 33 voted yea for the franchise, while 28 voted nay. (It was a reflection on Boss Platt's waning powers that four Republicans were among the nays.) Some of the absent Tammany men reentered the chambers. Two voted yea. Bronx Borough President Haffen, who hurried out to take a telephone call, returned scowling. As he conferred with other Bronx men a rumor raced through the chamber that Charles F. Murphy, who had emerged as the new boss of Tammany, had called to order Haffen to vote nay. But an angry-looking Haffen, suffering from a cold and sore throat, stood up and croaked his vote yea for the tunnels. At that, a Brooklyn alderman rushed over to change his yea vote to nay. Slowly, one after another, Haffen's Bronx Democrats followed their leader, and the vote for the tunnel franchise crept slowly up to 39.

At six o'clock when yet another Bronx Democrat stepped forward, the crowd quieted. That alderman looked around and voted yea, making 40 votes, exactly the number needed for passage. The chamber exploded in a rollicking roar of applause, groans, and hisses. The public reaction was jubilant. More than a year after Cassatt had first announced his tunnels, the PRR had their franchise and they had paid no boodle. "The great thing," wrote the *New York Times*, "the momentous thing, is that the way is now open for the Pennsylvania Railroad to begin work upon the

CLEAR THE TRACK.

A political cartoon about the tunnel franchise fight.

tunnel and terminal." For the PRR men, all the earlier frustrations and postponements and the failure of their North River Bridge plans could now be forgotten. They could luxuriate instead in the knowledge that their railroad would come into Gotham. Down in Philadelphia, Cassatt emerged from a Union League dinner smiling broadly, "It looks like clear sailing now." He would need every ounce of that optimism for the travails ahead.

PART II

THE CROSSING

"Oh River! darkling River! . . .
On glide thy waters, til at last they flow
Beneath the windows of the populous town,
And all night long give back the gleam of lamps,
And glimmer with the trains of light that stream
From halls where dancers whirl . . ."

—William Cullen Bryant, "Night Journey of a River" (1857)

THIRTEEN

"WE ARE NOT
MAKING A MISTAKE"

The Pennsylvania Railroad began its titanic battle with nature very quietly, just after ten in the morning on Wednesday February 25, 1903. On that day a bevy of distinguished-looking men in derbies and dark suits assembled in front of 557 West Thirty-second Street, a shabby five-story tenement house at Eleventh Avenue. The English tunnel maestro Charles Jacobs (the "Chief") was readily recognizable by his bald head and sweeping white handlebar mustache. Next to him stood the genial and portly Alfred Noble, renowned builder of western bridges and canals, now part of Alexander Cassatt's expert engineering corps. Numerous junior engineers milled about, including James Forgie, an angular Scotsman with a drooping dark mustache, trained by British tunnel pioneer J. H. Greathead, and now Jacobs's second in command. A crew of rough-clad workmen clattered up in a horse-drawn cart and unloaded tools in front of the vacant brick building. Across the cobblestone street, a camera expert from the *New-York Tribune* fussed with his bulky apparatus. Now he yelled to all the men—engineers and workers—to stand together. His camera flashed, capturing their solemn visages.

With that, one of contractor George W. Jump's workmen unlocked the front door of the former lodging house, the stale air of the entry hall still rancid with departed boarders and years of cheap meals. At precisely 10:30 a.m., amidst the faded wallpapers, a laborer ripped up a worn wooden floorboard, thus signaling the official start of the Pennsylvania Railroad's great New York Tunnels and Terminal Extension. Once Jump's wrecking gang had leveled this building, as well as the corner saloon next door and several small buildings on the adjacent Cooper & Wigand foundry, Charles Jacobs could launch the digging of the huge Manhattan shaft straight down, directly below where they now stood, to the musty depth of sixty-five feet. From there, Jacobs would begin tunneling toward the Hudson River, whose waters sparkled beyond the New York Central piers.

And so, on this dilapidated Eleventh Avenue block, on this breezy morning, there unfolded a historic beginning. This humble act of demolition would be the first visible work on a vast, transforming transportation enterprise, what the *Railroad Gazette* termed "an extraordinary example of imagination and daring," the connecting of the nation's mainland and its greatest railroad to its most important port and city. Everyone present had a heady sense of being part of something very big, something they could proudly tell their grandchildren.

The unprepossessing lodging house, with its dreary bed-sitters, would be the first of seven hundred buildings to be cleared, almost all those being further east in the Tenderloin. For the past year, real estate broker Douglas Robinson had been steadily "turning the tenement house dwellers and the storekeepers out by the wholesale, and the whole district seems at elbows and knees." And while the PRR had installed policemen rent-free in numerous homes it now owned, the neighborhood had become a strange ghost town in the very heart of this busiest of metropolises, an eerie urban wasteland of cheap brownstone double-decker lodging houses, shuttered saloons, dance halls, whorehouses, pool halls, vacated churches, derelict old three-story brick houses, and a few remaining Dutch-era residences.

The summer before, a *Tribune* reporter had described this forlorn and largely deserted section of the Tenderloin as "almost pathetic in its complete abandonment . . . Property owners say that every available doorknob, every letterbox and fully half of the lead piping have been stolen from the tenements and houses." The journalist wandering about on that warm June afternoon saw here and there "flowers and faces at the windows," but mainly, "everything is ramshackle. The windows have lost their panes and are stuffed with old rags, gaunt cats haunt the houses, and children are growing afraid . . . It would not be such a bad place for midnight murder."

The *New York Herald* waxed slightly more nostalgic for the passing of the heart of the Tenderloin, this "famous landmark of vice and blackmail," marking it with a tongue-in-cheek poem in its Sunday literary section:

> *Foul Tenderloin! Least wholesome spot in town,*
> *Where vice and greed full many a man brought down.*
>
> *The red faced drivers of the nighthawk cabs*
> *The wardman taking tribute of the drabs,*
> *The bold faced vixen mixing fizz and Scotch,*
> *The rural swain lamenting wad and watch—*
> *Sunk are your hovels, but in wholesome ruin,*
> *Freed from the stigma of much 'shady doin.'*
> *The iron horse has sent your dives to join*
> *The other nightmares of the Tenderloin.*

It was certainly not possible to wax nostalgic for the very far west avenues, tired blocks filled with "factories and rookeries, dingy buildings and the 'great unwashed' that lounge through its streets, giv[ing] it an aspect that is dismal at all times. There is no picturesqueness to be discovered here, not a vestige of the color and foreign chatter of the East Side." Fifty-car New York Central freight trains lumbered up and down their tracks on Tenth Avenue, spewing acrid clouds of cinders and smoke. An old man waving a danger flag rode a half block ahead on an aged nag.

Optimistic throughout the many uncertain and trying months of Tammany's intransigence over the franchise, Alexander Cassatt had been visiting Gotham regularly to quietly advance the PRR's plans. With mounting millions of dollars tied up in Manhattan real estate, the railroad had to press forward. In the beginning of 1902, Cassatt had appointed an eminent board of engineers to study, advise, and ultimately oversee construction of this behemoth and complex enterprise. Those five men gathered for the first time on January 11, high up in the railroad's offices at Cedar

Street, two long blocks from the ferries and overlooking Wall Street. Outside the windows, the skies lowered, threatening more light snow. The chairman was Colonel, soon to be General, Charles W. Raymond, sixty, top man in his West Point class, veteran of Gettysburg, the first army officer to explore Alaska and raise the American flag over the Yukon (an adventure that cost him his sight in one eye), and decorated engineer of many harbor works executed by the U.S. Army Corps of Engineers. His brilliant career and distinguished service at the busy Philadelphia harbor brought him to the PRR's favorable notice. Now he had been given special permission by the army to supervise this gigantic project.

The Board of Engineers: (left to right) Alfred Noble, Charles Jacobs, secretary Alexander Shand, Samuel Rea, George Gibbs, Charles Raymond.

Always a stickler, General Raymond had little patience with lesser scientific minds and brusquely reminded others (often long after the fact) of the many instances when his judgment had been right. What few present knew was that this brilliant but difficult man was slowly but surely losing the sight in his remaining eye to a cataract. Already, he could not properly appreciate the wonderful views from the PRR's aerie, could not clearly see the river busy with ships or the skyscrapers further uptown.

Charles Jacobs, the English tunnel expert, was of course one of the five members of Cassatt's board of engineers. He was, however, absent, for his steamship was late arriving from England, where he had spent his Christmas holiday in London with his wife. And then there was Alfred Noble, who started life as a farm boy, served in the Army of the Potomac, and then trained as a civil engineer. Based in Chicago, he was celebrated for building deepwater works all over the West, including a number of major Mississippi River bridges. A past president of the American Society of Civil Engineers, Noble was an endearing man, treasured for his self-possession and practice of "the simple homely virtues of truth, honesty, industry, and human kindness." In an era when many inflated their Civil War status and heroics, Noble wryly identified himself as part of "The great Corps of Privates." When asked what made a good soldier, he observed, "Ability to withstand hunger, fatigue, and hard marching were very essential qualities, but to be a good runner was also often a very useful attribute." Some years earlier, Noble had played an active role in the Nicaragua Canal Commission.

Also present for the first meeting that cold gray Monday was William H. Brown, the PRR's longtime chief engineer, a career railroad officer who had supplied the hard data for many an earlier scheme for entering Gotham. With his thick graying beard and precise ways, Brown had something of the air and appearance of a biblical prophet. Certainly engineering was almost a religion to him, a science that he savored in all its minutest details. Then there was Gustav Lindenthal, disappointed promoter of the now-forsaken North River Bridge; he would depart the board at the end of 1903 before construction began but would play a key role later.

Not until April was the board's final (and youngest) member appointed. This was the handsome George Gibbs, forty-one, an electrical engineer employed by Thomas Edison at his Pearl Street Station in the early historic days of electrification. Eventually Gibbs had gone into the coming field of electric traction, formed his own company, and then sold it to Pittsburgh industrialist George Westinghouse. The two became friends and collaborated all over Europe on building the new electric subways and trains. Now a partner at Westinghouse, Church, Kerr & Company in New York, the charming Gibbs would oversee all matters electrical. Each of these expert engineer consultants would be paid the then-princely sum of twenty-five thousand dollars a year.

At that very first January meeting, these eminent engineers were instructed to scrutinize the feasibility of every aspect of the PRR's monumental entry to Gotham. "Procure all additional information that may be needed," Alexander Cassatt wrote in a letter read aloud by Samuel Rea, "sparing neither time nor any necessary expense in doing so, for I am sure it is not necessary for me to say that, in view of the magnitude and the great cost of the proposed construction, and of the novel engineering questions involved, your studies should be thorough and exhaustive, and should be based upon absolute knowledge of conditions." "The main consideration," General Raymond would later write, "being safety, durability, and proper accommodation of the traffic. No expenditure tending to insure these conditions was to be avoided."

The big challenge, and a constant source of concern, were the underwater tunnels. The first huge problem was how to build them through glacial silt that *Engineering News* described as "about the most treacherous material through which submarine tunneling has ever been attempted . . . the silt is so yielding and semi-fluid in consistency that it is quite doubtful whether an ordinary cast-iron-lined tunnel would not be distorted and fractured by the movements of the trains."

Ten years earlier, when Samuel Rea had officially contemplated the PRR's various options and concluded a bridge was the best solution, he had bluntly asked, "Can a proper tunnel be constructed through the silt formation which is there encountered [in the North River] that will, after completion, withstand the rack and wear and tear of heavy trains passing through it at high speed? Would not the structure 'work' under the action of heavy trains? We have no precedent to go by, as all subaqueous tunnels of like construction are through a different formation than is found at New York. Therefore, it is largely a matter of speculation." A typical PRR passenger train replete with many comfortable Pullman cars weighed seven hundred tons. Cassatt envisioned hundreds of such trains pounding through the tunnels into and out of Manhattan every day.

In fact, while the problem of burrowing the tunnels under these two busy waterways was a serious one, the real specter haunting these venerable engineers as they met repeatedly during these years was the possible failure of the tunnels *after* vast millions had been spent to build them and the great terminal. As Charles Jacobs explained, the old Haskins tunnels, bedeviled by so many troubles, "led capitalists and engineers to believe that, owing to the very soft nature of the [North River] ground, a tunnel could not be built that would be sufficiently stable to withstand the vibration due to heavy traffic." Jacobs had convinced Alexander Cassatt that the New York tunnels were possible by designing and patenting a reinforced "tunnel bridge," whose supports would descend all the way to the river's bedrock. Many doubted this would solve the problem, and in certain private clubs amidst swirls of after-dinner cigar smoke, men murmured sotto voce that Cassatt's project was nothing short of reckless.

When, days into 1903, President Fowler of the New York, Ontario & Western Railroad defended Cassatt in the *New York Times*, writing, "I cannot believe that it is unduly adventurous or foolhardy to locate within [New York's] constantly expanding borders a second [terminal]," Cassatt penned a grateful note, hoping Fowler's opinion would have "a reassuring effect upon those of our friends, and I suppose there are a good many of them, who have doubted the wisdom of the project . . . We feel very confident we are not making a mistake."

Both Gotham's city fathers and members of the engineering world were thrilled by the coming of the Pennsylvania Railroad tunnels. But there were skeptics aplenty, and they would be neither persuaded nor silenced. For decades, the Pennsylvania Railroad had been a well-run, prudent road, faithfully delivering its 6 percent dividend to tens of thousands of stockholders, many of them English. Now Cassatt was controversially leading the road into a monumental, Pharaoh-like expansion, and he would soon be seeking more than $100 million in new stock and bond offerings to pay for it. Conservative financiers and investors were appalled and antagonized at the hubris, risk, and sheer scale of his vision. They were not at all sure that mere engineers could overcome the perils that lay deep under two swift-flowing rivers.

And so it was that month after month during 1903, PRR stock sank steadily. By early November, the *Tribune* reported the stock down from $170 to "112½, its lowest level since 1898 . . . the company might have difficulty in continuing its present dividends." The *Wall Street Journal* discounted persistent rumors that the Rockefellers were attacking the stock with an eye to acquisition. The issue was that "Mr. Cassatt has condensed ten years' work in two, and the magnitude of his operations has dazed people." Cassatt had little patience for all this shortsighted naysaying. As he wrote Rea, "We are planning for the future, as we ought to do, and not for the present only, and if any persons are doubtful . . . they fail to appreciate the great strength of [our] corporation, and those who doubt that it will ultimately pay have little faith in the future of this country."

As the New York Extension plans advanced, the safety of the tunnels was inevitably paramount. In this new age of industrial marvels and machines, some of the most excruciating disasters of recent decades had been engineering failures. The terrifying railroad bridge collapse at Ashtabula, Ohio—a combination of bad design and substandard iron— consigned eighty-one mangled passengers to die trapped in an inferno of flames at the bottom of a snowy ravine. Moreover, the Ashtabula bridge had collapsed after eleven years of service, underscoring that a structure that worked at first was still not necessarily safe over time. Far more deadly and nightmarish had been the Johnstown Flood in Pennsylvania, where a millionaires' private fishing club's badly designed and maintained earthen dam had ruptured after relentless rains, unleashing a towering torrent of water. This terrifying deluge, almost solid with deadly debris, roared down through the Conemaugh Valley, scouring, engulfing, and destroying more than two thousand souls.

On a regular basis, horrifying railroad accidents further underscored the fallibility of men and machines. Lest any member of this new PRR board of engineers forget this, just two days before their first meeting there had been a gory train wreck right in Manhattan. The engineer of an incoming New York Central White Plains train, failing to see the signals in the dark, smoky Park Avenue tunnel, had slammed straight into the back of the Danbury local, crushing its crowded last car and telescoping it into those in front. The pitch-black tunnel rapidly filled with smoke and echoed with such shrieks and groanings that rescuers groping their way through the dark and wreckage felt they had entered a charnel house. They were barely able to reach the panicked survivors. Fifteen passengers died gruesome deaths while twenty were badly injured.

With this catastrophic tunnel disaster fresh in his mind, Cassatt proposed that their river tunnels be single-track and have an innovative high side bench effectively hemming in the train. When E. H. Harriman, president of the Southern Pacific, had his secretary request information about the New York Extension, Cassatt, though he liked neither the railroad tycoon nor his tactics, wrote him personally to promote this high-bench innovation: "I think the section of the single-track tunnel will interest you . . . Accidents can only arise from two causes in single-track tunnels, either from a breakdown or from a tail-end collision. In either case we think the train will be held in place and that the sidewalks formed by the benches would not be obstructed, and also that telescoping would be prevented."

And so, for these veteran engineers on Cassatt's board of engineers, having decided on subaqueous tunnels, the present life-or-death conundrum was how best to actually build them under the two rivers. General Raymond and the rest of the board spent a solid year just soliciting engineering ideas and then sifting through all the alternatives, including many that "called for the construction of temporary structures in the rivers between the bulkheads," all of these being dismissed "on account of the heavy river traffic." Lindenthal teamed up with another engineer to propose a novel tunneling technique that involved freezing the ground first. In the end, the board concluded that the most logical method for tunneling through the silt was to use Greathead-style shields, designed by James Forgie, and compressed air. The shields, with their adjustable "doors," allowed tunnelers to excavate before each shove forward, and guaranteed a marvelous degree of control.

And then there was the challenge of the proper grades for the vast system of tracks and tunnels. "The limiting features were: the elevation of the tracks in the station area, which are from nine to twenty-three feet below mean high water; the depth of the river bulkheads, for it was necessary to pass under or through their foundations; the contour of the river beds, for it was necessary to establish the tunnel sufficiently below the dredging plane to insure them against possible injury from anchors or sunken vessels and to insure ample cover to retain the compressed air during construction without incurring danger from 'blow-outs'; and the rise and fall of the tide on the Hackensack Meadows—it being necessary for the water to drain away from the tunnel portals. The problem was solved so successfully that the grades to be surmounted are in all cases

less than 2 percent or about 100 feet rise per mile. The enormous electric locomotives have no difficulty starting and accelerating a 550-ton
train on the maximum grades."

All these decisions were merely preparatory to the truly herculean
task Cassatt had entrusted to his board of engineers: actual construction.
These men were Cassatt's generals, the leaders who would marshal
armies of engineers, laborers, animals, and machines as they invaded the
raw and perilous bowels of the ancient rivers and tamed them with civi-
lizing tunnels. The tunnel sections underneath Gotham itself would
present their own unique challenges, for the city's subterranean and
labyrinthine depths were perilous with unstable earth as well as manmade obstacles. Each of the engineers brought decades of real-world
experience to these problems, whether gained in the remote wilds of
India, Egypt, China, Mexico, or the American West, or in the most congested of modern cities. Imposing technological order upon unruly and
complicated landscapes had been their life's work and passion. Here in
America's greatest city, each would bring his talents and experience to
bear upon the most monumental and complex civil engineering project
of the time, the biggest since the Union and Central Pacific Railroads
raced to link the young nation.

Each man would lead according to his strengths. The first section and
most straightforward was the Meadows Division, which started in Harrison, New Jersey, outside Newark. The PRR's chief engineer, William
Brown, would direct the construction here of what would be known as
the Manhattan Transfer, where the steam locomotives would pull in and
pause for several minutes as powerful electric engines (still to be designed) were substituted for the trip into Manhattan. Brown would be in
charge of installing the five new miles of double tracks heading toward New York, all to be laid atop a steep, built-up twenty-five-foot-high
earthen embankment traversing the lovely but treacherous tidal wet-
lands. He would build a total of sixteen new railroad bridges, including a
drawbridge, as his double set of rails passed over the tracks of ten other
railroads, several turnpikes, and the Hackensack River, all enroute to
Charles Jacobs's North River Division.

Jacobs's section commenced with the Bergen Portals, the lower cliffs
of the ancient Jersey Palisades. Here crews would laboriously blast and
drill two single-track mile-long tunnels through what they soon learned

was exceedingly tough igneous basaltic traprock. The two tunnels would pass under Weehawken, descending steadily downward below the Erie Railroad yard on the river's edge near "King's Bluff," where Aaron Burr had killed Alexander Hamilton in 1804. Jacobs would command battalions of workers, called sandhogs, in both New York and New Jersey, for he intended to push the two tunnels simultaneously from each shore, his respective teams vying to be the first to reach the midriver state lines far below the river's tidal currents. There, so the plan went, the twenty-three-foot-wide cast-iron tunnels would be joined together.

Schematic drawing of the two PRR tunnels under the North River.

In Gotham, starting at Ninth Avenue where Jacobs's two mile-long tunnels would emerge, George Gibbs and Alfred Noble would take over. This was the New York Station and Approaches Division. Noble would first oversee excavation of the twenty-eight-acre station site and track yards in the bowels of the Tenderloin, an undertaking so immense it would quickly be hailed as the local version of the Panama Canal. As the buildings were steadily demolished and cleared, the New York sky suddenly seemed wonderfully wide and spacious, a proper frame for this gigantic engineering enterprise, an enthralling show of ambition and derring-do. The excavation itself would entail a spectacular and startling sight for the constant crowds of spectators: the propping up of all of Ninth Avenue across the ever-deepening pit, including the IRT's elevated tracks, which would come to seem like some oversized child's toy with trains traveling overhead.

Once Noble had completed the gigantic hole and the station's massive inclined concrete retaining walls, the debonair electrical engineer George Gibbs would lead construction of the actual seven-and-a-half-acre subterranean train terminal, including installation of the enterprise's novel and complex signaling and electrical systems. Gibbs was also responsible for erecting all the powerhouses providing compressed air for tunnel work and the electricity, the motive power, for the hundreds of trains that would eventually roll daily in and out of Gotham.

When trains left George Gibbs's station section, they entered the East River Division, also the bailiwick of Alfred Noble. Noble would be pushing the two (double-track) underground tunnels crosstown toward the East River—a complicated matter of navigating beneath the city's many sewer and utility pipes and brand new IRT subway line, and propping up the foundations of brownstones and large office buildings overhead. Just before diving under the East River, the two tunnels would become four single-track cast-iron tunnels (known as A, B, C, D) as they burrowed yet further down to pass deep under the heavily trafficked river, surfacing almost four thousand feet later in Long Island City. Two of the tunnels would carry the Long Island Rail Road, and the other two the PRR trains continuing on to the giant new Sunnyside yards in Queens, with room for four *miles* of train cars. Like Jacobs, Noble would push his four tunnels as fast as he could, with teams of sandhogs working toward each other from each shore. All these construction projects had to be coordinated and synchronized so that each advanced in time to complete the whole. The complexity and cost proposed were dazzling. And so, the PRR's stock kept sinking.

FOURTEEN

"A WORK UNSOUGHT"

Within days of Alexander Cassatt's announcement that the Pennsylvania Railroad was coming into Gotham, architects began their jockeying, some simply making their interest known, others brazenly nominating themselves for what had to be one of the most desirable commissions of the new century: the PRR's New York depot. This terminal was to be the public face of Cassatt's corporation in Gotham, the highly visible crown jewel of a colossal but largely subterranean engineering feat. The Pennsylvania Railroad's new station would be the city's great monumental gateway, the edifice where millions of commuters and travelers would surge off PRR and LIRR passenger trains.

By mid-January 1902, William Baldwin was proposing Bradford L. Gilbert, a seasoned architect "in the line of railroad and heavy construction . . . I also asked him to send me such plans as he had in print . . . He is a great big fellow, and his specialty is railroad and public structures." The firm of Howells & Stokes let it be known that they had a man already over in Paris studying the Gare du Quai d'Orsay. Another PRR officer sent a personal note to Samuel Rea on behalf of Samuel Huckel, a distinguished Philadelphia architect. Rea wrote back on April 10, 1902, saying Huckel had come by in person asking "for the privilege of competing on plans for our New York station when we are ready. As you may surmise, we have had a great many applicants of this kind, but have taken no definite action ... Mr. Huckel's work on Grand Central Station in New York, I understand, gave entire satisfaction."

Railroad stations in all their physical immensity and importance had emerged as the cathedrals of the industrial age, monuments to modernity and to the machine that at their best reflected and honored the full panoply of the train station's drama. In what urban crossroads in human history had so many multitudes high and low, so many varied nationalities, converged in such vast numbers for such different purposes? All those often inchoate human emotions tied to departures to far-flung destinations, to new beginnings and romance (had not George Westinghouse famously met his wife on a train?), even to human routine, deserved a suitably noble setting. Every architect who designed terminals coveted this prize.

Certainly Cassatt, who had passed through and savored the endless small dramas and theater of the world's great railroad depots, understood the wonderful possibilities here, as well as the considerable constraints of the particular site. As the railroad architects pursued the commission in their various ways, Samuel Rea advised one supplicant, "It is a matter which President Cassatt will look into personally." Indeed, Cassatt kept his own counsel, and on Wednesday April 23, 1902, he rode into Broad Street Station and dictated a telegram to a New York architect of great distinction.

Cassatt's Western Union telegram found Charles McKim of the celebrated firm of McKim, Mead & White not in his Fifth Avenue offices up in Gotham, but down in Washington, D.C., strolling about Capitol Hill with his friend Charles Moore, enjoying a warm spring day. It was perhaps fitting that these two gentlemen were at that moment surveying the site of yet another prospective train station. Their friend, Chicago architect Daniel Hudson Burnham, hoped to build there a suitably grand Union Station for Cassatt's PRR and the Baltimore & Ohio. (The bill to grant the land was still stuck in a Senate committee.) McKim and Burnham had been friends ever since the wildly successful and influential 1893 Chicago World's Fair, Burnham's creation that showcased a novel and astonishing vision of an America as City Beautiful.

The capitol's famously swamplike mugginess made it seem more like summer than spring as the architect opened the missive and read that Cassatt wished to see him the next morning, Thursday. McKim waved the telegram, saying in his usual self-deprecating way, "I suppose President Cassatt wants a new stoop for his house." Five foot seven, of slender build, the ever-effacing but charming Charles McKim looked very much the passionate aesthete with his high-domed forehead, balding head, and slender handlebar mustache. His droll, playful manner masked a rigorous intellect and decided ideas about cities, architecture, and beauty, ideas intensively cultivated during his youthful studies in Paris and subsequent roamings in Europe.

It was no surprise that Cassatt should seek out the architect widely hailed as the nation's best, the unquestioned dean of American architecture. His firm, McKim, Mead & White, ran "the largest and most important architecture office in America, if not the world. With a staff that grew to over one hundred, the firm became the model for the modern architectural practice." Like the Pennsylvania Railroad, McKim, Mead & White dominated and defined its field. McKim had never designed a

Architect Charles Follen McKim of McKim, Mead & White.

train station in his life, but no other man in America so understood grandeur, Gotham, and the monumental. The magisterial new uptown Morningside Heights campus of Columbia University was McKim's most recent triumph, displaying his consummate ability to think and design on a heroic scale.

Burnham's train station was just a secondary concern for McKim on that muggy spring day. In truth, he had journeyed down to Washington, D.C., expressly for a command visit with President and Mrs. Roosevelt. They had first summoned McKim nine days earlier for advice on how best to rebuild, remodel, and refurbish the worn and rat-infested Executive Mansion, appalling in its dangerously sagging floorboards (propped up from below for big receptions), "scuffed wooden stairs, the curly wallpaper and wainscots jaundiced with fifty years of tobacco spit . . . mustard carpets, the dropsical radiators, the sad-smelling laundry, the vertical wooden pipes that made flatulent noises in wet weather." The dowdy presidential residence was to be expanded and modernized as it was returned to its older, simpler historical character, and recast to gracefully house the large and young rambunctious first family and its menagerie of odd pets. Roosevelt, the author of numerous works of history, instructed McKim that his official residence and offices specifically be "restored to what it was planned to be by Washington." McKim had been giddy with delight. "The whole thing is so exciting and full of possibilities . . . am writing now in the frame of mind of a man more likely to go off on a spree than home to dinner."

Nonetheless, the next morning, still unseasonably warm, found McKim in Philadelphia promptly presenting himself at Cassatt's office. There, he was met by Cassatt's longtime personal assistant, William Patton, who kept a sharp eye on the wood-paneled corporate offices, vetting all the visitors and supervising the small phalanx of clerks. In his forties, Patton had rather staring eyes, middle-parted slicked-down hair, sideburns and a mustache. Many years earlier he had impressed Cassatt with his self-taught stenography skills. Subsequently, Patton had proved his worth in spheres of far more moment, becoming Cassatt's aide-de-camp and the PRR's unofficial political fixer.

McKim was welcomed and ushered into Cassatt's inner sanctum, a huge office starkly spare in its furnishings and lack of clutter: a gleaming mahogany and leather-topped desk holding but a blotter, a telephone, and a few papers. As McKim settled into one of several comfortable chairs, he noticed the large varnished globe, where the whole PRR system was outlined in red. There was also a luxurious private bathroom and a large private dining room where most days the road's top officers and any guests ate an excellent lunch together. Marveled one local journalist, "It is much easier to get an audience with the president of the United States than to gain admittance to the private office of Mr. Cassatt." And yet in the space of two heady days McKim had engaged in councils with both men.

"I passed the morning with Mr. Cassatt," McKim wrote that very evening to his friend, sculptor Augustus Saint-Gaudens, "leaving this afternoon. [He wants] a new terminal depot of the Pennsylvania Railroad to be built in New York, and which, as you will be glad to hear, was placed under our direction." McKim was typically self-deprecating and diffident about this most enviable of architectural plums—a monumental new train station costing $15 million for the nation's premier city, his own Gotham. When Daniel H. Burnham heaped congratulations, McKim wrote back saying it was "a work unsought, and which came as a complete surprise. They should have given it to you and I fully expected they would. Just after the interview, Newhall [a McKim friend and PRR officer] told me that they employed a New York man as a question of policy, and I ascribe our appointment chiefly to this cause." This was, of course, silly modesty.

The idealistic product of high-minded Pennsylvanian abolitionist parents, McKim spent a year at Harvard studying engineering before changing course. Soon after the end of the Civil War, he departed for Paris, where he trained for three years at the École des Beaux-Arts, returning to New York to serve an apprenticeship of sorts with master architect H. H. Richardson. Soft-spoken and scholarly, and rather particular about his clothes, McKim revered beauty above all things. For McKim, beauty was not "confined to architecture," wrote one colleague. "He saw beauty wherever it was; and he insisted that things accessory to architecture and to life in general should conform to his ideal of good taste."

Those who worked with McKim were soon aware of his extraordinary charm and his ability to bring others around to his point of view. Lawyer

Joseph Choate, an old friend, wrote, "I do not believe it was possible to know Charles McKim without loving him, or to have come in personal contact with him without admiring the wonderful features of his character." McKim harbored a special affection for Britain and Rome. Now, in his prime, he made an annual pilgrimage to "Albion," where one London ritual was the faithful purchase of a particular kind of beloved hat, a blue bag, and umbrella. Then it was on to the moors of the Scottish Highlands, for grouse shooting, golf, and the delicious coziness of peat fires on wet, chilly nights.

Yet, notes historian Paul R. Baker, "Some of those associated with him nonetheless considered McKim overly meticulous and even prim in his habits and overly rigid in his viewpoints." In fact, an early marriage had swiftly soured after the birth of one cherished daughter, ending in an ugly divorce and a custody battle that had devastated McKim. To make it all worse, his wife's brother, William Bigelow, was then his partner so that his professional life was sundered at the same time. Not quite a decade later, in early 1887, McKim's second wife died tragically in childbirth. All this heartache had undermined his health, leaving him prone to bouts of indigestion and melancholy.

Then in January 1899, to his great joy, his daughter, Margaret, twenty-three, sought him out. He had not seen her since she was three, when her mother had been remarried to a clergyman and started a new family with three sons. Charles McKim and his daughter became poignantly devoted to one another. "Everything is all right and happy," McKim wrote her as he was sailing out of the New York harbor to Europe on August 1, 1900, "or would be if only you were with me; but the next time we shall be together, I hope, and (as you said in your letter the other day) we shall always be together in spirit wherever we are, so *that* fact is settled comfortably forever." He delighted in being able to sign these letters, "Daddy."

Over the years, McKim had lavished most of his energies on his work, determined to bring a simple style of beauty and order to the chaotic American scene. His work on the Boston Public Library had made his early reputation. In recent years, the firm of McKim, Mead & White had ennobled Manhattan with one distinguished public building after another—the Herald Building, the University Club, the Century Club, Madison Square Presbyterian Church, and, of course, the new Columbia University campus. The Brooklyn Museum and the Grand Army Plaza were also magnificent exemplars of the firm's talent for civic splendor.

McKim's dear friend and partner, Stanford White, was a frenetic collector of beautiful things, a native New Yorker who had made a name designing (and often decorating) fabulous Gilded Age country mansions, important and exclusive New York venues like the Metropolitan Club, the Knickerbocker Trust on Fifth Avenue, and James Gordon Bennett's new Herald Building. Not only was White physically distinctive, a tall bristly haired redhead with a huge droopy mustache, he was always "bubbling with enthusiasm, always in motion, perpetually talking, usually loudly . . . In time, as he became known for his buildings, his civic activities, and his widely reported social life, he became a public celebrity" as neither of his partners ever was.

Charming, generous, ardent, restless, Stanford White was an architect

Stanford White.

of the picturesque, always in a whirlwind of designs and constructions. Above all, White was celebrated for the elegant and ornamental yellow-brick, white tile, and terra-cotta Madison Square Garden, an extraordinary Moorish pleasure dome that opened in 1890 with a concert hall, theater, and terraced Roof Garden dinner theater. Its 341-foot Spanish Renaissance tower became an instant New York landmark, topped by Augustus Saint-Gaudens's lithe nude *Diana*. White retained one of the seven apartments in the tower for himself as a studio and hideaway. A consummate sybarite, he was always pursuing yet another exotic *objet,* seducing yet another chorine, organizing yet another important festive occasion. One of the greatest of White's extravaganzas came soon after the opening of Madison Square Garden: a miniature indoor Venice complete with flooded waterways, gondolas, and thousands of twinkling lights.

William Mead, the third partner, was generally viewed as the man with his feet firmly on the ground, the "balance wheel" of the office. A Vermonter of few words, constantly smoking cigars, Mead had graduated from Amherst and then spent several years studying architecture in Florence. He was the practical one, the partner who "hired draftsmen, managed the Saturday night payroll, and let men go when work fell off. He kept the flow of projects moving along, supervised financial arrangements, and took charge of those technical elements of construction—heating, plumbing, and other aspects of building engineering." Sculptor Augustus Saint-Gaudens had designed a playful medallion showing Mead struggling to control two kites that were the wayward White and McKim. Notably handsome, with especially wonderful blue-purple eyes, Mead "brought in little business, designed little, and spent a lot of time draped on a chaise longue in his office. However, it was he who brought a business sense to the partnership."

Even as McKim journeyed home to New York in a PRR train, Cassatt was dictating a letter confirming their understanding. "I beg to say that your firm is appointed architects for the Terminal Station . . . your compensation to be the usual commission of five per cent . . . The part of the work which will be placed in your charge will be all that above the waiting-room level." The following Wednesday, McKim returned from yet another visit to Washington to consult with Teddy Roosevelt about the White House. The whirlwind renovations were about to begin and

McKim chortled, "I am thinking our noble President will find himself in such bedlam as he never dreamed of, even at Santiago." That same day the architect met with Samuel Rea in New York to show him some preliminary sketches of the station. Rea wired Cassatt, who was out in Pittsburgh on an inspection trip, that McKim's design included—as they had instructed—"an eighteen story building rising in centre over station."

In the past couple of years Charles McKim had become something of a regular at the capitol as a consequence of his friendship with Daniel Hudson Burnham. Not quite a decade after their Chicago World's Fair collaboration, Burnham, heavier but still handsome and energetic at fifty-one, had drafted McKim to join him on the Senate-appointed McMillan Committee, intended to beautify the ramshackle nation's capitol along the lines of their short-lived classical dream in Chicago. They recruited landscape architect Frederick Law Olmsted Jr. and sculptor Augustus Saint-Gaudens and all worked to resurrect Major Pierre L'Enfant's original 1791 plan of an official city arrayed around the stately greensward of a central mall. This required some optimistic imagining, for right in the middle of their prospective "mall"—between Sixth and Seventh Streets—stood the noisy, sooty Pennsylvania Station, "surrounded by a jumbled mass of shacks, assorted vegetable patches, and miscellaneous mounds of rubbish. Open sewers, euphemistically called canals, crisscrossed the Mall, while off towards the Potomac stank the largest marsh in the city." The commission hoped to clear all these unsightly intrusions away, and further, advocated the mall's graceful extension clear down through the hideous marsh to the Potomac River.

In the summer of 1901, less than a year before the fateful telegram from Cassatt, the commission members had traveled first to Paris and then to Rome for several weeks to study public design. Charles McKim could not have known it then, but this trip would play a central role in his PRR design. One languorous Roman afternoon the four friends had rested companionably amidst the Eternal City's evocative ruins, shaded by the towering brick walls and arches that were all that remained of the once luxurious Baths of Caracalla, talking as ever about architecture and cities. They agreed that the American capitol should and could be made a work of art along classical lines. "That afternoon," recalled Moore, who was part of the tour, "it seems as if the very spirit of Rome—its ordered bigness, its grandeur, its essence of the eternal—stole into their souls, lifting and transforming the men and giving them insight and power to compass achievements that belong to the ages."

Still concerned only about their collective vision of a classical (and imperial) Washington, D.C., they knew the removal of the PRR's railroad terminal was key, for this was an industrial blot in the midst of the future serene greensward of the mall. Fortunately, as the group soon learned in London from Cassatt himself, 'Since you gentlemen left the United States, a community of interests between the Baltimore and Ohio and the Pennsylvania Railroads has been brought about. We are willing to build a Union Station north of the Capitol.' "

Now at work on designs for the New York depot, McKim came up— as requested—with Pennsylvania Station sketches that featured an eighteen-story hotel. But he was determined to dissuade Cassatt from building a skyscraper atop his station, for McKim had never designed a skyscraper and he did not care to begin now. In subsequent meetings with his new client, relates Moore, "McKim argued that the great Pennsylvania Railroad owed the Metropolis a thoroughly and distinctly monumental gateway. Into his contention he threw every bit of that persuasiveness, all of that daring imagination, all that knowledge of world precedents, that made him irresistible. Of course he was fortunate in having a practical visionary like Mr. Cassatt to deal with."

After all, hadn't Cassatt already resited the Washington, D.C., station in part for aesthetic reasons? And while Mary Cassatt was not famous in America—in 1899 the *Philadelphia Ledger* wrote of her, "She has been studying painting in France and owns the smallest Pekingese dog in the world"—McKim well knew that the PRR president's sister was a serious artist. She had painted important murals for the 1893 World's Fair, exhibited with the Impressionists, and advised a number of serious art collectors, including her brother. Cassatt was a businessman and engineer, but he, too, savored beauty and refinement in his houses, paintings, gardens, grounds, and horses, and, most important, in his own railroad. McKim had found a like-minded soul in Cassatt, a corporate titan who cared deeply what his passengers would experience when they stepped forth into his new terminal, a railroad king who wanted to bestow upon New Yorkers something truly magnificent, a monument worthy of his road and their city.

Cassatt was won over. But not solely for McKim's aesthetic reasons. When the PRR considered the requisite engineering and foundation required for a tall hotel and office building over the station, it discovered a tall building would have "cut out two or more tracks, equivalent to one-tenth of the terminal, and filled that space with numerous large columns which would have impaired the future efficiency of the station . . . The Pennsylvania's directors felt that they could not cover the ground with anything more rentable than the present structure without making the railroad business a secondary feature." Cassatt was also worried about interfering with a third and fourth North River tunnel he expected would need to be built later. It was decided that no hotel tower or skyscraper would mar McKim's monumental gateway.

Over the decades of his distinguished career, McKim had admired and absorbed a wide range of Old World influences. "Confidence," he once said, "comes not from inspiration but from knowledge." Pennsylvania Station offered an unparalleled opportunity to distill the most noble influences into this, his greatest work, even as he kept in mind the practical demands of great crowds of travelers and trains. Recalled his friend Charles Moore, "While McKim had pinned over his designing table pictures of the facade of the Bank of England, and the Bernini colonnade enclosing the piazza of Saint Peter's, while he kept in mind the Roman baths and basilicas, and while he used the Roman Doric in all its stately simplicity, nevertheless he built what looks like a railway station—a monumental bridge over the tracks, with entrances to the streets on the main axis and on all four sides—a feature unique among the railway stations of the world, affording the maximum of entrance and exit facilities."

McKim was a man with very certain ways of doing almost everything. When he was ready to create a new building, he "liked to sit down at a draftsman's table," recalled one draftsman from the firm, "usually in his hat and immaculate shirt sleeves, and design out loud; the room reverberated with architectural terms: Cyma Tecta; Cyma Reversa; Fillet above; Fillet below; Dentils; Modillon. He was the most convinced authoritarian I have ever encountered." McKim did not draw himself. "Instead he would talk his way through a design, instructing a draftsman to draw a line and then, after much thought, tell him to erase it and draw it somewhere else. Often he would have a line redrawn many, many times." Such irresolute perfectionism, of course, drove some in the office mad.

When Alexander Cassatt first saw McKim's design for Pennsylvania Station, a majestic Doric temple, it must have stirred pleasant memories of his own trip to Italy with Lois the year he had retired. For McKim's classical design had its origins in his magical eight days in Rome with the McMillan Commission, when the summer sky had been indescribably blue, the Italian sunshine hot and golden, and the men immersed in places beautiful, hallowed, and ancient. McKim's dear friend Charles Moore recalled the pivotal [moment] as that afternoon "at the Baths of Caracalla in Rome . . . McKim's wildest dreams never gave him visions of opportunity to build in the stupendous manner. That afternoon it was simply artistic impulse that led him to hire the willing but astonished workmen to pose among the ruins to give scale and movement— movement, because in all his designing McKim ever had in his mind's eye the people, men and especially well-gowned women, who would sweep up and down his broad staircases. So the hours were spent in the luxury of visiting the halls and basilicas of Rome, purely for the enjoyment of the stupendous works of the past. And yet, within a twelve-month, both architects [Burnham and McKim] were planning buildings [for Alexander Cassatt's railroad] that rival the Baths of Diocletian and Titus and the Basilica of Constantine."

FIFTEEN

"DRILLING OF FIRST HOLE"

Never had the United States experienced such material abundance as it did during these first years of the twentieth century. American factories, mills, mines, and farms churned forth tremendous volumes of coal, steel, oil, glass, garments, grain, cattle, hogs, fruits—a veritable tsunami of industrial and agricultural wealth. The Pennsylvania Railroad was overwhelmed. On Sunday January 25, 1903, Cassatt sat at a rolltop desk in his Rittenhouse Square mansion, pondering his road's travails and writing a private letter to Henry Clay Frick, the PRR's largest stockholder and a major customer. Cassatt lamented "the present unfortunate and mortifying condition of the road," confessing, "The fact is we have reached the limit of yard & track facilities on several parts of the system, especially on the main line between Pittsburgh and Philadelphia."

One Pittsburgh reporter described rail yards "jammed with cars that could not be moved . . . thousands of workmen were idle for weeks waiting for materials that were rusting in cars blocked on side-tracks, within a few squares of their destination but inaccessible, and the owners of mills and of factories canceled orders, paid forfeits, and closed down their works." Cassatt just hoped they would have no serious problems two days hence when President Roosevelt and his cabinet would travel on private cars via Pittsburgh for a meeting of the Republican League in Canton, Ohio.

The year 1902 had almost certainly been one of the most trying of Cassatt's professional life. Not only had there been the galling political struggle with the Tammany aldermen over the franchise (thankfully won), but the PRR's collapsing freight service had customers apoplectic. Finally, in early December 1902, as the winter weather worsened, Cassatt stunned the railroad world by crowning William Wallace Atterbury, thirty-six, the little-known superintendent of motive power in Altoona, the new and youngest-ever PRR general manager. An engineering graduate of Yale who started his PRR career as a three-dollar-a-week shop apprentice, the unassuming Atterbury, a master of detail and organization, set to work untangling the PRR's freight business. But it was certainly too soon to see any major progress, as Cassatt candidly admitted to Frick.

And then there was George Gould, egged on by Andrew Carnegie to extend the Wabash Railroad into Pittsburgh, where five thousand manufacturers were desperate for reliable freight service. Cassatt was furious at this poaching, for he'd faithfully steered his road clear of Gould's territory. All through 1902, Gould's engineers and work crews hacked and blasted their way toward the industrial riches of the Smoky City at the prodigious cost of $380,000 a mile. In retaliation, Cassatt had first refused to renew the twenty-year Western Union contract providing the PRR's telegraph service, then requested Western Union remove its poles and wires. Gould sued. Two days after the PRR prevailed in the U.S. Court of Appeals on May 19, 1903, Cassatt dispatched an army of ten thousand Italian workmen along the PRR rails, armed with cross saws, axes, and wire cutters. In the next few days, they chopped down forty thousand Western Union poles and fourteen thousand miles of wire, inflicting $1 million in perfectly legal damage. Cassatt found the *New York Herald's* headline sweet reading: "Western Union Is Staggered By Railroad's Blow." To rub it in, Cassatt further billed Gould fifty thousand dollars for the cost of the "work." Even the PRR's own corporate historians conceded, "This was probably as drastic an act of eviction as has ever occurred in railroad history."

The year 1903, however, was shaping up well for the Pennsylvania Railroad. In Gotham, the PRR's Tunnels and Terminal Extension was finally under way, and on June 24 another historic tunnel moment was imminent. It had been four months almost to the day since Charles Jacobs and Alfred Noble and their engineers had watched George Jump's man pry up a floorboard from the forlorn lodging house at West Thirty-second Street and Eleventh Avenue. Now it was summer, that five-story building was demolished, and Jacobs and his top staff were assembled on the dirt floor of its old cellar, the site enclosed by plank fencing, the foundation stones creating a low wall. With the air surprisingly cool off the nearby river and the gray skies threatening rain, many of the engineers were attired in overcoats and carrying umbrellas. Aside from two young men sporting straw summer boaters, all the men wore their black derbies tilted at the jaunty angle befitting the momentous occasion.

A camera expert (hired by Jacobs to document progress on his tunnels) directed the fifteen engineers to stand to one side of a set of rough wooden steps ascending a small platform in the middle of the sloping hardpan floor. From an adjacent fire escape, a small child watched curiously as Jacobs mounted the wooden platform, turned on a hand-operated compressed-air drill, and a great RAT-TA-TAT-TAT blasted out. The camera expert clicked, cursing the several men who at that moment moved for a better view of what the photographer later titled, "Drilling of First Hole."

Jacobs saved this suddenly historic drill and, in a somewhat tongue-in-cheek gesture, had it silverplated and sent down to Cassatt at Broad Street Station, "with the hope that you may consider it as an interesting souvenir, inaugurating a work of such magnitude under your distinguished leadership." They were launching what *Engineering News* hailed as the "most extensive and difficult piece of submarine tunnel work ever undertaken," the first of the PRR's tunnels under the North River. Jacobs and his engineers jammed into field offices at the renovated but still-decrepit old brick foundry next door on West Thirty-second Street. There the medical officers examined the hearts and lungs of the hundreds of sandhogs who would soon be working in shifts round the clock. Elaborate locker rooms were set up with special clothes-drying facilities, showers, and plenty of strong "tunnel" coffee for all those working down under the earth. In all four divisions—in New Jersey, on the East River, and on Long Island City—work was now launched.

Even as George Jump and the other contracted building wreckers were noisily clearing the terminal site, creating mountains of debris and sending rats scuttling for new homes, Samuel Rea and realtor Douglas Robinson were still struggling to acquire the final pieces of property they needed, trying to avoid the slower route of condemnation through the courts. As always, Rea and Robinson first consulted the PRR's president about every purchase, in this instance about a strategic old brownstone at 233 West Thirty-third Street. "This is a very difficult property to deal for," Rea wrote Cassatt on January 12, 1904. "It is owned by two old ladies and Mr. Robinson has never been sure whether he could close with them or not . . . He doubts very much whether we can get it for less than $70,000, which, of course, is exorbitant, when we consider that we only paid $27,000 for #231. I will be glad to have your views." The stubborn old ladies got their price, making out far better than the Sire Brothers, "very unscrupulous" speculators who had snapped up a dozen properties they felt certain the PRR would want. By the time Robinson finally bought out the Sires, their carrying charges accumulating, they were grateful for a modest profit, and promised to buy no further buildings in the station vicinity.

President Cassatt, meanwhile, had decided to recoup some of their

TW 10. P. N. Y. & L. I. R. R. Terminal Station-West. House wrecking on the North side of 32nd Street from 9th Avenue, by the George W. Jump Co.
June 27, 06.

mounting land costs (and improve the neighborhood tone) by selling the large parcel between Eighth and Ninth Avenues to the U.S. Postal Service, then seeking a larger main post office in Manhattan. After all, the PRR trains carried 40 percent of the U.S. mail and a new post office structure (set atop the PRR's train tracks), could be specially designed to make mail handling efficient. On February 9, 1903, Cassatt offered the site to the postmaster general, noting that McKim's station would be "monumental in character and of very moderate height, [and is] of a style of architecture harmonious with the classic forms generally adopted by the Government, so that the two buildings ought to present a very fine effect." Further, the PRR would be happy to sell the land at cost.

Cassatt contacted Senator Matthew Quay to enlist his influence in this quest, for any such post office purchase required congressional budget approval. Douglas Robinson, down in Washington on a family visit to his presidential brother-in-law, duly scouted out the prospects with the secretary of the treasury at a Friday night soiree. Robinson bluntly warned Cassatt in a letter the next morning: "400 Congressmen must be convinced that the government has found a gold nugget for nothing in the street." Cassatt would have to "show that the Penna. R.R. is ready, to get the P.O., to lose a good many thousand dollars . . . you are the only one who can decide what loss to take." Undeterred, by the summer Cassatt had an agreement in the works.

Gradually, as one block after another was demolished at the station site and carted away, wondrous broad vistas of summer sky and cloud opened up, especially with Thirty-second Street closed off. Where once hundreds of dingy buildings had lined tired blocks, all that was left was an enormous earthen rectangle marked by the uneven smaller square imprints of hundreds of old cellars. Here and there, only the fronts of condemned buildings had been sheared off when the day's work ended, revealing warrens of small melancholy rooms with many aged patterns of wallpaper, scenes of who knew what joys and sorrows. And when the demolition men stopped their work in the evenings, a strange almost pastoral peace and quiet descended. To the east, the city's skyscrapers, tall church spires, and big department stores now hovered like faraway jagged cliffs. At almost any time of day and evening, the curious came to peer over the plank fencing festooned with advertisements for tailors and new vaudeville shows. Clusters of men in black derbies and

The cleared site of Pennsylvania Station looking east.

boaters, young women in Gibson Girl shirtwaists and hats, boys in their knickers, girls in their pinafores, all watched the many phases of the demolition and the gradual opening of this immense and unlikely urban plain.

For all the encouraging progress Cassatt and Rea had achieved on their monumental New York Extension and for all the satisfactions of the startling vista of the almost-cleared station site, the year 1903 had ended on an ominous note. On November 3, the Tammany Tiger roared back to electoral victory, deposing the honest, efficient, and effective Fusion mayor Seth Low, PRR ally and champion, after one two-year term in City Hall. The reason, explained journalist Lincoln Steffens, was simple: His Honor was a cold fish. "The appealing human element is lacking all through . . . His most useful virtues—probity, intelligence, and conscientiousness—in action are often an irritation . . . A politician can say 'no' and make a friend, where Mr. Low will lose one by saying 'yes.' Cold and impersonal . . . Mr. Low's is not a lovable character."

The grim, gray Tammany boss Richard Croker had largely retired to England with his ill-gotten millions, declaring as he departed on an ocean liner in the spring of 1902, "I am out of politics, and now I am going to win the Derby." Charles F. Murphy, a former horse-car driver and saloon owner who had become mysteriously rich while commissioner of docks, emerged as new chief sachem of the Tammany Wigwam. Famously taciturn, Murphy was also intelligent, canny, and far more progressive than Croker. Murphy persuaded the patrician congressman George B. McClellan, son of the Civil War general, graduate of Princeton and New York Law School, to run as the Tiger's mayoral candidate.

Many respectable voters—especially the Germans who enjoyed spending leisurely Sundays with family and neighbors in the beer gardens—resented Low's enforcement of Sabbath drinking laws. With Murphy ascendent, and memories faded of the Ice Trust scandal and vice run amok, all those voters in the tenement districts hankering after jobs or smaller forms of Tammany beneficence reverted in droves to the Tiger. George B. McClellan, a clean-shaven gentleman quite at home in a silk top hat, trounced the unlovable Low, 314,782 votes to 252,086.

Within days of the elegant McClellan's election as mayor, a clerk at the PRR's New York offices picked up the telephone and (as later reported to President Cassatt) was puzzled to be conversing "with a Mr. Gay, from New York, who said that Mr. Charles F. Murphy—whom he represented—would be very glad to see Mr. Cassatt the next time he was in New York." Could Mr. Cassatt telephone said Murphy? He did no such thing. About a week later in Philadelphia at the Broad Street Station offices, William Patton was surprised by the unexpected appearance of Mr. James E. Gaffney, a rather rough-looking, large and fleshy fellow wearing a loud suit and derby. Patton readily recognized him as Manhattan's Eighteenth District alderman, and one of Tammany's ringleaders in the fight to defeat Cassatt's winning the franchise.

Here in the PRR's home offices, Gaffney was the soul of shameless affability. He had traveled down, he confided proudly to Patton, as the emissary of Mr. Charles F. Murphy. "Mr. Murphy would be very glad," he suggested, "if Mr. Cassatt would give careful consideration to the bid made by the New York Contracting & Trucking Co., of which Mr. John J.

Murphy—brother of Chief Murphy—is President . . . Mr. Murphy is very anxious to see these people get the contract if their prices are anywhere near right." The Tammany Tiger was back in power.

Tammany's reemergence could not have been more ill-timed. Samuel Rea was about to seek the necessary franchise for the final phase of Cassatt's entry into Gotham: the New York Connecting Railroad, the road north to New England. As an exasperated Cassatt himself would later explain to a hostile Mayor McClellan, "The Connecting Railroad is to be twelve miles long, to run through a part of Queens borough as yet half rural . . . and, by a bridge authorized by the State and Federal Governments, to cross the East River at Wards and Randalls Islands.

"Its completion is obviously the key to the development thus proposed of commercial and manufacturing traffic in Brooklyn and Queens. We intend to connect this railroad by a short, direct line with the 'Tunnel Line,' thus permitting a new and direct all rail communication with New England and the north for Manhattan as well as for Queens and Brooklyn." As before, the PRR franchise required approvals from two boards and the mayor. When Rea attended the first hearing in late March before the Rapid Transit Railroad Commissioners, he wrote Cassatt that they were "very stiff in their first proposition, are unwilling to consider a fixed sum as an annual charge for our franchise . . . I argued with them for about an hour, but could make no impression on the rental, and in fact they raised other questions, notably, the right to regulate trains." It did not bode well.

As if the return of Tammany was not ill omen enough, back in Manhattan LIRR president William H. Baldwin faced the scheming of ever-vexsome August Belmont. Where exactly would the Transit King deign to expand his new subway system? The first Belmont subway line, set to open in the fall, would have a stop right at the Vanderbilt's Grand Central Station. However, "Belmont does not intend to make connection with [Pennsylvania] Station except by spur from Broadway," Baldwin wrote on January 28, 1904, in a confidential letter to Cassatt. He warned, "He is playing to bother you." If the PRR wanted absolute certainty that their terminal would be properly served by new subway lines, insisted Baldwin, they needed to control a subway company. "I believe that the whole situation can be worked out . . . you have no need of subway now."

But he warned Cassatt that he would. "You will need Metropolitan Subway by the time it is finished . . . I never saw such a situation."

Cassatt and Rea were also in the final throes of acquiring property for Penn Station. Among the more interested of the spectators watching the steady demolition and disappearance of the old Tenderloin neighborhood had been one John A. Gleeson, rector of the Church of St. Michael's. Gleeson's Catholic parish included a substantial church, school, rectory, and convent, all on the west side of Ninth Avenue between West Thirty-first and Thirty-second streets, just across from the PRR's known terminal boundaries. Gleeson had not yet been approached, but he had gazed out from his handsome red-brick complex with its mansard roofs and seen all those buildings give way to an endless expanse of dirt.

In late April 1904 the rector sent a handwritten letter to Alexander Cassatt: "Could I ask the favor in *strict confidence* of information" about which nearby streets they might still intend to acquire? . . . "not for purposes of speculation" but so he could plan—if necessary—for St. Michael's future and "the people whose spiritual wants I must attend." Both Cassatt and Rea had concluded some time before that their original plans for property acquisition were too conservative. Cassatt, for one, was already factoring in his intention to later construct yet *another* two North River tunnels into the as-yet-unbuilt terminal.

When Cassatt discovered Gleeson would sell only if the PRR replicated his magnificent church complex on a nearby block, the PRR president proposed to prop up Gleeson's property while they built under it. Gleeson emphatically declined. There ensued the most complicated, costly, and protracted of all of the PRR's many hundreds of New York real estate dealings. Back and forth the negotiations went, dragging on, culminating eventually in the PRR reluctantly purchasing a new site for St. Michael's three blocks north at West Thirty-fourth Street and building the shrewd Father Gleeson an entirely new and equally handsome complex, closer to his many parishioners in hardscrabble Hell's Kitchen. The new church incorporated portions of the old, including its magnificent marble altarpiece. All told, this one real estate deal cost the PRR more than $500,000. The total cost just for real estate was now heading toward $5 million.

A couple of months after Gleeson first contacted Cassatt, in early spring of 1904, a reporter for the *New-York Tribune* visited the Eleventh Avenue spot where Jacobs, Noble, and the engineers had posed for "Drilling of First Hole." The hardpan floor, the reporter found, had given way to a deep rectangular hole—thirty-two feet across—surrounded by onlookers peering nervously down into what had become a "subterranean wonder." He joined them and observed only "faint lights flashing below . . . confused murmurs of underground activity . . . [a fitting] entrance to Plutonian regions."

Well aware that no member of the New York press had yet been granted access to this new and mysterious underworld, the reporter boldly descended the narrow wooden staircase that zigzagged down. The cloud-flecked May sky above him became fainter and fainter, and the air colder and mustier. Sixty-five feet down in the strange earthen gloom, he could see "two ragged arches hewn in solid stone, and through them two narrow gauge tracks vanish into darkness, carrying tiny cars laden with rock blasted two hundred feet beyond, for the work has already marched this far toward the Jersey shore." At that moment, the engineers noticed the intruder and escorted him firmly back up whence he had come. When a Hearst reporter sneaked down on another occasion, the assistant engineer who confronted him encouraged the dumping of an "enormous bucket of mud" upon the hapless fellow before he was "frog-marched" back to the surface. These uninvited descents into the Manhattan shaft were as close as the voracious New York press would get for quite some years to the underground work on the North or East River tunnels.

Shortly thereafter, in early summer, LIRR president William Baldwin was diagnosed with intestinal cancer. With Tammany back in power, this was a real blow to Cassatt and Rea, for Baldwin was a well-connected Gotham leader who knew the key players and politicians, the feuds and factions, and could advise and strategize accordingly. It would be hard to proceed without his help as Rea began seeking the franchise to link up their Manhattan rails with New England.

"Mr. Baldwin is very sick," Booker T. Washington cabled a mutual friend on July 24. "Not expected to live. I go to New York today to see him." As Baldwin lay ill at his Locust Valley, Long Island, home, he confided to a family member, "I have been thinking of him [Washington] so often as I have been lying here. *He* is one of the *chief* reasons for my struggling to get well." In an era of entrenched Jim Crow, Baldwin, the first head of the Rockefellers' General Education Fund, promoting black education in the South, remained resolutely committed to racial advancement, an ardent advocate and fund-raiser for Tuskegee Institute and the black race. Baldwin did rally and Samuel Rea wrote Cassatt in early August, "I sincerely hope that he will recover, but I fear that what the doctors discovered on their first examination is too true."

While Baldwin valiantly battled his cancer that summer, William Patton, on a train speeding through New Jersey, received a telegram from Cassatt telling him to inform Tammany boss Murphy that "We propose letting the contract [for excavation of the twenty-eight-acre Penn Station site] to Isaac A. Hopper & Sons, who are the lowest bidders." The PRR's board of directors duly awarded the $5 million contract. Days later, William Patton, who specialized in delicate political dealings, heard from Hopper (himself a Tammany man) that he no longer cared to do the work and was yielding his prize to . . . the Murphy firm, which would match his low bid.

Exulted the shameless Alderman Gaffney, "You can bet all the money in New York that it is true and that we have got that contract." It was believed to be the biggest excavation contract ever awarded in the nation. Giddy with victory and feeling garrulous, Gaffney regaled a *Herald* reporter with the immensity of it all, the vast enterprise of excavating and clearing fifty feet down on the entire twenty-eight-acre site, all in a mere twenty-two months. "We will have to remove three thousand loads, that is sixty thousand cubic yards of earth and rock every day for the twenty-two months, put it on an elevated road, carry it to the North River, dump it in scows, tow the scows to Greenville, take it off the scows and place it in the swampy place of the big freight yards. It will keep nearly eight thousand men [a great exaggeration] busy day and night for the whole time." And there was the key to it all: Murphy and Gaffney hoped to have thousands of jobs to bestow upon the faithful followers of the Tiger.

Within two weeks, the enthralling spectacle of excavation began at the Penn Station site, Manhattan's own version of the Panama Canal. As the summer heat settled in, gangs of workers swarmed purposefully about, digging, drilling, dynamiting, and carting away. Steam-shovels gouged out the dirt and shattered layers of gneiss rock, slowly transforming what had been a flat dusty earthen plain into wilder terrain, featuring shallow valleys and stony outcroppings.

Through that late summer and lovely autumn, New Yorkers lingered to marvel over the astounding sight of the increasingly deeper and more gigantic Penn Station pit while all around them Gotham expanded rapidly both upward, and belowground. Ever taller skyscrapers vied for preeminence, while deep in the ground tunnels were being burrowed, tunnels for William McAdoo's New Jersey trolley lines, for the PRR, and for the long-awaited subway. Now, the first of those subways—August Belmont's IRT—was about to open. PRR officers were more than ordinarily interested, for they still feared that travelers might shy away from riding trains in tunnels, viewing them as somehow dangerous and unpleasant. But when the IRT opened to huge fanfare on the evening of October 27, 1904, and an amazing first-time flood of 150,000 eager riders besieged the City Hall line the PRR ceased worrying. Clearly, no one minded riding in tunnels. "It was carnival night in New York," reported

Little locomotive hauling cars full of station site debris.

the *New York Times*, marveling at how instantly and exuberantly New Yorkers embraced the subway. "Why, in two days it will seem to New York as if it had never ridden anywhere but in the subway."

The triumph of the subway served as a pleasant distraction from the presidential campaign between the Democrat's lackluster candidate, Judge Alton B. Parker, and the wildly popular Theodore Roosevelt. The very actions that made Teddy so beloved by the American people had angered powerful Republicans and corporate tycoons. First, he had sided with the coal miners during the strike of 1902. Then, he had dared to attack J. P. Morgan and his huge Northern Securities railroad trust, forcing its dismantling and causing the dyspeptic Henry Adams to cackle gleefully, "He has hit Pierpont Morgan, the whole railway interest, and the whole Wall Street connection, a tremendous whack square on the nose . . . they don't like being hit that way . . . The Wall Street people are in an ulcerated state of inflammation. Pierpont has declined the White House dinner." Wall Street's Republican titans, despite their deep suspicion of Teddy, dutifully anted up for this election: Senator Chauncey Depew gave $100,000 for the New York Central; Henry Clay Frick, $50,000; George Perkins of J. P. Morgan and New York Life Insurance, $450,000; George Gould, $500,000; John D. Archbold of Standard Oil, $100,000.

Roosevelt felt increasingly queasy and conflicted about concentrated wealth, power, and corporate millionaires writing checks. "It tires me to talk to rich men. You expect a man of millions, the head of a great industry, to be a man worth hearing; but as a rule they don't know anything outside their own businesses." From 1897 to 1904, 4,277 firms had merged again and again until they "consolidated into 257. The hundred largest concerns quadrupled in size and took control of 40 percent of the country's capital." If that was not enough to make Americans uneasy, half a dozen men controlled much of the nation's rails: Cassatt at the PRR, William K. Vanderbilt of the New York Central, Edward H. Harriman of the Southern Pacific, James J. Hill of the Great Northern & Pacific, George Gould of the Wabash and other western roads, and then there was Morgan who had huge and influential interests in these and other roads.

Publisher Joseph Pulitzer, an ardent Democrat, attacked Teddy on this tender issue of trusts. Two full splashy pages of the influential *World* featured headlines questioning Roosevelt's professed opposition to corporate rapacity and the deluge of trust dollars to his campaign. When the pallid Parker belatedly dared to raise the same questions, a furious Roosevelt struck back, reminding voters he had mediated the coal strike and taken on J. P. Morgan. Teddy need not have worried. On election day Tuesday November 8, 1904, he won in a thunderous landslide.

Meanwhile Baldwin, just forty-one, lay slowly wasting away all that autumn from his cancer. Ever a fighter, he survived many months longer than expected, dying on January 3, 1905, at 4:30 a.m., his wife and children surrounding him. Outside a fierce blizzard howled, high winds whipping the falling snow into huge drifts and fantastic shapes. By the next afternoon, as the storm eased, Manhattan was largely immobilized, but Cassatt, Rea, and Green made it to Manhattan and then crossed on the LIRR ferry to a special LIRR train that plowed slowly through the snow-shrouded landscape toward Locust Valley.

It was a dolorous day. William Baldwin, this unlikely railroad president, as ardently dedicated to reform and uplift as he was to profit and performance, had lived only just long enough to see the start of their great tunnels and terminal project, in which he took such pride. The PRR officers could not know, as they somberly rode through the pristine winter scene, that Baldwin's would be the first of many untimely deaths.

SIXTEEN

"THE SHIELD IS
READY TO BE SHOVED"

A ll through 1904, Charles McKim continued to perfect his designs for Pennsylvania Station, his monumental gateway to Gotham. From his apartment on West Thirty-fifth Street, he could walk to the Mohawk Building at Twenty-sixth and Broadway, where the firm of McKim, Mead & White occupied the whole fifth floor. The hushed reception rooms and partners' offices were decorated with French and Italian antiques and objets d'art, while the walls were hung with framed photographs and drawings of the firm's celebrated architectural work. However, most of the office was a beehive of activity, a huge open space with good natural light, where more than a hundred draftsmen—many of them young architects in training—were busy executing architectural drawings.

McKim was convinced that the rising American modern empire was more "nearly akin to the life of the Roman Empire than that of any other known civilization," so he turned to that ancient imperial scale to create for Cassatt a modern edifice of comparable magnificence. The Pennsylvania Station of McKim's first designs and models was an austere but imposing colonnaded Doric temple to transportation. McKim proposed giving a warmth to this simple exterior of towering pillars and attics with Milford pink granite. Inside Penn Station, McKim again paid architectural homage to the classical past with his luminous General Waiting Room, a space of extraordinary height and grandeur inspired by the

Baths of Caracalla, and to the industrial present with his vast and vaulting train concourse with its lyrical iron-and-arched-glass umbrella roofs. During these early phases of design, McKim found he had to fend off various ill-considered cost-cutting measures proposed by his thrifty PRR patrons. In late summer of 1904, Alexander Cassatt balked at the initial stated cost of the exterior's Milford pink granite. "We may have to give up using Milford stone," Cassatt wrote from Bar Harbor, "or perhaps any other kind of granite. I believe that the building would produce a very satisfactory effect if built of brick with granite columns, pilasters, sills, etc. and we would probably save half a million dollars. We shall, however, have to consider the whole question carefully when I return." Under McKim's persuasive counsel, however, the Milford granite remained.

Three months later, Cassatt, hoping to save $250,000, further alarmed McKim by suggesting he "leave off the elevated structure over the main waiting room . . . the saving is a large one, but, of course, we will come to no conclusion until we have an opportunity for a conference. Meanwhile I would like very much to have you prepare a sketch plan showing how you would treat the interior of this room without the elevated structure." Charles McKim again persuaded Cassatt this was false economy. Later, Cassatt would write McKim, "I am quite sure we are going to have a very handsome station, and so far as the elevated construction over the main room is concerned, I pin my faith upon your opinion."

Even as McKim was designing what would be his magnum opus, his friendship with Stanford White had become fraught with worry, embarrassments, and psychic pain. White's two decades of extravagant living, innumerable mistresses, and manic European shopping sprees (ostensibly for clients) had mired him in hopeless insolvency. By 1903 White's debts had spiraled up to the hard-to-believe sum of $790,000. The landlord of his lavishly decorated Gramercy Park townhouse was owed $53,000, and comparably vast sums were due wealthy friends and clients. Unable to rein himself in (White had *nine* exquisite harps in his house), Stanford had rigged up a mirror in his office window in the Mohawk Building so he could see tradesmen coming to dun him and skip out. McKim and Mead, owed $75,000, saw little choice but to put a lien on their partner's future profits. It had all been unspeakably painful.

In early 1904, White, determined to act responsibly and erase some of his most pressing obligations, had consolidated a portion of his hordes of antique furniture, paintings, tapestries, statues, and rugs into a West Thirteenth Street warehouse for a gigantic auction. But before the auction could take place, fire swirled through the building, and everything but the bronzes—all completely uninsured—went up in expensive smoke. White appeared at McKim's house in a state of "stony misery," McKim reported to Stanford's wife, Bessie, over in Europe, and remained immobile for two days. On the third day, "he broke down and sobbed at the breakfast table like a child . . . Then he made his mind up to it and threw it off so that one would think he had forgotten all about it."

All this took its toll on McKim, and, in early 1905, his precarious health collapsed completely. "I have had to carry more than one load this year," he wrote a friend, "and my nerves which have held out so well for so long have felt the strain, accompanied by disordered digestion and depression." Partner William Mead, ever the forthright Yankee, had described McKim as "alright physically, but when he attempts to do any work he goes to pieces."

By and large, the design for Pennsylvania Station was complete. But plenty of details remained to be resolved, and in 1905 McKim handed over much of that final work to William Symmes Richardson, a younger member of the firm who had worked extensively with Stanford White over the years. That summer, McKim recuperated in the restful sun and salt air of the Rhode Island beaches with his daughter, Margaret, before heading north with architect Daniel Hudson Burnham for a bit of fishing in the woodland lakes of rural Wisconsin.

Richardson took the terminal plans up to Bar Harbor so Cassatt could review them. "I went over with [Richardson] the revised plans of the New York Station," wrote Cassatt to one of his engineers. "I found that he was providing head room 13 feet in the clear for the baggage passageways and that this was accomplished with some difficulty and at the expense of putting quite a grade in the passageways, which ought to be as nearly level as possible. I told him that 11 feet was quite sufficient. Certainly that is higher than baggage ought to be piled upon a truck." It was just this capacity for such minutiae and detail—headroom and baggage trucks!—that so amazed those who worked for Cassatt.

McKim followed up his beach and fishing vacations with a quiet sojourn out at the Stanford Whites' Long Island seaside compound, St. James. The Whites had long served as McKim's surrogate family, and Charlie, as they called him, cherished his deeply affectionate friendships with both Stanford and Bessie, as well as with her parents, many sisters, and the Whites's college-age son, Larry. All this made it especially painful that McKim and Mead, fearful that liability for White's vast debts would ruin them, felt obliged that year to legally end his partnership in the firm, and put him on salary. The pathos of these practical steps had eaten away at McKim's fragile peace of mind.

While Cassatt worried about the myriad details of the Pennsylvania Station design, the tunnels were steadily progressing. On a late summer day in 1906 journalist Arthur Reeve, not long out of Princeton and a writer for the prestigious magazine *World's Work*, strode down the drab precincts of far West Thirty-second Street. A group of boys was playing ringalevio, shrieking and running as one boy counted. The smell of the river and the stockyards intensified as he neared the Hudson, and a long, lumbering New York Central freight train passed just ahead of his destination on Eleventh Avenue: Chief Engineer Charles Jacobs's bustling tunnel headquarters, wedged into the former Wigand Foundry on a cramped lot. Reeve stepped gingerly through the tumult of men busy with the boom derrick, feeding sand into the grinding cement mixer, and shoveling wheat coal into bins.

Reeve was delighted to be here. The offices were literally throbbing with activity, for the great steam-driven dynamos and the all-important compressed air machines were whirring away in the adjacent building. Jacobs had for several years forbidden entry to all reporters seeking to tour his Plutonian domain below the North River, so perilous and unpredictable was the work of subaqueous tunneling. But now the English engineer had relented and Reeve had landed this journalistic scoop. Even as he was shaking hands with several of the junior engineers, he began feeling a few qualms. To enter the tunnel, he was told, he would first have to submit to examination by Dr. A. J. Loomis, the PRR's "caisson's disease" specialist. The doctors rejected about six of every hundred men applying for tunnel work as unfit, usually for weak hearts or diseased lungs. To his relief, Reeve passed muster.

Reeve then followed his guide, a junior engineer, to the changing room, and donned tunnel gear: flannel shirt, oilskin overalls, oversized heavy yellow boots, and an oilskin sou'wester hat. Properly suited up, the two men clumped out to the top of the Manhattan shaft where a perilous-looking cagelike elevator awaited them. Looking down, Reeve saw nothing but a dark hole. The elevator cage door clanked shut, and at unnerving speed they dropped straight down fifty-five feet to the dark and dank bottom. The sunny day was gone.

Reeve was entering a peculiarly modern and claustrophobic nether-world, a damp space beset by relentless noise, heat, and giant machines. As they began to walk forward through this pounding chaos and then gradually downward, his eyes adjusted to the shadows. Reeve saw they were now in one of the vaulted tunnels, still rather raw looking, musty-smelling, dank water dripping all about and onto their hats, trickling down his neck, with noise and confusion echoing and a strange tribe of mud-smeared men scurrying here and there. Ahead loomed a wall with three massive iron doors blocking all access to the tunnel. These doors were the air locks, a large one for materials going in and river muck coming out, an emergency lock up above for escape, and an everyday lock where anyone going down into the tunnel had to spend time acclimating to the far higher compressed air pressure.

It was the compressed air that provided the pressure critical to keeping out the river water. Up top it had been George Gibbs's compressed air plants that Reeve had felt and heard steadily pumping the tunnels full of this all-important pressurized air, anywhere from ten to twenty-five pounds per square inch. On the way out of the tunnel, engineers, workers, and visitors had to pass through the air locks once again to acclimate to the lower everyday air pressure outside.

Reeve was told all this as he and his guide entered the ominous-looking air lock, studded with huge bolts like a powerful boiler. The reporter watched apprehensively as the heavy iron door clanged shut. "Your only view of the outside world is through two thick glass portholes in the doors," wrote Reeve later. "A valve is turned on and compressed air from the tunnel begins to rush in with a hissing as of escaping steam. Pound after pound to the square inch the pressure slowly rises. You feel it in the drums of your ears, which begin to press in as though they would burst." The guide, jaded veteran of the air lock, watched Reeve with amusement, and then showed the reporter how to hold his nose and blow to equalize the pressure. As the moist heat in the airlock became "insufferably hot and stuffy," Reeves, his flannel shirt already damp with sweat, began to imagine himself trapped in one of those "dungeons of deep moated castles of the Middle Ages." His guide suggested, "Whistle." Reeves was surprised to discover he could not comply. "You can't whistle in compressed air." By now, the hissing of compressed air had slowed to a wheeze and ceased. The air lock was full of mist.

Everyone working far below the surface of the earth in compressed air was at risk of "caisson's disease," or "the bends," an excruciating affliction set off when the sandhogs going back up to the surface exited too quickly and nitrogen bubbles in the bloodstream exerted pressure on organs and nerves, causing not only terrible pain but sometimes paralysis or death. Men subjected to this agony contorted into "doubled-up and distorted positions," hence the "bends." No one really understood the mechanism of the disease—they knew only that spending time in the air lock generally helped prevent it. As the PRR doctors tracked cases of bends, they discovered that the number rose noticeably when the weather up top became colder or whenever compressed air pressure had to be increased.

The PRR sandhogs working in compressed air were advised of the following rules: "Never [to] enter . . . on an empty stomach, not to use intoxicating liquors, to put on extra clothing when coming out, to get seven hours' sleep every day, to avoid sudden chills, and not to take cold baths on coming heated from the tunnels." Men who emerged from the tunnel air lock and began to suffer the bends were quickly escorted to a separate supervised medical air lock to be treated. "A man in a state of coma from compressed air is a man in an extremely serious condition, and . . . even though the life is saved, partial or complete paralysis of limbs or organs may result. In some cases, the paralysis disappears after perhaps several years, while in some cases it is permanent." In short, Reeve had good reason to be uneasy as he descended to gather his story.

What Reeve looked forward to seeing was the Greathead-style shield, a strange 193-ton behemoth of a machine, a gigantic mechanical mole that burrowed deep under the river as the tunnel's rings were assembled in its laborious wake. Charles Jacobs and James Forgie had designed their shields to be seventeen-foot-long cylinders that would snugly encase the forefront of each twenty-three-foot-wide tunnel as it was being built. The shield face itself, constructed with three strong layers of two-inch-thick steel plate, had nine compartments with doors so sandhogs could excavate from the face. Or those compartments could be carefully opened to let in river muck as the shield pushed forward. The tunnel itself was a series of gigantic cast-iron rings, each one two-and-a-half feet wide. Each ring was assembled with thirteen separate flanged segments, laboriously bolted together then attached to the previous ring. And so the tunnel advanced, two feet and six inches at a time.

Until now, for Reeve and most of Manhattan, the most visible work on the North River tunnels had been the extrication of the network of aged wooden piles (some eighty feet long) supporting the New York Central's huge wooden freight shed at Pier 62 at the end of West Thirty-second Street. Jacobs ordered a veritable forest of those piles—a total of 720—removed as both North River tunnels would pass right beneath the pier. And so for many winter weeks, while crowds of idling men and boys stood about watching, a powerful triangular-shaped machine slowly extracted the long poles from the mire.

Assistant engineer James Forgie stands in the center of the Greathead shield.

In early 1905 Jacobs had reported to Cassatt that he had made "rather less progress than we had anticipated, owing to the liability of the piles to break in drawing and the shallowness of the water at low tide . . . a few more than 500 have already been drawn." Speed was of the essence here, for the sooner the piles were out, the sooner the PRR could re-assemble the pier and complete the elevated wooden train trestle that would originate at the Penn Station site. Then the little black locomotives (which had worked the elevated lines before they went electric) could steam all the way from the station dig over to the river via a tunnel under Ninth Avenue, pass up onto the rough-hewn, elevated trestle, cross several more busy avenues, and finally pass over West Street, the busy New York Central freight yard and tracks, and straight out the long Thirty-second Street pier. From here, trainloads of Penn Station excavation "spoil" were dumped in a great whoosh and roar down numerous chutes onto waiting barges.

Each month now Charles Jacobs and Alfred Noble submitted to Cassatt brief, matter-of-fact progress reports along with documenting photographs providing detailed updates on their respective bailiwicks. Jacobs always sounded quite sanguine, even as he related one woe after another. Pushing the shields under Pier 62 was certainly arduous, but nowhere as perilous and complex as the next obstacle: getting through Gotham's heavy masonry riverfront bulkhead, all supported first by riprap, or big stones, and then more wooden piles. The shield had to push torturously through those twenty-five feet of riprap, the mud-smeared sandhogs working in teams of two in front of the tunnel shield, one armed with a bar that he used to carefully loosen the riprap stones. As the first man cautiously withdrew a stone, the other sandhog stuffed the hollow with a huge clump of mud to fend off "blows." And so each rock had to be plucked out and passed in through the shield, a dangerous and seemingly endless task made worse by the constant small blows that occurred in spite of their precautions.

Once they had worked through the worst of the riprap, the sandhogs in the shields then advanced at a snail's pace through thirty-five more feet of supporting piles, each of which "had to be cut into several pieces with axes to enable it to be removed through the shield doors." Not until March 2, 1906, could Jacobs report that on the North Tunnel the "100th or last pile was out." But then, the incredibly porous riprap just beyond the bulkhead allowed so much compressed air to escape, it "washed away the greater part of the mud cover." Jacobs stopped the shield, which, along with the portion of iron tunnel constructed thus far, now lay in sixty feet of water perilously exposed to the river. For four days, all work stopped on the North Tunnel while scows dropped a "blanket consisting of 16,000 sacks of mud" to once again bury the shield and the exposed tunnel. To fend off yet another bad blow when the South Tunnel shield, having cut through more than fifty piles, pushed beyond the bulkhead, Jacobs ordered "A blanket formed by canvas 30 feet wide by 60 feet long covered with 4000 sacks of silt laid on the riverbed just outside the bulkhead wall."

But that was all behind them as journalist Arthur Reeve prepared to exit the air lock. His guide thrust open the heavy door into the tunnel and Reeve, his shirt now completely soaked, stepped out into the shadow. The interior of the tunnel was twenty-one feet in diameter, though the dark and mist obscured the view. "You can feel that it is cooler in the tunnel," Reeve observed to his readers, "and yet you perspire almost as freely as in the heat of the lock . . . Along a suspended wooden platform through the tube you follow your guide, fanned by the moist breath of the tunnel. Every few feet an incandescent light gleams in the misty darkness. After perhaps a hundred paces, you have to duck down under a semi-circular partition covering the upper half of the tube." This Reeve learned was the emergency curtain. They walked on. "Should the tunnel start to flood, the other half of the emergency curtain can be dropped so as to cut off in-rushing water. The tunnel itself could be nearly flooded and safety could be found along the platform."

Now, as they entered the work zone, Reeve saw below them "men pushing little cars full of 'muck' or sand or rock taken out from before the shield. They and the men who do the shoveling are 'muckers.' Pipes laid along the side conduct compressed air and fresh water, while electric light and telephone wires are strung all about. These, together with the tools and other accessories strewn along the tunnel, obstruct the narrow passageway to such an extent that one must carefully pick his way between them." Reeve could not help but imagine muddy river water suddenly inundating this whole chaotic scene and men dashing panicked toward him, scrambling desperately for the air lock. The Haskins tunnel disaster was long ago, but well remembered. A god-awful way to die.

Again, as his eyes adjusted further to the dim light, Reeve could see from an overhead platform supported by timbers that a regular succession of heavy cast-iron rings formed the gigantic interior tube of the unfinished tunnel. The tunnel seemed drier. The guide explained that as each iron ring was erected, grout was pumped outside through a hole in each segment, creating a continuous sealed lining between the tunnel and riverbed. Reeve and his guide walked slowly along the slick wooden platform, the reporter still getting accustomed to the constant yelling and noise, clammy air, dim light, and the thin mud coating gleaming on every surface. It was unnervingly like one's vision of Hades. Finally, they reached the seeming chaos of the facing. They were now twenty-five feet below the silt riverbed itself. At high tide, they would have been ninety-five feet below the surface of the river.

Here Reeve beheld the 193-ton Greathead-style shield at the facing. "At first glance the sight seems little short of bedlam," he wrote. "Burly Negroes shout at husky Polacks as they load 'muck' on the cars. Other men are climbing about the compartments, excavating ahead of the shield. Another gang is erecting a segment of the newest ring. Everybody is apparently in everybody else's way. But you soon discover that what appears the most utter confusion is complete organization, considering the narrowness of the quarters. One gang excavates, another loads cars, another pushes cars back through the tunnel, another erects segments, and so on." In a twenty-four-hour period of three eight-hour shifts, the tunnel shield driving through silt advanced anywhere from three to eighteen feet. All this ordered chaos took place to the incessant and worrying hiss of the compressed air.

Reeve, in his uncomfortable rubber gear and wet flannel shirt, water dripping intermittently down on him from overhead, found this burrowing through the deep primeval river silt viscerally unsettling. Through the din, his guide indicated he should advance. Reeve went uneasily forward to better inspect the gigantic circular shield, with its nine adjustable forward compartments, several occupied by working sandhogs. Urged to enter, Reeve dutifully got down on his hands and knees and crawled tentatively through the slime into one of the shield's tiny mud-smeared compartments. Here at the raw front of the tunnel facing he could *feel* the compressed air escaping and see, smell, and feel the riverbed's musty ooze.

This was deeply disconcerting, and Reeve recoiled, experiencing for "the first time the weird realization that only the 'air' stands between you and destruction." Far up on the surface of the North River with all its maritime traffic coming and going, one of the few outward signs of the tunnel so far below had been actual "blows" or eruptions and much bubbling as the compressed air from the tunnel escaped up and out. But down here one realized only too well that if the air pressure dropped the river would rush in, with all its calamitous consequences.

When Reeve crawled back out of the Greathead shield, filthy and slimy with river mud, he had had enough. His guide took mercy on him and quickly escorted the reporter back to the air lock, which was in reality the most perilous part of anyone's visit. For even if men faithfully sat in the air lock for the prescribed fifteen minutes as the compressed air was slowly evacuated, no one could know whether they would be stricken with the bends. As Reeve sat in the lock, his flannel shirt totally wet, weighed down by all the heavy rubber protective gear, the air grew notably cooler, and a mist began to form. "By and by," wrote Reeve, "one of the men in the lock with you starts to whistle, 'Wait till the sun shines, Nellie' . . . At last the hiss of the escaping air ceases. The door to the dungeon grates open. You walk up the tunnel to the shaft and are hoisted up to God's air again. You gaze out across the river with its waves dancing gaily in the sunshine. Down beneath it the 'sand-hogs' are still rooting."

Later, Reeve asked one worker hospitalized with the bends what it felt like. " 'Like the jumping toothache and the worst kind of rheumatism,' the sandhog answered. 'If it hits you in the head you go daffy; in the stomach, it is like an awful colic; in the arms or legs, a painful numbness. Sometimes you are unconscious but more often you are keenly alive to the horrible pain.' " Like many another visitor to the world of tunnel building, Reeve wondered about the sandhogs who sought out such work. Yes, it paid reasonably well, but it was—he clearly believed—a hellish place to pass one's days. And yet there were legions of sandhogs who prided themselves on their skills and labored over the years in one tunnel works after another.

Of course, the rare visitor to the North River tunnels wondered how the two advancing faces heading toward one another from opposite shores could meet up almost precisely. In fact, the bulk of Charles Jacobs's engineers—the alignment corps—were dedicated to exactly this task:

A 39. P. R. R. Tunnels, N. R. Div. Sect. Gy. Showing Shield, (South Manhattan) in Hudson River Silt with one door of Shield open.   Aug. 24, 06.

properly aligning the tunnels as they advanced to their midriver meeting point. Reeve was told it was a "simple problem of trigonometry . . . Every time a new ring is laid the whole tunnel is resurveyed and the results in the two approaching headings compared. If the comparison shows an error, the shield is steered to right or left, up or down, as required to correct it; segments curved to just the necessary degree are then inserted in the next ring."

Jacobs's second in command, James Forgie, had never worked a tunnel job that required such meticulous and relentless aligning, all a consequence of the treacherous North River silt. "With the tunnels in a constant state of movement, both vertical and lateral," he explained in his Scottish burr, "and also showing constant alteration in shape after original construction, all of which movement had to be precisely measured and recorded both for the purpose of gaining an insight into the forces at work which produced such results, and also for the purpose of maintaining true line and grade at the working faces of the tunnel." The

North Star of all this aligning was a sixty-foot-high triangulation tower on the Jersey side.

Reeve, more than a little discombobulated by the Stygian tunnel, had little to say about the actual details of building, but the bookish secretary to Cassatt's board of engineers, William Coupland, also garbed in the oversized yellow rubber boots, jacket, and hat, journeyed down to the slimy tumult of the shield area and watched with great fascination. He too stood on the wooden platform at the muddy face, engulfed by the noise and apparent chaos. He had arrived just as the shield was being shoved forward.

"A flat car containing two segments is run as close to the shield as possible," wrote Coupland; "an iron chain is attached to the end of the revolving 'erector' and hooked on to one of the segments. This erector is then revolved, the segment pulled off the car and allowed to drop with a loud crash into the bottom of the 'tail' of the shield. Five or six men immediately jump down into the bottom with bolts and bolt this segment to the corresponding segment in the last erected ring. Another car containing two more segments has meanwhile been brought forward . . . This process is repeated over and over again until all the [thirteen] segments had been erected. The last segment to be put in place is the narrow 'key' segment. The whole gang then tightens up all the [127] bolts, and the shield is ready to be shoved ahead again." When the sandhogs first started in the tunnel, the installation of just one such two-foot-six-inch-wide iron tunnel ring had taken as long as five or six hours. But by the time of this visit, some seasoned sandhog gangs had the installing of a ring down to a two-hour process.

Before the shield could be shoved forward again, all had to be properly aligned. From his platform Coupland watched through the clangor and shadows as one man climbed into the shield's top compartment. He would control the shield, which would be carefully advanced by twenty-four jacks pressed firmly against the newly installed iron ring of the tunnel. The jacks, their position minutely calibrated, would be thrust slowly forward with a total pressure of thirty-four thousand tons. But first, four junior engineers, each with a foot rule, stationed themselves in the respective quadrants of the shield. As the jacks began to extend between the just-installed iron tunnel ring and the shield, the foreman carefully watched the readings on the four-foot rules. "As a result of those readings he calls out repeatedly instructions to the man in charge of the valves to turn off this one, and to open that one, so that by the time the shield has been pushed through the soft mud for the required distance of two feet six inches in order to permit the erection of one more ring, he knows that it has traveled on the line and on the grade he desires.

"Sometimes when the shield is being pushed forward, all of the doors in the front of the shield are closed tight, so that it pushed its way bodily through the soft ground. Usually, however, there is at least one door of the shield open, as this much facilitates its pushing. The mud streams in through this door in a semi-liquid mass like an enormous sausage. While the shield is moving forward and mud is flowing into the tunnel, cars are run up as near as possible on both tracks, and men who are not actually engaged in the shoving of the shield, shovel the mud into the cars as it pours through the shield. By the time the shield has advanced its stroke of two-feet-six-inches, half of the mud that was brought in has been usually cleared away."

All this transpired amidst the heat, noise, and mess of the mud, which seemed to coat everything, including the men, who were caked dark and shiny with it. Once the last of the muck had been shoveled in the cars and whisked away, the flatcar with the iron lining segments reappeared and the whole deliberate process began anew. Several hours later, the sandhogs would be ready for another shove. When the Greathead shield penetrated another two feet six inches forward, once again, one segment after another of the eleven-ton cast-iron ring was swung into place and bolted to the previous ring. And so, ring by cast-iron ring, the tunnel pressed forward deep under the ancient glacial riverbed, looking more and more like some gigantic segmented snake. And every fifteen feet, the cast-iron tunnel segments included a special "bore segment." This would allow the subsequent installation of screw piles that would attach the tunnel to the bedrock far below the silt, creating the tunnel bridge patented by Charles Jacobs. In sections where the tunnel passed between harder rock below and softer mud above, the tunnel rings were not iron, but steel.

What Reeve did not see or hear much about in his brief and uneasy tour were the vexing difficulties—albeit many of them anticipated—and outright disasters that Jacobs and his tunnelers had already encountered. One of the few actually reported in the press had struck back on

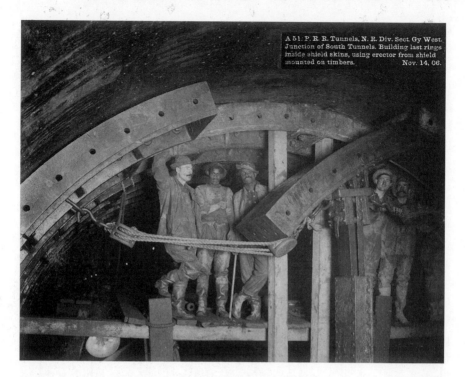

A 51. P. R. R. Tunnels, N. R. Div. Sect. Gy West. Junction of South Tunnels. Building last rings inside shield skins, using erector from shield mounted on timbers.   Nov. 14, 06.

February 14, 1905, yet another frigid morning in a brutal winter. Over in the PRR's Weehawken yard, gangs of sandhogs, clad in the required yellow oilskin overalls, coats, and hats, and primed with tunnel coffee, crunched through recent snowfall to the mouth of the hundred-foot-wide tunnel shaft. The PRR's rented property was a jumble of makeshift offices, air compressor buildings, mule stables, piles of iron ring segments to line the tunnels, mountains of wheat coal, and a cement plant. Above loomed the Palisades, their craggy heights crusted with snow and wintry trees. Jammed against the foot of the cliffs were the Erie Railroad's long, narrow, noisome cattle pens, full of lowing cows. Along the riverfront sprawled the Erie's train yard, old warehouse piers jutting into the Hudson. Manhattan hovered in the distance across the river.

As eleven o'clock approached, the sandhogs down in the North Tunnel were well settled in for another day of drilling, dynamite blasting, and mucking, making steady progress as they pushed to get under the river itself, where they would install the shield, the air locks, and begin the actual subaqueous tunneling. One of the men working on the top "heading" at the tunnel face inserted a stick of dynamite, and then retreated to set it off. They heard the muffled blast, and then as they sauntered forward, paused, sensing an unfamiliar sound, a muttering noise overhead in the earth. Alarmed, they retreated. The roof ahead began slowly crumbling, a soft muddy material squeezing through suddenly gaping holes. Then water burst forth, its gushing force explosive. Terrified, the sandhogs tossed aside their tools and raced for the shaft hundreds of feet back. Behind them, the face and then the raw pine-timbered tunnel itself were being engulfed in a dark slimy lava of mud and freshwater.

Up top, the engineers and contractors heard the muffled thunder of the collapse, and dashed from their offices into the blast of cold to witness over in the Erie yards an entire train being swallowed up by a fast-expanding sinkhole. The spectacular cave-in was described by a *New York Times* reporter, who saw "an immense circular hole . . . fully 50 feet across and as many deep. Inside are coal cars tilted at a dizzy angle, twisted rails, broken trucks, and one freight car overturned and lying with wheels up. The floor of the tunnel is about ninety feet below the track level at this point." A shaken Erie engineer and his fireman told the *Journal American*'s man how they had been routinely moving a string of loaded coal cars over some switches in the yard when—to their terror—the rails and earth simply gave way beneath them, as if the gates to hell were opening. The two men flung themselves off the engine, as it plunged slowly into the gaping maw of the crater, dragging five more cars down behind it, and settling finally into a topsy-turvy train wreck. The brakeman disappeared into the muddy void with the cars.

The contractor, John O'Rourke, airily dismissed the huge crater to journalists as "not a serious accident, didn't amount to much." In fact, the huge lavalike irruption of soft, muddy earth had filled the tunnel to almost half its height for a distance of about three hundred feet back of the face. Charles Jacobs reported to Cassatt that "Fortunately, the mud did not fill the tunnel completely to the roof, making it possible to lay planks on its surfaces and thereby reach a point about 60 feet from the break, where a bulkhead was commenced on the night of the 14th." In fact, it would take more than a month to reexcavate the tunnel and restore the Erie Railroad yard overhead to stability. As for the Erie brakeman, he was fished out, and escaped with just a broken leg.

SEVENTEEN

"SLOW PROGRESS HAS BEEN MADE"

C harles Mattathias Jacobs, fifty-four, chief engineer of the PRR's North River tunnels, looked very much like what he was—a British man of empire at the zenith of a colorful and accomplished career. Supremely confident, calm, and commanding in appearance and manner, he was in the prime of his manhood, easily recognizable with a noble bald head, distinctive sweeping white mustachios, and intensely blue eyes. Of medium height, he had a barrel chest and powerful build from decades of active work. Dispiriting and dramatic engineering disasters were just workaday challenges to him.

"Mr. Jacobs is not an office engineer," wrote one admiring reporter not long after the Weehawken tunnel cave-in. "He does not sit at his desk studying maps, charts, blue-prints and typewritten reports, and writing letters of instruction. He deals with real things and is out among his men. He holds frequent 'councils of war' with his assistants and foremen, and is ever ready to hear suggestions from any subordinate. 'I do not want a man in my employ,' he says, 'whose opinion isn't worth something.' But when he makes his decision, it is expected to go—and it does go; and oddly enough, every man somehow feels it is the proper thing to do. Familiar at all times with every detail of the work and the man doing it, always clear-sighted, resourceful, enthusiastic, he inspires his men, who, from assistant engineers who share his inmost councils to the men who handle the spades and drive the mules, recognize in him a chief

worthy to follow, who expects every man to do his duty. This helps to explain the remarkable success which Mr. Jacobs has had."

Born in Hull, Yorkshire, to a "substantial" family, ninth in a family
of fourteen, by age sixteen the privately educated Jacobs had been ap-
prenticed to an English engineering firm, Charles and William Earle,
specializing in ship and engine building. When Jacobs finished his five
apprentice years in 1871, the Earles showed their faith in this young
man by dispatching him first to the wilds of India and then to China to
build a number of bridges. Upon his return from the Orient, Jacobs continued his training, going to sea for several years to earn a certificate as a
First Class Marine Engineer. He then established his own offices at
Cardiff, Wales, but worked much on the Continent and as far afield as
Australia. As his reputation and commissions grew, he decided in 1887
to relocate to London, where he first worked on a subaqueous tunnel.
Three years later, Jacobs had his fateful meeting with LIRR president
Austin Corbin, who invited him to come to New York City to help solve
various engineering problems, above all that of tunneling under the rivers
encircling Manhattan. It was in that long-ago era that Jacobs had first
met Samuel Rea and Alexander Cassatt and begun talking bridges and
tunnels.

By early 1905, Jacobs was renowned in Gotham not just for the
decade-old feat of completing the eight-by-ten-foot natural gas tunnel
under the East River (the first subaqueous tunnel to reach Manhattan
and the first built using a shield and compressed air), but a far more
amazing and recent triumph. The previous March, Jacobs had completed
what many had long and loudly concluded was impossible: the seemingly
accursed Haskins tunnel from New Jersey to New York. Started in 1879,
the Haskins trolley tunnel had for more than twenty years defeated every
engineer and contractor who took it on. Its completion after two decades
by Jacobs was testament to his originality, skill, and sheer perseverance.
The opportunity (or challenge) presented itself in late 1901, just as Cassatt was launching the Pennsylvania Railroad's great tunnel enterprise.

William G. McAdoo, a young, ambitious Tennessee lawyer seeking
his fortune in Gotham, had contacted Jacobs, who had long advocated
completing the Haskins tunnels (to utter skepticism). The veteran engineer enthusiastically escorted McAdoo, tall, lanky, an almost Lincoln-
esque figure with striking bushy eyebrows, into the murky, half-flooded

tunnel works on a gray October day. The two men, dressed in hip boots and yellow oilskin coats and hats, carried oil lanterns as they descended sixty feet down a dark vertical shaft. "As I entered the tunnel," recalled McAdoo, "I had a powerful feeling of visiting a place I had known well many years ago . . . I was like a man who walks through a wrecked and dismantled house that he had lived in when he was a boy." It was pitch black, but you could hear the moisture trickling off the tunnel's old iron-plate walls. The narrow wooden boardwalk was slippery with oozing muck, and as the two edged carefully along, their lanterns cast "wavering, fantastic shadows. The gloom lay ahead of us like a long black section of nothing. When we spoke, it sent our voices back to us in metallic, unearthly echoes . . . The whole thing was so inanimate, so ponderous, and so lonely. It was not a ghost, or a skeleton, but a carcass. I felt as if I had seen the body of some long and enormously heavy animal that had lain down and died. Yet, from the moment I saw the tunnel I never doubted that I would get possession of it and complete it." While Reeve had disliked being in the PRR tunnel, McAdoo expressed that strange affinity and fondness, an almost mysterious bond certain men felt when immersed in the nethermost bosom of the elements.

Jacobs was equally committed to salvaging the Haskins tunnel and proceeded to solve engineering problems that would have vanquished lesser mortals. Twice the tunnel "blew" and flooded. For eleven months, Jacobs's men cautiously blasted and inched forward through a solid reef of rock. When they mercifully reached the end of it they encountered silt so porous they could not proceed. It just oozed through the shield in a glutinous mass. The ever-imaginative Jacobs decided to bake the stuff and sent in men with blowpipes. This ingenious solution worked and soon the Greathead shield was burrowing through plain old sandy silt, pushing swiftly ahead. "As soon as we began actual work," wrote McAdoo, "the sleeping tunnel awoke from oblivion into the glare of publicity as lively as that which surrounds a new operatic star. Everybody was interested. The people of New York looked on and stared as the people of Egypt must have gazed at the building of the Pyramids." (Of course, this being a tunnel, there was not much to see from the street.)

Once McAdoo and his backers in this $4 million cross-river venture saw they were truly likely to finish Haskins's old trolley tunnel between Hoboken and Morton Street, McAdoo had begun in early 1903 to seriously consider a second, complementary set of new subaqueous sub-way tunnels that would connect Jersey City and the Wall Street area. Knowing that these would siphon off passengers from the PRR's lucra-tive Cordlandt Street ferry, McAdoo decided to sound out Alexander Cassatt on the matter. The new Penn Station would serve those traveling and commuting uptown, but did the PRR intend to consign all its down-town passengers to the vicissitudes of the ferries? And so McAdoo boarded the PRR ferry to Exchange Place and journeyed by rail down to Philadelphia. Debarking at Broad Street Station, McAdoo strode up to the second-floor offices for his appointment, navigated the various fac-totums, and entered Cassatt's spacious office clutching his maps and plans.

The PRR president, attired in his usual black frock coat, dark vest with pocket watch, snowy white, high-collared shirt, and cravat tie, greeted McAdoo cordially. "My instinctive feeling for personality told me," re-called McAdoo, "before I had been in Cassatt's office five minutes, that any attempt at shrewd bargaining with him would not only be wasted effort, but might be harmful to my proposal. As a rule, great men do not haggle over details . . . The only way one can meet them on their own plane is by a frank and complete discussion of the subject in all its phases."

And so, McAdoo unrolled all his blueprints showing the revived Has-kins tunnel, and most relevantly the two new tunnels he and his partners proposed to build between Jersey City and the Wall Street neighbor-hood. Of course, each man knew Charles Jacobs well since the English-man was busy building tunnels for both. As McAdoo spread his plans out on the big wooden table, "I told Cassatt exactly what was in my mind. He looked over my maps and asked some questions. Then he glanced at me and smiled dryly, 'Well, it seems to me,' he said, 'that you're going to destroy our most profitable ferry.'"

Since this was certainly true, McAdoo waited politely but said noth-ing as Cassatt further studied the plans. Cassatt looked at his young visi-tor and continued rather genially, " 'You are about to put our ferries out of business, but the Pennsylvania Railroad believes in providing the best facilities for its patrons, and, as your tunnels will do that, we'll hook up with you.'"

McAdoo was agreeably amazed, for the two men had conferred for less than an hour. The New York lawyer had anticipated many drawn-out meetings and conferences, and, if the PRR was interested, certainly a presentation to the board of directors. This all seemed rather precipitous. "The brevity of the discussion and his readiness to come to terms on such an important question were somewhat disquieting . . . Of course, I wanted to get it all settled definitely, yet I did not want to ask him if he had authority to commit the road to this arrangement without seeing other people." Could Cassatt really speak so confidently for his road's board? McAdoo decided to reveal that his plan involved not just the building of new subway tunnels, but also two gigantic new office buildings that would rise above an underground terminal in Manhattan near the river (where the World Trade Towers later stood). He and his partner were already raising money and quietly buying the real estate. "If any hitch occurs in this agreement with the Pennsylvania Railroad," McAdoo told Cassatt, "it will put us in a bad hole."

" 'There'll not be any hitch,' Cassatt said. 'At any rate, none on our part. You can count confidently on us.'

"I left his office with full confidence in his word, and my confidence was entirely justified. He was the kind of man on whom one could rely absolutely." And indeed, just as Cassatt promised, his board approved, and McAdoo had his contract by mid-May 1903.

Less than a year later, on March 11, 1904, McAdoo received an excited phone call from Charles Jacobs, who was down in the tunnel. The lawyer-turned-tunnel-developer recalled, "I and a few others hastened across the river in a ferry-boat and went to the shaft on the New Jersey side." It was raining as they pulled on the usual yellow oilcloth coats and hats and the heavy waterproof boots. "We walked in the tunnel and passed through the air-locks until we came to the shield. The workmen were standing around. The men looked worn and tired; they were covered with mud, of course, from head to foot."

Chief Engineer Jacobs smiled. The two ends of Haskins tunnel had finally met up. Everyone present crept through the narrow passageway, dark and dripping, transiting from the Jersey side to the New York half of the tunnel. A historic half hour of walking later, and they had reached the Manhattan shaft, muddy and exalted. As Jacobs liked to say thereafter, "Henry Hudson was the first white man who crossed over the river, and Jacobs was the first who crossed under it." Sadly, DeWitt

Clinton Haskins had died broke and forgotten, long before his great dream was realized.

By July 1, 1904, the house-wrecking crews had completely cleared the Penn Station site, and work was beginning on the "Biggest Hole Ever Dug in the Island of Manhattan." Tammany chief Charles Murphy's company hired two thousand men to excavate around the clock, blasting and digging steadily down, while the small elevated steam locomotives hauled the spoil away to the scows at the West Side piers. By August 1905, half the digging—a million cubic yards of earth and rock—was already done. "It's an interesting job," said Murphy's chief engineer, "because of its size, but it's pretty prosy work. We haven't had any exciting incidents or made any interesting discoveries—haven't found gold mines, or human skeletons, or anything of that kind."

With summer once again upon the city, on the hottest days the *New York Herald* gave away free ice in the slum districts, while charities orga-

Penn Station site and Ninth Avenue and the Elevated before being propped up.

nized picnics and boat rides to get thousands of tenement children out in the fresh air. When the heat lingered and grew miserable, the "Fire Department flushes the tenement streets with streams of cold water, wetting down the panting horses and the hundreds of children who enjoy the shower-bath. Most of the horses, as in London, wear bonnets of straw all summer with the most coquettish effect. Free concerts are given on all the recreation piers . . . there are many public baths in both the Hudson and the East River where men and women can swim . . . [Nor] does it cost much time or money to reach the greatest pleasure circus in the world, Coney Island." There you could cool off in the Atlantic's surf, rise high up in the air on the Ferris wheel or hurtle down the giant Helter-Skelter slide. At Dreamland and Luna Park, you could ride a camel or the thrilling loop-de-loop, and then amble with the crowds to see all the queer sights—the six-tailed Bull Terrier or the human pincushion.

The Gotham of 1905 was growing like Topsy. No matter where ordinary citizens of New York looked, they could see their city being remade in every possible direction. Two years earlier, Daniel Burnham's twenty-two-story Flatiron Building became the tallest skyscraper in the city, its strange triangular shape topping 285 feet. Some skeptical New Yorkers called it "Burnham's Folly" and had wagers on when it would collapse. Over on the East River, the city was erecting new bridges. Up at Forty-second Street and Fifth Avenue, the old Croton Aqueduct had been demolished and the $5 million New York Public Library was arising in all its magnificence. Andrew Carnegie's gift to New York of $5.2 million promised dozens of new library branches. Below the streets and rivers, August Belmont's men and machines were burrowing new subway lines to connect Manhattan to Queens and Brooklyn. All this ambition and improvement was most exhilarating.

In mid-August 1905, soon after Samuel Rea returned from holiday, Cassatt wrote from Bar Harbor asking that their New York work be "pushed more rapidly. It seems to me that it has been going a little slowly." Chief Engineer Jacobs certainly found he needed every iota of experience gleaned from the McAdoo-Haskins tunnels as he and his men struggled to put through the PRR's North River tunnels. Yet the two projects—seemingly very similar—posed very different problems. First, the McAdoo tunnels were for electrified subway trolleys, and were consequently smaller in diameter than the PRR tunnels, which were designed to handle larger railroad cars and locomotives. No one worried that the Haskins tunnels might crack or break under the repeated journeys of their subways. But that was the constant fear of the PRR. For, as Jacobs himself conceded, "capitalists and engineers" had long believed (and a great many still did) that "owing to the very soft nature of the [North River] ground, a tunnel could not be built that would be sufficiently stable to withstand the vibration due to heavy traffic, and for this reason tunnels under the North River were not looked upon as practicable." Second, Jacobs was discovering that while the tunnels burrowed under the same river, the retreating glaciers had deposited very different substrata.

The Jersey side presented its own endless vexations, bringing work on the North Tunnel to a complete standstill in the summer of 1905. "The leakage of air through the ground was so great that it was impossible to maintain sufficient air-pressure to work both North and South Tunnels," reported Jacobs. The shield had also been installed in the South Tunnel from the Weehawken side but, wrote Jacobs, "Owing to the inability to maintain sufficient air-pressure to keep the face dry, slow progress has been made." From August 25 to September 12, 1905, Jacobs's sandhog teams managed to install only eight rings of tunnel lining. Since then, "the average progress has been one ring every working day. The material in the face is sand, gravel, and hardpan, with some large boulders. The entire face is timbered for each shove of the shield, and the water in the ground is about 9 feet above the invert . . . On Sept. 4th fire was discovered in the timber above the shield and tunnel. This was smothered by removing air-pressure from the tunnel for 12 hours, with no damage to the works.

"To date 62 rings of cast iron lining, equivalent to 155 feet of tunnel, have been constructed. The excavation done is approximately 5.7% of the total."

By the end of 1905 work was again progressing on the Jersey South Tunnel, and the shield "passed under the westerly side of the Fowler Warehouse on December 4th," reported Jacobs, "and immediately encountered wooden piles forming the foundation of the building. At about this same point the material in the face changed from red sand and gravel to black sand and river silt. The ends of seventy piles which came within the tunnel limits have been cut . . . The Fowler Warehouse, which is a heavy timber structure enclosed with a brick shell, has settled to some extent. Some cracks have shown." For the next several months, sandhogs worked in front of the shield under the benighted Fowler Warehouse. They laboriously hacked away with axes, slowly and carefully cutting up and pulling in the remaining 136 wooden piles in their path. Finally, in January of 1906 the shield in that South Tunnel passed under the Fowler Warehouse and out into the river.

Assuming the riverbed silt off Weehawken to be like that in the Haskins tunnel further south, on January 16 Jacobs ordered all the doors on the Jersey South Tunnel shield shut, preparatory to shoving full speed ahead. It was a jubilant moment, because from here on in, his men could shove rapidly forward without the mess and trouble of taking in muck. But when the crew of alignment engineers appeared at the facing to take measurements after several rings had been installed, they had startling and worrisome news. The South Tunnel was not on grade, but rising rapidly. They weighted the shield to counter this, but when they pressed forward the tunnel again failed to keep to grade, and the iron shell itself was "distorted . . . the horizontal diameter decreasing and vertical diameter increasing by as much as 11/4 in." Chief Engineer Jacobs came over in the freezing weather on the PRR's jaunty steam-powered despatch boat, the low-slung *Victor*, American flags flapping brightly in the river's breezes. But he and his engineers did not feel jaunty, just perplexed. Reported Jacobs, "The material in the face is soft mud of a peculiar consistency." But that did not explain the now slightly off-grade and distorted tunnel.

This was a very worrying issue, the worst they had yet encountered, for if the South Tunnel veered too much further off grade, it would become potentially defective. "A good many different theories were advanced as to the probable cause," wrote one of Jacobs's young engineers. "It was thought that the hood of the shield might have something to do with the trouble." So now the hood was removed, the doors remained shut, and the shield was driven forward. With great trepidation and anxiety, everyone waited for the findings of the alignment crew. Alas, all they documented was that the trouble persisted. "It was impossible to keep the grade." This was now a most serious matter. "Work was stopped, and the question was thoroughly debated." Jacobs decided to try another shove with one of the shield doors open as an experiment, allowing in 50 percent of the displaced muck. This time, when the alignment crew rapidly did their calculations, it was most welcome news. "The shield began to come down to grade at once," reported the delighted junior engineer, "and it soon became necessary to close the door partially and reduce the quantity of muck taken in, in order to prevent the tunnel from getting below grade. The other troubles from distortion, etc., ceased at the same time." There was great jubilation all round.

And so Jacobs and his men joyfully charged full speed ahead. During February 1906 alone on the Jersey South Tunnel, reported Jacobs to Cassatt, "166 rings have been built, an average progress of 14.31 lineal feet per working day. To date 436 rings of cast iron lining equivalent to 1091 lineal feet of tunnel have been constructed. The excavation done is approximately 38.5% of the total." The worst, they believed, was clearly over. All too soon, they would discover their celebration was most premature.

EIGHTEEN

"DISTURBED ABOUT
NORTH RIVER TUNNELS"

O n Monday April 2, 1906, an anguished Samuel Rea sat at a wooden desk in his spacious Bryn Mawr home and considered how best to begin his letter to Alexander Cassatt. Outside, after days of rain and squalls, it was a cold spring afternoon suffused with clear light. The PRR's third vice president was bone tired, recovering from tonsilitis, and feeling steady twinges of rheumatism in his knees, his back, and now his arm. His doctor was pressing him to go away for a bit, to make a quick but restful sail down to the warmer climes of Jamaica. Rea wearily took up his fountain pen, scrawled "Confidential" in his neat small script atop the half sheet of lined paper and paused. He decisively underlined "<u>Confidential</u>," and then plunged in: "Dear Mr. Cassatt, I have been disturbed about North River tunnels for some time—since I told you that General [Raymond] thought they were rising—He has verified this & Jacobs told me on the phone last Friday I think that he had suspended work and he thought they had risen about 6 inches, but he thought they would come to rest."

This was typical of Charles Jacobs—always sanguine. But Samuel Rea had just learned in a deeply distressing tête-à-tête that the eminent but prickly Brigadier General Charles Raymond very strongly begged to differ. Raymond, balding, his remaining good eye steadily dimming with its thickening cataract, was a formidable and punctilious military engineer. He was so esteemed that the PRR had pleaded with the War Department to borrow him to serve as chair of the PRR's board of engineers. In 1904, just before his military retirement, Raymond's stellar forty years of public service had been rewarded by promotion to brigadier general.

General Raymond had traveled especially to Rea's home to report his decided professional opinion that the as-yet-unfinished tunnels on the Weehawken side were shifting dangerously about in the river's infamous alluvial silt. Raymond, employing a large magnifying glass to aid his diminished vision, had painstakingly reviewed the daily figures and data produced by Charles Jacobs's own alignment crews. He had slowly come to believe that something was alarmingly amiss. Five days earlier, Raymond had for the first time confronted Jacobs with these disturbing facts at a board of engineers meeting. Both Alfred Noble and Jacobs scoffed, Rea told Cassatt in this letter, expressing such utter skepticism that they declined even to include Raymond's doubts or his data in the board's written minutes. But, wrote Rea, the "General was insistent on management being advised."

During their just-concluded private meeting, Rea wrote to Cassatt, Raymond had also revealed that his figures for the Weehawken tunnels showed "there had been a rise of about 2 feet in one place—This is alarming . . . If General was correct we must change method of construction—devise some way of anchoring tunnel and possibly doing that work as the driving of the tunnel progresses and that of course the work of driving must be suspended . . . Jacobs and Noble are now alive to the situation but for a long time didn't have much faith in General's theory or his results."

Was it possible that the naysayers were right? One man had written Cassatt early on, wondering if the bed of the river was still moving seaward, "like the movement of a glacier" and so might "be fatal to the stability of any structure imbedded in it?" Was it possible the PRR had indeed fatally miscalculated? The Pennsylvania Railroad had already spent the vast sum of $80 million on constructing its monumental entry to Manhattan, an enterprise many continued to condemn as an unnecessary and extravagant folly. If the trains could not roll into Gotham through the North River tunnels, it would be a humiliating corporate catastrophe.

And so began a season of unparalleled woe for Alexander Cassatt, Samuel Rea, and the Pennsylvania Railroad.

Up in New York, Alfred Noble and the many engineers working on the PRR's four subaqueous East River tunnels (known prosaically as A, B, C, and D) were as weary and frustrated as Samuel Rea. When they stood atop one of the Manhattan caisson shafts they beheld a beautiful swift-flowing river, its powerful tidal waters shimmering pewter as the sun rose and the batteries of ferryboats and steamers began their busy workaday schedules plying the industrialized waterfront. Soon, the more nimble fishing smacks, oyster sloops, and pleasure boats would breeze by, and on warmer afternoons even the occasional intrepid canoeist. As evening came, and the many vessels berthed and the city quieted, the East River gleamed with reflected lights and flowed a glossy indigo. But the riverbed deep below these scintillating tidal waters was proving a maddening and intractable mix for tunneling: a perilous underworld of quicksand, coarse sand, huge boulders, gravel, and clay—the bedeviling legacy of the ancient glaciers—lay between the water and the bedrock.

Not long after Rea confided his alarm over the North River tunnels to Alexander Cassatt in early April 1906, Alfred Noble, who had launched his East River tunnels two years earlier, detailed for the PRR president his own litany of setbacks: "In Line A, there has been no excavation done since December 29, 1905 . . . In Line C, work was continued until March 22nd when it became necessary to stop work on this line and bulkhead the face on account of the impossibility of supplying air for more than two tunnels . . . In Line D, the work has been extremely difficult during the entire month and progress has been very slow." Line D had been the first tunnel out into the river and the southernmost of the four, and now the recently erected iron tunnel rings were developing cracks. Finally, there were so many blows on Line D, despite the dumping of a twelve-foot layer of clay onto the riverbed, conceded Noble, "the heading was closed on the 31st." In short, three of the four East River tunnels were at a standstill. The two sets of subaqueous tunnels under the North and East rivers—the linchpins of this most ambitious of civil engineering projects—were now both in limbo.

Then there was the rising toll of fatal and sometimes macabre accidents under the East River. About nine in the morning on March 31 an Italian sandhog working with a big gang a hundred feet down in the warm, dank Tunnel B aimed his pneumatic drill at a ledge of rock. A thunderous blast ricocheted through the tunnel, the concussive force hurtling the sandhog and thirty nearby men onto the tunnel floor, rocks and dirt cascading down. A carelessly forgotten stick of dynamite. Most of the sandhogs slowly extricated themselves from the debris, bloody and shaken, as the junior engineers rushed in to the grim scene to help. The ambulance medics from nearby Bellevue Hospital carried out stretchers with three Italians so mangled and burned they were not expected to live.

Ten days earlier, a bored Negro watchman down by the air lock had snuck a cigarette (against all tunnel rules) at six in the morning. By the time the firemen put out the flaming salt hay (for patching blows), all that remained was a charred corpse. Back on January 15, there had been a far worse fire with even more fatalities. "DIE LIKE RATS IN TRAP" reported the *New-York Tribune*. "*Four Killed in Caisson* Smothered by Smoke and Drowned in East River Tunnel."

But what the sandhogs most feared were the bends. More and more often, it seemed, a brawny mud-smeared sandhog would exit the air lock, step free of the shaft, and collapse. It was a heart-wrenching sight, a large strong man gasping and writhing, groaning pitiably under the excruciating and peculiar torments of the bends. Succor was always swift. Yet, as fast as the sandhog might be rushed to the medical air locks or the hospital, often he was not seen again. Such a multitude of tunnel laborers came, worked, and quit in these ill-starred East River tunnels, so many of the men were new immigrants speaking no English—Italians, Bohemians, Swedes—that the longtime sandhogs knew little of the fate of the afflicted. How many men had been felled with bends in the three daily shifts? How many crippled? Dead? No one knew, but as the sandhogs sat in the air locks, they traded dark rumors of far too many among their ranks disabled and dead.

As the emergencies and troubles proliferated, Noble's second in command, Henry Japp, thirty-seven, a handsome, lantern-jawed Scotsman, had taken to sleeping nights in a little room off the company's offices by the Long Island City ferry slip. Japp, managing engineer for the PRR's East River tunnel contractor, the British firm S. Pearson & Son, was not infrequently jolted out of his light slumber by foremen telephoning from the tunnels with some new crisis. A graduate of Dundee University and a veteran of the Blackwell Tunnel under the Thames River and of London's Great Northern & City Railway tunnel, Japp kept the proverbial stiff upper lip as he, Alfred Noble, and their corps of engineers soldiered wearily on.

Down in Washington, D.C., President Theodore Roosevelt, triumphantly elected for a second term, was hell-bent on wresting a landmark piece of legislation—railroad regulation with real teeth—from an imperious and hostile Republican Senate. Long-simmering public anger was boiling over as the muckraking press dredged up new lows in railroad greed and malfeasance. "The cry arises from every part of the country," charged the influential *McClure's Magazine*, "that the railroad 'baron' . . . makes the [rates] low and easy for his rich favorites—the Rockefellers, the Armours, and their like . . . [but] high and hard for the farmer, the small struggling manufacturers and shippers and all the vast unorganized mass of producers and consumers."

Not since Abraham Lincoln had such an activist president occupied the White House. And never one so amusing, energetic, and combative. Theodore Roosevelt was determined to terminate forever the laissez-faire era of big business by ramming through the historic Hepburn bill, legislation that would at last give real muscle to the Interstate Commerce Commission, empowering the federal government to investigate secret corporate books and enforce fair railroad rates.

Senate majority leader Nelson Aldrich, son-in-law of Standard Oil's John D. Rockefeller, had come to view Roosevelt, his fellow Republican, as an impertinent rabble-rouser. Senator Aldrich adroitly and contemptuously consigned the vexsome Hepburn railroad bill to the care of Teddy's longtime Senate archenemy, South Carolina's "Pitchfork Ben" Tillman, a ferocious one-eyed backwoods Democrat who favored a black cowboy hat. Teddy and Tillman had not spoken since 1902 when Tillman had been stricken from a White House guest list for pugilistic assault upon another senator. To add insult to this blackballing, the snob in Teddy had quipped that Senator Tillman's politician brother had been "frequently elected to Congress upon the issue that he wore neither an overcoat nor an undershirt." Now, Teddy simply gritted his famous teeth and cultivated a working alliance with "Pitchfork." For the sake of railroad reform, the two antagonists held their respective noses and advanced the bill. The puissant Senator Aldrich was not pleased.

"Railroad rate regulation was the greatest challenge handed to Congress in forty years," writes Roosevelt's biographer Edmund Morris of the president's declaration of political war on the nation's most powerful and entrenched corporate interests. "More precisely, [the greatest challenge handed] to the Senate—the House voted to approve the [Hepburn] bill on 8 February by an astounding margin, with only seven negative votes. But the forces of reaction were confident that Old Guard delay tactics down the corridor would eventually make this victory Pyrrhic. 'No railway rate bill,' the [deeply conservative] New York *Sun* declared, 'will be passed by the Fifty-ninth Congress.' " U.S. senators, often castigated as the Millionaire's Club, were still (until 1913) elected by state legislatures, and cared little for popular opinion. Or, for that matter, for the young and presumptuous president.

During the 1904 elections, when the Democrats published their satiric, "An Alphabet of Joyous Trusts," R read: "R is the Railroad Trust, always on time/To Run over the People, and get their last dime." The fury aroused by the railroads largely boiled down to the dull-sounding issue of rate discrimination. The galling and inescapable reality in these early years of the twentieth century was that almost every American company, town, and farm found its economic well-being hostage to the local (and often high-handed) railway corporation. The railroad, as *McClure's* editorialized, "is not like any other industry . . . it is the essential tool of commerce. Other industries and men and cities, who must use this tool, rise to success or sink to poverty as it is handled well or ill."

Railroad freight rates—and the lack of any recourse if they were unfair—stirred vehement passions. The ever-sober *World's Work* declared: "Great corporations have grown rich because of such discriminations . . . They have broken laws and evaded laws . . . A small group of men control the great transportation lines; and the group becomes smaller every decade. Railroad property is tending towards one colossal 'combine.' It is this fact that stirs the public fear more and more seriously." More than anything, Americans wanted fairness. When they felt wronged, they wanted recourse.

President Roosevelt had already irritated important Republicans by intervening in the coal strike and attacking Northern Securities. Now, Roosevelt had really pushed beyond the pale, challenging the sacred concept of laissez-faire itself. Big business, which had contributed many millions to Teddy's presidential campaign, felt ill-used and wrathful. Hissed coke and steel king Henry Clay Frick, regretting his check for fifty thousand dollars, "We bought the bastard, but he didn't stay bought." Theodore Roosevelt, who understood the angry, impatient temper of the nation far better than the men he denounced as "malefactors of great wealth," was impenitent.

Soon after Roosevelt ascended to the presidency, a group of railroad chiefs had organized to express their intense displeasure at the mere rumor of regulation. Alexander Cassatt, that rare being, a rich corporate Democrat who welcomed regulation as necessary and inevitable, had curtly refused their invitations to join them: "I very much fear that in view of the diametrically opposite views which we hold, nothing would be accomplished by such a meeting." For years, Cassatt had been privately warning his fellow railroad kings and Wall Street's financiers that "the increasing power of the rapidly uniting systems of transportation must inevitably be counterbalanced by government control of traffic tariffs." When Roosevelt took over the presidency, he had assiduously courted Cassatt on railroad matters, asking in one 1901 letter, "Will you give me your views?" Then adding, "It was the greatest pleasure to have you to dinner the other evening. Remember, we are all going to go to that football game." Both men—the president of the United States and the president of its most powerful corporation—agreed that you could not have a healthy industrial democracy if the rich rigged the system to become even richer and bigger. Only the government had the power to tame the trusts.

Now, Roosevelt was fulfilling the worst fears of the railroad titans who abhorred the Hepburn bill as an outrageous assault on private capital. Armed with a huge war chest, they retaliated with a public relations barrage, stage-managing months of negative newspaper coverage and congressional hearings. Cassatt still abstained. "Let the government regulate us," he told one journalist. "For my part and for my associates in the Pennsylvania Railroad Company, I am generally heartily in accord with the position taken by President Roosevelt, and we have been all along; I told the President himself when he made his first recommendation on this subject to Congress, more than four years ago, that I believed him to be in the right."

Not only had Cassatt outlawed secret rebates on his own roads six years earlier, he had just abolished the free railroad pass, something he had wanted to do for decades. The free pass, which the Hepburn bill also sought to banish forever, was the deeply beloved, valuable perquisite of every journalist, entitled citizen, and above all, every petty or powerful politician. "The ability of a member of the legislature, or any other political leader, to get [free] trip passes for his constituents or partisans," writes historian Mark Sullivan, "was perhaps the most potent form of patronage he had. Any important political boss, such as Quay of Pennsylvania, could command trip passes by the thousand."

As the PRR's and Cassatt's personal letter books attest, the importuning for free passes never ceased. Every day the missives arrived—relatives, reporters, editors, archbishops, congressmen, businessmen of every hue, each expressing the desire to ride the PRR rails for free. People even pestered his sister, Mary, in Paris to ask for free passes on their behalf. On January 1, 1906, Cassatt decreed an end to it, saving the company $1 million annually. There was simmering resentment, worsened by the fact that complaining about the lack of passes made one look cheap. But this particular act of Cassatt, opined the *Wall Street Journal*, was "probably the most courageous of all his moves" because it so personally touched and riled the powerful.

While the fate of the Hepburn bill was still twisting in the senatorial winds that February and March, Cassatt made many forays to the capitol to advise the president and twist arms in the Senate. He expressed himself forcefully to President Roosevelt on the bill's ultimate shape, insisting that without certain changes, "You will deny the railroads the right to have orders of the [Interstate Commerce] Commission reviewed by the Courts as to their reasonableness and justness . . . I respectfully submit that we had a right to expect that a Bill would be framed which would be just to the railroads as well as to the public."

Even as those Republicans known as Railroad Senators did their imperious best to bury or neuter the Hepburn bill, the Interstate Commerce Commission came to life in early March, a recent U.S. Supreme Court decision enabling it to "examine railroad discrimination and monopolies in coal and oil and to report on same from time to time." Chief commissioner Martin Knapp announced a sweeping investigation of the half dozen biggest coal roads, including the Pennsylvania, and as March 1906 ended, all those roads were peremptorily ordered to produce lists of every single one of their stockholders, how many shares they held, and the ownership and control of any coal mines served by that road, "data that have hitherto been regarded as privileged and safe from publicity." A new day had abruptly arrived.

Alexander Cassatt was unconcerned, for he had long advocated just such government scrutiny. On April 9, he wrote to Knapp at the ICC, saying "If the Commission desires to examine me in connection with the investigation now being made of the coal and oil carrying railroads, I would be very much obliged if you could arrange to have me called some day this month, as I propose sailing for Europe on the ninth of May, and although I shall return the latter part of June, I expect to be at my office only for a few days, after which I shall go to Bar Harbor." ICC counsel William A. Glasgow Jr., forty-one, a southern coal lawyer with a deceptively "Aw shucks" manner, who had already developed a reputation as a soft-spoken bulldog in early hearings, reassured Cassatt that there was no hurry. Meanwhile, President Roosevelt continued battling to push the Hepburn bill through the Senate.

As spring unfolded in Gotham and the light lingered longer in the late afternoons, battalions of speed-mad bicyclists and automobilists zoomed up Riverside Avenue alongside the busy and beauteous Hudson. But for Samuel Rea and his distinguished board of engineers, the North River remained as alarming and perplexing an engineering problem as they had ever encountered. Rea had ordered Charles Jacobs, who conceded in a telephone conversation that the South Weehawken tunnel had indeed risen six inches, not to dig another foot further on the New Jersey side "until some agreement was reached . . . We must have the facts." Rea had also spoken rather bluntly with George Gibbs and Alfred Noble on the matter, reminding them that it was their beholden duty as members of the board of engineers to help the PRR obtain "absolute data."

Ironically, Gustav Lindenthal, the engineer and bridge builder who had preferred his North River Bridge project to tunnels, was now engaged to study what exactly was going awry under the river. Lindenthal's mandate was that "the stability of the Pennsylvania Railroad tunnels must be secure under all circumstances. For ample safety the worst known conditions must be considered." But the maddening North River glacial silt continued to confound him.

PRR President Alexander Cassatt (center) on an inspection tour.

Jacobs, ever the activist and ingenious problem solver, conferred at great length with his chief assistant, James Forgie. After all, Jacobs had neatly solved the earlier problem of the Weehawken South Tunnel shield advancing off-grade by taking in more muck. Jacobs now posited to Rea that this same tunnel had been moving about in such an unnerving manner—as General Raymond had shown—in response to the advance of the parallel North Tunnel shield just fourteen feet upriver. Exercising all his persuasive powers, Jacobs convinced Rea to let him cautiously push forward with the North Tunnel shield and see if, again, taking in more muck might correct the wayward South Tunnel.

On April 18, the experiment began. "Approximately 50% of the total excavation for a ring of iron has been taken out on every shove, in order to avoid possibility of disturbing the South Tunnel. So far, that portion of the South Tunnel contiguous to which the North Tunnel is working has not shown any discernible rise . . . The excavation done is approximately 44% of the total." The South Tunnel had, as Jacobs suspected, been thrust to one side by the passing of the North Tunnel and its shield.

Understanding why one of the Weehawken tunnels had been moving sideways was certainly gratifying. But Samuel Rea's alarm fastened now on the far graver issue of the overall long-term stability and safety of the North River tunnels. What the junior engineers nervously called the Panic of 1906 was just beginning. Why was it that *both* unfinished North River tunnels also seemed to be moving up and down? General Raymond's visit to Bryn Mawr and his data had prompted the deepest scrutiny and its early results were in no way reassuring. Lindenthal could see from his investigation that there was "bending and distorting" in the half-finished tunnels. Jacobs, after studying the matter in these early weeks, acknowledged that there were also "changes in the elevation of the tunnels . . . due to the effect of natural laws which are as yet imperfectly understood . . . Some other force than buoyant effort must be in action."

But what? The overriding fear fueling the PRR's Panic of 1906 was that whatever natural force this was would end up making the North River tunnels unsafe in the long run. If the tunnels were moving about, how would that affect the screw-piles of the subterranean "bridge" meant to connect them to the bedrock far below? These bedeviling but fundamental questions now hung ominously over Cassatt, Rea, and their engineers. By mid-April Cassatt decided to make the North River tunnels' cast-iron ring linings much heavier, increasing the weight of each lineal foot from 9,272 to 11,594 pounds, hoping the additional weight would better settle the tunnels. But the gnawing fear persisted that the answers they sought might be as unsettling as the questions.

NINETEEN

"WOULD MR. CASSATT
BE RESIGNING?"

I n late April 1906, Samuel Rea traveled not to Jamaica as his doctor had ordered, but to the Homestead resort in Hot Springs, Virginia. There he basked for a week in the southern sun and nursed his rheumatic joints in the mineral baths. Although Rea was a tall, robust man capable of prodigious amounts of hard work, a man who preferred chopping wood to golf, he fretted about his health. The previous summer, on a tour of Europe with his family, he had arranged to take the waters in Carlsbad, Austria, concerned that "my liver and kidneys were both impaired." He had written Cassatt, "We all live and work under so much pressure that our nervous systems get broken, which we only realize when off this way." He reported spotting Joseph Pulitzer, the publisher of the *New York World*, whose health was shattered, his eyesight mysteriously gone. Rea observed sadly, "It is an awful calamity for an active man to be blind."

Like Rea, Alexander Cassatt was bone weary and looked forward to sailing abroad for his annual European sojourn. The Hepburn bill, the perplexing tunnel woes, the escalating costs of expanding the PRR's complex and congested system, the depressed stock price, the vitriolic skepticism over his great New York project, the naysayers, all had taken a steady toll. There was also private heartbreak. Cassatt still mourned the death of his newly married older daughter, Katherine, who had died the previous year from goiter. This family tragedy had been compounded by the scandalous collapse of the marriage of his oldest son, Edward. His daughter-in-law's suit for divorce and subsequent remarriage had made the front pages.

And so, late on the wet gray Sunday of May 8, Cassatt, his wife, Lois, a young granddaughter, and their maid and valet rode a hansom cab through the squalor of Manhattan's West Side docks, past drays and wagons laden with cargo, their teamsters yelling and jostling, skirting the new electric traction streetcars and the ever-growing legions of noisy automobiles. Their destination was the White Star pier and the S.S. *Baltic*, sailing for England the next morning at six o'clock. In the rainy gloaming, the steamship was an impressive sight with its long ebony-black hull, gleaming white upper decks, two tan-and-black funnels, and four slender wooden masts bedecked with flags. Once aboard and settled in, his wife happily bustled about their luxurious staterooms. "I was so rejoiced," she wrote of her husband, "that he could go and enjoy a complete rest." As the ship sailed out at dawn the next morning with its escort of steam tugs, the skies were clearing. The ocean crossing was smooth, marked by restorative hours of sunning in deck chairs while stewards served tea, of leisurely strolls fore and aft, and the bracing elixir of copious sea air and breezes.

The *Baltic* docked in Liverpool Thursday May 17, and the Cassatts debarked with their steamer trunks to continue by train to London. That evening, as their cab drew up to the Berkeley Hotel in Knightsbridge near Hyde Park, newspaper reporters surrounded them. The PRR president was startled to hear: "Would Mr. Cassatt be resigning?" While he was at sea, two days of Interstate Commerce Commission hearings had engulfed the Pennsylvania Railroad in a sensational corruption scandal. "RAILROAD OFFICIALS GOT RICH GIFTS OF STOCK" read the front page of the *New York Times*. "Jamison Says He Paid Cassatt's Assistant $5,000/ Others Received Stock for Granting Favors in Coal Car Shipments." As the London evening air grew chilly, the journalists persisted: Were the rumors true that he would retire, aggrieved at his colleagues' deception? He waved them wearily aside. "I do not give interviews at home. I will not do so in England. I am here for a holiday and a rest." With that he bid them good evening and entered the lobby.

Back across the Atlantic Ocean, the next day's ICC hearings in Philadelphia were electric with tension as commission attorney William A.

Glasgow Jr., all affability and charm, probed relentlessly. The front-page headlines again said it all: "Gifts to High and Low on Pennsylvania Railroad," "$30,000 a Year From $500," "Even Clerks Got Stock for Favors— Pennsylvania Announces Abuses Will Be Stopped." Mercifully, when Glasgow finished grilling Friday's witnesses, he announced that there would be no further hearings until the following Wednesday. In Cassatt's absence, Captain John Green, first vice president, described the revelations of coal stock "gifts" to PRR employees and "acceptance of gratuities by its employees [as] a surprise to the management . . . [No such] ownership or practice . . . will be tolerated."

That night a beset Captain Green wrote Cassatt a long letter, both about the important and much-needed $50 million bond offering they hoped to float with French bankers, a pioneering financial first, and of course about the burgeoning ICC scandal. Green enclosed a newspaper story and editorial from the *Philadelphia Ledger*, expressing worry that "the public will be strongly impressed with the conviction that an improper state of things exists among our operating people." The letter was sent to London on the fastest steamship. Green hoped the worst was over.

As if the exploding ICC investigation was not woe enough, Alfred Noble's East River tunnel troubles had deteriorated from bad to dire. The tunnels were behind schedule and costs were mounting ruinously. The air blows were now so huge that spectators gathered in the balmy May sunshine by the busy river just to watch the small geysers of river water broiling up violently next to the new Long Island Rail Road ferry slips. Two of the four slips were so undermined they were listing and, of course, unusable. The problem, one idled sandhog told a *New York Times* reporter, was that just when the engineers thought the shield would be hitting rock, they struck quicksand. "The sand oozed into the shield like water . . . The air shot out with an awful noise punching a hole through the crust of the river bed. After that we were only able to work on one of the tubes, and now that one has a blow-out." Six air compressors were operating at full tilt to keep the river out of those tubes, while the PRR built additional compressor capacity at top speed.

The spectacle of intermittent geysers churning and gushing was complemented by the mesmerizing sight of hundreds of men in giant scows frantically dumping tons of bags filled with clay and cement into the river around the clock. Henry Japp confided, "It takes an enormous heap of clay to make the least bit of river bed, as the tide carries it away. But in the Thames River bed we did not find quicksand or silt such as we found here in the East River." As the compressed air pressure in the fourth tube rose before the last blow, there was yet another sandhog casualty reported in the newspapers, this time from the dreaded "bends." Hans Brinkman, twenty-nine, a big Swede nicknamed Blondy, had staggered out of the Manhattan tunnel shaft the evening of Friday May 19 after his shift and crumpled to the earth in pain. The PRR physicians rushed him to New York Hospital, where he was treated with oxygen, but died after twelve hours of agony.

And then, to add to the pall of corporate gloom, there was the sorry fate of the PRR sidewheeler ferryboat *Baltimore*. At the height of the evening commute on Wednesday May 16, the *Baltimore* departed the Jersey City slip at 5:05 p.m., heading diagonally across the Hudson for Desbrosses Street. Suddenly Captain George Fowler spied a lighter, the *Greenwich*, laden with pig iron, bearing down upon them. Even as the ferry's engines thrust into reverse, the *Greenwich* plowed into its hull, gashing a giant hole and tossing passengers about the deck. The *Baltimore* limped into the Desbrosses Street ferry slip, debarking its shaken passengers and four teams before half-filling with water and sinking.

In the midst of all these woes, the PRR's press bureau was very pleased—at long last—to be allowed to arrange the release of the first stunning drawings of Charles McKim's design for Pennsylvania Station. (A scale model had been on display in Saint Louis at the 1904 Louisiana Purchase Exposition.) There were bird's-eye views of an austere Roman temple exterior with its colonnade of towering Doric pillars, along with dramatic renderings of the General Waiting Room and the train concourse. In a three-page press release (embargoed until Sunday May 20), the PRR instructed, "In appearance [Penn Station] is a wide departure from the conventional railway station. One misses the turrets and towers and more than all the lofty arched train shed, but as the principal function of this station is performed underneath the streets, the upward and ordinary signs of a railway station are naturally absent." Here, finally, New Yorkers could get their first inkling of the full nobility of McKim's building, slated to arise from that gigantic hole on Seventh Avenue.

The many battling New York papers vied to prepare suitably grandiose Sunday coverage of these first views, devoting entire pages to McKim, Mead & White's striking architectural drawings. But then Pulitzer's *Evening World* broke the story on Wednesday May 16. The rest of the press, having been scooped, canceled their elaborate Sunday layouts and treated the station as old news. A chagrined McKim could only console himself that the world could see that the PRR was committed to erecting a magnificent New York terminal.

By now, McKim had sufficiently recouped from his breakdown of the previous year to spend several hours a day at his offices in the Mohawk Building. By and large, the design for Pennsylvania Station was complete. William Symmes Richardson, who had just been made a McKim, Mead & White partner, looked to many of the station's final details. While the station looked classical, the building techniques would be modern, featuring "a steel skeleton with curtain wall construction. A grid of 650 concrete-covered steel piers, spaced around the train tracks, [would carry] the weight of the structure down to bedrock. Above these footings [would rise] a complex steel structure that took engineers about two years to design."

Of the two construction companies bidding on the $25 million station contract, William Mead favored the Charles T. Wills Company, while Samuel Rea preferred the George A. Fuller Company, whose president was Paul Starrett. Rea had talked to Henry C. Frick, who was "very much down" on the Fuller Company after a dispute over their construction of his Pittsburgh office building, but Rea still believed that Fuller was "stronger and better able to carry out big work." And so Rea wrote Cassatt in late February of 1906: "Notwithstanding Mr. Frick's severe arraignment of the company, I believe they are the best people to do the work. If you would like to see them personally I can arrange [it] . . . You understand that they have their own iron workmen and could erect all the steel work in the building for us, as well as set the granite and do other things. [Starrett] said they would sublet the fine marble work."

By late May, Paul Starrett and the George A. Fuller Company had won the contract. Construction would soon start on one section, while the blasting and digging moved steadily along further east toward Seventh Avenue.

McKim's health was sufficiently improved that he and Stanford White had begun arranging a trip north to visit their old friend and sometime collaborator, the ailing sculptor Augustus Saint-Gaudens. White, all charm and exuberance, wrote Saint-Gaudens: "We are coming up to bow down before the sage and seer we admire and venerate so. Weather be damned; and roads too! . . . I am a pretty hard bird to snare, and, as for Charlie, he varies ten thousand times more than a compass does from the magnetic poles, so all this may end in smoke."

In truth, McKim was still deeply worried about his dear friend White. The two were inextricably bound by decades of personal and professional friendship, and a shared devotion to beauty. White, who had always reveled in the risqué and the tweaking of bluenoses, seemed to be getting more reckless. Back in 1895 he had organized the Pie Girl Dinner, a "stag event at which scarcely clad nubile and nearly nude young women served the wine—a blonde for the white and a brunette for the red—and a young woman called Susie Johnson jumped naked or clad in gauze (accounts differ) out of a pie, accompanied by canaries." When word of the dinner leaked out, White delighted in the scandal, unlike Mead and McKim, two of his guests. Now, McKim feared White was whirling toward self-destruction, what with his huge debts and insatiable appetites for collecting, for spending, for work, and for rapacious dissipation.

Over in London, Alexander Cassatt blithely pressed on with his enjoyable routine of fittings with his English tailors and outings to horse breeders. His longtime assistant Patton cabled on Tuesday May 22: "All well. Hope you will not allow sensational newspaper reports to interfere with your vacation. Your name has never been mentioned and there has been no intimation by [Interstate Commerce] Commission of their desire to have your testimony. Your offer to testify is well understood by public." In fact, things were not well. What Cassatt could not know as he rode horses in Hyde Park was that William Randolph Hearst, now an East Side congressman, had his eye on the New York governor's seat and his powerful papers were calling for blood, darkly predicting "criminal charges against a number of Pennsylvania officials."

Worse yet, the *Wall Street Journal*, long a faithful and vocal admirer of Cassatt's "tremendous courage in his attitude on the affairs of the corporation," reported that "It has been an open secret for some years that graft has pervaded the affairs of the Pennsylvania Railroad, and Cassatt has been aware of the feeling that such a state existed . . . It will be readily recognized how difficult his position has been in attacking men who have been with the system for years." One has to suspect that Cassatt, pushing forward his own vast, controversial projects, had chosen not to touch this explosive internal matter. And, one also suspects, Cassatt had no way of knowing the specifics that were now emerging in this embarrassing testimony. After all, if various small coal operators had not complained to the ICC when it began a general investigation of all the coal roads, who would ever have known? When the Roosevelt administration began pushing hard to reform the railroads and bring the worst to heel, who would have imagined that the forthright PRR would be their first big case?

The very next day, Wednesday May 23, when the ICC hearings resumed in Philadelphia's Federal Building, the atmosphere was again highly charged, with grim-faced lawyers facing off. William Patton, the reluctant star witness, found himself roughly interrogated. After three contentious hours on the stand, the *Wall Street Journal* reported, "It was brought out that of about 7,000 shares which Mr. Patton had acquired to the value of $307,000, while he was the assistant to President Cassatt, he had not paid one cent in cash." Moreover, as attorney Glasgow grilled his witnesses with silky finesse, he sought repeatedly to implicate Cassatt.

In the ensuing and increasingly adversarial hearings, there tumbled forth damning testimony showing high PRR officers accepting free coal company stock, petty clerks exacting large bribes, and men and coal companies claiming ruin when corrupt PRR employees discriminated against them in providing coal cars. The manager of one coal company testified that "owing to the lack of cars . . . [he] was almost driven out of business . . . When his company was rated at thirty or forty cars, it was supplied with four." Other testimony suggested ample PRR cars were available for large, favored coal companies like Berwind-White. Captain Green tartly pointed out that PRR officers had once been encouraged to invest in coal companies to promote business along their lines. Nonetheless, times had changed. The PRR board responded to these accusations by authorizing a sweeping and unprecedented internal investigation.

Unaware of the growing scale of the ICC scandal, Cassatt crossed the Channel to Paris on Thursday May 24, anticipating loan negotiations leavened with a leisurely visit with Mary at her country house. Instead the Cassatts learned by telegram what they also read in the Paris edition of the *New York Herald*: "GRAFT DISCLOSURES CREATING A PANIC" with the subhead, "Mr. Cassatt Held to Blame." His wife, Lois, later told her daughter, "As soon as I saw that I told your father there was but one thing for us to do and that was to return home at once, as I knew he would wish to help his friends and I felt the charges made could only be answered by him personally." Cassatt quickly saw his sister and launched the critical negotiations with French bankers for a $50 million loan. The next morning, Friday May 25, as they prepared to depart, Cassatt opened the *New York Herald* and read yet more bad press from the ICC hearings: "Railroad Man Admits He Got Coal Company Cash."

Later that Friday morning, Cassatt, his wife, granddaughter, and their two servants rushed into the cavernous Gare Saint Lazare with its familiar sooty smell and shrieks of coal-powered locomotives. They joined the crowds in the open terminal shed boarding the Hamburg-American steamship train for the port of Cherbourg and then boarded the fast line S.S. *Amerika* sailing for New York that very afternoon.

The Cassatts barely left their staterooms as ocean storms lashed sheets of rain upon their cabin portholes. Lois fumed at what she saw as "the outrageous action of the commission in Philadelphia and [its] criticism," while her husband struggled with his rising distress at the whole imbroglio. Why was the Roosevelt administration making such an example of his road? Yes, his own employees had betrayed the PRR, but surely other corporations—more corrupt in all ways—had far worse sins to be aired? But even as Cassatt sailed from Cherbourg, yet another coal operator angrily testified that his business had been "practically ruined" when the PRR reduced shipping cars for his coal from forty-one hundred cars in 1901 to five hundred in 1905. The reason, he told the ICC: "I suppose because I didn't give the railroad officials shares of stock in our company."

TWENTY

"DEATH STALKS
ALONGSIDE THEM"

On Sunday morning June 3, passengers on the S.S. *Amerika* began to gather on deck, savoring the last of the sea air and anticipating the familiar landmarks of New York harbor. The morning was already warm and hazy. The yellow revenue cutter *Hamilton* sped toward them and soon a dozen newspapermen, wearing light summer suits and clutching straw boaters against the breeze, were climbing up the steamship's wooden ladder and onto the deck.

The reporter for Hearst's *Journal American* raced ahead to Alexander Cassatt's stateroom, where the railroad president was staring out his porthole window. "Stalwart, deep-chested, but with shoulders bent and the massive, bowed head grayer by some degree than when he started abroad," wrote the reporter in the melodramatic style of the Hearst empire, "there was a semblance of tragedy to the tall, silent figure. His flushed face was seamed with care; the once powerful jaws twitched and the mouth drooped at the corners."

Cassatt, attired in his usual conservative vested dark suit with snowy starched shirt, high collar, and old-fashioned black cravat, paced back and forth. Visibly agitated, he declared he'd been "greatly surprised" by the scandal, and would never have gone abroad "had the situation, which now appears to exist, been disclosed or intimated to me in advance." Cassatt, who had already declared to the Associated Press in a telegram that he would not resign, vehemently dismissed rumors of resignation as "nothing but a canard." Otherwise, he had little to say. "My information is of the most meager sort, barely more than hearsay, and unconfirmed from any authoritative source . . . Hence, I am not really prepared to discuss my future actions."

He then wearily excused himself, put on his high-crowned derby, picked up his walking stick, and escorted his little granddaughter on deck to enjoy the ship's band as the *Amerika* sailed toward the Statue of Liberty. The Philadelphia reporters were shocked by Cassatt's haggard appearance. He "seemed like a man on the verge of a nervous breakdown . . . At times, when cross-questioned, his hands shook with the intensity of his inward excitement." Despite some initial loquaciousness, Cassatt asserted that he knew only the sparest outlines of the scandal, repeating, "I don't know," "I can't say," "I don't care to answer that." Finally, the reporters took pity and retreated.

To avoid the clamoring mob of yet more New York press awaiting outside the customs shed at the Hamburg-American docks in Hoboken, Cassatt and his party boarded the PRR tug *Lancaster* and sailed straight for the Jersey City Exchange Place Terminal, where the familiar comforts of private car Number 60 awaited them for the ride to Haverford. Ensconced again in his Cheswold estate, Cassatt met for hours with his top officers and attorneys. By evening, he had rallied. His formal statement to the Associated Press ceded almost nothing and took a truculent tone. He "would not sacrifice faithful and efficient officers to a manufactured and mistaken public opinion . . . There had always been a shortage of coal cars during periods of every year, and in recent years this had been greatly aggravated by the great increase in the production of coal, notwithstanding the very large increase the company had made in equipment."

He acknowledged some instances of wrongdoing, vowed to root it out, and offered to testify whenever called before the ICC. But he took umbrage at the press, chiding the newspapers for their shabby treatment of him and his company. Had they already forgotten that his management had "taken the company out of politics and done away with the free pass evil?" He decried politicians whipping up anticorporation fervor, a not-so-veiled rebuke of Roosevelt. The next morning, a hot muggy June day, Cassatt rode the local from Haverford to his Broad Street Station offices, declined to speak with the crowd of newspapermen, and closeted himself again with his officers.

Back in New York City, which was just as hot and soupy as Philadelphia, the PRR's four East River tunnels were coming to seem an almost accursed enterprise. Even as Cassatt ran a gauntlet of reporters at Broad Street Station that Monday, the Manhattan coroner, George F. Shrady, announced an official inquiry into possible criminal negligence for "the unusual number of men" who had died since January. Despite the new clay blanket in place, the raised level of compressed air—from thirty-two to thirty-five pounds, pressure critical to keeping the river at bay—was exacting its own toll. Far too many sandhogs were dying from the bends.

Splashed across the front page of the *New York Herald* was an article headlined: "Say Death Stalks Alongside Them in Tunnels." The newspaper estimated anywhere from thirty to fifty men had died since January. A tunnel medical attendant testified that in those five months "he had seen hundreds of men taken with the bends, and known of eleven men dying from the bends." The PRR tunnel physician employed just since March 29 knew of three fatalities. The family of one Robert Griffert, deceased, was suing for fifteen thousand dollars, asserting that he was hired without a proper medical examination and had died "that same day at midnight after emerging from the tunnel."

The workers complained bitterly of laxity in operating the all-important air locks, and the actual removal of the air gauges so no one knew just what the pressure was. The air in the tunnels was especially foul because the intake was near a gas house, the sandhogs charged. Everyone understood that digging tunnels was dangerous work, but Coroner Shrady accused S. Pearson & Son, the English contractors, of criminal negligence. Replied Pearson's supervisor at the tunnels, "I do not see that this is the public's affair. It is a matter concerning only the company and the men." Shrady responded by empaneling a jury.

And so it was on Wednesday June 6, his third day back from Europe, that Alexander Cassatt found the Pennsylvania Railroad facing bitter and unflattering attacks on two fronts. The morning began with ICC attorney Glasgow cross-examining Joseph Boyer, the $225-a-month chief clerk of the PRR's superintendent of motive power, a grim-faced balding man with a thin mustache. Responsible for purchasing all the coal for the PRR's locomotives, Boyer reluctantly admitted that for three years he had received kickbacks of three to five cents a ton from several coal companies anxious to curry his favor and land big contracts with the mighty PRR. These pennies of graft had accumulated into the startling sum of $46,000.

"What did you do with the money?" asked Glasgow in his soft, southern accent.

"I kept it all," admitted Boyer. And then there were the $14,000 worth of stocks Boyer also "kept."

Cassatt promptly fired Boyer. The next day he dismissed a second clerk complicit in the same scheme. But still no heads higher up had rolled.

Each time Cassatt departed his Broad Street Station office now, he passed through a jostling crush of reporters. As the rumors of graft, illicit fortunes, and undue influence swirled around him, Cassatt seized the high ground by releasing his entire personal financial portfolio. He declared unequivocally that he held no stock—and never had since becoming president—in any coal company. Nor had he ever received "gifts" from any man or company doing business with his road. Henry Clay Frick, the PRR's largest individual stockholder and a man once described as possessing "a hunk of iron for a heart," came forward to say, "Mr. Cassatt is not only a very great man, but he is a very honest man . . . The most astonishing thing to me is that such a name and such a career should not have been enough to protect any American citizen against mere insinuation and malicious gossip." The beleaguered Cassatt immediately wrote Frick, "I cannot adequately express my deep and grateful appreciation." However, Cassatt admitted to one friend about the PRR, "Enough has been disclosed to show there must be a thorough housecleaning. This the Board has already undertaken in a most vigorous way." Like Cassatt, every PRR officer and employee would now have to reveal his personal holdings.

In certain clubs there were satisfied whisperings and knowing insinuations that the Pennsylvania Railroad's president was getting his just desserts. Had he not foolishly helped President Roosevelt push the invidious Hepburn bill, legislation that would further empower the interfering ICC? To the astonishment of the Old Guard and the jubilation of Roosevelt, the Hepburn bill and real railroad reform now looked headed for certain passage. The *Wall Street Journal* decried the unseemly glee over Cassatt's woes and the "spirit of exaltation in the humiliation of the greatest railroad corporation in the country." Still the rumors about the PRR flew and multiplied, including that of Cassatt's imminent dismissal. This was certainly the fervent hope, wrote the (London) *Times*, of minority shareholders outraged "over the lavish expenditure sanctioned by Mr. Cassatt in connection with contemplated improvements."

As the rainy dawn sky lightened on Thursday morning June 21, the 6:15 Long Island Rail Road ferry had just departed to cross the East River toward Manhattan and the Thirty-fourth Street slip. At that moment, the crew and the few passengers heard a shuddering roar, followed by the terrifying sight of a gigantic muddy geyser, spewing slime and sand, exploding out of the river ahead. They watched in awe as the huge, pulsing column of filthy water shot higher and higher, thirty, forty feet, while all around the river boiled and bubbled. The ferrymen knew exactly what it was—Tunnel D, the southernmost, had just blown again, the worst blow they'd ever witnessed. On the New York side, the ferry house men rushed to the shaft elevator cage, squeezed in, and plunged down.

Far below the boiling East River, terrified sandhogs were already stumbling wildly through the muck of the five-hundred-foot-long tunnel, racing back toward the safety of the air locks. Minutes earlier they had been installing an iron ring after making a shove. Every man there had heard through the usual din of work a sharp fearful crack, followed by a gigantic whooshing, sucking noise as the compressed air roared out and into the river, swirling up into the gigantic geyser. Moments later, river water gushed in through the shield, trapping and drowning a Pole, Jacob Krass, and a West Indian Negro, James Williams, who had been shoveling blasted rocks out of the facing. The river poured with fearful force into Tunnel D as the sandhogs fled. Ten terrifying minutes later, the survivors emerged filthy, soaked, mud-caked, trembling, and grateful to feel the light rain on their faces. If this were not enough corporate calamity for one day, later that morning Manhattan coroner Shrady's jury severely censured the PRR's East River tunnel contractors S. Pearson & Son for negligence in preventing the bends. The city's Board of Health now vowed to supervise the tunnel works.

As the steamy heat wave lingered and the two sandhogs lay dead in flooded Tunnel D, all four of the PRR's East River tunnels were once again at a halt. Many New York engineers now dared to say aloud what had been only spoken of sotto voce before: the PRR's East River tunnels were defective. Specifically, "the contractors when beginning the tunnel did not sink their shaft deep enough before attempting to bore under the East River. Just what they will do to continue the work is a problem at present unsolved." Alfred Noble and Henry Japp set about pumping out their flooded tunnel, while the sandhogs decided to form a union and strike, demanding better pay and safer conditions.

Alexander Cassatt and Samuel Rea immediately traveled to New York, just as Ernest W. Moir, vice president of S. Pearson & Son, providentially arrived from England. The torrid heat finally broke, and the ensuing rain left the air mercifully cool and fair. Reporters were invited for mollifying interviews. Rea explained that PRR engineers knew from the first that "the difficult feature of this whole work was the East River tunnels." He revealed that not a single responsible American contractor had bid. And even S. Pearson & Son, which had built the Blackwell Tunnel under the Thames, had taken the contract only on a percentage basis. Noble was there to deny the coroner's negligence charges, conceding only that "Occasionally a man will escape from the foreman's vigilance and come out through the mud lock . . . in less time than he ought."

Over at the Hotel Netherland on Central Park that evening, Pearson partner Moir, a jolly man with a large handlebar mustache, strode about his luxurious room with its brocaded walls, waving away all the gloom and laughing as he chatted with a reporter. "Most of the alarm about these tubes seems to have been felt by the newspapers, not by those who are doing the work." They were, he acknowledged jovially, two months behind. He fully expected they would complete the tunnels, but declined to predict a completion date. "Everybody that knows anything about tunnel work knows that one can't make prophecies about it. The only certainty about it is its uncertainty, so to speak. It's not like bridge building, in which stress and strain can be calculated with mathematical accuracy. For you never know what you are going to meet under the bed of a river." Especially under the East River, which was shaping up as the worst "he had ever seen in his tunnel building career." Moir insisted only fourteen men had died of the bends and disputed Coroner Shrady's charges of lax safety. "We are very careful to give the men good air . . . carefully analyzed all the time . . . We have a complete hospital work force." As for the strike and the formation of a sandhog union, he pooh-poohed that, too.

On the same Friday Alexander Cassatt traveled to Gotham to quell the troubles engulfing the East River tunnels, William A. Patton telephoned the New York office to leave good news heard from Washington, D.C.: "the Interstate Commerce Commission has finished its work and adjourned sine die . . . they consider their work ended and the Commission feels that they will probably not require Mr. Glasgow's services any further." Patton discounted rumors reported in the newspapers of impending ICC prosecutions, writing "there is no truth in the sensational despatches from Washington, which appear in the morning papers." In short, Patton was once again assuring Cassatt that "All is well."

However, the venerable *Sun*, voice of conservative Wall Street, forecast otherwise. Its front-page headline read: "AFTER A RAILROAD PRESIDENT Roosevelt Hopes to Convict One or More." And by Monday, the *New York Times* concurred, reporting in its lead story, "MAY PICK CASSATT FOR PROSECUTION Federal Lawyers Plan to Center Attack on One President." It was a sad irony that the one railroad president who had openly supported President Roosevelt, who had actively backed government regulation, and whose railroad had taken such pride in serving the public was now the first railroad president rumored to be targeted by the ICC. The White House legal strategy was said to revolve around conspiracy charges, which "if proved will carry a penalty of imprisonment."

Near midnight that very same Monday June 25, Charles McKim, visiting with his daughter, Margaret, his health still uncertain, was surprised to hear the telephone jangling insistently in his apartment on East Thirty-fifth Street. He picked up the receiver and a *New York Times* reporter breathlessly told him Stanford White had just been gunned down and killed at the rooftop theater at Madison Square Garden, White's masterpiece. White, he said, had been sitting alone at opening night of *Mamzelle Champagne*. During the song, "I Could Love a Million Girls," three shots rang out. White, in his formal dinner suit, slumped to the floor, and a pool of blood began to spread.

"My God—good God!" groaned McKim. The murderer, said the excited newsman, was Pittsburgh millionaire Harry Thaw, who muttered as a policeman led him away, "He deserved it. I can prove it. He ruined my wife and then deserted the girl." At first, there was just silence as McKim absorbed this horror. Then he said slowly into the receiver, "I cannot conceive of any possible ground upon which such a statement could be made." Upon hanging up, McKim telephoned William Mead, who raced back into town. While Gotham slept, Mead had draftsmen search White's private office hideaway at the Mohawk Building and burn all his pornographic photos.

The next day, every one of Gotham's dozen newspapers devoted pages to this cold-blooded high-society murder and the loss of one of the nation's greatest architects. A picture of White, the beau ideal of the gentleman-architect, was in one paper surrounded by the firm's great works—including Penn Station. "There is hardly a city of importance in the country that does not boast at least one building designed by this firm," wrote the *New York Herald*, lauding White not only as the firm's "guiding spirit," but as an artist larger than life: "Stanford White was known all over Europe and America as the most companionable and lovable man of his time." McKim and Mead could not realistically hope this respectful coverage would last long.

Indeed, all of Gotham and the nation would learn in the coming days that White, a married man with a nineteen-year-old son at Harvard, had seduced Evelyn Nesbit, Thaw's wife, when she was an unmarried showgirl of just sixteen. Now twenty-two, Nesbit was described by a *World* reporter as "exquisitely lovely," having "the slim quick grace of a fawn, a head that sat on her faultless throat as a lily on its stem, eyes that were the color of blue-brown pansies . . . a mouth made of rumpled rose petals." Moreover, as extra editions hit the streets, far worse revelations came, with Hearst's *Journal American* leading the pack: "WHITE—THE WAGES OF HIS SIN IS DEATH/ Leader in Immoral Clubs, Watched by Detectives." Or worse yet, "WHITE'S ORGIES HELD IN TREASURE HOUSE OF ART." In recent years, as press stories made clear, White had perfected a repellent talent for complex, and sometimes serial, seductions of young, often barely pubescent actresses. Tenderloin cabmen who knew White expressed little surprise at his murder, one saying, "But I thought that it would be a father that would do it, not a husband." Within days, the celebrated Stanford White had been reduced in public print to a despised "voluptuary and pervert."

Charles McKim suffered agonies to see his dear friend so reviled, and White's son and long-suffering widow bearing the brunt of it. Moreover, McKim had the further burden of knowing that it was he who had, all those years ago, introduced, Bessie, White's widow, to her husband. McKim's devotion to Bessie was heartfelt and he wrote her to say that for him she had "for years made life more worth living" and would always be "the dearest Friend I have on Earth—because the one who has taught me the most and to whom I owe the most."

In the coming weeks, he reassured friends who wondered about his own frail health and the future of the firm that the "past month has been one of terrible strain," but McKim, Mead & White had not been "dismasted nor demoralized, and we shall go on to the end together, whatever happens." He arranged to take Bessie and her son away to Europe to escape the ugly aftermath of White's murder. Of course, they all could only dread the coming trial of Harry Thaw.

As Charles McKim prepared to leave for Europe, booking adjoining staterooms and three steamer chairs on the S.S. *Baltic*, a besieged and exhausted Alexander Cassatt was gratefully heading north to Four Acres, his handsome seaside "cottage" in Bar Harbor for a working vacation. Once out to sea, McKim wrote his daughter, "This ship is a miracle of steadiness, cleanliness, law and order. Til today it has been hot and clammy owing to the Gulf Stream, but heavy coats, wraps and rugs are in order this morning and life once more worth living."

When Stanford White's murder took over the front and inside pages of every newspaper, the stories about Cassatt's imminent prosecution disappeared, as did any further such talk. Instead, in the wake of Ida Tarbell's scathing nineteen-part series in *McClure's* titled "The History of the Standard Oil Company," which had stirred up a storm, the Roosevelt administration was preparing to prosecute John D. Rockefeller and his much-hated monopoly, Standard Oil.

TWENTY-ONE

"THE SHIELDS
HAVE MET EXACTLY"

Wednesday September 12, 1906, dawned gray and wet in Manhattan. The tops of the taller skyscrapers pierced the drifting mist, while the cobblestone streets gleamed slick, full of filthy puddles as the morning commuter traffic built to a roar. By eleven o'clock, a warm drizzle was falling steadily. At the West Thirty-second Street pier abutting the New York Central's rail yard, a throng of damp men attired in oilskin caps, oilskin tunnel coats over dark suits and ties, and sturdy rubber boots boarded two tugboats. With shrieking whistles, the boats steamed out into the Hudson. The river was choppy, pea green in the silvery light.

Back in Gotham, the city was tense with political strife. William Randolph Hearst was running hard for governor of New York State, electrifying huge crowds at elaborately orchestrated campaign rallies. A political loner and natural autocrat, Hearst had parlayed his mother's fortune and his years of bare-knuckled press attacks on corporate and Tammany greed into a juggernaut candidacy. The previous night, followers waving American flags had jammed Carnegie Hall to hear Hearst, roaring to their feet in great waves of ovations and flags when he appeared, a stiff, uneasy figure in his now trademark somber long frock coat. Irate Tammany bosses, who had thwarted Hearst's 1905 mayoral bid by deep-sixing stolen ballot boxes in the rivers, knew they had little choice but to accept Hearst as the Democratic candidate. Hearst operatives had plastered the city with campaign posters featuring his formal portrait.

From the White House, an alarmed President Roosevelt wrote privately to one editor: "I so thoroly dislike and despise . . . Hearst . . . [His] private life has been disreputable. His wife was a chorus girl or something . . . He preaches the gospel of envy, hatred, and unrest. His actions go far to show that he is entirely willing to sanction mob violence . . . He is the most potent single influence for evil we have in our life."

On the water, those visceral power struggles seemed far away, as the PRR tugboat chugged past Albany day steamers, coastal steamers up from New Orleans, oyster sloops, and tugs towing Erie Canal coal barges. Gulls wheeled in the breezes. Downriver, the railroad ferries lumbered back and forth, plying their routes, whistles hooting.

Charles Jacobs was waiting at the Weehawken pier, clad in a plain work suit. He greeted the group stepping off the tugboat, shaking hands with a clutch of excited newspaper reporters, effusively welcoming Alfred Noble and Henry Japp of the struggling East River tunnels, General Charles Raymond, James Forgie, and the other engineers. In high humor, he led the way down into the North Tunnel, riding in the Weehawken cage elevator with the dimple-chinned John F. O'Rourke, famously silent president of the tunnel's construction company. As a young engineer, O'Rourke had erected some of Manhattan's early elevated lines as well as the Poughkeepsie Bridge, and in recent years his firm had built (by the caisson method) the foundations of many of the city's celebrated new skyscrapers, including the Commercial Cable Building.

The entire large party, now forty-five strong, passed through the dungeonlike air lock apparatus in two groups for the requisite ten claustrophobic minutes, acclimating to a tunnel air pressure of twenty pounds. "No great discomfort was experienced," the man from the *Herald* reported of his own passage. However, "one of the press agents of the company fainted in the air lock in a realistic manner." That abashed fellow was escorted back up to the surface. Upon entering the bowels of the North Tunnel, the *Evening Post* reporter peered about in the shadowy netherworld, noting that the usually cluttered, slimy tunnel workings had been "cleaned out for the occasion and ten long lines of electric lights were festooned over the steel ribs of the sheathing." The chatter of the men echoed eerily in the damp metallic space. What no reporter knew (or would be told) on this festive tour was why the work of cementing had not been started. That would require revealing Samuel Rea's closely held secret and continuing affliction.

Alfred Noble is in oilcloth coat and bow tie to left of Charles Jacobs, center. Charles Raymond is to right with dog.

Despite Rea's fears, Jacobs had pressed the work on the North River tunnels using the much heavier iron segments. But to their collective dismay, they had had no visible effect in resolving the mysterious oscillations. All the engineers agreed now that the North River tunnels were moving, but they could not agree on whether it was *both* up *and* down. Worse, they still did not know *why* they were moving. All through the spring and summer, the board of engineers had held tortured sessions examining all manner of measurements and scrutinizing various screw piles—would steel be better than iron?—and then how best to anchor the tunnels. On September 7, even as the board was once again meeting, Rea had written Cassatt a very grumpy letter, complaining that "Mr. Jacobs probably still believes implicitly that there never can be any occasion for holding the tunnels from any upward movement, and both he and Mr. Noble believe that there will be some downward settlement of the tunnels, but neither of them can say why the tunnels should settle other than the fact that they believe [William McAdoo's] Hudson Tunnels have acted in that way."

From the very start, when Rea had contemplated how best to span the Hudson River, he had wondered, "Can a proper tunnel be constructed through the silt formation which is there encountered that will, after completion, withstand the rack and wear and tear of heavy trains passing through it at high speed?" He had been convinced it could, but since learning that the tunnels were moving about in the silt, now wondered anew, "Would not the structure 'work' under the action of heavy trains? We have no precedent to go by, as all subaqueous tunnels of like construction are through a different formation than is found at New York. Therefore, it is largely a matter of speculation."

Now that they *still* did not know why the tunnels moved or what this movement might portend, Rea had no problem imagining the worst. What if a crowded passenger train weighing seven hundred tons rumbled down under the river en route to Penn Station some years hence and the tunnel began to crack? The ensuing calamity would be too awful to contemplate. The specter of flooded trains full of drowned passengers had haunted Rea ever since General Raymond had come to see him at his home the past April.

Consequently, Rea had been in no mood for rejoicing a week earlier when he alerted Alexander Cassatt by cable up in Bar Harbor: "The distance between the two ends of the north tunnel is one hundred and fifty feet, so that they will meet before long . . . Jacobs just advised me that the alignment on the north tunnel is within one eighth of an inch . . . there can be no doubt about the result. I think it is highly satisfactory." At this historic moment, when the two tunnel halves were about to meet up so perfectly, deep under this ancient alluvial riverbed, Rea could take only perfunctory pride in the feat.

Even as Jacobs's first tunnel was reaching completion, Rea complained to Cassatt, "I am not satisfied with the way we have gone on heretofore, and have told Mr. Noble and Mr. Jacobs . . . that it was up to the Board of Engineers to determine what was the very best thing to do and then complete a final plan and proceed with its execution . . . if we, with the very best data we can secure, build our tunnels in a way that they are absolutely secured against any upward or downward movement, we can feel that we have done our full duty and are absolutely safe, and I am not going to approve anything until I am satisfied that what we are doing will be within the range of any possible future maximum and minimum pressures." Rea was simply in no mood for celebrations.

Chief Engineer Jacobs, however, was understandably jubilant. After all, for decades experts and know-it-alls had insisted such tunnels under the North River could not be built. There had been the many months of laboriously removing all those piles, some by machine, many by ax, overcoming the endless riprap, making sure not to damage the New York piers or harbor bulkhead, besting the irksome quicksand, countering the deadly air blows, and waiting out the worrisome halts when the alignment seemed off. Two workers had given their lives, one a sandhog who "was suddenly submerged in the quicksand" ahead of the shield and another a man who had died of the bends. It was true that the tunnel movements remained a mystery, but Jacobs was confident that answers and solutions would come in good time. Last May, just before sailing for London for vacation, he had written Rea, "I sincerely believe that the questions on the tunnel construction are absolutely clearing themselves up, which will free you and all from anxiety as to their stability."

Jacobs was not the only one brimming with pride. On the Gotham side of the tunnel, the New York sandhog crews had raced to best their Jersey rivals, erecting their heavy iron rings at breakneck speed to be first across the underwater state line. On August 28, they had bolted together the ring that touched New Jersey. All told they had installed 692 rings of ordinary iron, and then 571 of the heavier rings, for a total of 1,263. To make their point, the New Yorkers pressed victoriously on through Jersey silt, erecting another three tunnel segments on subaqueous Jersey territory. Thus, the New York sandhogs upheld Gotham's reputation for push, drive, and gumption. *And* its status as the most cosmopolitan of cities. For, noted the *Evening Post* reporter, "Men of all nationalities have built the Pennsylvania tubes under the Hudson, negroes having done a large part of the job . . . there must be something about the compressed air which generates energy and enthusiasm, for the men vied with one another to make the record number of rings."

Even as the two sandhog crews were racing one another to the state line, Jacobs and his engineers descended into the tunnels near the New York side of the river and spent several days meticulously checking the alignment measurements, to ensure that the two tunnel halves were truly on course to match up. Expounded Jacobs to a reporter, "Here we have two enormous iron tubes of twenty-three feet in diameter driven for 6,000 feet under water, and yet expected to join as accurately as the sections of a bridge which can be continuously measured . . . We feel confident that our work will be a success. Nevertheless, it is only when the actual fact is proved that we can heave a sigh of relief and be refreshed to continue our labors."

To measure the final alignments of the two tunnels, Jacobs had his engineers bore a hole through the side of the North Tunnel's cast-iron lining in three places—near New York, near New Jersey, and in midriver. Then, they forced a six-inch hollow pipe through each hole and through the mud and silt until it touched the side of the nearly completed southerly tunnel. Next they drove each of those pipes through that tunnel's lining. "After these connections had been made the 'review' developed into a study of angles," explained one engineer. "When the four lines through the centres of the tubes and the six-inch pipes were joined, these four lines formed four similar angles." To be but an eighth of an inch off after three years was, as the *New York Times* exclaimed, "hardly short of wonderful, even among engineers used to mathematical exactness," especially when the tunnels were advancing toward each other "not in broad daylight" but "beneath all that mud and water."

When the two shields of this first almost-completed North River tunnel had approached within feet of meeting up, the engineers stopped work to gauge the exact distance. From a shield compartment, the men pushed a long six-inch-wide hollow pipe out into the river muck, probing, prodding, and finally pushing right through the other advancing shield. The exultant engineers and New York sandhogs peered through that pipe, razzing their rivals on the New Jersey crew. With good grace, the Jersey sandhogs ceremoniously pushed a box of cigars through the pipe, a victory trophy to the conquering New Yorkers. On both sides of the shields, men were giddy and gleeful. Now the engineers very gingerly pushed forward again until the shields truly met metal-to-metal, deep under the middle of the river at 7:50 p.m. September 11, 1906, like giant mechanized kissing moles. It was just as planned, but wondrous nonetheless.

The next day, a proud and delighted Charles Jacobs led an inspection party through the tunnel out to the very center of the river. This newest and deepest section of the tunnel lay ninety-seven feet below the high tide mark. It did not do to dwell too much on the fact that far above, all manner of ocean liners and laden barges were passing overhead. As the merry group neared the Jersey shield, the Weehawken sandhogs spotted Jacobs and unleashed raucous whoops, hoots, and wildest clapping, generating a wall of noise that rang up and down the iron and steel lining of the tunnel. Red, blue, and white electric lights blazed all around the Greathead shield.

As the applause and laughter subsided, Jacobs mounted a wooden, mud-smeared ladder propped against the shield and announced in mock solemnity, "I am proud to lead the way for the first time through the Pennsylvania tunnel from the Jersey shore into New York City."

The aligning of the North River tunnels.

With that, he stepped through the New Jersey shield, crossed a little plank bridge built just that morning, and passed into the outer compartments of the New York shield. Gleeful pandemonium erupted. A photographer began flashing one picture after another, catching Jacobs in a blaze of phosphorescent light as he took that historic step. More flashes and cheers followed, as the tunnel engineers and sandhogs proudly posed for posterity, including General Raymond, who was walking through the tunnel with the help of his dog. At long last, despite the doubters and many travails, the first railroad tunnel had connected Manhattan to the mainland. The most crucial link in the Pennsylvania Railroad's gargantuan civil engineering project was now a reality. It was, as the *New York Times* wrote, "one of the greatest feats in the history of modern engineering."

As soon as Jacobs emerged from the tunnel works and into the busy world of rainy Manhattan, he dispatched a Western Union telegram to Alexander Cassatt in Bar Harbor that was a model of modest understatement: "I am pleased to report that we have just come from Jersey to New York through the North tunnel and that the shields have met exactly on line. All is satisfactory."

And then Jacobs, O'Rourke, and their large gang of engineers and reporters made their way uptown to the splendid Delmonico's at Fifth Avenue and Forty-fourth Street. With the orchestra playing and the French wines and champagnes flowing freely, everyone dined superbly on lobster à la Newberg, quail, and of course, well-aged steaks. Later, amidst the sated merriment and cigar smoke, Charles Jacobs stood up and raised his glass to O'Rourke: "You and your staff have accomplished what was thought a few years ago to be an impossibility!" Raucous applause and roars! Mr. O'Rourke stood to toast Jacobs: "The credit is yours! To the best tunnel engineer in the world!" General Raymond graciously stood and acknowledged O'Rourke and Jacobs: "For the excellence of the construction!" Then, caught up in the fun, the general added, "There is more danger from Mr. O'Rourke and his automobile than there is from his tunnel." Jacobs sprang up, exultant: "Today is the happiest moment of my life!" The men rose to their feet and burst into lusty song as the champagne and wine flowed on.

Samuel Rea was notably absent from both the historic saunter through the tunnel and from the champagne and fun at Delmonico's. Rea, feeling conspicuously unhappy, could be found brooding in the PRR's Cedar Street skyscraper offices, its windows wreathed in mist. That afternoon at 3:45 p.m. he sent Alexander Cassatt a terse telegram: "North tunnel hudson river joined shortly after ten o'clock engineering party walked from New Jersey into New York." Rea could not comprehend, in light of what they knew, how Jacobs could be so sanguine and certain about the tunnels.

When Jacobs hosted a second triumphant tunnel walk less than a month later on Tuesday October 9, Rea was again notably absent. "For the first time in history," noted the *New York Times*, "a party of men walked from Manhattan to Weehawken yesterday, and walked back by a different route . . . The occasion was the opening of the second bore of the Pennsylvania Railroad tunnel; the realization of the greatest engineering feat ever attempted." Now, however, no further work would be done in the tunnels—the thick layers of concrete, the electric wiring, or tracks—until the board of engineers knew why the tunnels were shifting. And what to do about it.

Up in Bar Harbor, Cassatt had been personally reviewing all the studies and reports and sharing Rea's qualms. He had caught a bad bout of whooping cough from his grandchildren, and he was deferring his return until he felt more fully recovered. On September 12, as Jacobs was celebrating the completion of his first North River tunnel, Cassatt had responded to Rea's missives with this curt message for his board of engineers: "This whole subject should be exhaustively studied. The Board has nothing so important before it at this time."

The completion of this first North River tunnel was a great astonishment to the public, which had heard no tunnel news except the very public woes and disasters besetting the PRR's East River tunnels. As far as New Yorkers were concerned, in that fall of 1906, the imminent completion of any of the city's many long-aborning subway and railroad projects could only be good news. Every commuting citizen of Gotham and its suburbs daily experienced the considerable travails of traveling in and out of Manhattan under current conditions, a sorry situation well summed up by the *New York Times*: "The somewhat antiquated and greatly overburdened Brooklyn Bridge used to its full capacity as limited by its old and totally inadequate terminal facilities; the Williamsburg Bridge used to the capacity of its trolley tracks, with the elevated section neglected and rusting; no tunnels under the East River; no tunnels under and no bridges over the North River." In coming years, all that would be changing, as this tunnel tour showed. Until then, the public jammed across the Brooklyn Bridge or patiently boarded the crowded ferries.

Jacobs's tunnel tour—with its many reporters—reflected a major rethinking of the PRR's usual tight-lipped attitude toward the press. In the wake of the ICC scandals, Cassatt had hired the youthful Ivy Lee, an enthusiastic pioneer in the nascent art of corporate public relations. The young firm of Parker & Lee was to deal with journalists and present "our side of the various railroad questions." A Princeton graduate, Lee, twenty-nine, had worked as a reporter for both Pulitzer and Hearst, and thus knew the New York press, and had done p.r. for Mayor Seth Low's second (losing) campaign in 1903.

When Lee received the telegram from Cassatt, he was visiting the Panama Canal, another wonder of the new century. Lee cut short his stay and hastened north to New York by ship. "The Pennsylvania job gets bigger every day," rhapsodized Lee to his father that fall. "The activities of the Pennsylvania are of an exceptionally high order, everything they do being carried out in the best way possible, regardless of expense. The consequence is that we have beautiful raw material with which to work." Certainly, stories like the impending completion of the North River tunnels were easy sells since they remained a mystery, largely unseen by reportorial eyes. Not only was Jacobs finishing the North Tunnel a year ahead of schedule, the two halves of the South Tunnel had been joined only a month later.

Five grueling years had passed since Alexander Cassatt and Charles Jacobs had debarked from the S.S. *Celtic*, two engineers afire with huge ambitions, determined to tunnel deep under the Hudson, Manhattan, *and* the East River and bring the Pennsylvania, the nation's greatest railroad, at long last into the heart of New York. Over these years, Cassatt had endured no end of naysayers and skeptics jeering at what they viewed as reckless "Cassatt madness." Nowhere was that more vividly reflected than in the PRR's stubbornly undervalued stock. In the first year of Cassatt's reign, before the New York Extension was announced, PRR stock had hovered above $170, already less than the $185 most financiers thought its underlying worth.

By late 1903, as Cassatt began his high-profile borrowing and his feud with George Gould festered, the stock had sunk to an anemic $110. The nation's economy boomed, the PRR's income and profits swelled, and the stock gradually inched back up to $145. But Cassatt's monumental expansions demanded vast financings, a $50 million stock offering here, a $100 million convertible bond sale there. The latter, floated in May 1905, was the largest of its kind in railroad annals. Only 10 percent was subscribed by existing stockholders before Kuhn, Loeb stepped in to sell the rest. By the dreadful spring of 1906, further gigantic borrowings, combined with the Interstate Commerce Commission hearings and the East River tunnel troubles, made for chary stockholders. The PRR stock price sank to $129.

The editors of the *Stockholder* heatedly denounced Cassatt for "the most deplorable management of this great property . . . Conservatism thrown to the winds, and money perhaps wasted like water. Additional income from these costly improvements is a matter of the distant future . . . How does the Pennsylvania expect to make $6,000,000 a year net out of the New York tunnels?" It seemed to make no difference that the PRR earned greater profits than ever, hauled fully *half* the nation's coal, and faithfully paid its 6 percent dividend. Back in June 1906, when Cassatt was floating his latest $100 million in bonds, reported the *Wall Street Journal*, "A dozen of the best bond houses of Wall street are advising, coaxing, even imploring their clients to buy these bonds, as one of the best and safest issues of the market. The clients turn from them."

The problem, explained the newspaper, is that "The Pennsylvania [Railroad] is too vast to be grasped by the lay mind . . . Its growth is too big to be understood . . . The tradesman, the clergyman, the country lawyer or doctor out in Pennsylvania, who has owned Pennsylvania stock for twenty years, does not think in hundreds of millions at once. He hears that the New York terminals are to cost $100,000,000 . . . It is an 'awful lot of money.' He hears of a $50,000,000 flotation in New York, and another, the next week in Paris. He thinks the Pennsylvania must be hard up . . . In the end he sells the stock, and buys a mining stock with the proceeds."

The PRR's main Wall Street investment banker, the courtly Jacob Schiff, just back from a journey to the Far East, cautioned Cassatt in that benighted summer of 1906, amidst the lingering torments of the ICC graft investigations and the stalled East River tunnel diggings, "Do no more financing in this market for some time to come. We must not shut our eyes to the fact that your company's immense requirements are beginning somewhat to frighten its shareholders."

Such was the brouhaha in the business world over Cassatt's expensive ambitions that in the early fall of 1906, the eminent English railroad expert, W. M. Acworth, crossed the pond to "form for myself a definite opinion whether the Pennsylvania Railroad is, as I have always believed, an ultra-conservative company, or whether, as many people in England and some in America believe, it has abandoned its old traditions, been badly bitten with megalomania, and gone in for a policy of reckless extension which may end in imperiling the modest 6 per cent dividends of its common stockholders." Acworth scrutinized the PRR from top to bottom, noting the road's excellent infrastructure, starting with its far-flung tracks and lines, all serving prime industrial territory and of the highest quality construction: "the most solid and modern type with masonry viaducts, stone ballast, 100-lb. rails." And then there was the Pennsylvania's well-built equipment, a vast fleet made up of "3,000 locomotives, 2,000 passenger cars, and 63,000 freight cars."

So immense was the American industrial heartland served by the PRR, and so rich the nation's current business boom, Acworth heretically concluded that Cassatt and the PRR could be expanding faster and Cassatt spending more. Moreover, reasoned Acworth, "If it is worthwhile for the New York Central to spend seventy millions to remain where it is [and build a new terminal], it surely must be at least as well worth while for the Pennsylvania to spend a hundred million to get there." Nor was Acworth the only expert to extol Cassatt's PRR. In 1905, broker James T. Woodward had issued a detailed study and hailed gross earnings that rose during these years of Cassatt's reign from $152 million to $238 million, a rise of 57 percent, while net earnings had risen from $45 million to $67 million, or 49 percent. Thanks to Cassatt's "community of interest," the PRR's average freight rates per ton mile had risen 25 percent, leading this Wall Streeter to hail the PRR as "the highest type of an

American railroad company, and because of this, unequalled in the world."

And then there was the windfall that came from ending the free pass. When the White House moved north for the summer to Oyster Bay, William Patton wrote President Roosevelt's secretary, William Loeb, on May 29, "all arrangements have been made for the shipment of the President's horses, carriages, etc. . . . a bill for which will be rendered later." Like all politicians of any importance, it had been a long while since Teddy had paid his own way to ride a train. The president was shocked by the bill for $150.29 that arrived. William Patton responded to Loeb with a detailed rendering of costs, perhaps relishing this small infliction of distress on Roosevelt, whose ICC had so thoroughly humiliated him. He signed off, "My best wishes to you for a pleasant summer."

Cassatt made no exceptions. When his own daughter traveled with her family to Bar Harbor that August, he paid the $168 bill for her use of his private car. After all, for decades he had itched to make the self-important nabobs pay full freight. *And* his road had higher earnings for passenger travel in the first half of 1906, thanks to "the cutting off of free passes," a situation he found "very satisfactory."

To some extent, the shareholders were mollified—especially when Cassatt raised the dividend to 7 percent. Through the late summer and fall, the stock inched back up to $145. Samuel Rea, who was vacationing in England, wrote Cassatt in late August, "I am very glad to see our stock advancing—& hope it will get above 150." But at $145 it stubbornly remained.

All that October, William Randolph Hearst barnstormed the state in his private Pullman car, Reva. He and his powerful newspapers blasted away at the Republicans, exhorting the voters to elect a governor unbeholden to corruption or corporations. Even his enemies credited Hearst and his crusading newspapers with bringing to heel the Ice Trust, the Coal Trust, the New York water board, the New York gas board, and all manner of "corporations caught trying to sneak under or around a law." But they also loathed his autocratic ways and slippery notions of truth. Roosevelt and the Republicans resolved to destroy the publisher once and for all. Roosevelt was well aware of the power of Hearst's appeal. The president understood the rising public anger against the "money power," but he intended to deal with the nation's "malefactors of great wealth" in his own way. As for the office of the governor of New York, it was far too important to cede to a Democrat.

The agent of Hearst's ruination was Roosevelt's secretary of state, Elihu Root, a brilliant corporate lawyer. At a political rally in his hometown of Utica, the tall, thin Root took the podium, introducing himself as an emissary of the popular president. In the dark days after President McKinley's assassination, Root reminded the crowd, Roosevelt had blamed those who "appeal to the dark and evil spirits of malice and greed, envy and sullen hatred." Now, Root revealed, Roosevelt "had Mr. Hearst specifically in mind." It was a sensation. The president of the United States was blaming Hearst's vitriolic anti-McKinley stance for provoking the president's murder! "ROOSEVELT CALLS HEARST INCITER OF THE ASSASSIN" blared the morning paper.

With this, Tammany leader Charles F. Murphy chimed in about his party's candidate, "I don't like Mr. Hearst anymore than Mr. Hearst likes me." Hearst had, after all, tagged Murphy "The Colossus of Graft." For Hearst, these were staggering blows. Come Election Day, a hostile Tammany did not bestir itself, and the voters of the Empire State rejected Hearst. But in a warning to the status quo, Hearst lost by only 60,000 votes of 1.2 million cast.

TWENTY-TWO

"THE ONLY RAILROAD
STATESMAN"

C harles McKim stood on the deck of the S.S. *Provence* as it sailed toward Manhattan under late October skies. He was slipping quietly back from Europe with the widowed Bessie White and her son Larry. The view that met his gaze as the liner steamed into the harbor was one of aggressively tall buildings. As H. G. Wells, a contemporary ocean voyager, described the vista, "The sky-scrapers that are the New-Yorker's perpetual boast and pride rise up to greet one as one comes through the Narrows into the Upper Bay . . . [They] stand out, in a clustering group of tall irregular crenelations, the strangest crown that ever a city wore. Happy returning natives greet the great pillars of business by name, the St. Paul Building, the World, the Manhattan tower." Wells marveled, too, as did every visitor, at the frenetic crowded chaos of Gotham, first palpable on the busy waterways. "Across the broad harbor plies an unfamiliar traffic of grotesque broad ferry boats, black with people, glutted to the lips with vans and carts, each hooting and yelping its own distinctive note, and there is a wild hurrying up and down and to and fro of piping and bellowing tugs and barges, and a great floating platform, bearing a railway train . . . Everything is moving at a great speed and whistling and howling."

McKim, who had turned fifty-nine while in France, leaned into the breeze watching Gotham come closer, observing the skyline with unhappy heart. These ever-taller behemoth buildings that now dominated his adopted metropolis offended his sense of aesthetics. But worse was the melancholy prospect of a world bereft of one of his oldest, dearest friends. In the wake of Stanford White's murder, McKim had found solace in his leisurely shooting holiday on the moors of Scotland and "the simple diet of fresh air and oat-meal of my Highland ancestors." He had then lingered in London, feeling under the weather, before rejoining Bessie and her son in Paris for further recuperative travels motoring through Normandy and Touraine. Now, as their French liner steamed toward Manhattan, there was little illusion about what lay ahead. "I fear nothing—anymore," Bessie had written one of her sisters, "and am laying in a good stock of strength and courage to be ready for the winter which is bound to be a hard one."

Manhattan skyline in 1908.

McKim and the Whites landed and emerged with their trunks from the perils of the U.S. Customs shed into the pleasant day, threading their way through the melee of West Street. Each dreaded Harry Thaw's impending trial for murdering White—sure to be a lurid and painful legal circus. Bessie quickly departed to live in Cambridge, where her son would begin his final year at Harvard. McKim settled back into his third-floor apartment at 9 East Thirty-fifth Street and faced the Augean task of untangling White's large and labyrinthine debts, and somehow salvaging something for Bessie. McKim, Mead & White alone was reportedly owed $600,000. Before departing, McKim had ordered that in their own offices all White's "pictures, tapestries, bronzes, marbles, stuffs, objects, whatsoever, in the reception rooms (large and small), as well as in Stanford's office, should at once be placed in storage."

With White dead and his treasures packed away, McKim returned to find his firm's offices sadly altered. "Our sense of personal loss," wrote McKim to a friend, "and loss to the office and the profession, is only exceeded by Mrs. White's courage and fortitude under so crushing a blow."

McKim's immediate professional concern when he returned to work were certain pressing Penn Station design questions. He was aghast to learn about the siting of the station's planned powerhouse. He protested to the PRR, "There can be no question that the construction of two steel chimneys of a height of 180 feet, in such close proximity to the terminal would strike a fatal blow at the new station." And yet the evolving site of his magnificent railroad temple—just eleven blocks north of his office—had become one of the wonders of Gotham.

The vast Penn Station canyon was rimmed by brownstones bedecked with clotheslines and family laundry, a homely contrast with the monumental enterprise below. All day and night, onlookers were omnipresent, drawn by the spectacle of legions of men and powerful, noisy machines working around the clock to gouge away at this gaping valley now nicknamed "The Culebra Cut," after the similar digging underway at the Panama Canal. "As quickly as the buildings disappeared from this once closely populated district," observed a journalist from the *New York Herald*, "an immense amount of excavating machinery was installed. Railroad tracks were laid in every direction [to remove spoil] and the ground soon lost all semblance to its former civilization. Today the resemblance to the canal zone is complete. The land . . . has been ridged and furrowed until its original topography is but a memory. Long, uneven alleys stretch east and west upward of half a mile in length, through which noisy [work] trains pass on a very busy schedule. The depths of these valleys at many points completely hides the trains from the surrounding country. At several points the tract is dominated by several hills which rise twenty feet

A May 7, 1908, *Harper's Weekly* illustration of
the Penn Station excavation shows a propped-
up Ninth Avenue Elevated and the locomotive
pulling a train of debris toward a Hudson River
pier.

or more above the level of the valleys. There are several miles of railroad tracks in constant use, with switches and crossings—a complete
railroad system." The public was beguiled by the sheer bold scale of the
enterprise.

While in Britain and France, McKim had heard the rumors that
Alexander Cassatt, now sixty-seven, was in poor health, but found them
hard to believe. After all, the PRR president was a big, physically powerful man, a lifelong athlete and equestrian, equally at ease charging across

the hedgerows foxhunting and handling the demands of driving a four-in-hand. Yet, word had it, the indomitable Cassatt was far from well. Any man would have felt the accumulated strain of Cassatt's outsized labors. For six years now, he had been engaged in gargantuan corporate undertakings. He had fought battles with Andrew Carnegie, George Gould, Tammany, and all those who opposed Teddy Roosevelt's railroad rate regulations.

The revelations of the Interstate Commerce Commission had exacted a toll, but the PRR's internal investigation had found the kickbacks limited to a handful of cases: Of "more than 300 operators of bituminous coal mines, situated on the lines of the Pennsylvania Railroad, less than 10 operators in all have testified that they believed themselves to have been unfairly discriminated against." The fifty trained accountants unleashed to delve into the holdings of 2,501 PRR officers and employees concluded that "few, if any" of the ICC charges of rate discrimination and favoritism bore up under detailed study. This was, Cassatt wrote from Bar Harbor, a great relief. "I have been somewhat fearful all along that the result might be the reverse . . . [and] might be used in evidence in suits." Cassatt had not had the heart for any further firings, certainly not his own longtime assistant and aide-de-camp, William Patton. Instead, every PRR employee was ordered to divest himself of all coal holdings. And so, as the summer had waned, Cassatt could feel that the worst of the ICC firestorm was behind him and he could enjoy his sojourn in Maine.

The Bar Harbor summer colony preferred its money quiet (automobiles were banned from town) and its social life genteel—tennis, picnics, regattas, and dog and horse shows. Its summer "rusticators" were substantial men like Cassatt, publisher Joseph Pulitzer, financier Jacob H. Schiff, former New York mayor Seth Low, and distinguished lawyers, physicians, and professors. Their large picturesque shingle-style "cottages" lined the seashore, set amidst manicured lawns, flowerbeds, and rambling gravel paths. Some years J. P. Morgan caused a stir by sailing in with guests (none his wife) on his yacht, the *Corsair*. Here the excesses of Newport, Rhode Island, evoked scorn. In Bar Harbor, no bored millionaires in Versailles-like palaces hosted dinner parties to meet one Prince del Drago, who turned out to be a monkey. Nor would any local hostess fete one hundred pampered dogs as her guests of honor, some reportedly dining in fancy dress.

The Cassatt family had arrived on July 5 at Four Acres, their Arts and Crafts mansion overlooking the jagged coast of Bar Harbor. On the best of days, when the morning fog lifted, the Maine sky scintillated blue, the sun warmed, and the copses of towering pines perfumed the air. Cassatt always brought his horses and carriages north, but on summer mornings he liked nothing better than heading to the Yacht Club to sail his thirty-foot sloop, *Scud*. With all the sailing and sea air, Cassatt felt better every week.

On August 8, the Cassatts' married daughter, Mrs. W. Plunkett Stewart, had arrived at Four Acres with her small son and daughter, who both promptly fell ill with whooping cough. It was then that Cassatt, the doting grandfather, contracted it as well. His family watched in alarm as his coughs swiftly worsened. "It was so severe," his wife, Lois, later wrote, "that I feared he might die in one of the spasms of coughing. I took the precaution of having a nurse in the house all the time, and finally got a young physician to sleep in the house as the worst spells were only in the nighttime." By August 20, Cassatt was sufficiently recovered to wire William Patton that he was feeling much better, but that he would stay longer in Maine to fully recoup.

Cassatt was even willing to endure a visit from Edward H. Harriman, the short, bandy-legged president of the Union Pacific Railroad, who came from Boston by steamer for advice on his upcoming ICC grilling. Shifty-eyed, Harriman wore "wire-rimmed spectacles, an unkempt mustache, and a peevish expression," writes historian Ron Chernow. "Harriman was a market operator—more a raider than a deal maker." Cassatt believed men like Harriman inflicted pointless economic wreckage, stirring up further antirailroad antagonism. Lois wondered, as she saw the Union Pacific president depart their private dock in his steamboat, why Cassatt had not invited him to dine? "No Harriman will lunch at my house," he answered curtly.

Each late summer day now, as part of his convalescence, Cassatt walked slowly along the piney paths to the yacht club. In the years since he had become president, his tall, strong frame had become more noticeably stooped, his blue eyes ringed by dark circles and pouches. Still debilitated from the whooping cough, Cassatt clambered carefully aboard the *Scud* and let his crew do most of the sailing as they trained for an end-of-season regatta. On the race day, the weather was raw and wet, the winds blustery. Cassatt insisted on piloting the *Scud* himself to a respectable finish. He returned home soaked, cold, and more exhausted than he liked to admit.

When the Cassatt family finally returned on September 21 to Cheswold, Cassatt was still too fatigued to return to the office. As rumors flew, the *Wall Street Journal* reported the PRR president would not take up "active duties at his office until he has completely recovered." Even when Cassatt did return to Broad Street Station on October 17, the rumors persisted. A *New York Times* article declared that Cassatt "will go South for his health on an indefinite leave of absence." He would, however, remain the PRR's titular head, for "Mr. Cassatt wishes the completion of the New York terminal to be associated with his management, and he wishes to be present when it is dedicated. This done, he will step out, giving way to a man more capable physically of meeting the trying conditions." The railroad angrily denied the story as "maliciously false."

Yet, how did one run the nation's greatest corporation during a prolonged convalescence? Before his illness, Cassatt's presidential letter books brimmed with directives resolving every possible trouble. Now, the relentless inpouring of correspondence was largely referred to other PRR officers. In Gotham, the benighted East River tunnels progressed slowly, still afflicted by recurring disasters. On October 11, a bad electrical fire in Tube D killed three workmen. On November 7 and 16, there were two more fatal cave-ins, one in Tube C and one in Tube A. Then, on Sunday afternoon October 28, on the newly electrified Camden–Atlantic City line, the PRR suffered one of the worst train wrecks in its history. A three-car train careened off the rails while doing forty miles an hour. The locomotive plunged off a drawbridge into a river, condemning fifty-seven passengers to a frigid death. Most telling of all, the annual October inspection trip, when the president of the Pennsylvania Railroad and his top officers steamed forth to review firsthand the state of their road, had been indefinitely postponed.

There was no shortage of financial troubles to beset the convalescing Cassatt. The PRR's shareholders were still perennially disgruntled. "It is a commonplace of banking offices," the *Wall Street Journal* explained, "that neither the success of the company's engineers under the North River nor the heavy earnings of this year and last have restored the stock to its old place . . . [Investors] don't like the idea of the company going abroad for new capital; they don't like the expenditure of such an immense amount of money on a passenger terminal," and so forth and so on.

Cassatt could only be grateful that these stockholders knew nothing of his greatest woe: the disastrous conundrum of the two North River tunnels. Charles Jacobs had now completed both tunnels and led triumphant underwater walks through each. But as the days shortened and winter neared, the board of engineers had yet to explain to Samuel Rea and Alexander Cassatt the deeply vexing movements of the completed tunnels. These two top officers of the Pennsylvania Railroad knew better than any what it would mean for their beloved road if the North River tunnels—the linchpin in this whole $100 million project—turned out to be defective and unusable.

As the last autumn leaves fell and morning frosts covered the lawns and meadows of Cheswold that November, Cassatt and his family moved back into Philadelphia for the winter. Their red-brick triple-wide Second Empire Revival townhouse at 202 West Rittenhouse Square was located next door to Holy Trinity Church. The Cassatt mansion, overlooking the formal Rittenhouse park with its geometric gravel paths, had handsome double bay windows at street level, a charming bowed window on the third floor, and a copper mansard roof with little dormers. Each morning, Lois watched with a pang as her once-vigorous husband, attired in a warm winter coat and wearing his high-crowned derby and gloves, climbed slowly into his carriage and set forth to drive the few blocks to his office at the train terminal.

Up in busy, chaotic Gotham, Charles McKim prepared on November 12 to send Cassatt some further Penn Station drawings showing a new "perspective of the waiting room looking towards the Seventh Avenue arcade." McKim reported, "I arrived back from Europe a fortnight ago, feeling much better, and, in writing this letter to you, at the request of my partners, I want to express the great pleasure it gave me to learn, on landing, that the published reports in regard to your own health were without foundation." Two days later, Cassatt replied, approving the General Waiting Room, writing, "It is going to be very fine. I am glad to hear that you have been benefitted by your trip abroad. Am glad to say that I am in much better shape." Yet the rumors and reports of Cassatt's ill-health persisted after Cassatt telegraphed to the secretary of the New York, New Haven & Harlem Railroad on December 5 to say he would not be able to be present at the meeting of the board of directors in New York.

On Friday December 8, Cassatt drove as usual to Broad Street Station. It was his sixty-eighth birthday and he remarked to some of the staff that no other PRR president had ever attained such an age. Two years hence, he would reach seventy and mandatory retirement. As the trains rumbled in and out of the station below, he dictated letters responding to half a dozen matters, ranging from the need for grade crossings in Buffalo, to progress on the new passenger station in Baltimore, to the Pittsburgh Coal Company's acquisition of certain PRR lands. When he returned to Rittenhouse Square that afternoon, Cassatt acknowledged a bone-weary fatigue. He was ready to accede to both his wife's and physician's repeated pleas that he work from home for a time, away from the hurly-burly of the office.

And so each December morning, Cassatt's chief clerk, O. J. De Rousse, appeared at the townhouse, as did various officers of the road, bringing correspondence, talking strategy, and pondering problems amidst the silk-damasked walls of the ground-floor rooms. PRR stock still languished, hovering in the mid $130s. The irksome business with the U.S. Post Office dragged on. The previous March, when Cassatt had sought to get the actual deed signed and monies paid, he had been astounded to learn that Postmaster General George B. Cortelyou "thinks the whole scheme is bad, the law unfortunate, and the price too high." Believing it would "be wise to run down and have a talk with Mr. Cortelyou," who was McKinley's former secretary and a major Republican operative, Cassatt left the next day for the capitol. The deed was eventually forthcoming, but now on December 14, the PRR president dictated a letter urging Samuel Rea that "A strong effort should be made at this session to have Congress appropriate $450,000 or $500,000 for the foundations and steel platforms upon which the Post Office is to be built." Even as

Cassatt grappled with all these matters, Mrs. Cassatt and a trained nurse ensured no one stayed too long. Her husband chafed at his confinement.

Christmas came and went, the weather turned cold, with snow flurries and blustery winds. On Wednesday December 26, Cassatt could not, as he had planned, personally nominate Henry Clay Frick as a director. Only his portrait, painted by John Singer Sargent, would represent him in the opulent Broad Street Station boardroom. The three-quarter portrait of the PRR president, done in 1903, showed him standing, dressed in a formal frock coat and vest (gold watch chain just visible) with a stiff high collar and cravat. Cassatt's air was alert and vigorous, his right hand holding a paper, his left hand notched from his pant pocket. Sargent, during that whirlwind American painting tour (he had also painted the president), had captured Cassatt's reserve, thoughtfulness, and vision. But the artist, although famous for his society portraits, had come to loathe these highly lucrative five-thousand-dollar commissions, and thus one also sensed a certain perfunctory quality to the picture.

On Friday December 28, when Cassatt's aides came to Rittenhouse Square, the PRR president dictated a placating letter to the head of Trenton Potteries, angered by a rude porter on the New York ferryboat *New Brunswick*. Cassatt also signed a pro forma letter directing special arrangements for "movement of private car 'Idle Hour' with Mr. W. K. Vanderbilt and party from Washington to Jersey City Jan. 6th." At midmorning on Friday, Dr. J. H. Musser came by, the PRR men were sent away, and Lois summoned a second nurse for the night. Outside, it was still cold and gray.

Around noon, Cassatt, resting in the back upstairs bedroom, asked for his valet, Joseph. Told he was eating lunch, Cassatt said he would wait. When Joseph appeared, he helped Cassatt slowly to the bathroom and then settled him back down. Lois bustled in with their daughter, Eliza, and a wan Cassatt said he would remain in bed a bit before going downstairs again. Two of his top officers were coming for an appointment. A clock chimed one o'clock. As Cassatt lay there, he suddenly looked startled and fearful, gasping, "I feel faint." The nurse rushed into the bedroom to administer medicine. Cassatt sighed, looked at his wife, put a hand to his heart, and closed his eyes. He was dead. When Dr. Musser appeared, he reassured Lois, distraught, tearful, that nothing could have been done for such swift heart failure.

"Word was immediately sent to Broad Street Station," wrote the *Philadelphia Inquirer*, "and a moment later the news was radiating throughout the financial, political, railroad and social circles of the world that the master mind of the great Pennsylvania Railroad was gone." Even as the porters at the Philadelphia station began draping black mourning crepe and many employees in the offices openly wept, "personal dispatches were at once sent to President Roosevelt, to the great bankers of New York, London and Paris, to the president of every great railroad in the United States, and to the scores of corporations with which Mr. Cassatt was directly connected." All along the line the PRR's thousands of locomotives would soon be draped with black, too, as they steamed over the mountain passes, rivers, and through the nation's great midwestern and eastern cities on new tracks laid as part of Cassatt's gigantic expansion. W. W. Atterbury ordered all flags flown at half-mast at the company's far-flung operations until January 10.

William Patton, Cassatt's longtime assistant and friend, raced over from Broad Street Station. All through that doleful winter afternoon, the doorbell rang again and again at the Rittenhouse Square mansion. The cream of Philadelphia society and business—among them almost all of the PRR's directors—drew up in elegant carriages and chauffeured motorcars to leave cards expressing their condolences. Late into the evening the mourners came, as did a steady stream of uniformed Western Union and Postal Telegraph Cable boys delivering telegrams of condolence.

While Alexander Cassatt's family and intimates knew he had heart disease, few dreamed he was on death's door. Samuel Rea, who worked as closely with Cassatt as had anyone in the company, was far away in Pittsburgh when he heard the news. Nor was he free to return, for he was at the bedside of his ailing eighty-six-year-old mother, Ruth, at the exclusive Kenmawr Hotel. Rea wrote immediately to Lois, "The sudden passing away of Mr. Cassatt has shocked me beyond expression . . . I had often promised to have [the New York extension] done before he reached the retirement age. But it was not to be. He was an extraordinary man— one so noble and inspiring—I have never had so much pleasure in my life as the seven years of association with him." Rea confided to a friend in England, "While I knew he had some heart trouble, I held the opinion that he would get better, though perhaps never entirely well, and that he would be enabled to serve out his allotted time with the Company and see the greatest of all our great improvements completed, that is the extension into and through New York."

The sudden demise of the president of the Pennsylvania Railroad was front-page news. Moreover, it was played as both a satisfying Horatio Alger story—he had started as a lowly rodman (despite his family's wealth) and risen to the presidency. But even more dramatically, it was played as a corporate Greek tragedy. "A. J. Cassatt Dies; Of Grief, Friends Say," wrote the *New York Times*, with the subhead, "Pennsylvania President's Heart Broken by Graft Exposures." The headline in Hearst's Philadelphia newspaper blared, "Prominent Financiers Think Cassatt Died of Broken Heart." The story went on to say that "Many men prominent in the railroad and financial worlds . . . unhesitatingly declare that he really died of a broken heart due to the sensational revelations made in the course of the recent coal inquiry conducted by the Interstate Commerce Commission." J. P. Morgan partner George W. Perkins, handsome, roguish, and facing legal troubles of his own for scandals at the New York Life Insurance Company, was his usual outspoken self. Quick to laud Cassatt as "a great public servant," he then took a satisfying swipe at government prosecutors daring to bother their corporate betters. Perkins declared that Cassatt had "died of a broken heart—a heart broken by the constant hounding of iconoclasts."

Some friends blamed President Roosevelt for unleashing the ICC and stirring up scandal. Privately, Lois believed her husband was also still grieving for their daughter Katherine. "Her loss to us and her husband was irreparable, and I feel now that your father was never able to get over the shock of her death."

Considering the pummeling he had taken just months earlier in the press, Cassatt would almost certainly have been gratified to read his glowing obituaries, the ensuing editorials, and the many letters of condolence. William McAdoo, whose own visionary Hudson River tunnel system had been possible only because of Cassatt's magnanimous views of public service, wrote, "He was not only one of the great men of the day, but he was the only railroad statesman this country has ever produced."

Cassatt's worldview that pure laissez-faire capitalism was detrimental to the nation had put him at loggerheads with his fellow Gilded Age railroad potentates. The deceased PRR president, noted the *New York Times* in an editorial, "was among the first [and] . . . certainly was the most prominent and powerful of the railroad men who . . . advocated a cordial co-operation [with government]" Cassatt was also unique, the *Times* said, for practicing "the doctrine that the true policy of a public service corporation was to deal candidly, fairly, and honorably with the public." And what, wondered the more embittered of his family and friends, had he and the PRR gotten for these enlightened views?

Monday December 31, 1906, was cold and dreary, with a steady drizzle creating a fitting atmosphere for the funeral obsequies at the Cassatt mansion. Across the street in Rittenhouse Square Park, beneath the dripping winter trees, hundreds of curious onlookers jostled under umbrellas, craning and hoping for a glimpse of the nation's rich and powerful. Policemen stood uneasy guard at the mansion's front entrance, elaborately draped in black crepe, keeping a wary eye out for troublemakers and bomb-throwing anarchists. At noon, the mourners began to appear, led by a delegation of Pennsylvania Railroad employees. The men removed their derbies as they passed within to the solemn hush of the front parlor, furnished in antiques, oriental rugs, and modern paintings. They nodded and murmured their condolences to William Patton and Cassatt's two grown sons, Robert and Edward, all seated at the head of the open black wooden casket. Once again, a PRR president had died in office. Delegations from the railroad's rank and file and every top Pennsy officer passed through to murmur their respects. Samuel Rea was still in Pittsburgh with his sick mother.

When the men reminisced about their boss, they shared one especially famous Cassatt story. The PRR president had boarded the morning local as usual at Haverford Station on the Main Line for his commute into Philadelphia. When the train came to an unscheduled stop, Cassatt noticed that the trainman, one he did not recognize, was not, as company rules dictated, standing behind the train waving a red flag. Instead, he was lounging on the train's back platform. Cassatt opened the back door and inquired quietly if this was proper procedure? Obviously unaware who the well-dressed Cassatt was, the trainman squirted forth a great stream of tobacco juice and replied, "I don't know if it is any damned business of yours." Cassatt, taken aback, responded, "Certainly not, certainly not," and retreated to his seat. Once in his office at Broad

Street Station, Cassatt summoned the trainmaster, who swore he would immediately fire the lounger. "No, you won't fire him," Cassatt said. "But tell him not to be so disrespectful to people who ask for information in the future."

Cassatt was always popular with his officers, who had a whole song they liked to sing at get-togethers (to the popular Irish air, "Tessie—You Are the Only, Only, Only") that had a final lyric:

> Harriman may struggle for the N.P. stock;
> Hill may try to keep the interests pooled;
> Vanderbilt of Atchison may get a block;
> Pittsburgh may be opened up by Gould
> But the Pennsylvania need never fear,
> While the helm is held by A.J.C.
> With his men behind him he can safely steer,
> And his railroad first always will be.

Outside the Cassatt mansion, the hundreds of damp onlookers in the park ignored the steady rain, relishing the luxurious pomp of magnificent horse-drawn carriages and chauffeur-driven motorcars splashing up through the rain. The crowd gawked as dozens of somber railroad presidents, a U.S. senator, and several eminent financiers emerged from these splendid conveyances, men large in girth and corporate power, sporting silk top hats, clutching canes. Many murmured curiously, wondering just how rich Cassatt had been? Not until the will became public would the sum be known: $10 million. There was a satisfied stir at glimpses of such millionaire titans of Wall Street as Edward Harriman, J. P. Morgan, and Henry Clay Frick, dour, fearsome men well known from the nation's front pages.

Inside the increasingly crowded parlor, the clock struck one, and William Patton stood up and reverently closed the lid of the coffin, gazing down on his patron for the last time. Perhaps he felt a twinge of guilt for his role in the ill-starred ICC scandal, for he had acquired one of the larger fortunes in "free" coal stocks. On the lid lay two bouquets of purple violets, Cassatt's favorite flower, and wreaths from Cassatt's sister Mary, in Paris, and his brother Gardner. By now three hundred guests had squeezed in, filling all the chairs in the parlor, adjacent music room, and entry hall. Even a few millionaires were obliged to stand, pressed in back along the walls and in the corners. Suddenly the whisperings and murmurings were pierced by the sweet boyish strains of choir boys singing "O Paradise." As the music filled and quieted the rooms, Lois and other family members, all dressed in deepest mourning, walked slowly into the parlor and stood by the closed casket for the service.

Later that afternoon, a far smaller group reassembled in the rain out in Bryn Mawr at the rustic stone Church of the Redeemer. Lois, a sad figure in her dark coat, black-veiled hat, and muff, had prevailed in keeping the graveside service more private. President and Mrs. Roosevelt had sent a wreath of dark greens and white hyacinths, an offering some felt should not have been accepted. As the mourners ringed the large muddy grave, the heavens opened and the rain drummed down so ferociously few could hear the readings.

In this most respected and meritocratic of great American corporations, the accession to president was swift and orderly. James McCrea, a tall, bearded Scotsman who had also begun at the bottom as a rodman many decades earlier and who had long run all the PRR lines west of Pittsburgh, was promoted to president. Samuel Rea, who long ago had had his first job under McCrea, became second vice president. It would now fall to Rea to guide the great New York tunnels and terminal to completion. Rea wrote a Wall Street friend about Cassatt, "He was a great man and a noble character, and aside from the great loss officially it is a severe personal loss, and the last seven years association with him was the pleasantest period of my life."

TWENTY-THREE

"NEW YORK CITY SHAKEN"

O n May 25, 1907, the usual hundreds of idlers and spectators were leaning on the rough plank fence along Seventh Avenue, enthralled by the show far below their feet in the gigantic Penn Station excavation, New York's "Culebra Cut." Ignoring the busy traffic and throngs of Saturday shoppers, the men and boys along the fence chatted among themselves, commenting on this and that as the army of dusty workmen labored away in the vast man-created canyon now thirty and forty feet deep. It was a gratifying drama of perpetual motion: roaring steam derricks jerkily scooped up dirt and blasted rock, heaving them with a resounding crash into the waiting lines of battered freight cars. Small black locomotives steamed about, whistles shrieking, trundling the laden cars toward the North River, disappearing into the tunnel under the propped-up Ninth Avenue El, where every few minutes uptown and downtown IRT trains passed high above. And then there was always the excitement of the blasting.

Across the wide avenue, jammed with horse-drawn trucks and wagons, Isaac Finesilver and Jacob Kosty were enjoying the balmy morning, conversing in front of their secondhand clothing store on the corner of West Thirty-second Street. Upstairs in the Finesilvers' second-floor apartment, their wives were just sitting down to lunch in the dining room with its panoramic (if noisy) view of the great Penn Station dig. Mrs. Finesilver was serving her four small children, while Mrs. Kosty shushed her baby. One block south on West Thirty-first Street, a Mrs. Melonius was up on the roof taking advantage of the fine weather to hang her family's laundry to dry on a clothesline. Less industrious souls in the neighborhood were passing Saturday bellied up to the bar drinking beer in Bob Nelson's corner saloon down on Seventh Avenue and Thirtieth.

Those men and boys lining the Penn Station fence noticed the work gangs across the deep canyon moving back as flagmen waved red warning flags to signal that blasting was imminent. Excavation had so advanced that it had been down to hard rock for some time now. As the PRR's publicist, Ivy Lee, was happy to point out, this was no ordinary excavation, but required "the supporting of streets, including three main north and south avenues carrying the city's heaviest traffic; the closing up of Thirty-second Street between Seventh and Tenth Avenues; the removal, care and support of miles of water, gas, and fire mains; telegraph, telephone, electric light, police and fire alarm wires." Before actual construction could proceed for the new station, twenty-eight acres had to be dug down forty-five feet, which meant removing a mind-boggling three million cubic yards of material—mainly rock—from the terminal and track yards. And so the blasting had become a thrilling commonplace. The perimeters of this four-block site were being shored up by a mile and a half of ten-foot-thick concrete retaining walls. With the workmen backed far away, the signal was given to detonate.

In the next moment, a volcanic explosion ripped through the neighborhood, hurling the lounging spectators violently, and spewing a bombardment of hundred-pound boulders, big and small rocks, and a heavy hail of pebbles high up above Seventh Avenue. A towering dust cloud swirled out of the great pit, billowing skyward, reeking of nitroglycerin, and briefly engulfing the street in its gritty pall. After a lull of shocked silence, there was pandemonium.

Police patrolmen came running in their tall helmets and blue coats, while from the brown fog came yelling, wailing, and groans. Shattered glass glistened on the sidewalks while the brick fronts along Seventh Avenue were full of bulletlike holes. Debris and thick dust settled heavily into a rocky carpet. Mr. Finesilver picked himself up to see a huge gaping hole in the front wall of his own second-floor apartment. One of the bigger boulders had "plowed through the wall into the room where the women and children were . . . through the brick masonry as if it was so much pasteboard. The [150-pound] rock knocked the chandelier down, and then ricocheting across the room, tore away about fifteen feet of plastering, after which it fell to the floor and rolled under the table. Not a person in the room was so much as scratched. The hole in the wall measured four by five feet."

High up on the roof, six stories above the street, Mrs. Melonius was not so lucky. One moment she was hanging wet clothes and adjusting the wooden clothespins, next she was face first on the tar roof, badly injured by a large rock. In Bob Nelson's saloon, three blocks away, the plate glass shattered explosively as a twenty-pound rock crashed through. There, again miraculously, no one was hurt. But the barroom was a wreck. The cause for what seemed a volcano and an earthquake combined? At the Penn Station excavation, several forgotten and unexploded sticks of dynamite in some rocky crevice (a so-called "loaded hole") had ignited unexpectedly.

As the breeze blew away the last of the dust and grit cloud, ambulance crews from three hospitals arrived to tend and remove the groaning, weeping victims. Despite the many hundreds out doing their weekend shopping, those badly hurt totaled but ten. The worst injured was a young boy of nine who had been watching the excavation and whose leg was badly crushed. The police found and arrested "John Fitzpatrick, the Superintendent in charge of the work, who was promptly bailed by his employers, John J. Murphy, a brother of Charles F. Murphy, leader of Tammany Hall, who is President of the contracting company." The Murphy firm issued a statement notable for its insouciance: "This happens occasionally in all blasting work, and is an unavoidable accident."

Unnerving accidents and fatalities had punctuated and marred the steady progress of the tunnels under the two rivers, but of late, the construction mishaps had become far more public and embarrassing. As the Pennsylvania Railroad's gargantuan civil engineering project relentlessly advanced, untoward dangers were being visited upon an unsuspecting citizenry. Two months before the manmade "volcanic" eruption at the station site, there had been a far more terrifying earth-shaking episode. Twelve minutes after midnight on Sunday March 3, the whole of Manhattan *and* the New Jersey opposite woke to a stupendous jolt. In Gotham, "firemen from all the engine houses in the city were ordered out at once to try to locate the trouble. Police Headquarters, in Mulberry Street, was shaken by the shock, and each police station was at once communicated with to learn quickly what had happened."

But the epicenter of the trouble was far across the river in Homestead, New Jersey, and the PRR's Bergen Hill tunnel. Minutes after midnight the residents of nearby Union Hill "were awakened from their sleep by a trembling of the earth, followed by a terrific crash. They groped blindly about for lights, and then stood back aghast at the destruction. Shutters, window panes, and sashes were missing, and the cold wind poured into the rooms. On the floor lay pictures, bric-a-brac, and other trinkets . . . they rushed from their homes to the street." At first, panicked families fleeing their battered houses into snowy yards wondered if an earthquake had set off some kind of brief cyclone. On both sides of the Hudson River, calls flooded into police stations, fire stations, and the newspapers, seeking the cause. In Jersey City, one man wandered the streets asking if Judgment Day had arrived. New York reporters descending upon Union Hill were astonished—hundreds of modest homes in a one-mile radius "looked as though they had been subjected to a severe bombardment . . . Many of the houses were so badly wrecked that they will have to be rebuilt or renovated." The casualties included the local silk mill, where every single window was blown out, and the home of the very unhappy mayor, who had been ejected from his warm bed onto a floor littered with broken glass.

It quickly emerged that the cause was dynamite and sheer carelessness. This time, it was not an overlooked "loaded hole" but an entire storage magazine that had exploded. "It may be that the building was overcrowded with dynamite, and some of the boxes therefore too near the stove," reported Charles Jacobs at the next meeting of the board of engineers. In fact, flaunting all the local rules, the PRR Bergen Hill contractor, William Bradley, had stockpiled far more dynamite than legally allowed. The mile-long Bergen Hill tunnels, where the electric PRR trains would begin their descent into the North River tunnels, were being advanced through extraordinarily hard rock. The contractors called one tough section "bastard granite." No official cared to admit just how much dynamite was on hand when it blew up, but there was talk of one to four tons, a truly prodigious stash, and certainly sufficient to explain why the blast left a blackened crater thirty-six feet wide and ten feet

deep and was felt for a radius of twenty miles, as far away as Connecticut. At first, the morning papers reported, "30 May Be Dead, Town
Wrecked," "Score Injured in Dynamite Explosion in Pennsylvania Tunnel at Homestead, N.J.," "New York City Shaken." Amazingly, when the
dust settled and heads were counted, only one workman was slightly
injured, and three members of one family cut and bruised by falling picture frames. Indignant local officials arrested a supervisor, who was quickly
bailed out.

And then there were the unanticipated troubles with the crosstown
tunnels in Manhattan. The original plan for the two double-track tunnels, which would connect the East River tunnels to Penn Station, was
to burrow away quietly sixty feet below all the brownstone row houses,
the Pilgrim Baptist Church, the Alpine Hotel, and various apartment
buildings lining East Thirty-second and Thirty-third streets, sparing residents living and working there any noise, chaos, or traffic snarls. The first
hint that perhaps all was not well had come in mid-January when a horse
and coal wagon were "swallowed up" in a cave-in on Thirty-third Street
just behind the Waldorf-Astoria Hotel. A fortnight later, the Pennsylvania
Railroad admitted the crosstown tunnels were "at a standstill" having encountered quicksand, but worse yet, half-dried-up underground streams.

The only safe way to proceed, they told the city's Rapid Transit Commission, was to tear up Thirty-second and Thirty-third streets between
Madison and Seventh avenues "from curb to curb, a wooden roadway being substituted for the present asphalt surface, and the buildings which
line those thoroughfares may all have to be shored up from beneath."
Each night, the wooden roadway would be lifted while tunnel crews excavated down sixty feet. They predicted a timetable of ten months. After
a brief fight, the property owners—including such powers as Alfred and
Cornelius Vanderbilt, John Jacob Astor, and William Havemeyer—
relented, and the ripping up of the streets proceeded.

The winter and early spring of 1907 served up their own tumult for
Charles McKim. Even as the workers at one section of the Penn Station
site were about to begin constructing its foundation, the ethereally lovely
Evelyn Nesbit Thaw, dressed like a schoolgirl in simple smocks with large
collars and wearing veiled hats, began testifying in the trial of her husband,

Harry, for the murder of Stanford White. The afternoon papers of February 7 fulfilled McKim's worst nightmares. With graphic candor, Evelyn told all: Her ascension into New York show business as a Floradora Girl at age sixteen, Stanford White's wooing her at small dinner parties in his Madison Square Garden hideaway, and the evening she was deflowered. As she testified, Harry Thaw filled the courtroom with racking sobs. Evelyn said, "Stanford told me to finish my champagne. I said I didn't care much for it. He insisted that I drink this glass of champagne."

Here the New York newspapers reported, "She told of awaking later, to find herself in a bed surrounded by mirrors. She screamed and Stanford White asked her to please keep quiet . . . Then she went home and sat up all night." McKim still remembered running into White that very day ushering Evelyn around their Fifth Avenue offices. "This little girl's mother has gone to Pittsburgh and left her in my care," he said. McKim had eyed her and said, "My God!" As sensation, the trial did not disappoint: Harry Thaw was a cocaine addict, he may or may not have tied Evelyn down and beaten her, Stanford White paid Evelyn's fancy boarding school fees, showered her one Christmas with white-fox furs and diamonds, loved to push her naked on a red velvet swing.

Through it all, Charles McKim soldiered on. His usual bouts of depression and weariness were now joined by what he termed "ear trouble." McKim, not yet sixty, was losing the hearing in his left ear. He could still, despite all these travails, write wryly to his daughter about this new affliction. "I am afraid *deaf* is the word!" When beset by his own infirmities and the murder trial, Charles McKim could console himself that professionally he was at the pinnacle of a distinguished career.

The previous fall, he had completed an Italian Renaissance library for financier J. Pierpont Morgan's collection of rare manuscripts on East Thirty-sixth Street and Madison Avenue (conveniently just a block north of his own apartment). Morgan tended toward the cantankerous, so McKim stole in and out of the construction site, avoiding the imperious financier he had dubbed Lorenzo the Magnificent. When the library, with its wondrous jewellike interiors, was finished in November 1906, McKim exulted, "The sky is blue and there is no cause for worry," for the difficult Mr. Morgan "expressed great pride and satisfaction in the building."

Moreover, McKim could rejoice to know his long-cherished dream of an American Academy in Rome was a solid reality, with a powerful board (including Morgan), a rich endowment, and a villa for its students. In Washington, D.C., he and Daniel Hudson Burnham had successfully revived L'Enfant's original vision of the Mall. They had persuaded the federal government that the nation's capitol should feature imposing classical buildings worthy of ancient Rome. Moreover, McKim's design for a Lincoln Memorial was gaining favor.

And then, of course, there was New York's Pennsylvania Station. In early 1907, New Yorkers saw a gigantic and rocky canyon rimmed by run-down brownstones and filled with armies of excavators. But McKim knew that very shortly the Fuller Construction Company would be erecting a steel frame that would begin to convey the magnificent dimensions of his railroad temple. While Stanford White, the private man, was being daily scourged in the press, McKim encouraged young Larry White's interest in his father's profession. In mid-February, McKim sent Larry photographs of the "Pennsylvania Terminal record, including those of stone quarried, cut, and awaiting transportation, as well as models, etc. There are fields of this cut stone lying ready for shipment near South Framingham, and some day, when the weather is fair, it would be a good object lesson for us both to go out . . . The quarry itself is well worth the short journey of an hour from Boston. The drawings show the work in its various stages of progress. I send them to you for this reason."

When McKim was feeling well, he helped William Mead organize auctions of Stanford White's thousands of objects of desire and exotica. He also oversaw White's grave site out at the St. James cemetery, "transplanting a large white pine tree, much box wood . . . [and erecting] a Greek stele, nine feet high." Then, on April 12, as thousands of New Yorkers mobbed the courthouse to hear Thaw's murder trial verdict, the judge declared a mistrial. A second murder trial would reprise the whole sordid tale. For McKim, it was too much to bear.

It was now the spring of 1907 and Samuel Rea *still* did not know why the now-completed North River tunnels continued to move about in the silt forty feet below the riverbed. They could proceed no further with finishing these tunnels until they understood what the problem was. The previous September, not long after his triumphant public walks through the tunnels, Charles Jacobs had finally responded in writing to Rea's repeated and increasingly exasperated demands for his professional opinion. It did not help Rea's mood when Jacobs had conceded, "Since we commenced to construct these tunnels we know very little more about the nature of the mud—its specific gravity may have been determined more closely . . . but we have no knowledge of its future action during the permanent use of these tunnels in railroad service." Rea found this completely unacceptable. He was equally angry to read Jacobs's assertion that, "We are faced at the present with the certainty that these tunnels go down and not up. We do not know why they go down."

"The Behavior of the Subaqueous Tunnels," as the issue was now blandly referred to in meeting after meeting, was causing a bitter split between Brigadier General Raymond and, it appeared, the rest of the board of engineers, led by Jacobs. General Raymond's cataract had been operated on, but with little success. Now, when he descended under the North River for his investigations, "he had to be personally led to and through the tunnels, and could examine drawings only with the aid of a strong glass, magnifying one spot at a time."

Understandably, Raymond had taken deep professional umbrage at Jacobs's lackadaisical and skeptical attitude on the tunnel issue, wondering caustically, "Does Mr. Jacobs believe that a tunnel can be built scientifically if it cannot be scientifically designed, and does he propose to build the tunnels at hap-hazard and design them scientifically after their completion? . . . He has driven four tunnels completely across the river and has removed or displaced several hundred cubic yards of the material concerning the nature of which he is still ignorant . . . The plain truth is that Mr. Jacobs has made no serious effort to investigate this important question. Even the specific gravity determinations, which he reluctantly admits may have been made, were not obtained by him. A lack of information on this subject may involve the company in the useless expenditure of hundreds of thousands of dollars and in the construction of tunnels not well adapted to the surrounding conditions."

In the wake of this acrimonious exchange, Rea and his board of engineers managed to agree on one matter: Perhaps the tunnels were moving about because they were not yet watertight. Back on November 8, 1906, Jacobs had ordered caulking commenced on the North Tunnel in the middle section from Ring 735 to Ring 1,135. The first phase had been finished the day Alexander Cassatt died, December 28. But there was still considerable leaking. During the ensuing months, Jacobs built a dam at each end of a thousand feet of tunnel to wall off the water from the uncaulked portions of the tunnel, and then "re-tightened and red-leaded [those thousand feet] . . . in addition to [more] caulking and grummeting [of] the tunnel lining [and] the joints between the bore-plugs and bore-segments. [All] were made tight with wooden wedges driven as tightly as it was possible to drive them." But despite Jacobs's efforts, it was now spring of 1907, the tunnels were still not watertight, and Rea still had no answer.

Moreover, even as they were bewildered by the mysterious oscillations of the tunnels, Rea and the board of engineers still had to decide whether they should proceed with anchoring the tunnel to the riverbed in some fashion. And if so, how? They were actively studying different systems of screw piles to provide supports. On June 5, 1907, Rea weighed in. He believed that if the North River tunnels were anchored by screw piles of any kind to bedrock, "any appreciable movement would tend to rupture the shell." If they attached screw piles that allowed for motion of the tunnels, the very nature of those attachments would cause "more or less leakage into an otherwise dry tunnel." He proposed they consider reserving the ability to install screw piles if needed, but to strengthen the tunnel instead by "the insertion of steel rods in the concrete lining."

Only days later, on June 8, 1907, Rea opened his *Scientific American* to find an editorial titled "Tunnel Tubes in Soft Material." It began as a discussion of the East River Rapid Transit tubes. But it also dealt with their own work, and the further he read the more his heart sank: "The success of the work under the Hudson and East rivers proves that it is entirely possible to build as many tunnel tubes as may be desired. But the question which has yet to be proved . . . is how far will the vibration set up in the metal tubes by the passage of the trains tend to agitate the surrounding material . . . [If] bending stresses developed . . . far in excess of the resisting power of the tubes . . . fracture must ensue. But whatever theory may indicate, time alone can tell." And so, for safety sake, the editors of *Scientific American* strongly endorsed exactly what Rea now opposed: piles "sunk through the bottom of the tubes until they reach rock or some other sufficiently firm bearing."

Rea did not need any lectures or advice. This matter, "The Behavior of the Subaqueous Tunnels," along with the related issues of attaching piles, had become his constant preoccupation and worry. At such moments, he sorely missed Cassatt. James McCrea was a fine president, but McCrea's whole career had been in the Lines West of Pittsburgh, his duties far removed from the entanglements of Gotham. With Cassatt dead, Rea had to carry the full burden of the New York Extension. And the problem of whether or not to install screw piles was sowing discord among his board of engineers just as he most needed their counsel and advice.

As if that were not sufficiently galling, on Saturday June 29 Rea was perusing the *Philadelphia Inquirer* when he saw an editorial headline titled, "The Philadelphia Tunnels Condemned." To his horror, the newspaper editors had read the *Scientific American* article and were parroting its assertion that without piles anchoring the PRR's two North River tunnels, "the strain from pressure and vibration will be so great as to make the tubes break." Inveighed the Philadelphia editors: "Here is a question in which the public is vitally interested, not only through its ownership of the securities which built the tubes, but because it is to become a vast artery of travel. The thought of a breaking down of the tunnel is too horrible for contemplation." Was this not precisely the possible calamity that had haunted Rea for more than a year?

"My first impulse on Saturday morning when I saw this editorial," Rea confided to McCrea later when he had calmed down, "was to write the Editor of the paper at once denying the truth of it . . . But after conferring with our Board of Engineers, I feel inclined to drop the matter. To get into a discussion with a daily newspaper on a technical question is fruitless, but at the same time I realize that such articles as these lead to other comments . . . I would prefer not to do [anything] pending our experimental tests which I am watching continuously."

All that spring and summer of 1907, Charles Jacobs worked on those experimental tests, trying to make a thousand feet in both North River tunnels truly dry. By September, when both were deemed watertight, Jacobs installed an Edson Recording Gauge in each to monitor "any movement of the tunnel." A week later, he noted that these gauges had revealed "the interesting fact that the tunnel bodily rises at low tide and subsides again at high tide." Despite Rea's inclinations not to have screw piles, he and the board had decided to proceed with the installation of various test screw piles to see how they worked. When the board met again on October 3, 1907, Jacobs reported that using the Edson Gauges, "The actual time and elevation of high and low tide in the river at this point are observed daily, and the time of high tide is found to agree identically with that at which the tunnel reaches its lowest position."

A month later, at the November 7, 1907, meeting of the board of engineers, Jacobs further reported, "That the tunnels (and piles also) move down at high tide and up at low tide is now a certain fact. This is shown clearly not only by the Edson Recording Gauges . . . but also by the pile test observations." And so it was that Samuel Rea finally learned in part why the PRR's North River tunnels were moving about in the silt: they were responding to the changing pressures of the incoming and outgoing tides. Once known, it seemed so simple and so obvious. They now had a full scientific explanation for the *upward* movement of the tunnels. They all knew the North River was a tidal body, but never dreamed these tides were powerful enough to affect their deeply buried tunnels. Rea also now knew that making tunnels watertight had slowed their gradual downward settling. So they could say that the *downward* drift of the tunnels was partly a function of leaking. But there still remained a terrifying unknown: Situated in this soft North River silt, would the tunnels continue to subside downward year after year? And if so, would they finally sink so far in the fluid silt that they would rupture?

Rea had already expressed the opinion that screw piles seemed more of a danger to the tunnels than a solution. By November, General Raymond had come round to that same stance. Unhappily, Alfred Noble, Charles Jacobs, and George Gibbs, three engineers with decades of hands-on experience, remained completely unpersuaded. "In recent discussions," wrote Noble, "the question has been asked frequently of those of us who favor the use of supports what we propose to do if the subsidence of the tunnels proves to be rapid. It is equally pertinent for us to ask those who propose to omit supports what they would do if the tunnels, unrestrained by supports, should wallow in the mud . . . [If] a large and continued downward movement should occur, the condition of the tunnel project would be very serious and supports on a more comprehensive scale than has yet been contemplated might be the only alternative to the abandonment of the project." There in a nutshell was the fearsome truth. Might they have to abandon the two finished North River tunnels as unsafe?

The backdrop to this engineering debate was an escalating mood of financial jitters infecting the New York Stock Exchange. All that summer, stocks had been in a nervous swoon. Pennsylvania stock was sinking back to previous lows, reaching $117 by August. Wall Street financiers blamed Roosevelt's high-decibel crusade against entrenched corporate malefactors and their "successful dishonesty." Cascading bankruptcies culminated in crowds of desperate depositors besieging the Knickerbocker Trust, a revered marble temple to mammon on Fifth Avenue. At this moment, J. P. Morgan rushed back from an Episcopal conference in Richmond to rescue the nation. Now seventy, Morgan had become a caricature of a plutocrat, with his gigantic belly, ferocious, arrogant eyes, and monstrous nose, red and deformed from acne rosacea. Ensconced now in the inner sanctum of his sumptuous new Madison Avenue library, the great financier smoked his Cuban cigars and huddled with the rich and powerful, consulting the U.S. secretary of the treasury, conferring life or death to banks, trusts, and firms teetering on the brink.

The day the Knickerbocker collapsed, President Roosevelt emerged from a fifteen-day hunting trip deep in the Louisiana bayous. Energized and exuberant, he regaled reporters with tales of shooting bear, turkey, opossum, squirrel, and wildcat. "We ate them all," he enthused, "except the wildcat." As for the Panic of 1907, the president accepted no blame, wondering privately in a letter whether certain titans had not provoked the financial crash "so that they may enjoy unmolested the fruits of their own evil-doing." The panic merely added another layer of difficulty to the PRR's troubles, forcing layoffs and slowdowns. President McCrea blandly announced they would not push the work in New York "as vigorously as had been done in the past."

TWENTY-FOUR

"THE WAY IS STONY AND WET"

That same fall of 1907, Charles McKim returned from his annual outing to the Scottish moors, where he had hunted grouse and ignored his birthday. "When we turn our 60th corner and face 70, the less said the better," he wrote his daughter, while sailing toward New York on the leviathan ocean liner, the S.S. *Celtic*. "So I kept it wisely to myself. . . . I am coming home—if not yet quite well and strong—better in every way than when I went away. I am advised to start in gradually to work . . . [I] propose, if possible, to get well enough, deaf or dumb, to get back to my work, and to take care of you for a while longer!" McKim lingered only briefly in Gotham before retreating to St. James out on Long Island and the simple beauties of its sea air, thatch meadows, orchards, and clam flats.

By early 1908 McKim was back in Manhattan and settled into a new apartment, still on East Thirty-fifth Street but a few doors closer to Fifth Avenue. His daughter, Margaret, moved in to keep house for him. The two could stroll downtown just two blocks, head west, and join the perennial gawkers watching the wonder of the Pennsylvania Station construction site. The blasting still went on day in and day out over toward Ninth Avenue, but on Seventh Avenue, the station's foundation was in place and the steel frame was readily visible. "The new Pennsylvania Railroad Station in New York," reported *Harper's Weekly*, ". . . is slowly rising out of the gaping depths . . . The vast extent of the excavation, in which gangs have been delving and building night and day during the last three years, gave the spectator a sense of wonder at the gigantic task that was being undertaken. It seemed almost beyond physical powers to complete it. But it is being accomplished. The foundations are laid, and little by little the steel framework of the central building rises above the surrounding houses." In January, Samuel Rea, an avid reader of thick tomes of history, had a copper box with the project's history and plans placed in the cornerstone at Seventh Avenue and Thirty-third Street.

On January 6, Harry Thaw's second murder trial had begun, the whole rancid circus once again undermining McKim's faltering health. It was not possible to venture forth on the streets of Manhattan without encountering some scruffy herd of newsboys bleating about Evelyn and Harry and Stanford. This time, mercifully, the trial had moved swiftly, with Thaw's lawyers arguing that their client was crazy and should thus be acquitted. On February 2, the jurors had agreed, finding "Mad Harry" not guilty of murder by reason of insanity. But that had not put an end to the whole sordid saga. Harry Thaw lost little time seeking to be declared sane, while his family worked on annulling his marriage to Evelyn. In mid-February, William Mead had written to Daniel Burnham, "Poor McKim has had another knock out, and quite severe this time. He is getting on all right and out in the country, where he is receiving good care. I am afraid, however, it will be some months before he shows up here." One consolation was that Larry White had finished Harvard, and he and Bessie were far away in Paris, where he was studying architecture.

As for the rest of Gotham, they were soon distracted. On February 12, 150,000 strong, they squeezed into Times Square to watch the thrilling start of the New York to Paris Automobile Race sponsored by the *New York Times* and *Le Matin*. The Hotel Astor was festooned with flags and bunting, while mounted police kept the street clear. Westward the six autos roared (stopping soon enough, of course, to cross on the ferries), and a nation increasingly mad for motorcars cheered the American team as it raced toward Alaska, and ultimately, on to Siberia, Russia, Europe, and the finish line in Paris.

———

Even as Samuel Rea and his board of engineers wrangled over how best to protect the North River tunnels, the seemingly accursed quartet of East River tunnels were at long last nearing completion. In the wake of all the spectacular blowouts, fires, cave-ins, floodings, explosions, injuries, deaths, and various strikes, Ernest W. Moir, Scotsman by birth, veteran tunnel builder, and vice president of S. Pearson & Son, had taken decisive charge, rallying the men onward. A constant presence in the tunnels for the past eighteen months, Moir maintained a penthouse in the skyscraping Belmont Hotel with a view of the East River. "When he goes to bed, which is seldom according to the sand-hogs, Mr. Moir has a telescope glued to his never-closed eye. Certain it is from his aerie den you can see the air bubbles in the river . . . he has always turned up on the job before the telephonic message of a 'blow-out' or some other of the hundred and one obstacles which have beset the undertaking."

In the realm of subaqueous work, it was widely acknowledged that the East River tunnels had posed nearly insuperable conditions, especially in the central sections where the top of the tunnel passed through sand and the bottom hit up against rock. Many had been quick to call it impossible and the designs fatally flawed. Dozens of sandhogs and other laborers had been carried out of the tunnels, suffering ghastly deaths during the always-behind-schedule job. In early February 1908, the two sections of Tunnel D neared one another after four grueling years. The alignment engineers cautiously thrust an eight-inch-wide steel pipe forward fifty feet from one shield face to the other. Rapturous cheers greeted the pipe's final successful push into the other shield. The two sides were about to meet!

When the elated sandhogs in one half of Tunnel D felt the strong air current flowing through the connecting pipe, they rushed out and "procured a toy train [a replica of the *Congressional Limited*] . . . Placing it in the pipe, it was forced through at a high rate of speed. This was the first train to actually pass through the tunnels." On February 20, 1908, the two halves of D became the first of the PRR's benighted East River tunnels to meet up. Anticipating no further major obstacles, a jubilant Ernest Moir swiftly dispatched engraved invitations to celebrate the long-anticipated "Junctioning of the Four East River Tunnels." The formal dinner was set for Thursday evening April 2 at Gotham's most fashionable restaurant, the opulent Sherry's. Rea, happily responding to Moir's invitation, lamented only that Cassatt, "who devoted so much personal time and attention [to the project] . . . was not spared to join with us."

Rea had already taken concrete action to ensure posterity would never forget Alexander Cassatt's visionary leadership. At his suggestion the PRR board of directors voted to honor Cassatt with a larger-than-life bronze statue. Fittingly, this memorial of their company's seventh president would be enshrined in the monumental Manhattan terminal. Rea had assumed charge, going in person to 160 Fifth Avenue to consult with Charles McKim, who had returned from his rest in the country at a sanitarium.

McKim, in his usual fastidious way, considered all the ins and outs of his station design and then advised: "There is one space which particularly suggests itself . . . the head of the flight of steps leading from the Arcade into the General Waiting Room." McKim proposed "a niche out of reach and considerably above the line of the eye, designed to contain an heroic figure which would be seen by all entering the Station on its main axis, as well as from the Waiting Room . . . its elevated and retired position, while being seen by all, would escape the charge of conspicuousness, which above all things would be distasteful to Mr. Cassatt." To Rea, it seemed most apropos that Alexander Cassatt could keep a benevolent eye on the millions of railroad passengers arriving and departing from the station he did not live to see.

With McKim's health still wobbly, William Mead shepherded through the commission for the Cassatt statue. He engaged, for a twelve-thousand-dollar fee, Adolph A. Weinman, the New York artist already sculpting the station's gigantic stone statues of robed women, allegories of Day and Night, and stern eagles that would flank each of the giant seven-foot clocks decorating the four main entrances. In March, Mead asked the PRR if Weinman could have "both a heavy and a light overcoat of Mr. Cassatt's, a cutaway coat, vest, pair of trousers, as well as a pair of shoes. If he could also have a collar it would be useful. I think Mr. Rea had a certain type of coat in mind which Mr. Cassatt usually wore." Mead suggested he and Weinman meet with Lois Cassatt "for any suggestions she may desire to make."

Meanwhile, the board of engineers *still* could not agree about the necessity of screw piles, nor was there consensus about whether the tunnels would keep settling until they cracked. But even as the board clashed over these dilemmas, the other phases of the gigantic enterprise were falling gratifyingly into place after six hard years. By mid-March, after so many travails, the mood was ebullient when the remaining three East River tunnels connected well before Moir's formal affair at Sherry's. The workmen in Tunnel B, "not to be outdone by those in 'D,' procured a rag doll representing a lady and sent it through the [aligning] pipe . . . heralding it as the first lady to make the trip. This doll was preserved, framed and presented by the contractors as a souvenir to the engineers in charge of this tunnel."

For the hundreds of engineers and sandhogs who had struggled through so much disaster and uncertainty, these triumphant early months of 1908 were a fitting time for sentiment, pride, and souvenirs. The East River sandhogs bestowed a munificent gift upon their boss, Ernest Moir, veteran of the original ill-starred Hudson River tunnel, who had reappeared at the East River tunnels' darkest hour to lead his sandhog troops to glory. The gift was an impressive model air lock measuring "two feet six inches long and . . . nine inches in diameter. The interior is lit by electric lights, and compressed air is supplied by pumps. There is a miniature hospital bed . . . There is also a chronometer inside the little room; also pressure gauges."

Much to Ivy Lee's delight, he was allowed to organize a press tour for journalists ("should be men who can stand an air pressure of 34 pounds") to witness the actual breakthrough for the northernmost and final East River tunnel, Tunnel A. "In the mud and the mist and the drenching fog ahead," wrote one Philadelphia reporter, thrilled to be walking under the river from Manhattan in one of the infamous, off-limits tunnels, "we could see the glint of the shield that had traveled from Long Island City, and we could see that the two powerful engines were only 18 inches apart. The jacks were started, the shields quivered and shook, they moved forward like caterpillars, resting on their tails, and soon they touched all round the circumference, but for an impertinent rock lodged in one corner.

"Jimmy Sullivan was for blowing the thing to smithereens, but Moir said, 'No bulldozing, boys, now, least of all when we have got the East River, backed by the Atlantic Ocean, just where we want 'em.' Quietly he plotted the destruction of the rock, and together we climbed into the Long Island shield while both gangs cheered the completion of the work." It was a deliriously thrilling and historic moment. As thanks, the workers were given two days paid vacation.

However, bemoaned the reporter for the *New York World*, relishing all the drama of the drippy, shadowy iron tubes where men had struggled and died to penetrate these antediluvian depths, "The millions of people who will use these tunnels in getting to and from their business will see nothing of them but a blur at the car window, and will scarcely realize that they are passing through tubes which have proved to be the most difficult of any driven, nor will they comprehend the stupendous nature of the labor that has been expended in their construction." All those future Long Island Rail Road commuters whooshing through these hard-won tunnels would know only that swift trains made possible their family's move from a crowded, expensive apartment building to a home of their own, with trees and a garden for the children.

On the morning of April 1, as a steady rain began, Ernest Moir left a telephone message for one of the PRR officers about his elaborate dinner, detailing its many courses, planned toasts, talks, and vaudeville entertainment. Consequently, Moir was disappointed to learn later that afternoon that Rea had been summoned to Pittsburgh to the bedside of his dying mother. Before leaving, however, he had dictated a message of congratulation for the party. Such was the occasion that PRR president James McCrea and vice president Green would both journey up from Philadelphia to attend.

Moir's dinner, however convivial, was almost certain be a far more sedate affair than the gigantic bash Charles Jacobs had thrown at Sherry's in March 1907 for the four hundred men involved in finishing the long-aborning McAdoo tunnels. That evening, following the usual flowery speeches and cigars for all, a Sand Hog Band decked out in yellow oilskins had mounted the stage under the crystal chandeliers to torture the banqueters by caterwauling on tin instruments, imitating the sounds of air blows, foghorns, and tunnel explosions. The jeering, boisterous audience expressed its appreciation first by tossing "rolls, then pickles, and within a few minutes the place was in an uproar with 400 tunnelers pelting the Sand Hog Band with loaves of bread, chunks of beef and other things handy on the tables. The army of waiters became frightened and ran pell mell from the great dining hall, but Chief Engineer Jacobs restored order."

Samuel Rea departed his Bryn Mawr home in a rush, anxious to reach Pittsburgh and his mother, Ruth Moore Rea. As his wood-paneled PRR parlor car rumbled through the Alleghenies, the engineer in Rea appreciated the notable reductions in his road's grades and curves. He also worried, for his was a coal-carrying road and once again labor unrest and wildcat strikes were roiling the Pennsylvania coal mines. The morning's papers wrote of twenty-five thousand men out. As for Rea's ailing mother, he was quite resigned to her death—"it is be expected"—for she was eighty-eight years old.

In truth, Rea was more concerned about his grown son, George, twenty-eight, a civil engineer, married and a new father. For almost a week, George had been down with the grippe, a malady his mother, Mary, feared he had contracted working in his father's New York tunnels. After graduating from Princeton in 1904, George Black Rea had joined the large army of junior engineers toiling away in the PRR's New York Extension. Because their only son had suffered rheumatic fever when young, the Reas still worried about his health.

In Pittsburgh, Rea debarked his train to find winter, for snow, accompanying a cold wave, had howled in, briefly making the Smoky City white. Over at Duquesne Gardens, crowds filled the second annual Automobile Show, covetously eying new models of Franklins, Packards, Raniers, and Maxwells. The Ford Motor Company ("More Than 20,000 Fords Have Been Sold") boasted that its utilitarian six-hundred-dollar black roadsters were "equal in value to any car at double the price."

Rea drove through the elegant precincts of Shadyside to the Kenmawr Hotel, hoping as he neared Mrs. Rea's suite in the Italianate villa residence on its terraced grounds that he was not too late. Rea found his mother failing but alive and spent the next several days by her side. Then, on Monday April 6 at four in the afternoon, Ruth Moore Rea died of a cerebral hemorrhage.

Two days later, soon after he had bid his mother farewell, a telegram arrived from home in Bryn Mawr. Rea opened it, glanced at the message, and felt a wave of misery. Many men had lost their lives working on the PRR's tunnels and terminal, and now, in an unspeakable sacrifice, George, his son, had joined their ranks. Alfred Noble had noted to Rea just the previous year, "Long continued work in compressed air is very serious in its effects, the men all show them." If any one knew the exact number dead from working on the PRR's New York Extension, they did not speak it out loud. Now, his own son had joined those largely anonymous fatalities. Worse yet, from an illness contracted in the poor, always damp air of the PRR tunnels. It was as cruel a blow as could befall any loving father. For five years, men working for the PRR's contractors had died from the bends, from floods, blowouts, collapsing headings, and in careless dynamite explosions and fires. Not quite two months earlier, three more men had died in the North River tunnels from yet another mishap with dynamite. All those men had families—mothers, fathers. Some had wives and children. And all had been mourned. Now he and his wife and daughter-in-law would join the bereaved. He thought of William Baldwin, the LIRR's president, dead too young of cancer. And his own dear chief, Cassatt, whose big and courageous heart had simply stopped beating. But most wrenching for him, his own son.

Life pressed relentlessly on and Samuel Rea with it. Three days after George's death, the first of the Bergen Hill tunnels that would carry the PRR tracks from the Meadowlands down to the North River tunnels was to be blasted fully open. Ivy Lee was allowed to invite all the New York and Philadelphia reporters who had been clamoring (usually to no avail) to see the PRR's manmade netherworld. By seven o'clock on April 11, a mild Saturday morning, a gaggle of journalists, engineers, and tunnelers had gathered in the shadowy rocky bore deep inside Bergen Hill, a musty, dank place. "At 7:05 o'clock the blast was set off, and as the smoke cleared there came a glimmer of light through the cracks in the dividing wall," wrote the *Times* man. "This traprock, right where the tubes were scheduled to join had been found among the worst met by tunnel workers at any point of their labors, and has taken an average of three pounds of dynamite for every cubic yard of rock removed. So another blast was set and this time when the smoke cleared there was an opening large enough for the engineers to make their way through without much difficulty."

With a shout, the engineers and tunnelers inside Bergen Hill, ignoring all the smoke, dust, and grime, clambered through the jagged hole, followed close behind by the crowd of journalists. After three years of around-the-clock work, the men were over the moon at being the first through. At that dusty moment, Cassatt's dream had been fully realized. You could now enter a tunnel at Bergen Hill and, following it down under the North River, as the *New York Times* reported, "Walk from Hackensack Meadows to Long Island, but the Way is Stony and Wet." More than five miles of PRR railroad tunnels, starting in New Jersey and ending in Long Island were now bored completely through. This moment of corporate and engineering triumph was nonetheless somewhat muted, for all knew of the tragedy that had befallen poor Samuel Rea, his wife, and young widowed daughter-in-law. The untimely death of George Rea was alleviated only by the fetching two-month-old granddaughter who understood nothing yet of her own loss. Samuel Rea and his wife, Mary, who from that day on wore black mourning, had buried their son in Church of the Redeemer, the same shady Bryn Mawr church cemetery where Alexander Cassatt lay.

Bergen Hill contractor William Bradley organized *his* celebratory dinner at Sherry's for Thursday May 7 to honor Chief Engineer Charles Jacobs and his staff. On May 2, one of Rea's assistants wrote Bradley saying his chief had received the "polite invitation," but declined, "owing to the recent bereavement which has come to him." On the very day of the dinner, Charles Jacobs had detonated the final blast opening the second Bergen Hill tunnel, signaling the completion of all the PRR tunnels. All told, almost four hundred tons of dynamite had been exploded to blast away—inch by inch and foot by foot—the Bergen Hill's tough rock interior. As Rea wrote in a congratulatory note, "The Pennsylvania Railroad is now into New York City."

The May 7, 1908, dinner at Sherry's was exceedingly jovial. Jacobs, in formal dinner suit, waxed nostalgic, recalling, "On June 24, 1903, I had the honor of starting the first drill on the first piece of the work of this huge undertaking, viz.: the shaft at 33rd Street and 11th Avenue . . . Today I have had the extreme pleasure of firing the final blast that brought down the last heading of the North tunnel under the Bergen Hill, which will now enable an inhabitant of the United States to pass under Bergen Hill, the North River, New York City, and the East River and on to Long

Island." After a few more remarks Jacobs sat down to another wild burst of applause.

The evening rollicked on, with sentimental toasts, Sherry's excellent dishes and wines, raucous renderings of popular songs, silly skits, and jokes about the Tunnel Bowling League (pitting the Bergen Hill engineers against those of the East and North River tunnels), doggerel verse extolling their tremendous triumph, all culminating in a specially written song, "The Pennsy Tunnels," sung to the well-known political song, "Tammany."

All through that spring, the board of engineers continued to meet and dispute bitterly over the North River tunnels. On May 6, 1908, the board had convened for its 204th meeting. Not quite six years before, Alexander Cassatt had instructed these men to proceed always with "absolute knowledge of the conditions." But now, despite their best efforts, General Raymond, Charles Jacobs, Alfred Noble, and George Gibbs all had to concede "it had not been possible to do so in every instance." Two years had passed since General Raymond had journeyed to Bryn Mawr to alert Samuel Rea to the disturbing movements in the unfinished North River tunnels. Now, as they sat around the meeting table, they lacked the "absolute knowledge" that would allow a definitive decision. On the matter of how best to secure and protect the North River tunnels, these engineers could only offer their best professional opinion.

"In my opinion," General Raymond had written months earlier in arguing against screw piles, "such supports will endanger the safety of the tunnel instead of insuring it . . . Construction of a satisfactory sliding joint [to attach the screw piles] will sooner or later bind or leak, or do both, introducing conditions that will be troublesome and dangerous." But Noble, Jacobs, and Gibbs were still in favor of screw piles. The board remained split.

At the 204th meeting, a letter from Samuel Rea was read laying out all the reasons that "I have, after most careful consideration, reached the conclusion that piles, not being a necessity or advisable, we should not install them." He then instructed "that the North River Tunnels be at once made absolutely watertight, or as nearly so as may be possible; and that they shall be lined with concrete, reinforced with steel to such extent as may be considered desirable by the Board, in such manner as to admit of the installation of piles thereafter if deemed advisable." Soon, gangs of workmen down inside the PRR's sixteen miles of completed tunnels would be busily coating the iron tubes with two-foot-thick inner walls of reinforced concrete mixed and minutely monitored by PRR engineers to ensure its absolute integrity.

Samuel Rea could only hope now that he and General Raymond were right in their professional opinions and that the calamity they all feared would not come to pass. They had exercised their best judgment in pursuit of making the North River tunnels safe. But the truth was that they

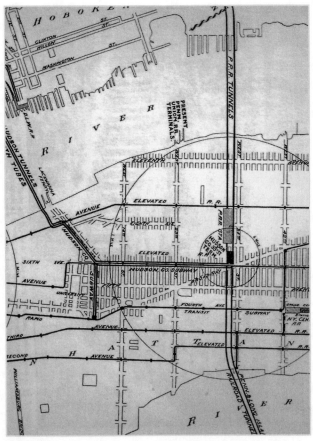

The PRR tunnel route from New Jersey to Long Island.

would not know definitively if they were right until years in the future after the tunnels had endured the continual pounding of hundreds of trains day after day, week after week and year after year.

By the fall of 1908, New Yorkers were amazed at the grandeur arising on Seventh Avenue. For months, the gawkers and passersby had watched as a veritable army of men assembled the colossal steel shell, a resplendent silhouette that bespoke the latest construction techniques. From the track bed, 650 steel columns rose up to support the massive structure that McKim had designed. But it was only when the men began to install the Milford pink granite facade that the station's somber beauty and power appeared. As one majestic Doric column after another rose thirty-five feet into the air, they began to form a monumental Roman colonnade—fronting, of all plebeian places, Seventh Avenue. On a blue September day, one could now stand at West Thirty-third Street staring dreamily at the busy construction site and imagine onself transported to ancient imperial Rome. It was an odd but inspiring sight, to see such rosy classical splendor materializing in the middle of Manhattan's Tenderloin.

The construction of Penn Station in October 1908.

On February 21, 1909, the final piece of the stonework was completed on Penn Station's Seventh Avenue facade. Now one could stand at the junction of Broadway and look west down Thirty-second Street to behold the unlikely classical vision of the station's main entrance, a "great central pavilion" set off from the long front of Doric columns by its greater height and double row of ten columns. "Above the columns," reported the *New York Times*, "is an entablature surmounted by a stepped parapet and sculptured group [*Night* and *Day*] supporting a clock with a dial 7 feet in diameter." When the Brooklyn Bridge had been built decades earlier, the whole of Gotham could easily observe the steady advance of that beautiful behemoth. But most of the PRR's New York Extension—the tunnels—remained out of sight. Only as the terminal began to rise in all its Doric glory did New Yorkers begin to realize that an immense change was upon them.

As the station took magisterial shape, Chief Engineer Gibbs grappled with two critical decisions about motive power. First, what kind of electricity—alternating current or direct current—should power the New York Extension's 110 miles of rails, starting in Harrison, New Jersey, and continuing into Penn Station and then on to Long Island? "The Manhattan terminal . . . [of] the Pennsylvania involved electrical systems of such magnitude," writes historian Carl W. Condit, "embodied so many novelties, and grew from such an intricate complex of urban factors, [it] . . . may be described [along with Grand Central Station] as the greatest unified engineering and architectural work ever undertaken in the United States."

As the end of 1908 neared, Gibbs had fully considered all aspects of the situation. While alternating current systems offered greater flexibility, they were also newer and less tested. For several years, LIRR trains running on the Atlantic Avenue line through Brooklyn had been powered by direct current electricity via a third rail. And it was that road's intention to simply extend its D.C. third rail all the way to Penn Station. This alone "argued more strongly for the Pennsylvania's own use of direct current than any other factor." Moreover, D.C. traction technology had been around longer, and thus was more familiar and reliable. Add to the equation the many travails the New Haven Railroad had suffered on its newly electrified A.C. lines out of Gotham and it was easy to understand Gibbs's inclination to err on the side of certainty. "Any serious operating failures," he later said, "would have jeopardized the whole investment and put electrification back years." One had also to consider the flexibility of interchanging cars with other local transit systems using the same D.C. system. And so, in early December 1908, Gibbs endorsed D.C. to the board of engineers, who agreed they should opt for the tried and true—direct current electricity.

The second major question then was what kind of electric locomotive would best serve the PRR's brand-new all-steel fleet of passenger and Pullman cars that Cassatt had insisted on to prevent train fires in his New York tunnels. Gibbs had been helping with experimental designs for new kinds of electric locomotives, collaborating with the Westinghouse Company and Baldwin Locomotive Works. They had been methodically testing locomotives over the past several years. "It was decided to make quite a radical departure from general practice," said Gibbs, "in the final design of high-speed locomotives for the terminal equipment." By the time Gibbs was done, he had indeed come up with something unprecedented. His engine looked nothing like the hulking, ripsnorting steam locomotives Americans had long admired as they roared along the rails. Instead, the DD1, as it was dubbed, appeared to be just two joined passenger cars, and it could operate in either direction, a great plus. With its two front oval windows looking like sad drooping eyes, the DD1 looked disconcertingly like a big mechanical basset hound rather than a powerful locomotive.

Yet the DD1 immediately became the most powerful locomotive—steam or electric—of its day. The DD1s "showed not the slightest strain," says railroad historian Michael Bezilla, "when called upon to start 850-ton trains on the steep 1.93% grade westbound in the Hudson tunnels—a task which would have set the drivers of a steam locomotive spinning helplessly." They rocketed along reliably at eighty miles an hour. In the coming years, the DD1s would operate for an average of 11,458 miles for every *minute* they were down from engine failures. They would cut the trip between Harrison (its station, soon to be renamed the far more resonant and romantic Manhattan Transfer) and Penn Station down to thirteen minutes. Under the best of circumstances, the ferry crossing had taken fifteen minutes, and one still landed in the dreary wilds of West Street. When railroad men and the public first saw the DD1 in action, they were struck not only by its meek and homely appearance, such a contrast to its power, but also by its quiet. Americans were not used to locomotives that did not belch and steam and shriek. When the mighty but modest DD1 entered a station, it glided in almost silently.

Through Charles McKim's Roman temple to transportation, the citizens of Gotham were slowly coming to comprehend the magnitude of Alexander Cassatt's vision and how this vast enterprise would reconfigure their world by opening up New York City to the shores beyond its rivers. In late April 1909, an infirm McKim had returned to Manhattan from a sojourn in Washington, D.C., for work on the design of the central Mall. Acknowledging his declining health, McKim had first signed over power of attorney for his business affairs to William Mead, that Vermont rock of reliability, then closed his New York apartment for good.

Ensconced temporarily at the Hotel Netherland overlooking Central Park, McKim wrote to Larry White, about to enter the École des Beaux-Arts in Paris, saying, "When you . . . come home ready to build, you will find opportunities awaiting you that no other country has offered in modern times. The scale is Roman." McKim exulted at the new classical buildings he had seen beautifying and permanently redefining the nation's capitol. "As Mr. Root says, 'Enough pegs driven to make it impossible for anybody to pull them up.'"

But New York was another matter altogether. McKim chafed at the towering new skyscrapers sprouting up everywhere, the growing congestion, and incessant commercialism. In mid-May, he wrote Larry, "I think the sky line of New York grows daily more hideous." He had never much cared for skyscrapers and hated to see architects vying to erect what he viewed as misbegotten behemoths. Since 1908, the forty-seven-story Singer Tower downtown had reigned as the world's tallest building. Topping six hundred feet, made of ornate brick and terra-cotta, the Singer Tower was almost twice the height of the 362-foot Times Tower. And now, the Singer Tower was to be eclipsed by a building McKim disliked even more. He wrote Larry: "The new Metropolitan Life Insurance tower, 700 feet high, makes [Burnham's] the Flatiron building look like a toy and puts every building within a mile in the shade. But all the same, Madison Square tower [Stanford White's creation], one-third of its height, is by far the greater of the two as David than Goliath. The first has the merit of bigness and that's all."

McKim lamented the imminent widening of Fifth Avenue, and the consequent removal of stoops, the narrowed sidewalks, and the discombobulation of the existing graceful streetscape. "The constantly increasing traffic on the streets and the crowded sidewalks have made this imperative and I suppose it is a choice of evils that must be accepted. What New York is coming to, Dieu sait!" Still suffering over the Stanford White scandal and its aftermath, McKim had become so fearful and anxious at times that he required an attendant.

In June, Samuel Rea, back from several weeks motoring around France, had dispatched a photograph of the nearly completed exterior of Penn Station and a letter of congratulation to McKim. "It is a wonderful building, and as time goes on will justify its cost." To William Mead, he wrote of the station: "It is regarded, not alone by ourselves but by everybody who is competent to judge, as a magnificent building." On July 31, 1909, the PRR announced that the last section of Milford pink granite stone had been cemented into place, signaling the completion of Penn Station's imperial Roman Doric exterior. Ivy Lee delighted to tell all that, among many other stupendous facts, "It took 1,140 freight cars to transport these 47,000 tons of stone from Milford, Mass." Covering seven and a half acres, Penn Station was going to be not just the world's largest train station, but the world's fourth-largest building, with the three bigger ones—St. Peter's Basilica, the Tuileries, and the Winter Palace—all ancient monuments that had been built and expanded over the centuries.

When hot weather enveloped New York, McKim and Margaret migrated north to Narragansett Pier, their favorite resort in Rhode Island. On July 23, 1909, William Mead, about to depart for a European jaunt on the S.S. *Lusitania*, sent McKim a short note of farewell. Mead was in good spirits because work was now well underway on another of the firm's plum Gotham commissions: the new main U.S. Post Office across Eighth Avenue from Penn Station. They had designed a stately Corinthian edifice to complement McKim's Doric temple. This would have pleased Cassatt, for back in June 1904 he had written to the secretary of the treasury, taking "the liberty of suggesting to you, quite unofficially" that they give the work to McKim, Mead & White. "I know you appreciate how important it is, from an artistic standpoint, that your building should accord with ours in general style."

Mead regretted not having time to visit McKim before he left for Europe, but wanted him to know in his quick goodbye note, "Larry White was in the office this morning, looking very well . . . Webster was in the office at the time, and I had him take Larry over to the Station and show him around, and I am sure it was a pleasure to both of them. Larry has seen the outside, and said it was the finest thing on earth. I shall be back before you miss me."

TWENTY-FIVE

"OFFICIALLY DECLARE
THE STATION OPEN"

The first day of August 1910 was a warm and sunny Monday in Gotham. On Seventh Avenue, the lunchtime traffic rumbled by, the automobilists in their Pierce Arrows and Whites impatiently blasting past horse-drawn carts and electric trolleys. Newsboys in ragged knickers and bare feet yelled the day's big story: the murderer Dr. Hawley Crippen had been dramatically arrested at sea. Inside the still unopened Pennsylvania Station, the modern world with all its hurly burly and vehicular cacophony seemed far away. Several PRR men, who had just entered from the station's colonnaded loggia, paused atop the forty-foot-wide Grand Stairway, awed anew by what Charles McKim had wrought: They looked up and about, admiring the vast and luminous space that was the General Waiting Room, McKim's masterpiece of Roman grandeur.

Towering sixty-foot-high Corinthian columns topped with carved acanthus leaves lifted the eye up 150 feet to the soaring groin-vaulted coffered ceiling, which framed eight huge and lovely semicircular lunette windows. Through these windows poured lambent shafts of moted sunshine, bathing the stone floor with moving pools of light. The warm honey-colored travertine of the stairway, walls, and massive fluted pillars was a clever blend of real marble brought all the way from Roman quarries, and a more economical matching faux-marble mixture. Travertine, as the PRR proudly noted, was the stone of ancient Roman monuments and never before used in the United States. Charles McKim had so skill-fully evoked classical monuments that the very air seemed ancient, golden, suffused with quiet and timeless drama. Samuel Rea had already decreed that no advertising or even seating would mar the stateliness of this wondrous space.

During those languorous days in Rome a decade earlier, McKim had been enthralled by the antiquity, grandiose scale, and grace of the Baths of Caracalla. Now, as the PRR men strolled down into Penn Station's im-mense, glorious, and misnamed waiting room, they could see how the architect had incorporated that golden memory, giving to Gotham his last and greatest building, one of appropriately imperial formality, scale, and nobility. "The conditions of modern American life in which under-takings of great magnitude and scale are carried through . . ." noted McKim, Mead & White partner William Symmes Richardson, "are more nearly akin to the life of the Roman Empire than that of any other known civilization."

It was perhaps fitting that McKim had gone the Romans one better, making his American homage even bigger than those ancient baths. His General Waiting Room was the largest room in the world. Its dimensions were colossal—two city blocks wide and 150 feet high, enough to hold Gotham's City Hall and then some. Its spare and somber beauty was lightened by Jules Guerin's elegant pale blue map murals depicting the territory served by the Pennsylvania and Long Island railroads. The only other sign that this was the beginning of the twentieth century was the incandescent lighting. A double row of electrolier candelabra atop bronze pillars and marble pedestals created a pretty walkway through the im-mensity of the marble floor. In each corner were arrayed a marble-clad information desk, a ticket window, a parcel room, and a telephone and telegraph office.

All this impending PRR grandeur had not been lost on the Vander-bilts. In 1902, they had announced that the New York Central would also build a brand new terminal, one equally magnificent, and invited a quar-tet of major firms, including McKim, Mead & White, to submit plans. When the railroad's president chose a design (not Stanford White's) with a huge, revenue-producing hotel atop it, chairman William K. Vanderbilt intervened, rejecting such crass considerations. Gustav Lindenthal wrote to Samuel Rea, "Everyone concedes that the Pennsylvania Railroad has been at extraordinary pains to make its railroad station in this city architecturally beautiful, and that fact may be said to have induced the New York Central Railroad to go to the very large expense of a new terminal building for its own road, conceived also on monumental lines." Without a doubt.

Penn Station's General Waiting Room looking north to West Thirty-third Street in 1911.

New York's Penn Station was to be its own small city. Travelers coming through the main Seventh Avenue double-colonnaded pavilion and into the arched doors entered a graceful high-ceilinged arcade, a 235-foot "boulevard" lined with artful bronze shop fronts, their modern motifs set into the honeyed travertine marble walls of Ionic pilasters. The natural light pouring through the arcade's lunette windows illuminated the luxurious displays of candies and flowers, as well as more practical goods dear to the traveler. At the end of the large and airy arcade, just before the grandeur of the General Waiting Room, were the station's two restaurants. The one on the south side was the formal Corinthian Room, where tea was poured from fine silver, while the one on the north side was a lunch buffet with counter seating.

Penn Station also offered the latest word in barbershops, haberdashers, shoeshine stands, both a gentlemen's and a ladies' waiting room, a men's smoking lounge, luxurious pay toilets and changing chambers equipped down to silver-handled broom whisks, special waiting rooms for bereaved funeral parties, full-service baggage rooms, a small police station and two-cell jail, a staffed medical clinic, and all manner of amenities. On the Eighth Avenue side, there were new executive offices for the PRR and the LIRR. Above those, the station's third and fourth floor were given over to a YMCA serving the road's employees, offering not just sleeping quarters for 175 men, but a gym, a bowling alley, billiard room, library, and lecture and assembly rooms.

On this momentous Monday, the small group of PRR men strolling through the luminous splendor of the General Waiting Room savored its timeless quality, knowing that soon enough its ethereal silence would give way to busy throngs of purposeful voyagers. Walking down the stairs from that magnificent waiting room into the train concourse, they left behind the past and entered an utterly inspired industrial present. McKim had reconfigured the familiar Victorian glass train shed into a complex railroad cathedral of light and dramatic motion, an airy rhythmic space of repeating, vaulted lacy steel-truss umbrella arches and glass skylights supported by tall slender steel pillars. The glass-block floors echoed the airiness, filtering natural light down to the eleven subterranean train platforms serving the twenty-one tracks. McKim (and then Richardson) had thought long and hard about the experience of train travel, designing the terminal so that departing passengers entered the train platforms through this upper concourse, while those arriving by train exited out from a lower separate concourse and onto the city streets. It was not hard, even in the warmth and quiet of this August afternoon, to envision the hurrying crowds of travelers moving through McKim's version of the modern train shed, almost unconsciously savoring the dramatic possibilities of their travels, a drama heightened by the dreamy, shifting play of light through the vaulted glass ceilings. Charles McKim's astute eye, his delight in detail and light, his pleasure in the romance of departures, arrivals, and novel sights, had all been embodied in Penn Station.

Penn Station's concourse in 1911.

In his train station, McKim had called on a lifetime of architectural knowledge and passion to celebrate the human spirit and civilization itself. "While amply equipping Penn Station to sort and handle vast numbers of people and trains, and to sustain the fast-paced life of the city," writes art historian Hilary Ballon, "McKim tried to temper the brute claims of efficiency with the reassuring comforts of historical tradition. Guided by a vision of civic grandeur, he translated the mundane business of boarding trains into a stately procession, and subsumed the commotion of constant movement and disorganized crowds into the station's overriding order."

As the PRR men descended the steel concourse stairs they became players in their own corporate drama, awaiting a special two-car train arriving from Philadelphia, carrying President James McCrea, the board of directors, many officers, and Alexander Cassatt's two sons and his son-in-law. (From Bar Harbor, Lois Cassatt had wired: "Poor health makes journey from here unwise for me.") This day, August 1, 1910, was the official opening of the terminal, even though it would be months before the station truly opened for regular service. When the DD1 rolled quietly into the platform President McCrea, natty in white vest, bow tie, and Panama hat, stepped out, flanked by Samuel Rea and Captain Green, each attired in dark suits, ties, and summer straw hats. All the railroad men as a matter of punctilious habit checked their pocket watches to see how long the trip had taken from Manhattan Transfer—a highly satisfactory thirteen minutes.

Charles McKim could not be present. He had died almost a year earlier, just sixty-two, his early demise precipitated, his friends and family believed, by the shock and heartache of Stanford White's murder. Not long after Bessie White and Larry had sailed home from Paris and settled back into Long Island the previous summer, Bessie had invited McKim, now almost an invalid, to come to them to convalesce. Mead wrote, "Mrs. White feels that McKim always loved St. James, and everything is familiar to him down there, even the old horses on her place, and that he would be not only contented but encouraged." And so McKim returned to the bucolic seaside of so many fond memories—the clamming and sea bathing, the good meals and conversations—the better to nurse his failing health. Bessie fixed up "the Red Cottage for him. She put in gateposts adorned with beskirted bronze horses that had been figureheads for gondolas in Venice . . . She furnished the house with, among other things, a five-foot-high Tyrolean chest . . . a Swiss gaming table . . . a corner cabinet that Stanford had improvised out of some ornamentally painted wooden panels from a Bavarian church."

McKim had not been there long when in mid-August 1909 he was stricken by a heart attack. "For a time," reported the *New York Times* "his condition was critical, but it was believed now that he will recover." Despite the cool and languid ocean breezes, "the serene sky and the white clouds and the friendly sea and the old horse and the dog," the gentle ministrations of his beloved daughter and the matronly Bessie, Charles Follen McKim grew weaker and weaker. At one o'clock on September 14, 1909, with Margaret by his side, he died quietly in the Red Cottage. Like Alexander Cassatt, Charles McKim would never see his greatest work— the Pennsylvania Station—fully completed. McKim's was the final un- timely death among those great-hearted leaders who had planned the New York Extension to be a magnificent paean to a great city.

Now, almost a year later, fourscore of PRR officers and directors passed into the stillness of the General Waiting Room. Here the Philadel- phians greeted the New Yorkers: General Charles Raymond, wearing bottle-thick eyeglasses and a plain black suit and bow tie; engineers James Forgie and George Gibbs; architect William Symmes Richardson of McKim, Mead & White; sculptor Adolph A. Weinman; and Gustav Lindenthal, serving happily now as chief engineer for the Hell Gate Bridge section of the PRR's New York Connecting Railroad. Alfred Noble was away vacationing on the North Shore of Lake Superior.

About ten days earlier, Samuel Rea had proposed to President McCrea that "as we have determined, and determined rightly, that we will have no elaborate opening [of Penn Station], my suggestion is that we hold our dividend meeting early on August 1st, and then that we come over to New York and that you will unveil the Statue . . . This trip will be short and informal . . . As those present . . . will have been personal associates of Mr. Cassatt's it seems to me that we can avoid elaborate arrangements or speech-making."

Rea had expected Penn Station to be open by now, alive with passen- gers and hundreds of trains rolling in and out daily. But bitter strikes at the car factories had delayed delivery of almost a third of the PRR's order of 1,988 fireproof all-steel passenger cars, without which the company would not begin using the tunnels. Now, as the hands of the huge wait- ing room clock moved ponderously to 2:30 p.m., the group quieted and arrayed themselves on the Grand Stairway facing Weinman's sculpture of Alexander Cassatt. Still draped and hidden by a large cloth, the statue had been duly located, as McKim had proposed, in a special elevated niche.

"With the unveiling of the statue before which we stand, it is pro- posed, sir," intoned PRR director Thomas Cuyler, nodding to President McCrea, "that you should officially declare the Station open . . . these massive walls and columns speak in their severe simplicity and majestic silence far more eloquently than human tongue could give utterance to." Edward Cassatt tugged off the cloth, revealing an impressive bronze sculpted likeness of his father. Cassatt's statue showed an imposing man, tall, dressed in an old-fashioned suit and great coat, his right hand touching a book of engineering blueprints, his left hand clutching his familiar derby, gloves, and walking stick. The sculptor, working from photos, had captured Cassatt's laconic intelligence and power. The bronze plaque below was engraved with his name, title, and years as president, and the simple phrase: "Whose foresight, courage, and ability achieved the extension of the Pennsylvania Railroad system into New York City."

Every man on that stairway must have marveled at it all, as the applause faded and they waited for the photographer to click away, capturing for posterity in a formal portrait this sentimental tribute and historic PRR occasion. The New York Tunnels and Terminal Extension had finally come to be, just as Alexander Cassatt had envisioned when he stepped off the S.S. *Celtic* almost exactly nine years earlier. As one engineer would later write, "When one considers the magnitude of this undertaking even after the engineering plans were approved and found feasible—the tremendous scope of the work, the purchase of the enormous amount of necessary property in the heart of a great city, the financing of the venture and the thousand and one other difficulties to be met and overcome—one cannot but admire and applaud the stout and brave heart of the chief whose foresight planned, whose splendid courage inspired, whose counsel guided and whose ability mastered it!"

As Charles Raymond stood on the Grand Stairway, he felt a pang of melancholy that Cassatt was present only as a bronze statue. Raymond's thick eyeglasses did not much help his near blindness. He could not see the magnificence of the station as the others did, but even the blurred sight of the statue stirred many memories of their collective effort. Living now out at the Water Witch Club in the New Jersey Highlands, Raymond had met many of the titans of his time, but he considered Cassatt "almost unequaled, owing to the breadth, originality, and decisiveness of his character." Beyond Cassatt's brains and brilliance, what had so touched Raymond about the man was that "his manner to his subordinates was so direct and simple that he seemed unconscious of his own superiority."

It was a rare quality that had endeared Cassatt to almost all who worked for him.

Charles Jacobs, with his job as chief engineer completed, was back in England, as he was every summer. Later that day Samuel Rea, first vice president since Green's retirement a year earlier, wrote Jacobs, saying, "I am personally very sorry that you could not have seen this simple

The memorial statue of Alexander Cassatt in Penn Station.

unveiling ceremony to our old chief, but will look forward to you being here in the Fall when the regular operation begins." As for Rea, the moment Cassatt's statue was unveiled he knew the face was too dark. Before the week was out he had Weinman lightening up the bronze patina. But all in all, Rea confided to an aide, "I am quite well pleased with the statue and like it more than ever." Lois Cassatt would not have her first view until September.

The previous December at the annual formal dinner of the PRR's board of directors, Rea had reminisced about the perils, pitfalls, and frustrations of their road's prolonged forty-year quest to enter Gotham. An impressive, rugged figure as he entered his fifty-fifth year, his brushy hair and mustache gone salt-and-pepper gray, Rea reminded these powerful men of "the severe criticism—written and spoken—which rained upon the Company for a so-called needless and extravagant expenditure of money that would never bring any return directly or indirectly, but happily that is past . . . I for years had my doubts whether the present generation would fully appreciate this work, and more than once remarked [about this] to Mr. Cassatt . . . I am happy to feel, however, as the work is nearing completion, that people are beginning to see and appreciate what it really means . . . to have this extension into and through New York City, and a station erected there creditable to our system and well worthy of the greatest city of the country, if not of the world . . . Had it not been undertaken at the proper time, it would be practically prohibitive today by reason of cost and physical impediments. The whole work speaks for itself and will stand for all time as a monument to the Company, to the Directors and stockholders . . . [and] to the engineers in charge of construction and to the whole staff of the Pennsylvania Railroad."

Rea acknowledged the project's costs, heading now toward $111 million. But he assured the directors what they knew full well: "Every agreement [was] negotiated by the best talent we could secure, and every expenditure so scrutinized that adequate value has been obtained, and every dollar of this large sum has been regularly and properly disbursed and audited." And so, as the evening grew later, Rea came to the end of his almost nostalgic review of the company's many travails and triumphs in Gotham, saying, "It should be a great satisfaction to us to have lived to see the great work completed, and the anticipation of so many years realized." But there was always, as Samuel Rea now said, "the sorrow ever present that Mr. Cassatt was not to see the completion of the work in which he took such a deep interest." Unspoken was Rea's other even greater sorrow and loss—his only son, George Black Rea, who had died as a junior engineer building those tunnels.

It was still pitch-black in the wee hours of Thursday September 8, 1910, and the night air distinctly chilly, when a small group of men and women began to gather on the West Thirty-third Street side of Penn Station. McKim's austerely simple classical walls made for a strange contrast with the worn tenements and shops across the street. Amidst the early admiration, already some architects and critics were grousing at the "archeological" quality of McKim's work, while others would bemoan the heaviness and monotony of the great expanse of granite pillars. In June, the *Architectural Record* lamented "the sadness of the interminable fronts . . . A stranger set down before the Seventh Avenue front . . . would be apt to guess it a good substantial jail, a place of detention and punishment of which the inmates were not intended to have a good time." And then there was the matter of the many blocks immediately surrounding the station that still looked raw and unfinished after all the years of demolition and construction.

More and more people drifted up to join those waiting at the LIRR station, and a blue-coated police sergeant and seven traffic cops kept a close eye on them, ready for any unruliness. The crowd tensed as at 3:00 a.m. the doors to Penn Station's (comparatively modest) Long Island Rail Road section swung slowly open, ready to receive these eager inaugural riders. Today was the first day of regularly scheduled service and the first train would soon be departing. The waiting crowd sprinted in to the ticket booth, each hoping to buy the first tickets for the historic first ride on the first train out of the new Penn Station and through the East River tunnels.

All were disappointed to learn that the pioneering first train, scheduled to depart at 3:36 a.m., was a two-car baggage train carrying chiefly newspapers. So the history-minded passengers made do with the Number

1702 departing five minutes later at 3:41 a.m. on Track 19 for Winfield Junction, whence they could connect with trains for Babylon, Hempstead, Whitestone Landing, and Port Washington. One passenger bestowed a congratulatory bottle of champagne upon LIRR motorman T. W. Fields, who would drive No. 1702. A gaggle of newspaper reporters, the stationmaster, his aides, and numerous porters gathered on the pristine platform to watch as, promptly at 3:41, No. 1702 glided out under Manhattan, the East River, and on toward its first stop at Long Island City. This new all-rail journey would cut in half almost every Long Island commuter's travel time. The *New York Times* had devoted an entire special section on September 4 (crammed with real estate ads) to the opening of LIRR tunnels and the huge and inevitable suburban housing boom coming to the bucolic spaces of Long Island. With commutes so much simpler and shorter, the breadwinners of New York families could move their wives and children, now jammed into small apartments, out to the island's fresh air and seashore. The great transformation of the New York region was about to begin.

Exactly one hour after the first LIRR passenger train had departed Penn Station, intimations of opening day trouble surfaced. Three veteran LIRR commuters, men holding monthly tickets, boarded the 4:40 a.m. New York–bound train in Jamaica, settling in as usual in the smoking car. When the LIRR conductor came through to exact the 14-cent day surcharge for the new (nonferry) service, the trio were outraged. One "argued with the conductor a while and finally handed over 15 cents, with the remark: 'Keep the change—my contribution to the tunnels.' Another man puffed his cigarette and offered to draw a check on the National City Bank for 14 cents. A third declined to pay anything and asked the conductor to put him off under the river." Considering that the East River tunnels had just reduced their usual forty-four-minute commute to nineteen minutes, their tight-fisted chagrin must have seemed churlish.

At 8:30 a.m., middling disaster struck at Winfield. There had been "imperfect installation of a section of third rail which knocked the shoes off from two electric trains," explained LIRR president Ralph Peters. "This stalled the trains, and it was necessary to get locomotives to pull them out of the way. The damage was repaired promptly," but not before causing an hour's worth of LIRR rush-hour trains to be ten to forty minutes late. All over Long Island on what turned out to be a September day of sunshine and breezes, country towns rejoiced with "tunnel" parades and festivities celebrating their speedier and more convenient connection to Gotham's wealth and opportunity. But as village bands played, schoolchildren marched, and politicians speechified, chaos was building on the LIRR.

Longtime LIRR riders fumed at having to exchange their old commuter tickets for new ones (at the cost of an additional dollar) and again at having to pay new tunnel surcharges. "For some weeks past," asserted the LIRR the next day, the company had used every endeavor "to inform its patrons of the new tariff . . . strange to say, very few patrons paid any attention." But worse yet, commuters discovered all the old familiar schedules had been changed. Infuriated mobs of passengers besieged overwhelmed ticket agents at every station along the various lines, their ire rising yet further as the long waits to exchange or buy tickets caused them to miss trains. Riders of the Far Rockaway Branch learned their trains had disappeared from the schedule altogether. In the LIRR section of Penn Station, police had to quell outbreaks of fisticuffs among rival newspaper hawkers and other assorted thuggish vendors staking out valuable new sales terrain. All told, thirty-five thousand people rode the first LIRR "tunnel" trains, and many were mad as wet hens. The LIRR put the best spin on it they could: "There were no personal injuries to passengers or employes, and that is really the most important thing." Matters improved steadily from there.

The opening of the LIRR section of Penn Station underscored an appalling oversight: There was not a single subway or elevated line connected to the PRR's mighty terminal. More amazing, none was as yet even planned. As the PRR prepared to open the entire station, the nearest subway—August Belmont's IRT—was four long blocks distant. The Ninth Avenue El and the more popular Sixth Avenue El were each a long block away. Only the slow-moving Seventh Avenue trolley car was close at hand. In infuriating contrast, the Vanderbilts' Grand Central Station had been served for six years by the IRT, which had a subway stop conveniently under the terminal.

Back in early 1904, now-deceased LIRR president William Baldwin had warned Cassatt in a private letter that the PRR could guarantee sub-way service at the terminal only by taking control of the rival Metropolitan Subway. Cassatt, in a serious miscalculation, demurred. August Belmont pounced, bought the Metropolitan, and proceeded to reign for a good half-decade as the intransigent and wily Traction King (complete with his own private subway car, *Mineola*), blocking all rivals and any and all subway development that might eat into his fabulous IRT profits. As Manhattan came to be one of the most congested places on earth ("More people resided on this small, twenty-three-square-mile island than in thirty-three of the nation's forty-six states"), transit politics became cor-respondingly more byzantine. Tammany under Boss Murphy, Belmont's staunch ally, evinced as little interest as ever in serving the public. Fi-nally, dire need and utter stalemate propelled the state legislature in 1907 to ram through a new state Public Service Commission dedicated solely to getting New York City's subways built.

During all those years, Pennsy officers had exhorted, pleaded, demanded, and entreated Belmont, transit commissions, and city and state officials to do their civic duty and launch construction on a Seventh Avenue sub-way line to serve the city's other big railroad terminal, their Pennsylvania Station. Said Rea, "This line on the west side of the city is imperatively needed . . . unquestionably it should be built at the earliest possible oppor-tunity." As of 1910, it had all been to no avail. Penn Station would open not only without a subway. It would open without even the prospect of a sub-way. All agreed this was a civic scandal. But no one had a ready solution.

The day after the LIRR inaugurated its train service into Penn Sta-tion, William Randolph Hearst's *Journal American* jeered in an editorial, "How red are the flushes of the Public Service Commission as it comes trailing with empty hands . . . on this day of jubilee? Where is its tale of subways to match the Pennsylvania tubes and terminal . . . a work com-parable in difficulty and magnitude to the building of the Panama Canal? What can [the Commission] show for its three years of costly lucubra-tions and its vast acreage of blue-prints? Nothing but ample terminals for long trains of thought?"

And then there was the sorry state of the surrounding neighborhood. Later in 1910, Samuel Rea would write a long, detailed letter to the

Penn Station just before it opened in 1910.

president of New York's Municipal Art Society, regretting "the rather cheap character of the property adjacent to our Station, [we feel] this section of the City could be very much beautified by an architectural treatment of the entire surroundings, and the territory between Broadway and the Station, and Twenty-third and Forty-Second Streets, enlarged by new streets and traffic facilities to ease congestion . . . Little has been done for this section of the City . . . which badly needs improvement." The lack of a subway only exacerbated this unfortunate situation. Without proper mass transit, the neighborhood would continue to languish, an inconvenient area with a bad reputation.

On the cold autumn night of Saturday November 26, 1910, following two months of elaborate dress rehearsals, the Pennsylvania Railroad was at last ready to run its Tuscan red passenger trains into the heart of Gotham. By nine o'clock, excited New Yorkers, bundled up against intimations of snow or freezing rain, were converging upon the station's Doric colonnades. Outside and in, the terminal was brilliantly lit, ablaze with the electricity that made the tunnels possible.

When the station's massive doors opened officially for business at

9:30 p.m., mobs of curious but well-behaved citizens and a few bona fide train passengers streamed inside. All were suitably awestruck when they emerged into McKim's monumental General Waiting Room. The play of light and shadow in McKim's high curved ceilings and pillared walls was evocative and deeply poetic. "A Frenchman standing beneath the dome of the splendid waiting room sobbed aloud because such a 'beautiful affair' was 'just a railway station,' " the *World* reported, "while friends explained to him that in this commercial country commerce is idealized in art and beauty."

The citizens of Gotham embraced the magnificent station as their own, with many proudly declaring it one of the wonders of the world. "In thousands they flooded the acres of its floor space," wrote the reporter from the *Tribune*, "gazed like awestruck pygmies at the vaulted ceilings far above them, inspected curiously the tiny details of the place, so beautifully finished, on their own level, and pressed like caged creatures against the grill which looked down upon subterranean tracks, trains and platforms." What particularly struck the *Tribune* reporter as he watched the awed and curious crowds swirling about McKim's masterpiece was the building's ability to absorb this much humanity and hoi polloi, such opening night bedlam, while retaining its magisterial calm and dignity.

Elsewhere in the terminal a bemused reporter for the *Herald* watched jaded New Yorkers turn into veritable rubes as they spent their Saturday night testing out this new civic space. Fellows in rakish derbies strolled into the men's waiting room and plopped into the deep leather-cushioned seats or drifted off to puff cigarettes in the men's smoking lounge. A few had their shoes shined, while many citizens stopped to stare at the statue of Alexander Cassatt. Women in the latest huge beribboned hats dined in the Ladies Café, inspected the arcade shops, and strolled down to see the trains. Everyone, it seemed, had to get a drink of the free ice water at one of the 158 fountains and line up to ask questions of the inundated PRR clerks at the information booth. The Corinthian Room and the café were mobbed and noisy as New Yorkers sampled the PRR's famous cuisine.

By ten o'clock, many passengers and families had boarded Pullman sleeping cars departing early Sunday morning to points south and west, but few considered retiring to their berths. They milled about on the platforms and visited the General Waiting Room again to crane their necks up at the coffered ceiling and study the mural maps. There was just too much excitement and hubbub to settle in to sleep. Some bought newspaper extras and shook their heads at the somber details of the horrific factory fire over in Newark. Twenty-three young seamstresses at the Wolff Muslin Undergarment Company had died in the roaring flames, roasted alive, while another forty were injured throwing themselves desperately out the windows of a firetrap of a building with useless fire escapes. The details were gruesome, with some jumping girls holding hands as they leaped, only to be impaled on a fence surrounding the property.

As midnight neared, thousands of New Yorkers made their way onto the skylighted concourse to be there when the first PRR train pulled out at 12:02 a.m. In truth, it was just a local five-car accommodation train going to South Amboy, crammed with those wanting to make a small piece of history. Many suburbanite theatergoers (just in from the Bijou, the Lyric, and the Casino) streamed on, chattering, and installed themselves in the green plush seats, luxuriating in a trip home that entailed no ferry. Onboard, amid the excited crush of passengers was William Atterbury, Cassatt's protégé now ascended to PRR fifth vice president. Veteran locomotive engineer Leon Bedman leaned out the side window of the DD1 as, at 12:01, conductor Henry Orner yelled "All Aboard!" and waved his lantern. With that, the doors closed and at 12:02 precisely they were off, sailing out on the electrified tracks into the open train yard before whooshing under the North River, rushing through the well-lighted tunnel, and emerging from the Bergen Portal to roll across the marshes of the Jersey Meadowlands and on to Manhattan Transfer. There, while the steam locomotive was exchanged for the electric, many New York passengers debarked to wait for the next train into Gotham.

Back at Penn Station, at 12:50 a.m. the *Washington Express* pulled in from Philadelphia and points south with President James McCrea and several other PRR officers aboard, all come to experience firsthand this momentous occasion, the true opening of their company's monumental gateway. As the passengers streamed off, many having attended the traditional Army-Navy game that afternoon, several rhapsodized to the *Journal American* reporter about what a relief it was not to find themselves facing the ferry ride, and after that, the drab prospect of getting a cab or trolley car at West Street. "The dense crowds at the rush hours, the delays, fogs, floating ice, and river collisions," prophesied a *New York Times* reporter, ". . . will be remembered only vaguely." These first arriving passengers were greeted by Stationmaster William H. "Big Bill" Egan, a man of massive physique and matching charm who had risen from freight brakeman to parlor-car conductor to stationmaster in Trenton, before ascending to his present Olympian responsibilities and a staff of 250. He possessed a soon-to-be-legendary courtesy and grasp of p.r. and fun.

In contrast to the small gathering when Cassatt's statue was unveiled back in August, the vast terminal now pulsated with life, filled with expectation and excitement as well as the smooth movement of the on-time trains and people and luggage. The PRR's publicity bureau estimated a hundred thousand people were present that first evening. All that night and the next day horse-drawn carriages, chauffeured automobiles, and electric taxis swept up to unload and pick up the first train travelers through the North and East River tunnels. But those who came merely to see and savor this extraordinarily gracious public space greatly outnumbered actual travelers. Many who had "never been west of Eleventh Avenue" came to watch trains depart to such faraway cities as Chicago and St. Louis, and down to Port Tampa, Florida. The trains came and went close to clockwork.

Among the swarming good-natured crowds that night stood Scotsman James Forgie, chief assistant engineer to Charles Jacobs and now a member of Jacobs's New York firm. On Monday Forgie wrote to Samuel Rea, saying, "Yesterday I witnessed the inauguration of the traffic of the Pennsylvania Railroad from New York City by the North River Tunnels with feelings very different, I have no doubt, from those of the average spectator who went to see the opening of the Station." There were few who knew better than Forgie the agonizing tribulations and commensurate triumphs of their arduous tunnel boring deep under the river's ancient bed.

"Therefore," enjoined Forgie, "permit me to offer you my most hearty congratulations on the final attainment of the greatest engineering scheme of the age, to which you have devoted the past twenty years more or less—not a long time, considering the magnitude of the scheme—and for which, also, you are so greatly responsible." Forgie acknowledged and alluded to their bitter differences on screw piles, "The subject of so much deep concern." He ended with felicitations and best wishes. In truth, only time would tell if Samuel Rea had made the right decision, if the North River tunnels were safe. But on that wonderful day the tunnels worked and the PRR's debut was near flawless. Samuel Rea's wire to Charles Jacobs in London was the understated work of an engineer: "Station operating successfully." The Pennsylvania Railroad had conquered Gotham.

THE PENNSYLVANIA STATION, NEW YORK CITY.   INCOMING TRAIN WITH ELECTRIC ENGINE.

TWENTY-SIX

CODA

Alexander J. Cassatt and Charles Follen McKim had bequeathed to Gotham a magnificent monument in Pennsylvania Station, drawing inspiration from one great and ancient empire to create a modern temple of transportation worthy of their own ascendant American empire. Perhaps no one ever captured so beautifully the timeless essence of McKim's architectural masterpiece as did Thomas Wolfe in his novel *You Can't Go Home Again*, published posthumously in 1940: "Few buildings are vast enough to hold the sound of time. . . . There was a superb fitness in the fact that the one which held it better than all others should be a railroad station. For here, as nowhere else on earth, men were brought together for a moment at the beginning or end of their innumerable journeys, here one saw their greetings and farewells, here in a single instant, one got the entire picture of human destiny. Men came and went, they passed and vanished, and all were moving through the moments of their lives to death, all made small tickings in the sound of time—but the voice of time remained aloof and unperturbed, a drowsy and eternal murmur below the immense and distant roof."

And yet all of Penn Station's monumental grandeur could not compensate for certain intrinsic problems. When an ailing James McCrea retired early on November 13, 1912, Samuel Rea ascended to the presidency of the Pennsylvania Railroad still engaged in a herculean—but

Samuel Rea (right, in derby) and Gustav Lindenthal
(left, white hair) dedicate the Hell Gate Bridge March 9,
1917, thus completing the New York Tunnels and Terminal Extension begun in late 1901.

as yet futile—struggle to secure a West Side subway line for the station. If it were not so galling, it would be almost funny that in 1917,
four and a half years later, Penn Station could boast a more convenient
connection to Boston than it had to other parts of New York City. On
March 9, 1917, Rea and Gustav Lindenthal dedicated the final piece of
Cassatt's dream, the Hell Gate Bridge across the East River (at 1,017
feet the world's longest steel arch bridge) from Queens to Ward's Island,
thus completing the PRR's New York Connecting Railroad to New England. On this red-letter day, the Seventh Avenue IRT was still not finished. Not until the next year, 1918, could passengers debarking LIRR
and PRR trains finally step onto a Seventh Avenue subway from a Penn
Station stop—sixteen years after Cassatt and Rea first requested such
service and eight years after the station opened. So convoluted were

New York subway politics, it would be yet another decade before the Eighth Avenue subway finally connected to Penn Station.

Not only did this early lack of real mass transit undermine the success of Penn Station, so did its inauspicious location. The Tenderloin neighborhood was no longer the raucous Satan's Circus of old, but enough saloons, dance halls, and bordellos lingered on to make those West Side blocks seedy. When Rea tried to recruit real estate developers to upgrade and beautify Penn Station's immediate vicinity, he was told by one realtor, "It is not a question of more transportation facilities (though these are always helpful) as much as the purifying of the neighborhood by the occupancy of the streets by respectable people doing business or living in hotels there." Another potential developer pointed out to Rea that his own passengers did not care to linger in the vicinity, preferring to "take cars and escape almost as if the station were in a plague spot."

Unfortunately, the top PRR brass, being largely Philadelphians, failed to grasp that they would have to boldly lead the way as investors and even builders to transform the neighborhood into a worthy setting for their New York station. True, the PRR had, albeit with considerable difficulty, wooed the U.S. Post Office to build atop their tracks on Eighth Avenue. McKim, Mead & White's attractive Corinthian temple, the new main branch of the New York Post Office, opened in December 1913. A quote from Herodotus about Persian couriers chosen by the architects and inscribed on its Eighth Avenue frieze soon became the agency's unofficial motto: "Neither snow, nor rain, nor heat, nor gloom of night stays these couriers from the swift completion of their appointed rounds."

Cassatt and Rea had always envisioned their Pennsylvania Station as the catalyst for a neighborhood real estate boom: modern office skyscrapers rising on avenues busy with important men wearing top hats, fancy hotels and theaters displacing saloons, and smart shops, boutiques, and bustling cafés giving new polish to nearby blocks. They had hoped to see the city widen Seventh Avenue, along with Thirty-Second Street, creating a handsome plaza. But the PRR failed to control the requisite sites and Tammany, which still ruled Manhattan, was not about to bestir itself for corporate foes. Two years after the station opened, the Seventh Avenue Improvement Association complained that the PRR itself was stymying new development. Their overpriced and unsold holdings were sitting "vacant or covered with old rookeries . . . In the meantime the section south . . . was being built up as a loft or factory section. If the present situation continues, factory building will gradually close in on the station. When this happens Mr. Cassatt's dream will have failed . . . For want of investing $10,000,000 or $15,000,000 of additional capital the Pennsylvania Railroad is impairing the value of the $125,000,000 already invested."

To its great and lasting detriment, as art historian Hilary Ballon writes, "The Pennsylvania did not see itself in the business of real estate development. Its business was the railroad." Consequently, this rich and powerful corporate giant had not gained possession of sufficient adjacent territory—as had the Vanderbilts and New York Central around their terminal—nor did the PRR officers have the mind-set to aggressively and strategically use what they did own to reshape the surrounding district. As one developer upbraided Rea, "I find my endeavors thwarted at every step by the constant opposition of my [real estate] clients, because of your apathy as compared with the zeal and activity of the New York Central people."

Finally, desperate to demonstrate their support for desirable buildings, the PRR helped underwrite the Hotel Pennsylvania, a comfortable business hotel that opened directly across from the station's Seventh Avenue entrance, but not until January 1919. The 2,200-room hotel, also designed by McKim, Mead & White, became the city's largest hotel, but possessed no great cachet. It was the PRR's first and last foray into active development. Between the late arrival of the IRT subway and the even later opening of the Eighth Avenue IND, the seedy character of the nearby streets, and the timidity of the PRR's own efforts, the blocks and avenues around Penn Station languished. No fancy skyscraper office buildings arose, nor fashionable hotels. The Penn Station neighborhood remained a disappointing backwater.

As for Penn Station itself, New Yorkers harbored mixed feelings. They adored its glamour and grandeur, the sense it gave one of embarking on a magnificent journey. They loved the convenience of catching the all-Pullman *Broadway Limited* to Chicago or the *Orange Blossom Special* to Florida right from Manhattan, as well as the prospect of glimpsing a star like Charlie Chaplin or political bigshot being squired about by Stationmaster Egan, jovial and elegant in his top hat, gray spats, and trademark mahogany cane. (Reportedly, "Mr. Egan was the only man with whom the late President Coolidge ever spent three hours chatting.") Travelers felt part of something momentous just by entering the station, important players in the great human drama.

The Hotel Pennsylvania being built across Seventh Avenue from Penn Station.

Amidst the crowds surging through McKim's General Waiting Room, wrote Thomas Wolfe in *You Can't Go Home Again*, "There were people who saw everything, and people who saw nothing, people who were weary, sullen, sour, and people who laughed, shouted, and were exultant with the thrill of the voyage, people who thrust and jostled, and people who stood quietly and watched and waited; people with amused, superior looks, and people who glared and bristled pugnaciously. Young, old, rich, poor, Jews, Gentiles, Negroes, Italians, Greeks, Americans—they were all there harmonized and given a moment of intense and somber meaning as they were gathered into the murmurous, all-taking unity of time."

For some New Yorkers, the glamour and rich human theater were offset by the station's shortcomings. "The average traveler will be dumbfounded when he views the magnificent waiting room and concourse for the first time," wrote railroad man John Droege in 1916, "but in more cases than a few the immensity of things and the magnificence will lose their luster when he has traversed the 'magnificent distance' from the sidewalk to the train or vice versa. It cannot be denied that this is a disadvantage." This criticism struck such a nerve at the PRR that, true engineers that they were, they assembled detailed statistics on walking distances at numerous major train stations—including Grand Central Terminal—to prove that walking a thousand feet to catch a train at Penn Station was no worse (or not *so much* worse) than elsewhere. Another longstanding gripe among the natives was "The ambiguity of the many exits from the trains, some leading to the second level and some to the third." This, wrote architecture critic Lewis Mumford, "is baffling to anyone attempting to meet a person arriving on a train." Over the years, the PRR continually adjusted the station—making platforms longer, installing

The General Waiting Room in 1930.

escalators—including one right up the center of the Grand Stairway. But they never really addressed these principal design flaws.

Ironically, the Long Island Rail Road, something of a stepchild in the original enterprise—it was allocated five of the station's twenty-one tracks in 1910—turned out to be the more important source of passengers. In 1911, the first full year of operation, the LIRR carried six million riders. LIRR President Ralph Peters reported that in one year 7,793 houses were built along their lines in Queens and Long Island, forty factories, 773 stores, and 792 other buildings. By 1917, the number of LIRR riders had doubled to twelve million, making them two-thirds of Penn Station's eighteen million annual passengers that year. The preponderance of suburban commuters at Penn Station was not just unanticipated, it was "a problem because the station, from track layout to support spaces, was not designed to serve commuter traffic. The large majority of users were confined to cramped quarters. They moved underground, from commuter shuttles to subways and streets, without cause to enter McKim's uplifting vaulted spaces. Millions of people were using Penn Station, but not as McKim had intended and, more urgently, not as the Pennsylvania Railroad projected on their balance sheets."

Moreover, Penn Station had been built to handle far greater numbers—a hundred million people a year—than the eighteen million being served in 1917. Consequently, President Rea found himself once again defending the whole Gotham enterprise from attacks: "The Pennsylvania Station," he wrote, "instead of being a monument to inefficiency and waste and a white elephant, is a monument to foresight and the necessities of New York City and the whole country with which it does business . . . The station was constructed for the future." Two years later, in 1919, Penn Station's passenger numbers had almost doubled to thirty-four million, surpassing Grand Central Terminal, and vindicating the PRR's belief that ever larger numbers would flow in and out of the nation's greatest city.

On September 30, 1925, at Broad Street Station in Philadelphia, Samuel Rea, still tall and commanding, but more heavyset, his thick shock of hair almost white, walked into the opulent wood-paneled meeting room of his road's board of directors, with its oriental carpet and carved mantel. Oil portraits of the previous eight presidents (all deceased) kept corporate vigil. The gathered directors no longer sported the fussy dark frock coats, high white collars, and silk cravats of old. The new corporate attire was the modern business suit, vest (with watch and chain), and tie. Outside, under a gray sky, the powerful locomotives screeched and rumbled as they came and went. How many times had Rea come into this room, suffused with the railroad's history and so many memories of his own? Just nine days earlier Rea had celebrated his seventieth birthday and today he would officially retire. The previous April, Rea had given his valedictory speech to the shareholders at their annual meeting in the grand foyer of Philadelphia's Academy of Music. On that occasion, Rea lamented that "We have had a continuous struggle to prevent the confiscation of the railroad investment and service by unwise, wasteful and hostile legislation and regulation which, happily, a fully informed public opinion has tempered."

Today when he retired, as called for in the company rules, Rea would become the first PRR president ever to reach three score and ten and to leave this famously "killing" job in good health. His was a true Horatio Alger story, from humble beginnings fifty-three years earlier as a rod and chain boy to the twelve years he had just completed as the activist ninth president of the company. This had made Rea one of the nation's most powerful men, for his railroad employed 165,000, carried an eighth of the nation's freight, transported sixty-seven million passengers, and was valued at $136 million. And yet, marveled the *Wall Street Journal*, Rea possessed an "almost singular combination of modesty, steadfastness and unselfishness."

Today was, of course, a day of sentiment and praise. The board of directors, arrayed around the highly polished doughnut-shaped wooden meeting table, honored Rea's role as the steady guiding hand behind the New York Extension by voting to engage artist Adolph A. Weinman to create a second monumental bronze statue for Penn Station. This one would be of Rea and occupy the niche across from Cassatt. Back in March 1911, Rea had rejected a proposal to place a statue in that niche that would honor the project workmen who had perished, along with a plaque listing their names. No explanation was given. Perhaps he did not feel the sandhogs and other laborers merited the honor. Perhaps he preferred not to dwell on those who died building the company's great work—because his own son had been among them. Rea's wife, Mary, still wore black mourning. Or perhaps he felt the honor should be his, for he had been Cassatt's right-hand man for the first five years and then seen the project through its darkest hours.

In the fifteen years since Penn Station had opened, there had never been any detailed public discussion of what had inarguably been the most anguishing struggle of Samuel Rea's career: his decision—against the advice of three of his own outstanding engineers—not to attach screw piles to the North River tunnels. Time had borne out the wisdom of Rea's choice, for the tunnels—constantly surveyed and watched—had proven to be completely safe. They had not, as had been Rea's worst fear, continued to sink inexorably deeper and deeper into that ancient silt or shown any sign of strain. Instead, as the PRR's own meticulous measurements showed, the tunnels continued to oscillate very slightly with the tide of the great river that flowed in and out high above them.

Like Rea, the North River tunnel engineers viewed that work as the highlight of their careers, a project of such magnitude and importance, so fraught with travails and triumphs, that they hated to part. And so, under the aegis of the Pennsylvania Tunnels Alumni Association of the North River Division, for years they threw merry, elaborate reunion dinners at Healy's Restaurant on Columbus Avenue. Menus featured "Chicken Gumbo à la Terminal West" and "Grapefruit in Half Section apparently severed by some sharp instrument." In the early days, Charles Jacobs and James Forgie had presided at these jolly soirees, winding up after many courses and cocktails, Roman punch, and other libations, singing the many verses of their own sentimental anthem, "Tunnel Days."

The PRR board of directors was looking on this September day not just to the past, but to the company's future. With Rea's retirement, they elected W. W. Atterbury tenth president of the PRR. Promoted not quite three decades earlier by Cassatt to unsnarl Pittsburgh, Atterbury over the ensuing years had demonstrated great range and charm as an executive. Having started as a three-dollar-a-week shop apprentice, Atterbury prided himself on cultivating the best in everyone he worked with. During World War I, he had served in France, constructing railroads almost from scratch for the Allies and then running them, earning the rank of brigadier general. Today, Atterbury expressed his considerable pleasure at becoming president, saying, "I like to think that the Pennsylvania railroad has a soul and that its soul has been created out of the lives of men who devoted themselves to its service . . . the Pennsylvania Railroad has a great destiny."

In a final gesture of appreciation to Samuel Rea, Effingham B. Morris bestowed upon the retiring president a personal gift from the board of directors, rare English silver plate made in London in the reign of Charles II. This was a most apropos memento because Rea, who so loved history, confessed "a weakness for studying old English silver craftsmanship and its distinctive hall marks of which there is a record for about six hundred years." Further, he savored "the pleasure of constantly using these works of art." During his presidency, Rea, now wealthy, had built a beautiful fieldstone mansion on 104 rolling acres in Gladwyne. He named this graceful Main Line estate Waverly. "Tramping and working about my home farm give me all [the exercise] I need," he said during one interview, with wood chopping a favorite activity. Now, Rea looked forward to having more hours for tending his peach orchards there.

Whenever Rea spoke with reporters, he never wavered in his advice for the young and ambitious: Read! Books, especially biography and travel, he said; "give us insight into the lives of successful men and heighten the imagination and increase knowledge of other countries. If neglected by the young businessman, he will find himself lacking in culture, vision and balance of life. His sympathies will be narrow and selfish. He must stand for the best things in life and use his service, influence and money to advance them. The world gets nowhere with stand-patters or indifferent people." A few years later, on March 24, 1929, Samuel Rea—who had thrown himself into Al Smith's unsuccessful White House campaign the year before—died at home from a heart attack after a bout of the flu. He had believed deeply in his railroad and his country, and had relished working with the giants of his day, ushering in the astounding prosperity of the industrial age. He had outlived not just Cassatt, his revered boss, but also Charles Raymond, dead in 1913, Alfred Noble, who died a year later, and Charles Jacobs, who died in 1919.

Rea was a famously modest man, but it certainly would have pleased him to see the more than a thousand people gathered in Penn Station's General Waiting Room on April 9, 1930, a fair spring day, for the unveiling of his statue. Even as crowds of passengers streamed by the Pennsy men commanding the Grand Stairway, great shafts of light illuminated McKim's timeless space and organ music swelled up, deep notes slowly floating through the air. George Gibbs and Gustav Lindenthal, grayer, older, stouter, were both present, the sole remaining members of the original board of engineers. After a few words, they did the honors, pulling the cloth cover off the statue of their old boss and friend. Weinman had done Rea full justice. The sculpted Rea, wearing a modern business suit, overcoat draped over his left arm, fedora hat in hand, looked as vigorous in bronze as he had in real life. In his niche, he appeared to have just stepped in to look over the situation at the station. Like Cassatt, Rea was identified as an engineer by the blueprints clasped lightly in his right hand. The face was intelligent, considering. Two decades had passed since the unveiling of Cassatt's statue on that hot August day in 1910. At that original ceremony, all the men then present could only marvel at the power of the Pennsylvania Railroad, the triumph of its entrance into New York, its radiant prospects.

The mood today was far more elegiac. The nation was mired in a wrenching Depression, hard times such as had not been seen in decades. But the greater melancholy was that Samuel Rea and all those present had lived long enough to know that the glory days of the Pennsylvania Railroad and every other American railroad were over. Back in 1906, when Alexander Cassatt had bucked all his peers in supporting President Roosevelt on railroad regulation, he thought it a sensible way to deal with their competitors—other railroads. But now there were different competitors, and they were not shackled by regulation. "The ICC," writes business historian Robert Sobel, "improvised, temporized, mediated, and in the end acted in such a fashion as to leave the industry starved for capital and on the defensive, at a time—on the eve of the automobile and aviation ages—when massive funding was necessary for improvements." Shortly after Rea's death, a survey of regular PRR passengers revealed their own declining opinion of "The Standard Railroad of America." They complained of rude service in the stations and trains and poor food on the dining cars. General Atterbury, the last of the Cassatt men to rule the PRR, would survive only five years longer than Rea. Exhausted by the ardors of running his beloved road during the darkest days of the Great Depression, the general would step down in 1935, not yet seventy, and die soon thereafter.

For decades Americans had resented the power and arrogance of the railroads. Now, disgruntled passengers had a liberating alternative: the automobile. It is impossible to overstate the bracing, heady freedom, the delicious convenience of the motorcar. You came and went on your own schedule, self-sufficient, setting the heat and air to your own liking, stopping as you pleased, sharing your car with no annoying strangers who talked too much. Back in 1910 few imagined—certainly not the railroad kings like Cassatt or Rea—that balky expensive motorcars, largely the gleaming playthings of the rich, might ever become a reliable (much less competing) form of long-distance transportation. But then came Henry Ford and the Model T. It was true that as yet the nation had no real highway system. It was an ominous sign of the times for the PRR that the next (and longest) subaqueous Hudson River tunnel, the state-financed Holland Tunnel, dedicated on November 13, 1927, served only cars and trucks driving between New York and New Jersey.

If it had been hard to imagine the car as a competitor to the railroad, airplanes seemed an even more far-fetched rival. It was only after World War II that the true dimensions of the combined threat hit home. In 1958, the Pennsy and other railroads, which had long run their sprawling rail empires with private capital, spent $1 billion of their own funds for maintenance of their facilities and paid $180 million in taxes. That same year, the U.S. government spent six times that sum—$10.3 billion—building highways for automobiles, trucks, and buses, thus helping to siphon off rail customers. While the federal government built the forty-thousand-mile interstate highway system as part of national defense, the *Wall Street Journal* pointed out trucks were hauling more and more freight "with the roadbeds being supplied at public expense." Government then spent yet another $431 million that year on the nascent airlines and airport construction. The PRR, which carried far more passengers than any other road, was competing on very unequal terms with its new tax-payer subsidized rivals. Moreover, the glamour and excitement once attached to private cars and luxurious trains hurtling to distant big cities or resorts, chic couples enjoying sunsets through the dining car windows, was shifting inexorably to cars and airplanes.

Back in 1939, railroads carried 65 percent of intercity passenger traffic. In 1945, when MGM set key scenes of the Judy Garland love story *The Clock* in the General Waiting Room, Penn Station handled 109 million passengers, an all-time peak. But when World War II ended, so did those huge crowds. By now the Lincoln Tunnel was also open, giving yet more motorists and buses easy entry to midtown Manhattan. PRR officials watched with alarm as their share of Penn Station passengers plummeted from wartime highs of forty-four million riders each year to a quarter of that. By 1960, railroads carried only 29 percent of intercity passenger traffic. A quarter of travelers were boarding sleek airplanes and soaring through the clouds to their destinations. The PRR saw their losses balloon to $70 million a year as they indignantly protested (to no avail) the double standard that had their postwar rivals operating out of brand-new government-built bus stations and airports, while the PRR struggled to pay New York City $1.3 million in taxes for Penn Station. It was absurdly unfair.

As for Penn Station, even back in 1937 the PRR knew it needed freshening up and refurbishing. At almost thirty years old its beautiful pink granite facades had grown dirty, its golden Travertine marble interiors dingy, and its walls cluttered with advertising and ill-conceived signs. Designer Raymond Loewy, who had so brilliantly redesigned the look of the PRR's locomotives, proposed cleaning and painting the arcade, cleaning the General Waiting Room and lighting Guerin's map murals, almost invisible under accumulated grime, then creating new drama by floodlighting both the arcade and the General Waiting Room. He thought the concourse skylight ribbings should be painted light gray rather than black. But in that Depression year, nothing came of his suggestion.

Twenty years later, the station was filthier than ever and its grandeur badly faded. New Yorkers and modern architecture critics became scornful of the sadly neglected train station as outmoded. A half-hearted cleaning of the bottom ten feet led one New Yorker to liken the PRR officers and their station to "a small child who would wash his hands but never his wrists; either there should have been no cleaning at all, or the whole building should have been given a gentle washing." Author Lorraine B. Diehl in *The Late, Great Pennsylvania Station*, describes how "the glass-domed roof in the concourse was darkened, grimy with soot. Broken windows were replaced with sheets of metal. 'They didn't take good care of it,' said Archie Harris, a former baggageman for the old station ... In the main waiting room the six lunette windows were clouded with dirt, and the Jules Guerin murals beneath them were little more than dark, colorless expanses."

Now, the beleaguered PRR, which was openly talking about selling air space to build a skyscraper over the station to lessen its deficits, defaced McKim's General Waiting Room with what came to be disdainfully called "the clamshell." Designed by architect Lester C. Tichey and presumably intended to signal airportlike modernity, the monstrous crescent-shaped plastic clamshell served as the illuminated canopy roof of a highly visible new ticket counter, replete with television monitors and garish fluorescent light. Occupying the whole middle of the General Waiting Room and tethered with many wires to McKim's monumental pillars, this modern excrescence mainly acted to "block access . . . to the concourse," writes Diehl. Moreover, to make space for it, "both the ladies' and the men's waiting rooms were removed, and in a half-hearted gesture to the comfort of passengers who would no longer have anyplace to sit, the railroad installed a few benches in the concourse. To reach these, passengers were forced to take a labyrinthine path . . . It was during this time that automobile displays, fluorescent-lighted advertisements, and flashy glass-and-steel storefronts invaded the station."

Critic Lewis Mumford could not believe his eyes when he saw the clamshell, which he denounced as "the great treason to McKim's original design." He wondered, "What on earth were the railroad men in charge really attempting to achieve? And why is the result such a disaster?" Mumford said one could only be grateful Cassatt was not still alive to see what his successors had wrought. "The only consolation," he wrote innocently, "is that nothing more that can be done to the station will do any further harm to it."

Desperate to raise money and indifferent to its own monumental gateway, the PRR promoted one plan after another to exploit the valuable air rights above Penn Station. In 1954, Lawrence Grant White, son of Stanford White and now head of McKim, Mead & White, heard that the PRR had secretly struck a deal and arranged to meet the developer. "I lunched yesterday with William Zeckendorf, who said that he was negotiating with the P.R.R. for the Pennsylvania Station in New York, with the avowed purpose of tearing it down and erecting a 30 story building upon the site. I had already told him at a previous dinner that I deplored tearing down such an important building, but was afraid neither I nor my firm could do anything to stop it; and that if it was to be torn down we should like, as architects for the P.R.R., to have some professional connection with the building that was to be erected ... After an excellent lunch in his fabulous setting, he promised to keep us in mind." That deal—Zeckendorf's "Palace of Progress"—came to naught. Still, writers like Lewis Mumford clearly had no inkling even four years later, in 1958, that the PRR was actively seeking deals that required demolishing McKim's station.

On July 21, 1961, the PRR finally announced with great fanfare that it had its deal, with developer Irving Felt. A new Madison Square Garden would arise above the station, a $75 million "entertainment center" featuring a thirty-four-story office tower, a twenty-five-thousand seat sports arena, a twenty-eight-story luxury hotel, parking garages, and bowling alleys. Nowhere did the article actually mention the necessary razing of Charles McKim's great temple. (Oddly, newspapers had taken to identifying the station's architect as the far more famous Stanford White.) By the time the PRR had its long-sought deal, Lawrence White had been dead five years, a devoted husband and father who had left behind a large brood of grown children. As for engineer Gustav Lindenthal, he had finally seen constructed what he had never ceased to promote—a bridge spanning the Hudson River. Alas, the handsome George Washington Bridge was not his design, and served only motorized vehicles. The dashing and cosmopolitan George Gibbs had been the final member of the board of engineers to go, dying in 1940.

Only Evelyn Nesbit survived from Gilded Age Gotham, her ethereal girlish beauty long gone. After the Thaws had abandoned her, she had triumphed in a series of smash hit vaudeville shows, but these interludes of showbiz success merely masked her private struggles with alcoholism, morphine addiction, suicide attempts, and the necessity of earning a living. Over the years she sold her story again and again to various newspapers and publishers. In 1955, the movie *The Girl in the Red Velvet Swing* made Evelyn, now age seventy and given to wearing heavy spectacles, briefly known to a new generation. "You must be wiser than most women and wealthier than most women if you are beautiful," Evelyn told an interviewer then. "For there is no way to avoid danger if you are beautiful." She had raised a son she said was fathered by Thaw (he denied it), and in her old age was living modestly in Los Angeles and teaching ceramics. She had long outlived Harry Thaw, dead in 1947 of a heart attack. Mad Harry had gained his freedom, only to revert with a vengeance to his wastrel ways, a regular item in the yellow press with his brawls, sordid flings, costly cover-ups, and bailouts.

Through the ballyhoo of the new Madison Square Garden deal, a handful of Manhattan architects discerned that the Pennsylvania Railroad Company intended to demolish its classical New York station. In spring 1962, this small group raised the alarm, banding together as the Action Group for Better Architecture in New York. On August 2, 1962, they marshaled two hundred concerned architects and others, elegant in their suits, the women in pearls and high heels, and set up a picket line outside the station at five o'clock as the sea of humanity flowed in and out for the evening rush hour. The architects, many of them renowned modernists, marched carrying picket signs emblazoned with slogans: "Don't demolish it! Polish it!" and "Save Our Heritage" or "Action Not Apathy!" They buttonholed commuters and gathered several hundred signatures on petitions to stop the demolition.

Later that evening, several journeyed out to the Port Authority's Idlewild International Airport to greet Mayor Wagner as he jetted back from a European vacation, pleading with him to join their crusade. Eventually, prodded by James Felt, chairman of the City Planning Commission and, oddly, brother of the very developer planning to destroy Penn Station, the mayor appointed a Landmarks Preservation Commission. But it had no real power yet. And there were rebuffed suggestions that the Port Authority take over Penn Station, as it had McAdoo's New Jersey trains, which became known as the PATH, or the Port Authority Trans-Hudson.

The AGBANY architects were stunned at how few of their fellow citizens seemed to care. "People never heard of landmarks in 1962," said Norval White, chairman of the group. "They didn't realize what they were about to lose." Norman Jaffe, another member, recalls his boss, architect Philip Johnson, warning, "You can picket all you want, but it's not going to do any good. If you want to save Pennsylvania Station, you have to buy it." "There was not consciousness among most New Yorkers of the value of old architecture," said Elliot Willensky. "People wanted automobiles, suburban houses," explained Kent Bartwick, a future chairman of the city's Landmarks Preservation Commission. "There wasn't much affection for the city itself around the country."

Perhaps the hard truth was this: New Yorkers had never come to really love Penn Station. Charles Follen McKim, an architect rankled by the very skyscrapers, crowds, and cacophony that embodied modern New York, had designed a classical monument out of step with its own time and place. In 1939, *Fortune* magazine had ungraciously described McKim's masterpiece as "a landmark from Philadelphia [that] squats on the busiest part of underground New York." The *Fortune* article about the station, while affectionate about men like "Big Bill" Egan and station cats (two mousers), was otherwise grudging: "Pennsylvania Station affronts the very architectural rationale on which New York is founded by daring to be horizontal rather than a vertical giant. Many New Yorkers unconsciously resent the Pennsylvania Station for that reason . . . To sensitive New Yorkers the station's body is on Seventh Avenue, but its soul is in Philadelphia . . . The New York Central Railroad, on the other hand, was put together in New York and New Yorkers think of the Grand Central Terminal as a native . . . it has the grace to be newer, more vertical, and compactly efficient in a way New Yorkers admire." In short, the Pennsylvania Station was the work of men who did not love New York. It seemed that the subsequent decades—as even Penn Station's grandeur had faded with grime and neglect—had done little to overcome that lingering native resentment. And so, the plans advanced for the destruction of one of the city's noblest civic spaces and monuments.

Aside from the AGBANY architects, a few lone voices expressed outrage. The *New York Times* and its architecture writer, Ada Louise Huxtable, inveighed against "carte blanche for demolition of landmarks . . . We can never again afford a nine-acre structure of superbly detailed solid travertine . . . The tragedy is that our own times not only could not produce such a building, but cannot even maintain it." The president of the PRR, A. J. Greenough, defended the impending destruction, saying in a letter to the *Times* that "Pennsylvania Station is no longer the grand portal to New York that it was in the days of the long-line passenger travel." One city official said in an interview, "Pennsylvania Station is one of the city's great buildings of our time. I'm working on a plan to save the columns." Even that rather pathetic gesture was beyond the city's ken.

On October 28, 1963, as the very skies seemed to weep a gentle rain, desecration and demolition began. By eleven o'clock, the first of sculptor Weinman's twenty-two imperial Roman eagles, symbol of the Caesars, had been detached from its aerie and lowered to the pavement. There that imposing stone raptor looked trapped, the three-ton centerpiece of a group photo of grinning officials wearing hard hats. The station's main clock was sentimentally set at 10:53 to signal the opening date of the station, 1910, and its lifetime, fifty-three years. That afternoon the AGBANY architects reappeared to march silently in protest, wearing black armbands and hoisting picket signs reading simply, "SHAME!" as the wrecking team attacked with jackhammers.

"Until the first blow fell no one was convinced that Penn Station really would be demolished," editorialized the *New York Times*, "or that New York would permit this monumental act of vandalism against one of the largest and finest landmarks of its age of Roman elegance . . . Any city gets what it admires, will pay for, and ultimately, deserves. Even when we had Penn Station, we couldn't afford to keep it clean. We want and deserve tin-can architecture in a tin-horn culture. And we will probably be judged not by the monuments we build but by those we have destroyed."

By the summer, the wrecking crews, working carefully in the sticky New York heat not to disrupt the regular comings and goings of the six hundred trains in the station below them—the part built by George Gibbs—were desecrating McKim's General Waiting Room, with its great lunette windows streaming in huge shafts of light. "A half century of emotion hung in the air," writes Lorraine B. Diehl, "textured with memories of two world wars, a worldwide depression, and the private histories of people coming and going, meeting and parting. So many Americans passed through this room, leaving so much of themselves behind, that it seemed to belong to all of them."

Now, as the wreckers pressed on, it "looked like the bombed-out shell of a great cathedral. Coils and wires hung like entrails from its cracked and open walls. The men with jack-hammers filled the air with noise and dust. The noise violated memory; the dust smelled of death."

And so, slowly, McKim's great temple built for the centuries was methodically dismantled over four years. By July 1966 the demolition crews were ready to remove Weinman's quartet of female statues, each pair representing Day and Night and arrayed around one of the enormous outdoor clocks. Some were saved, but like much of Penn Station, the rest were unceremoniously dumped in the swamps of the Meadowlands, along with the gigantic Doric columns that had once lined Seventh Avenue. This strange instant ruin, complete with snapped and strewn columns and tumbled statuary, was all sadly visible to the passing Pennsylvania trains. By the time winter arrived in 1966, the destruction was complete. McKim and Cassatt's monumental gateway was gone. Several weeks later, on January 18, 1967, Evelyn Nesbit died in a nursing home in Santa Monica. Just before Thanksgiving, the last of the Hudson River ferryboats made its final crossing, the Erie-Lackawanna's service between Hoboken and lower Manhattan, departing for its terminal voyage at 5:45 p.m. from Barclay Street. Most of the three thousand passengers who "still rode the comfortable, broad-beamed boats chose to do so not so much for convenience as for romance." Perhaps they would now drive their cars. It was the end of an era.

The statue of Cassatt, that visionary corporate leader, had been plucked from its niche and consigned to his alma mater, Rensselaer Polytechnic Institute, in Troy, New York, where it passed many years in storage before finding a home in the Pennsylvania Railroad Museum in Strasburg, Pennsylvania, along with his Sargent oil portrait. Samuel Rea's statue was relocated to the outside Seventh Avenue entrance at 2 Penn Plaza, along with two of Weinman's stone eagles. There Rea still stands, a monumental bronze sentinel looking much diminished and out of place, eternally watching the automobile traffic roar downtown, a poignant, little-noticed reminder of splendor lost. As for the new Penn Station, it was and is a mingy low-ceilinged affair little better than a bus depot. But neither the PRR's desperate despoilment of its magnificent temple nor its doomed 1968 merger with its old rival the New York Central could save those proud old empires of passenger rail. Grudging government ownership was their unfortunate fate. And yet, when developers came to destroy Grand Central Terminal, outraged New Yorkers rallied to its defense, invoking a now powerful landmarks law.

All these decades later—as our love affair with cars and airplanes has soured—there is hope that New York can once again reclaim the grandeur of arriving by train in Gotham. Little could Alexander Cassatt have dreamed that the land his corporation sold on Eighth Avenue for a central post office would become so important. But it is this austere Corinthian

General Post Office Building (a New York landmark long known as the James A. Farley Building) that opened in 1913 and its large 1934 addition that offer salvation. These elegant structures are now the centerpiece of a plan that envisions them reconfigured to serve the riders of New Jersey commuter trains. There is also serious talk of demolishing hideous Madison Square Garden and once again erecting a new train station worthy of New York.

Gotham's Pennsylvania Station. "Through it one entered the city like a god," wrote architect Vincent Scully of that old wondrous monument in his *American Architecture and Urbanism*. "Perhaps it was really too much," Scully pondered, lamenting that "One scuttles in now like a rat." Maybe now we can hope for a return to the grandeur of the past.

The statue of Day in the Meadowlands.

ACKNOWLEDGMENTS

Conquering Gotham has been in the works for a long time and I have accrued many debts.

First, I would like to thank my agent, the always wonderful Eric Simonoff of Janklow & Nesbit, and my two excellent editors at Viking, Rick Kot and Hilary Redmon, whose work measurably improved the manuscript, as did that of copy editor extraordinaire Elaine Luthy.

Early on, I worked at the Hagley Museum and Library, where Chris Baer continues to be the ultimate expert on the Pennsylvania Railroad, promptly answering all the many, many questions that have arisen in the course of research and writing. During a half dozen years at the Pennsylvania State Archive in Harrisburg, I was helped by good-natured staffers there: Bill Gordon, Brett Reigh, Michael Sherbon, Willis Shirk, Rich Saylor, Jason Amico, Jonathon Stayer, Jerry Ellis, Judie Marcus and Cynthia Margolies. Gerald A. Francis of the Lower Merion Historical Society outside Philadelphia kindly answered various inquiries. As ever, I have depended on the knowledgeable staff of the Milton S. Eisenhower Library at Johns Hopkins University.

Mark Reutter, editor of *Railroad History*, has been endlessly helpful and truly generous. He has fielded innumerable e-mails, carefully read the manuscript, proffered invaluable advice, and been a good dinner companion. In Philadelphia, Jeff Groff of Wyck House has been similarly generous, providing entree to the Philadelphia side of the story and also thoroughly reading the manuscript. Through him I met Pliny Jewell, the great-grandson of Samuel Rea. I was also very fortunate to have the help of Cassatt descendants, Jacques de Spoelberch and Polly Maguire, whose husband, Robert, kindly handled my many inquiries and provided materials, including photos. John Marshall, who is writing a biography of PRR president William W. Atterbury, graciously shared a trove of materials. Both Larry Grubb and Dave Sonderblum read early versions of the manuscript, for which many thanks.

Lorraine B. Diehl, whose classic *The Late, Great Pennsylvania Station* is the original excellent history and photo documentation of Penn Station, has been kind and very helpful, especially as I was gathering photos. John Turkeli gave a fascinating tour of the present Penn Station, shared his impressive collection of images, and kindly lent several for illustrations. Cyndy Serfas wielded her technological prowess on behalf of the photos, as did Viking's Jacqueline Powers.

Karen Hansen and David Melnick put me up many nights in Delaware, as did Peggy and Bob Sarlin in New York, and were, as always, good company.

NOTES

All material attributed to "PRR Archives, Harrisburg, Pennsylvania" is from the group of papers to be found in the Cassatt Presidential Correspondence, Pennsylvania Railroad Archives, MG 286, Penn Central Railroad Collection, Pennsylvania State Archives, Harrisburg.

1. "WE MUST FIND A WAY TO CROSS"

5   *"one of the handsomest"*: "The P.R.R.'s New Station," *New-York Tribune*, February 12, 1899, p. 13.

6   *"Gentlemen will not"*: Philip Burne-Jones, *Dollars and Democracy* (New York: D. Appleton & Company, 1904), pp. 27–28.

6   *"most brilliant railroad official"*: "A. J. Cassatt Unanimously Chosen," *Philadelphia Ledger*, June 10, 1899, p. 1.

7   *"The Pennsylvania"*: George H. Burgess and Miles C. Kennedy, *Centennial History of the Pennsylvania Railroad Company 1846–1946* (Philadelphia: Pennsylvania Railroad Company, 1949), p. 363.

7   *"We are now taking up"*: A. J. Cassatt to General William J. Sewell. April 3, 1900, carton 2, folder 2/39, PRR Archives, Harrisburg, Pennsylvania.

7   *"These railway kings"*: James Bryce, *The American Commonwealth* 3 (London: Macmillan, 1888), pp. 412–13.

7   *"We stand on our last railroad tie"*: "The Centre of the Universe," *New York Herald*, Sunday Magazine, Oct. 24, 1909, pt. 2, p. 9.

10   *"bits of wood, straw"*: Rupert Brooke, *Letters from America* (New York: Charles Scribner's Sons, 1916), p. 8.

11   *"Waterfront as squalid"*: E. Idell Zeisloft, ed. *The New Metropolis* (New York: D. Appleton & Company, 1899), p. 586.

11 *"one of the most inconvenient"*: Kurt Schlicting, *Grand Central Terminal* (Baltimore: Johns Hopkins University Press, 2001), p. 53.

11 *"Through the fog"*: William G. McAdoo, *Crowded Years: The Reminiscences of William G. McAdoo* (Boston: Houghton Mifflin, 1931), p. 66.

12 *"In daylight, dusk, and darkness"*: Maximilian Foster, "The Waterways of New York," *Munsey's*, November 1900, pp. 200–201.

14 *"I have never been able to reconcile myself"*: "Long Island's New Era," *New York Times*, Sunday September 4, 1910, pt. 7 (Special Long Island Section), p. 1.

2. HASKINS'S TUNNEL AND LINDENTHAL'S BRIDGE

15 *"Of all the great improvements"*: "The Hudson River Tunnel," *New York Times*, May 25, 1880, p. 4.

16 *"It is built"*: "Down Under the Hudson," *New York Times*, July 18, 1880, p. 1.

16 *"That we have gone 300 feet"*: "Science in Tunnel Building," *New York Times*, Oct. 1, 1880, p. 8.

16 *"slippery blue black"*: "Down Under the Hudson," *New York Times*, July 18, 1880, p. 1.

17 *"to furnish a brace"*: Ibid.

17 *"a thin semi-circular"*: Ibid.

18 *"Everything about"*: Ibid.

18 *"My God! The water is gaining"*: "A Collapsed Tunnel," *New York Herald*, July 22, 1880, p. 1.

19 *"Engineering skill"*: Ibid.

19 *"This tunnel scheme"*: "Science in Tunnel Building," *New York Times*, October 1, 1880, p. 8.

19 *"Many of these roads"*: John Moody, *The Railroad Builders* (New Haven: Yale University Press, 1919), p. 215.

19 *"The sun is no longer"*: Ian R. Bartky, "The Adoption of Standard Time," *Technology & Culture* 30 (1989): 49–52.

20 *"in national importance"*: "Bridge Across the Hudson River at New York City," House of Representatives, 51st Cong., 1st sess., report no. 928, p. 37.

21 *"We are not disposed to disturb"*: Francis N. Barksdale, "The Pennsylvania Station in New York," Samuel Rea Papers, Accession 1810, carton 146, folder 10, The Hagley Museum and Library, Wilmington, Delaware.

22 *"perpetual control"*: Ibid.

22 *"hard work tramping . . ."*: "A. J. Cassatt Stricken by Sudden Death," *Philadelphia Record*, December 29, 1906, p. 1.

22 *"Cassatt reeled off the figures"*: Patricia T. Davis, *End of the Line: Alexander J. Cassatt and the Pennsylvania Railroad* (New York: Neale Watson Academic Publications, 1978), p. 22.

23   *"seemed to grasp"*: Ibid.

23   *"a natural talent"*: Ibid.

24   *"that important territory"*: Samuel Rea, *Pennsylvana Railroad New York Tunnel Extension: Historical Outline*, December 15, 1909 (Philadelphia, 1909), p. 4. Hagley Museum and Library, Wilmington, Delaware.

24   *"You sing divinely"*: Davis, *End of the Line*, p. 26.

24   *"I see you now"*: Ibid., p. 30.

24   *"I had to send back"*: Ibid.

25   *"The road's employees"*: "The Pennsylvania Crowd in the Public Eye," *New York Times*, June 10, 1906, pt. 3, p. 3.

26   *"railroad managers"*: Alfred Chandler: *The Essential Alfred Chandler: Essays Toward a Historical Theory of Big Business*, Thomas K. McCraw, ed. (Cambridge, Mass: Harvard Business School Press, 1988), p. 208.

26   *"than had occurred in"*: Harold C. Livesay, *Andrew Carnegie and the Rise of Big Business* (New York: HarperCollins, 1975), pp. 31–32.

26   *"No private enterprise"*: Robert V. Bruce, *1877: Year of Violence* (Chicago: I. R. Dee, 1989), p. 43.

26   *"When the master"*: quoted in Walter Lord, *The Good Years: From 1900 to the First World War* (New York: Harper, 1960), p. 70.

27   *"Why, it is nothing less"*: Ron Chernow, *Titan: The Life of John D. Rockefeller Sr.* (New York: Random House, 1998), p. 201.

27   *"I thought it my duty"*: *Pennsylvania Report of the Committee Appointed to Investigate the Railroad Riots* (Harrisburg, Pa.: Lane S. Hart, 1878), p. 691.

27   *"I went down"*: Ibid., p. 692.

27   *"They all seemed to be shouting"*: Ibid., p. 693.

28   *$5 million in prime PRR property*: Bruce, *1877: Year of Violence*, p. 180.

28   *"This may be the beginning"*: Paul Dickson, "The Great Railroad War of 1877," *American Heritage* 29, No. 2 (February–March 1978): 56.

30   *"Through this secret arrangement"*: James Creelman, "All Is Not Damned." *Pearson's Magazine*, 15, no. 6 (June 1906): 547.

3. "THE ABLEST MAN THIS RAILWAY EVER PRODUCED"

31   *"How do you manage"*: Katharine Cassatt to A. J. Cassatt, December 7, 1881, Philadelphia Museum of Art.

31   *"When you get these pictures"*: Nancy Mowll Mathews, *Cassatt and Her Circle* (New York: Abbeville Press, 1984), p. 161.

31   *"to have more time"*: Francis Nelson Barksdale, "A. J. Cassatt," *World's Work* 2 (July 1901): 973.

32   *"It changed my life"*: Nancy Mowll Mathews, *Mary Cassatt, a Life* (New York: Villard, 1994), p. 114.

32   *"The truth is"*: Ibid., p. 68.

32   *"Had to do it,"*: Patricia T. Davis, *End of the Line: Alexander J. Cassatt and the Pennsylvania Railroad* (New York: Neale Watson Academic Publications, 1978), p. 99.

33   *"We listened to any scheme"*: William D. Middleton, *Manhattan Gateway* (Waubesha, Wis: Kalmbach Books, 1996), p. 17.

33   *"For seventeen years"*: James Creelman, "All Is Not Damned," *Pearson's Magazine*, 15, no. 6 (June 1906): 549.

33   *"Seagram's . . . only win"*: A. J. Cassatt to William Patton, Feb. 5, 1894, private family papers from the estate of Mrs. William Thayer, Shoreham, Vermont.

34   *"Mother seizes the paper"*: Mary Cassatt to A. J. Cassatt September 21, 1885, and September 2, 1886, quoted Mathews, *Cassatt and Her Circle*, pp. 196 & 201.

34   *"furnished in bird's eye maple"*: Davis, *End of the Line*, p. 123.

34   *"I am glad to say"*: Ibid., p. 128.

34   *"massive elevated stone causeway"*: Nathaniel Burt, *Perennial Philadelphians: Anatomy of an American Aristocracy* (Boston: Little, Brown, 1965), p. 193.

34   *"He is by no means a genius"*: Davis, *End of the Line*, p. 127.

35   *"first place in world's production"*: John L. Cowan, "Freeing a City from a Railroad's Control," *World's Work* 9 (1905): 5712.

36   *"disaster was imminent"*: George H. Burgess and Miles C. Kennedy, *Centennial History of the Pennsylvania Railroad Company* (Philadelphia: Pennsylvania Railroad Company, 1949), p. 455.

37   *"a droll city"*: Quoted in Russell Weigley, ed. *Philadelphia, A 300-Year History* (New York: Norton, 1982), p. 471.

37   *"No person understands better"*: "Alexander J. Cassatt," *New York Times*, June 18, 1899, p. 2.

37   *"the most intelligent and thoughtful"*: Samuel Rea, *Pennsylvania Railroad New York Tunnel Extension, Historical Outline*, Dec. 15, 1909 (Philadelphia, 1909), p. 17. Hagley Library, Wilmington, Delaware.

4. "THE NORTH RIVER BRIDGE MATTER"

38   *"Permit me to suggest"*: Gustav Lindenthal to A. J. Cassatt, Nov. 29, 1899, carton 2, folder 39, PRR Archives, Harrisburg, Pennsylvania.

38   *"Your decision"*: Gustav Lindenthal to A. J. Cassatt, July 11, 1900, carton 2, folder 39, PRR Archives, Harrisburg, Pennsylvania.

39   *"The anchorages"*: "The Proposed Great Bridge between New York and Jersey City," *Scientific American*, March 15, 1890, p. 167.

39   *"The grandeur of the project"*: Quoted in "Bridge Across the Hudson River at New York City," House of Representatives, 51st Cong., 1st sess., report no. 928, p. 40.

39   *"To propose a bridge"*: Samuel Rea, *Pennsylvania Railroad New York Tunnel
      Extension, Historical Outline*, December 15, 1909 (Philadelphia, 1909), p. 9,
      Hagley Museum and Library, Wilmington, Delaware.

39   *Though Rea had finally:* J. Lawrence Lee, "Baltimore's Belt," *Railroad His-
      tory, Spring–Summer 2005*, pp. 30–51.

40   *"In 1891 I resigned my position"*: Samuel Rea, *Pennsylvania Railroad New
      York Tunnel Extension, Historical Outline*, December 15, 1909 (Philadelphia,
      1909), p. 13, Hagley Museum and Library, Wilmington, Delaware.

41   *"I would be glad"*: Ibid., p. 14.

41   *"The railroad situation"*: Ibid., p. 57.

41   *"foot of West Thirty-fourth"*: Ibid., p. 79.

42   *"but only for small-sized cars"*: Ibid., p. 80.

43   *"back door" entry*: Ibid., pp. 7–16.

43   *"This . . . solves the problem"*: Ibid., p. 65.

43   *"No half-way solution"*: Ibid., p. 68.

44   *"Did you make an engagement"*: Samuel Rea to A. J. Cassatt, October 24,
      1899, carton 2, folder 39, PRR Archives, Harrisburg, Pennsylvania.

45   *PRR made no public announcement*: Memorandum on Great North
      Bridge, September 12, 1900, carton 2, folder 39, PRR Archives, Harrisburg,
      Pennsylvania.

45   *"a thing whose existence"*: John Moody, *The Railroad Builders* (New Haven:
      Yale University Press, 1919), p. 230.

45   *"The struggle for competitive traffic"*: George H. Burgess and Miles C. Ken-
      nedy, *Centennial History of the Pennsylvania Railroad Company* (Philadelphia:
      Pennsylvania Railroad Company, 1949), p. 455.

45   *"Cassatt had not occupied"*: Francis Barksdale, "The Pennsylvania Station in
      New York," carton 146, folder 10, Samuel Rea Papers, PRR Archives, Acces-
      sion 1810, Hagley Museum and Library, Wilmington, Delaware.

46   *"through the great volume"*: M. M. Bosworth to A. Carnegie, May 4, 1907,
      Andrew Carnegie Papers, Manuscript Division, Library of Congress, Wash-
      ington, D. C. Bosworth wrote this after Carnegie criticized the conduct of
      other millionaires active in the stock market. Bosworth was bitter because he
      had worked for Carnegie for twenty years securing secret rebates, but Carne-
      gie had failed to share "the swag."

46   *"Mr. Cassat's [sic] action"*: Andrew Carnegie to Charles Schwab, October 9,
      1900, Andrew Carnegie Papers, Manuscript Divsion, Library of Congress,
      Washington, D.C.

47   *"Overworked engines failed"*: C. M. Keys, "Cassatt and His Vision," *World's
      Work*, July 1910, p. 13199.

48   *"You have returned to harness"*: Andrew Carnegie to A. J. Cassatt, Dec. 31,
      1900, Andrew Carnegie Papers, Manuscript Division, Library of Congress,
      Washington, D.C.

48   *"Carnegie is going to demoralize"*: Joseph Frazier Wall, *Andrew Carnegie* (Pittsburgh: University of Pittsburgh Press, 1989), p. 784.

49   *"a twenty-fifth of the whole national wealth"*: Andrew Sinclair, *Corsair: The Life of J. Pierpont Morgan* (New York.: Little, Brown, 1981), p. 125.

49   *"Pierpont Morgan is apparently trying"*: Jean Strouse, *Morgan: American Financier* (New York: Random House, 1999), p. 405.

49   *"We have trampled out"*: James Creelman, "All Is Not Damned," *Pearson's Magazine* 15, no. 6 (June 1906): 552.

5. "A SEVERE DISAPPOINTMENT"

50   *"The Pennsylvania Railroad is"*: "North River Bridge Plan," *New York Times*, June 26, 1901, 6:7.

51   *"Heat was so intense"*: "Heat Brings Death To Over 200 Persons," *New York Times*, July 3, 1901, p. 1.

51   *"all the trunk lines,"* *Wall Street Journal*, July 6, 1901.

51   *"the financial syndicate"*: Gustav Lindenthal to A. J. Cassatt, September 21, 1901, carton 2, folder 39, PRR Archives, Harrisburg, Pennsylvania.

52   *"in bad repute"*: Charles F. Adams, *An Autobiography* (Boston: Houghton Mifflin, 1916), p. 193.

52   *"he was the soul of chivalry"*: "The Career of Mr. Baldwin," *Review of Reviews* 31, 2 (February 1905): 142.

52   *"freight depots"*: George H. Burgess and Miles C. Kennedy, *Centennial History of the Pennsylvania Railroad Company* (Philadelphia: Pennsylvania Railroad Company, 1949), p. 474.

52   *"quite a remarkable faculty"*: "William. H. Baldwin, Jr." *American National Biography* (New York.: Oxford University Press, 1999), p. 68.

52   *"I just want to write a line"*: *The Booker T. Washington Papers*, ed. Louis R. Harlan and Raymond W. Smock, vol. 5, 1899–1900 (Urbana: University of Illinois Press, 1977), p. 236.

53   *"That an army of strumpets"*: John Graham Brooks, *An American Citizen: The Life of William Henry Baldwin, Jr.* (Boston: Houghton Mifflin, 1910), p. 255.

53   *"fear of ridicule,"* Ibid., p. 257.

53   *"You see how impossible"*: George F. Baer to A. J. Cassatt, June 18, 1901, carton 2, folder 39, PRR Archives, Harrisburg, Pennsylvania.

54   *"If the Pennsylvania R.R. desired"*: Samuel Rea to A. J. Cassatt, carton 102, folder 32, Memorandum December 16, 1901, p. 2, PRR Archives, Harrisburg, Pennsylvania.

54   *"I should very much"*: A. J. Cassatt to John M. Hall, president New Haven line, telegram, July 3, 1901, President's Telegram Letterpress Book, no. 2, p. 203, PRR Archives, Harrisburg, Pennsylvania.

6. "IT MIGHT OFFER THE SOLUTION"

55   *"To the great majority of visitors"*: "The Park Pay Chairs," *New York Times*, July 10, 1901, p. 6.

56   *"After all it is a work of art"*: Nancy Mowll Mathews, *Mary Cassatt, a Life* (New York: Villard, 1994), p. 171.

57   *"Business very good"*: William Patton to A. J. Cassatt, Aug. 15, 1901, President's Telegram Letterpress Book, PRR Archives, Harrisburg, Pennsylvania.

57   *"No disorder,"* Ibid.

57   *"The inability to carry out"*: Samuel Rea, *Pennsylvania Railroad New York Tunnel Extension, Historical Outline*, December 15, 1909 (Philadelphia, 1909), p. 20, Hagley Museum and Library, Wilmington, Delaware.

58   *"he was much impressed"*: Ibid.

59   *"I believed it was"*: Ibid.

59   *"It was my duty"*: Ibid.

59   *"Give me a plant"*: Zach McGhee, "Charles M. Jacobs," *World's Work* 9 (January 1905): 5965.

60   *"Seldom has a construction"*: Gosta E. Sandstrom, *Tunnels* (New York: Holt, Rinehart & Winston, 1963), p. 211.

61   *"She seems to dwarf"*: "Mighty Celtic Arrives," *New-York Tribune*, Aug. 5, 1901, p. 3.

61   *"this object"*: Francis Barksdale, "The Pennsylvania Station in New York," Samuel Rea Papers, PRR Archives, Accession 1810, carton 146, folder 10, Hagley Museum and Library Wilmington, Delaware.

7. "GET A LITTLE OF THE TENDERLOIN"

64   *"I am an anarchist"*: "The Assassin Makes a Full Confession," *New York Times*, September 8, 1901, p. 1.

64   *"Now look—that damned cowboy,"* Edmund Morris, *Theodore Rex* (New York: Random House, 2001), p. 30.

64   *"Do you know that man"*: Mark Sullivan, *Our Times: The United States, America Finding Herself 1900–1925* vol. 2 (New York: Scribner's, 1927), p. 367.

64   *"We immediately started"*: Samuel Rea, *Pennsylvania Railroad New York Tunnel Extension, Historical Outline*, December 15, 1909 (Philadelphia, 1909), p. 21, Hagley Museum and Library, Wilmington, Delaware.

64   *"Last week Mr. Samuel Rea"*: Gustav Lindenthal to A. J. Cassatt, Sept. 21, 1901, carton 2, folder 2/39, PRR Archives, Harrisburg, Pennsylvania.

65   *"Even a slight settlement"*: Ibid.

65   *"the iron tunnel lining"*: Ibid.

65   *"exposed to the danger"*: Ibid.

65   *"A bridge is more"*: Ibid.

65   *"expensive to maintain"*: "Bridge Across the Hudson River at New York City," House of Representatives, 51st Cong., 1st sess., report no. 928, p. 37.

66   *"The bridge is specially designed"*: Gustav Lindenthal to A. J. Cassatt, Sept. 21, 1901, carton 2, folder 2/39, PRR Archives, Harrisburg, Pennsylvania.

66   *"with the complete plan"*: "Discussion: New York Tunnels, Pennsylvania Railroad Company," *Transactions of the American Society of Civil Engineers* 69 (October 1910): 402.

66   *"given up to the French"*: E. Idell Zeisloft, ed., *The New Metropolis* (New York: D. Appleton & Company, 1899), p. 628.

67   *"As much property as possible"*: Samuel Rea to A. J. Cassatt, memorandum, December 16, 1901, p. 2, carton102, folder 32, PRR Archives, Harrisburg, Pa.

67   *a hundred known whorehouses*: Timothy J. Gilfoyle, *City of Eros: New York City, Prostitution, and the Commercialization of Sex, 1790–1920.* (New York: W. W. Norton, 1992), p. 201.

68   *"I've been living on"*: Luc Sante, *Low Life: Lures and Snares of Old New York* (New York: Vintage: 1992), p. 17.

68   *"cheap, low-class"*: William. Baldwin to A. J. Cassatt. Memo, October 14, 1901, carton 15, folder 32/1 v. 2 PRR Archives, Harrisburg, Pennsylvania.

69   *"decent, respectable but cheap"*: Ibid.

70   *"drinking places"*: Zeisloft, *New Metropolis*, p. 626.

70   *"center for the criminal classes"*: W. T. Stead, *Satan's Invisible World Displayed* (New York: Arno Press, 1974 [1902]), p. 81.

70   *"a good class of apartment"*: William. Baldwin to A. J. Cassatt. Memo, October 14, 1901, carton 15, folder 32/1 v. 2, PRR Archives, Harrisburg, Pennsylvania.

71   *"Rule No. 1"*: Richard Butler and Joseph Driscoll, *Dock Walloper: The Story of "Big Dick" Butler* (New York: Putnam, 1933), p. 113.

72   *"on a salary of $2,750 a year"*: "Williams on the Stand," *New York Times*, December 29, 1894, p. 6.

72   *"I'm so well known"*: "Williams Denies All," *New York Times*, December 27, 1894, p. 2.

8. "CROOKED AND GREEDY"

73   *"Like many other millionaires"*: Lloyd Morris, *Incredible New York: High Life and Low Life of the Last Hundred Years* (New York: Random House, 1951), p. 229.

74   *"Croker's greatest fun"*: Lothrop Stoddard, *Master of Manhattan: The Life of Richard Croker* (New York: Longmans, Green & Co., 1931), p. 169.

75   *"Think of the hundreds of foreigners"*: Lincoln Steffens, *The Shame of the Cities* (New York: Hill & Wang, 1965 [1904]), p. 205.

75   *"They speak pleasant words"*: Ibid.

75   *"a small figure"*: William Allen White, *Masks in a Pageant* (Westport, Conn: Greenwood Press, 1971 [1928]), pp. 57–58.

76   *"use his political position"*: Theodore Roosevelt, *Theodore Roosevelt: An Autobiography* (New York: Macmillan, 1913) p. 301.

77   *"Then you are working"*: New York State Legislature, *Report of the Special Assembly Committee to Investigate the Public Offices and Departments of the City of New York* (Albany: New York State Printing Office, 1900), I:353.

78   *"There are more gambling houses"*: Ibid., 1591.

78   *"Touchin' on the question of gambling"*: City Club of New York, *Ten Months of Tammany* (New York: City Club, October 1901), p. 30.

79   *"Last fall there arose in this city"*: "Cheers for Mr. Carnegie," *New York Times*, March 18, 1901, p. 3.

79   *"honest graft"*: William Riordan, *Plunkitt of Tammany Hall* (New York: Signet Classics, 1996), p. 3.

79   *"four or five houses of ill fame"*: Committee of Fifteen, 19th Precinct Reports, Box 19-20, Humanities—Manuscripts & Archives Division, New York Public Library.

80   *"The girl in there"*: Alfred Hodder, "Fight for the City," *Outlook* 73 (January 31, 1903): 254–5.

80   *"If the people find anything is wrong"*: Stoddard, *Master of Manhattan*, p. 229.

80   *"would find his business responsibilities"*: People's Institute et al., *A Memorial to William Henry Baldwin, Jr. Cooper Union, Sunday, February Fifth, 1905* (New York: DeVinne Press, 1905), p. 12.

81   *"I have taken up this work"*: Ibid.

81   *"She got on the bed"*: Committee of Fifteen, 19th Precinct Reports, Box 19-20. Humanities—Manuscripts & Archives Division, New York Public Library.

9. "SOMEONE IN THE PENN IS LEAKING"

83   *"From early morning"*: Lothrop Stoddard, *Master of Manhattan: The Life of Richard Croker* (New York: Longmans, Green & Co., 1931), p. 252.

83   *"The purchase of that property"*: A. J. Cassatt to Samuel Rea, phone message, November 8, 1901, carton 15, folder 32/1, vol. 2, PRR Archives, Harrisburg, Pennsylvania.

84   *"We have gone systematically"*: Douglas Robinson to A. J. Cassatt, November 13, 1901, carton 15, folder 32/1, vol. 2, PRR Archives, Harrisburg, Pennsylvania.

84   *"There has been so much talk"*: Samuel Rea to A. J. Cassatt, November 13, 1901, carton 15, folder 32/1, vol. 2, PRR Archives, Harrisburg, Pennsylvania.

84   *"Do you not think"*: Ibid.

84   *"The actual work"*: Recollections of Douglas Robinson, 1910, Samuel Rea Papers, Accession 1810, carton 149, folder 7, PRR Archives, Hagley Museum and Archives, Wilmington, Delaware.

85   *"The owners being of moderate"*: Ibid.

85   *"If his price"*: Ibid.

85   *"I'm afraid someone"*: Douglas Robinson to William Baldwin, Nov. 21, 1901, carton 15, folder 32/1, vol. 2, PRR Archives, Harrisburg, Pennsylvania.

85   *"Within two weeks"*: Recollections of Douglas Robinson, 1910, Samuel Rea Papers, Accession 1810, carton 149, folder 7, PRR Archives, Hagley Museum and Library, Wilmington, Delaware.

86   *"It may be well"*: William Baldwin to A. J. Cassatt, November 21, 1901, carton 15, folder 32/1, vol. 2, PRR Archives, Harrisburg, Pennsylvania.

86   *"real estate dealers"*: "Reported P.R.R. Purchase," *New-York Tribune*, Dec. 1, 1901, p. 7

86   *"The reports about land"*: William Baldwin to A. J. Cassatt, Dec. 2, 1901, carton 15, folder 32/1, vol. 2, PRR Archives, Harrisburg, Pennsylvania.

86   *"like a Chinese wall"*: Hilary Ballon, *New York's Pennsylvania Station* (New York: W. W. Norton, 2002), p. 35.

10. "THE TOWN IS ON FIRE"

88   *"It was hoped"*: A. J. Cassatt, memorandum, December 23, 1901, board file 269, carton 39, PRR Archives, Harrisburg, Pennsylvania.

88   *"It was deemed necessary"*: Ibid.

88   *"Until the announcement"*: "Pa. Road To Tunnel Into City," *New York World*, December 12, 1901, p. 1.

88   *"The line as adopted"*: Ibid.

89   *"one of the greatest"*: Charles Jacobs to James McCrea, July 31, 1909, carton 102, folder 32/22, PRR Archives, Harrisburg, Pennsylvania.

90   *"Tunnels of the kind"*: Charles W. Raymond, "The New York Tunnel Extension of the PRR," *Transactions of the American Society of Civil Engineers* 68 (September 1910): 21.

90   *"believed there was a drift"*: Samuel Rea, "Engineering and Transportation," *Journal of the Franklin Institute*, June 1926, p. 685.

90   *"sublime exhibition of faith"*: "The Faith that Digs Tunnels," *Wall Street Journal*, March 26, 1903, p. 1.

90   *"an underground bridge"*: "Five Great Trunk Lines," *New York Herald*, December 13, 1901, p. 5.

90   *"Electricity and modern science"*: "Tunnel Station at Quai D'Orsay," *New York Herald*, December 14, 1901, p. 3.

90   *"There will not be any smoke"*: "Pa. Road To Tunnel Into City," *New York World*, December 12, 1901, p. 1.

92   *"The town is on fire"*: William Baldwin to A. J. Cassatt, December 14, 1901, carton 102, folder 32/25, PRR Archives, Harrisburg, Pennsylvania.

93   *"George wore fine clothes"*: Maury Klein, "George J. Gould" in *Railroads in the Age of Regulation, 1900–1980*, ed. Keith L. Bryant, Jr., *Encyclopedia of American Business History and Biography* (N.Y.: Facts on File, 1988), p. 168.

93   *"Oh, Hell!"*: Lothrop Stoddard, *Master of Manhattan: The Life of Richard Croker* (New York: Longmans, Green & Co., 1931), p. 210.

94   *"Had Mr. Roebling"*: David McCullough, *The Great Bridge* (New York.: Touchstone, 1982), p. 493.

94   *"A good part of"*: Ibid., p. 288.

95   *"more than ten thousand miles"*: Charles S. Gleed, "A.J. Cassatt," *Cosmopolitan* 33 (Aug. 1902): 421–23.

95   *"The New York law"*: Memorandum of report to PRR board, April 22, 1902, carton 102, folder 32/23, PRR Archives, Harrisburg, Pennsylvania.

96   *"inconceivably low"*: *Beatrice Webb's American Diary, 1898*, ed. David A. Shannon (Madison: University of Wisconsin Press, 1963), p. 63.

96   *"I have been all over"*: Samuel Rea to A. J. Cassatt, telephone message, Dec. 24, 1901, carton 15, folder 32/1 vol. 2, PRR Archives, Harrisburg, Pennsylvania.

97   *"Before you decide"*: Samuel Rea to A. J. Cassatt, telephone message, Jan. 7, 1902, carton 15, folder 32/1 vol. 2, PRR Archives, Harrisburg, Pennsylvania.

97   *"coming up Cortlandt Street"*:"The Head of the Pennsylvania," *New York Times*, December 28, 1902, p. 22.

98   *"In his presence"*: Frank H. Spearman, *The Strategy of Great Railroads* (New York: Scribner's, 1906), p. 32.

98   *"The very dogs"*: Eliot Gregory, "Nation in a Hurry," *Atlantic Monthly* 85 (May 1900): 609.

11. "WE SHALL MAKE OUR FIGHT ABOVEBOARD"

100   *"If I help you"*: James Creelman, "All Is Not Damned," *Pearson's Magazine* 15, no. 6 (June 1906): 554.

100   *"We shall require some legislation"*: A. J. Cassatt to Senator Quay, January 16, 1902, carton 15, folder 32/29, PRR Archives, Harrisburg, Pennsylvania.

101   *"silent in sixteen"*: James A. Kehl, *Boss Rule in the Gilded Age: Matt Quay of Pennsylvania* (Pittsburgh: University of Pittsburgh Press, 1981), p. xv.

101   *"Mr. Frank Platt"*: William Baldwin to A. J. Cassatt, January 21, 1902, carton 15, folder 32/29, PRR Archives, Harrisburg, Pennsylvania.

101 *"On further reflection"*: A. J. Cassatt to T. C. Platt, January 24, 1902, Thomas Collier Platt Papers, Yale University Library, New Haven, Connecticut (hereafter referred to as Platt Papers).

101 *"You have placed us"*: A. J. Cassatt to T. C. Platt, February 27, 1902, Platt Papers.

102 *"did not comprehend"*: William. Allen White, *Masks in a Pageant* (Westport, Conn.: Greenwood Press, 1971 [1928]), p. 21.

102 *"sitting around the corridors"*: Citizens Unions, *The Best Administration New York Ever Had* (New York: Committee on Press and Literature of the Citizens Union, 1903), pp. 63–64.

103 *"There was no secrecy"*: "The Pennsylvania Tunnel," *New-York Tribune*, March 22, 1902, p. 8:1.

104 *"To get a perpetual charter"*: "Tunnel Bill Opposed," *New-York Tribune*, March 22, 1902, p. 3:1.

104 *"perfectly willing to pay"*: "More Opposition to Pennsylvania's Bill," *New York Times*, March 21, 1902, p. 5:1.

104 *"from the record made"*: "For Its Exclusive Use," *New-York Tribune*, March 25, 1902, p. 3:2.

104 *"There will be no room"*: Ibid.

104 *"No one in this community"*: "Thought Low Would Veto," *New-York Tribune*, March 25, 1902, p. 3:2.

105 *"We do not know just"*: "For Its Exclusive Use," *New-York Tribune*, March 25, 1902, p. 3:1.

12. "UGLY RUMORS OF BOODLE"

106 *"It is infamous"*: "A Colossal Robbery of the People," *Journal American*, March 26, 1902.

106 *"an administration of men"*: "The Trouble with Reform," *Journal American*, March 4, 1902.

106 *"[Low] does know"*: Ibid.

107 *"Though he continued to dress like a dandy"*: David Nasaw, *The Chief* (Boston: Houghton Mifflin 2000), p. 106.

108 *"Pulitzer was left"*: Ibid., p. 105.

108 *"Pulitzer had become"*: Ibid.

109 *"The Board of Aldermen"*: "Now For P.R.R. Tunnel," *New-York Tribune*, April 16, 1902, p. 4:6.

109 *"Mr. Carvalho assured me"*: George Boyd to William A. Patton, April 17, 1902, carton 15, folder 32/29, PRR Archives, Harrisburg, Pennsylvania.

110 *"city has received"*: "Approve P.R.R. Franchise," *New-York Tribune*, June 16, 1902, p. 14:4.

110 *"one face more repulsive"*: Beatrice Webb's American Diary, 1898, David A. Shannon, ed. (Madison: University of Wisconsin Press, 1963), p. 63.

111 *"that the company would not pay"*: "Fear A Franchise Lobby," New-York Tribune, July 10, 1902, p. 14:3.

111 *"No vote of mine"*: "Aldermen Fight the Pennsylvania Franchise," New York Times, July 12, 1902, p. 1.

111 *"scab labor"*: "Seven Aldermen Opposed," New-York Tribune, July 12, 1902, p. 3:1.

111 *"Great public improvement"*: "Our Obstructive Alderman," Commercial Advertiser, July 23, 1902.

112 *"It is a veiled"*: "The Aldermen and the Tunnel Franchise," World, July 23, 1902.

112 *"Let us give credit"*: "Refusing a Railroad's Bid Does Not Make Aldermen Criminals," Journal American, Juy 24, 1902, p. TK

112 *"straightforward and manly"*: "Mayor on Aldermen's Action on the Tunnel," New York Times, July 24, 1902, p. 2:8.

112 *"true Roosevelt style"*: Kathleen Dalton, Theodore Roosevelt: A Strenuous Life (New York: Knopf, 2002), p. 218.

113 *"No sane man"*: "PRR and Eight Hour Law," New-York Tribune, August 6, 1902, p. 1:3.

113 *"We have come here"*: Ibid.

113 *"Had to listen"*: Capt. Green to A. J. Cassatt, August 6, 1902, carton 15, folder 32/33, PRR Archives, Harrisburg, Pennsylvania.

113 *"The rights and interests"*: Edmund Morris, Theodore Rex (New York: Random House, 2001), p. 137.

114 *"I am at my wits':"* Ibid., p. 151.

114 *"It is asking very much"*: A. J. Cassatt to Abram S. Hewitt, Sept. 28, 1902, carton 15, folder 32/33, PRR Archives, Harrisburg, Pennsylvania.

115 *"miracle . . . of connecting"*: "Tunnel Franchise Clauses Discussed," New York Times, October 3, 1902, p. 5:1.

115 *"It has made its proposition"*: Ibid.

115 *"Public opinion"*: "The Pennsylvania Franchise," New York Times, October 11, 1902, p. 8:2.

116 *"The Dollar-Rooting"*: "The Dollar-Rooting Swine of the Anthracite Fields," Journal American, December 11, 1902.

116 *"throwing up my hands"*: Dalton, Theodore Roosevelt, p. 237.

117 *"the railroad interests"*: "Bitter words at Hearing on P.RR. Tunnel," New York World, November 27, 1902, p. 2.

117 *"If this rich corporation"*: Ibid.

117 *"I am sure"*: Ibid.

117 *"If we don't get permission"*: Ibid.

117   *"clique . . . determined to extort"*: "PRR Gives Warning," *New-York Tribune*, November 27, 1902, p. 1.

117   *"We have come to New York"*: "Ugly Rumors of Boodle," *New York World*, November 29, 1902, p. 4:4.

118   *"There is not an honest"*: "Appealing to the Legislature," *New York Times*, December 8, 1902, p. 8:1.

118   *"one of the most shamefaced"*: "The Pennsylvania Railroad Tunnel," *Scientific American*, December 6, 1902, p. 372.

118   *"a perpetual menace"*: "The Aldermen and the Pennsylvania Tunnel," *New York Times*, December 7, 1902, p. 32–33.

118   *"every daily newspaper"*: "The Pennsylvania Tunnel," *Railroad Gazette*, December 12, 1901, p. 94.

119   *"not to deprive"*: " 'Little Tim' Says 'No,' " *New-York Tribune*, December 14, 1902, p. 2:4.

119   *"No power on earth"*: Ibid.

119   *"an example to other corporations"*: "The Franchise," *Railroad Gazette*, December 19, 1902, p. 962.

120   *"It means, if accepted"*: "The Franchise Goes Over," *New-York Tribune*, December 10, 1902, p. 1.

120   *"during every minute"*: "Pennsylvania Tunnel Franchise Passed," *New York Times*, December 17, 1902, p. 1.

120   *"If you pass"*: Ibid.

121   *"The great thing"*: "The Aldermen Yield," *New York Times*, December 17, 1902, p. 8:1.

122   *"It looks like"*: "Victory for Pennsy Tunnel Franchise," *New York World*, December 17, 1902, p. 1.

13. "WE ARE NOT MAKING A MISTAKE"

128   *"almost pathetic"*: "Deserted Part of the City," *New-York Tribune*, June 5, 1902.

129   *"Foul Tenderloin!"*: "The Deserted Village in the Tenderloin," *New York Herald*, May 10, 1903, Literary Section, p. 6

129   *"factories and rookeries"*: E. Idell Zeisloft, ed., *The New Metropolis* (New York: D. Appleton & Company, 1899), p. 616.

131   *"The simple homely virtues"*: "Memoir of Alfred Noble," *Transactions of the American Society of Civil Engineers* 79 (December 1915): 1357.

131   *"The great Corps of Privates"*: Ibid.

131   *"Ability to withstand"*: Ibid.

132   *"Procure all additional"*: William Couper, ed., *History of the Engineering, Construction, and Equipment of the Pennsylvania Railroad Company's Terminal and Approaches* (New York: Isaac H. Blanchard, 1912), p. 10

132   *"The main consideration"*: Charles Raymond, "The New York Tunnel Extension of the Pennsylvania Railroad Company," *Transactions of the American Society of Civil Engineers* 68 (September 1910): 17.

132   *"about the most treacherous"*: "The Pa. and LIRR Extensions Across the North and East Rivers," *Engineering News*, December 19, 1901, p. 473.

132   *"Can a proper tunnel"*: Samuel Rea, *Pennsylvania Railroad New York Tunnel Extension, Historical Outline*, December 15, 1909 (Philadelphia, 1909), p. 13, Hagley Museum and Library, Wilmington, Delaware.

133   *"led capitalists and engineers"*: Charles Jacobs, "The New York Tunnel Extension of the Pennsylvania Railroad Company: North River Division," *Transactions of the American Society of Civil Engineers* 68 (September 1910): 42.

133   *"I cannot believe"*: A. J. Cassatt to Fowler, Jan. 5, 1903, and clipping of that day's *New York Times*, carton 15, folder 32/33, PRR Archives, Harrisburg, Pennsylvania.

133   *"to 112½, its lowest"*: "Pressure on P.R.R. Stock," *New-York Tribune*, November 12, 1903, p. 4:3.

134   *"Mr. Cassatt has"*: "Mr. Cassatt's Policy," *Wall Street Journal*, July 13, 1903, p. 2.

134   *"We are planning"*: A. J. Cassatt to Samuel Rea, August 29, 1904, carton 21, folder 32/157 v. 1, PRR Archives, Harrisburg, Pennsylvania.

135   *"I think the section"*: A. J. Cassatt to E. H. Harriman, July 16, 1902, carton 17, folder 32/76–90, PRR Archives, Harrisburg, Pennsylvania.

135   *"called for the construction"*: Couper, *History of Engineering, Construction, and Equipment*, p. 11

135   *"The limiting features"*: Ibid.

14. "A WORK UNSOUGHT"

139   *"in the line of"*: William Baldwin to A. J. Cassatt, Jan. 14, 1902, carton 15, folder 32/20 v. 1, PRR Archives, Harrisburg, Pennsylvania.

139   *"for the privilege of competing"*: Samuel Rea to Wayne MacVeagh, April 10, 1902, carton 15, folder 32/20 v. 1, PRR Archives, Harrisburg, Pennsylvania.

140   *"It is a matter"*: Ibid.

141   *"I suppose President Cassatt"*: Charles Moore, *The Life and Times of Charles Follen McKim* (Boston: Houghton Mifflin, 1929), p 273.

141   *"the largest and most important"*: Samuel G. White, *The Houses of McKim, Mead & White* (New York: Rizzoli, 1998), pp. 10–11.

142   *"scuffed wooden stairs"*: Edmund Morris, *Theodore Rex* (New York: Random House), p. 174.

142   *"restored to"*: Ibid.

142   *"The whole thing is so"*: Moore, *The Life and Times of Charles Follen McKim*, p 206.

143   *"It is much easier"*: Patricia T. Davis, *End of the Line: Alexander J. Cassatt and the Pennsylvania Railroad* (New York: Neale Watson Academic Publications, 1978), p. 137.

143   *"I passed the morning"*: Moore, *The Life and Times of Charles Follen McKim*, p. 274.

143   *"He saw beauty"*: Ibid., p. 58.

144   *"Some of those associated"*: Paul R. Baker, *Stanny: The Gilded Life of Stanford White* (New York: Free Press, 1989), pp. 81–82.

144   *"Everything is all right:"* Moore, *The Life and Times of Charles Follen McKim*, p. 284.

145   *"bubbling with enthusiasm"*: Baker, *Stanny*, p. 83.

146   *"hired draftsmen"*: Ibid.

146   *"brought in little business"*: Suzannah Lessard, *The Architect of Desire: Beauty and Danger in the Stanford White Family* (New York: Dial Press, 1996), p. 83.

146   *"I beg to say that your firm"*: A. J. Cassatt to Charles McKim, April 4, 1902, carton 15, folder 32/13–19, PRR Archives, Harrisburg, Pennsylvania.

147   *"I am thinking"*: Moore, *The Life and Times of Charles Follen McKim*, p. 214.

147   *"an eighteen story"*: Samuel Rea to A. J. Cassatt, telegram April 30, 1902, carton 15, folder 32/13–19, PRR Archives, Harrisburg, Pennsylvania.

147   *"surrounded by a jumbled mass"*: Christopher Weeks, *AIA Guide to Architecture of Washington, D.C.*, third edition (Baltimore: Johns Hopkins University Press, 1974), p. 54.

147   *"That afternoon"*: Moore, *The Life and Times of Charles Follen McKim*, p. 192.

148   *"Since you gentlemen"*: Ibid., p. 198.

148   *"McKim argued"*: Ibid., p. 274.

148   *"She has been studying"*: Davis, *End of the Line*, p. 129.

149   *"cut out two or more tracks"*: "New York Terminal Situation: Central and Pennsylvania," *Wall Street Journal*, September 4, 1912.

149   *"Confidence"*: Hilary Ballon, *New York's Pennsylvania Stations* (New York: W. W. Norton, 2002), p. 53.

149   *"While McKim had pinned"*: Moore, *The Life and Times of Charles Follen McKim*, p. 276.

149   *"liked to sit"*: Lessard, *Architect of Desire*, p. 83.

150   *"at the Baths of Caracalla"*: Moore, *The Life and Times of Charles Follen McKim*, pp. 274–75.

15. "DRILLING OF FIRST HOLE"

151 *"the present unfortunate and mortifying"*: A. J. Cassatt to H. C. Frick, Jan. 25, 1903, Archives, Frick Collection, New York.

151 *"jammed with cars"*: John L. Cowan, "Freeing a City From a Railroad's Control," *World's Work* 9 (1905): 5713.

152 *"This was probably as drastic"*: George H. Burgess and Miles C. Kennedy, *Centennial History of the Pennsylvania Railroad Company* (Philadelphia: Pennsylvania Railroad Company, 1949), p. 516.

153 *"with the hope"*: Charles Jacobs to A. J. Cassatt, March 14, 1904, carton 18, folder 32/14–155, PRR Archives, Harrisburg, Pennsylvania.

154 *"This is a very difficult"*: Samuel Rea to A. J. Cassatt, January 12, 1904, carton 2, folder 32/1, v. 2, PRR Archives, Harrisburg, Pennsylvania.

155 *"monumental in character"*: A. J. Cassatt to Henry C. Payne, February 9, 1903, carton 17, folder 32/195, v. 1, PRR Archives, Harrisburg, Pennsylvania.

155 *"400 congressmen"*: Douglas Robinson to A. J. Cassatt, February 14, 1903, carton 17, folder 32/195, v. 1, PRR Archives, Harrisburg, Pennsylvania.

156 *"The appealing human element"*: Lincoln Steffens, *The Shame of the Cities* (New York: Hill & Wang, 1957 [1904]), pp. 200–201.

157 *"I am out of politics"*: Lothrop Stoddard, *Master of Manhattan: The Life of Richard Croker* (New York: Longmans, Green & Co., 1931), p. 258.

157 *"with a Mr. Gay"*: William Patton to A. J. Cassatt, memorandum, December 18, 1903, carton 15, folder 32/20, v. 1, PRR Archives, Harrisburg, Pennsylvania.

157 *"Mr. Murphy would be very glad"*: Ibid.

158 *"The Connecting Railroad"*: "Communication to Hon. G. B. McClellan and Hon. Alexander Orr from A. J. Cassatt," January 18, 1906, p. 6, carton 47, folder 12/59, PRR Archives, Harrisburg, Pennsylvania.

158 *"very stiff"*: Samuel Rea to A. J. Cassatt, March 26, 1904, carton 15, folder 32/20, v. 1. PRR Archives, Harrisburg, Pennsylvania.

158 *"Belmont does not intend"*: William Baldwin to A. J. Cassatt, January 28, 1904, carton 18, folder 32/132–32/139, PRR Archives, Harrisburg, Pennsylvania.

159 *"Could I ask the favor?"*: John A. Gleeson to A. J. Cassatt, April 30, 1904, carton 15, folder 32/1, v. 2, PRR Archives, Harrisburg, Pennsylvania.

160 *"faint lights flashing"*: "Tunneling the Hudson," *New-York Tribune*, May 29, 1904, sec. 2, p. 3:2

160 *"two ragged arches"*: Ibid.

160 *"Mr. Baldwin is very sick"*: Louis R. Harlan and Raymond W. Smock, eds., *The Booker T. Washington Papers*, vol 8, *1904–6* (Urbana: University of Illinois Press, 1979) p. 28

161 *"I have been thinking of him"*: Ibid., p. 36

161   *"I sincerely hope"*: Samuel Rea to A. J. Cassatt, August 5, 1904, carton 15, folder 32/1, v. 2, PRR Archives, Harrisburg, Pennsylvania.

161   *"You can bet"*: "Aldermanic Firms Gets 'Pennsy' Job," *New York Herald*, June 21, 1904, p. 1.

161   *"We will have to remove"*: Ibid.

162   *"It was a carnival night"*: "Our Subway Open, 150,000 Try It," *New York Times*, October 28, 1904, p. 1.

162   *"He has hit Pierpont"*: *The Letters of Henry Adams (1892–1918)*, Worthington Chauncey Ford, ed. (Boston: Houghton Mifflin, 1938), p. 373.

163   *"It tires me"*: Edmund Morris, *Theodore Rex* (New York: Random House, 2001), p. 360.

163   *"consolidated into 257"*: Jean Strouse, *Morgan: American Financier* (New York: Random House, 1999), p. 396.

16. "THE SHIELD IS READY TO BE SHOVED"

165   *"nearly akin to the life"*: William Couper, ed., *History of the Engineering, Construction, and Equipment of the Pennsylvania Railroad Company's New York Terminal and Approaches* (New York: Isacc H. Blanchard, 1914), p. 77.

166   *"We may have to give up"*: A. J. Cassatt to Samuel Rea, September 1, 1904, carton 17, folder 32/61, PRR Archives, Harrisburg, Pennsylvania.

166   *"leave off the elevated"*: A. J. Cassatt to McKim, Mead & White, December 2, 1904, carton 15, folder 32/13–19, PRR Archives, Harrisburg, Pennsylvania.

166   *"I am quite sure"*: A. J. Cassatt to McKim, Mead & White, May 1, 1905, carton 15, folder 32/13–19, PRR Archives, Harrisburg, Pennsylvania.

167   *"broke down and sobbed"*: Suzannah Lessard, *The Architect of Desire: Beauty and Danger in the Stanford White Family* (New York: Dial Press, 1996), p. 217.

167   *"I have had to carry more"*: Paul R. Baker, *Stanny: The Gilded Life of Stanford White* (New York: Free Press, 1989), p. 353.

167   *"I found that he was"*: A. J. Cassatt to J. T. Richards, July 18, 1906, carton 15, folders 32/24, PRR Archives, Harrisburg, Pennsylvania.

169   *"Your only view of the outside"*: Arthur B. Reeve, "The Romance of Tunnel Building," *World's Work* 13 (December 1906): 8338.

170   *"A man in a state of coma"*: Reeve, "Romance of Tunnel Building,"

172   *"rather less progress"*: Charles Jacobs to A. J. Cassatt, April 7, 1905, p. 2, carton 18, folder 32/156 v. 1., PRR Archives, Harrisburg, Pennsylvania.

172   *"had to be cut"*: B.H.M. Hewett and W. L. Brown, "The New York Tunnel Extension of the PRR—The North River Tunnels," *Transactions of the American Society of Civil Engineers*, 68 (September 1910): 248.

172 *"100th or last pile"*: Charles Jacobs to A. J. Cassatt, April 12, 1906, p. 1, carton 18, folder 32/156, v. 1., PRR Archives, Harrisburg, Pennsylvania.

173 *"washed away"*: Ibid.

173 *"blanket consisting"*: Ibid.

173 *"A blanket formed by canvas"*: Charles Jacobs to A. J. Cassatt, May 11, 1906, carton 18, folder 32/156 v. 1, PRR Archives, Harrisburg, Pennsylvania.

173 *"You can feel that it is cooler"*: Reeve, "Romance of Tunnel Building," p. 8338.

173 *"men pushing little cars"*: Ibid., p. 8339.

174 *"At first glance"*: Ibid., p. 8349.

175 *"the first time"*: Ibid., p. 8341.

175 *"By and by one of the men"*: Ibid., p. 8342.

175 *"Like the jumping toothache"*: Ibid., p. 8349.

176 *"simple problem of trigonometry"*: Ibid., p. 8348.

176 *"With the tunnels in a constant"*: James Forgie, "Construction of the Pennsylvania Railroad Tunnels Under the Hudson River at New York City," *Engineering News* 57, no. 9 (February 28, 1907): 228.

177 *"A flat car"*: William Couper, ed., *History of the Engineering, Construction, and Equipment of the Pennsylvania Railroad's New York Terminal and Approaches* (New York: Isaac H. Blanchard, 1912), p. 48.

177 *"As a result"*: Ibid., p. 49.

180 *"an immense circular hole"*: "Erie Yard Falls Into Pennsylvania Tunnel," *New York Times*, February 15, 1905, p. 1.

180 *"not a serious,"* Ibid.

180 *"Fortunately, the mud"*: Charles Jacobs to A. J. Cassatt, March 11, 1905, carton 18, folder 32/156 v. 1, PRR Archives, Harrisburg, Pennsylvania.

17. "SLOW PROGRESS HAS BEEN MADE"

181 *"Mr. Jacobs is not"*: Zach McGhee, "Charles M. Jacobs," *World's Work* 9 (Janaury 1905): 5966–67.

183 *"As I entered the tunnel"*: William G. McAdoo, *Crowded Years: The Reminiscences of William G. McAdoo* (Boston: Houghton Mifflin, 1931), p. 73.

183 *"As soon as we began"*: Ibid., p. 79.

184 *"My instinctive feeling"*: Ibid., p. 86.

184 *"I told Cassatt"*: Ibid., p. 87.

185 *"The brevity of the discussion"*: Ibid.

185 *"I and a few others"*: Ibid. p. 87.

185 *"Henry Hudson"*: Zach McGhee, "Charles M. Jacobs," *World's Work* 9 (January 1905): 5966.

186 *"It's an interesting job"*: "Biggest Hole Ever Dug in the Island of Manhattan," *Washington Post*, August. 20, 1905, p. G3.

187 *"Fire Department flushes"*: Rupert Hughes, *The Real New York* (New York: Smart Set Publishing Co, 1904), p. 297.

187 *"pushed more rapidly"*: A. J. Cassatt to Samuel Rea, August 14, 1905, carton 37, folder 48/6, PRR Archives, Harrisburg, Pennsylvania.

188 *"capitalists and engineers"*: Charles Jacobs, "The New York Tunnel Extension of the Pennsylvania Railroad, The North River Division," *Transactions of the American Society of Civil Engineers* 68 (September 1910): 42.

188 *"The leakage of air"*: Charles Jacobs to A. J. Cassatt, Oct. 5, 1905, carton 18, folder 32/131–39, PRR Archives, Harrisburg, Pennsylvania.

188 *"Owing to the inability"*: Charles Jacobs to A. J. Cassatt, Dec. 7, 1905, carton 18, folder 32/131–39, PRR Archives, Harrisburg, Pennsylvania.

188 *"the average progress"*: Ibid.

188 *"passed under"*: Ibid.

189 *"distorted . . . the horizontal"*: Charles Jacobs to A. J. Cassatt, February 7, 1906, carton 18, folder 32/131–39, PRR Archives, Harrisburg, Pennsylvania.

189 *"The material in the face"*: Ibid.

189 *"A good many different"*: Charles W. Raymond, *The Pennsylvania Company New York Tunnel Extension–North River Tunnels*. Report and Conclusions on Proposed Supports and Foundations, December 1, 1911, p. 37, PRR Archives. Railroad Museum of Pennsylvania, Strasburg, Pennsylvania.

189 *"It was impossible"*: Ibid.

190 *"The shield began to come down"*: Ibid.

190 *"166 rings"*: Charles Jacobs to A. J. Cassatt, March 8, 1906, carton 18, folder 32/131–39, PRR Archives, Harrisburg, Pennsylvania.

18. "DISTURBED ABOUT NORTH RIVER TERMINAL"

191 *"Dear Mr. Cassatt"*: Samuel Rea to Alexander Cassatt, April 2, 1906, carton 2, folder 32/170, PRR Archives, Harrisburg, Pennsylvania.

192 *"General was insistent"*: Ibid.

192 *"there had been a rise"*: Ibid.

192 *"like the movement"*: Theodore Heizmann to Alexander Cassatt, February 17, 1902, carton 15, folder 32/12, PRR Archives, Harrisburg, Pennsylvania.

193 *"In Line A"*: Alfred Noble to A. J. Cassatt, April 11, 1906, carton 18, folder 32/132–139, PRR Archives, Harrisburg, Pennsylvania.

195 *"The cry arises"*: Ray Stannard Baker, "Railroad Rebates," *McClure's Magazine*, December 1905, p. 180.

195 *"frequently elected"*: Edmund Morris, *Theodore Rex* (New York: Random House, 2001), p. 443.

196 *"Railroad rate regulation"*: Ibid.

196 *"An Alphabet of Joyous Trusts"*: Roger Butterfield, *The American Past: A*

History of the United States from Concord to the Great Society (New York: Simon & Schuster, 1966), p. 329.

196   *"is not like any other industry"*: "The Railroads on Trial," *McClure's Magazine*, November 1905, p. 672.

196   *"Great corporations"*: "The Case Against the Railroads," *World's Work* 9 (1905): 5890.

197   *"We bought the bastard"*: Samuel A. Schreiner, *Henry Clay Frick* (New York: St. Martin's Press, 1995), p. 237.

197   *"I very much fear"*: Patricia T. Davis, *End of the Line, Alexander Cassatt and the Pennsylvania Railroad* (New York: Neale Watson Academic Publications, 1978), p. 177.

197   *"the increasing power"*: James Creelman, "All Is Not Damned," *Pearson's Magazine* 15, No. 6 (June 1906): 550.

197   *"Will you give me"*: Theodore Roosevelt to A. J. Cassatt, October 19, 1901, Papers of President Theodore Roosevelt, Manuscript Division, Library of Congress, Washington, D.C.

197   *"Let the government regulate"*: Creelman, "All Is Not Damned," p. 552.

198   *"The ability of a member"*: Mark Sullivan, *Our Times: The United States, 1900–1925, vol. 3, Pre-War America* (New York: Scribner's, 1971 [1930]), p. 205.

198   *"probably the most courageous"*: "Cassatt and the Pennsylvania," *Wall Street Journal*, May 22, 1906, p. 6.

198   *"You will deny the railroads"*: A. J. Cassatt to Theodore Roosevelt, Feb. 26, 1906, Papers of President Theodore Roosevelt, Manuscript Division, Library of Congress, Washington, D.C.

199   *"If the Commission desires"*: Davis, *End of the Line*, p. 184.

199   *"until some agreement"*: Samuel Rea to Alexander Cassatt, April 4, 1906, carton 21, folder 32/170, PRR Archives, Harrisburg, Pennsylvania.

200   *"the stability"*: Charles W. Raymond, *The Pennsylvania Company New York Tunnel Extension–North River Tunnels*, Report and Conclusions on Proposed Supports and Foundations, December 1, 1911, p. 37, PRR Archives, Railroad Museum of Pennsylvania, Strasburg, Pennsylvania.

200   *"Approximately 50%"*: Charles Jacobs to A. J. Cassatt, May 11, 1905, carton 18, folder 32/156, v. 1, PRR Archives, Harrisburg, Pennsylvania.

201   *"bending and distorting"*: Raymond, "Report and Conclusions," p. 45.

201   *"changes in the elevation"*: Ibid., p. 46.

19. "WOULD MR. CASSATT BE RESIGNING?"

202   *"We all live"*: Samuel Rea to A. J. Cassatt, June 11, 1905, carton 37, folder 48/6, PRR Archives, Harrisburg, Pennsylvania.

203   *"I was so rejoiced"*: Patricia T. Davis, *End of the Line: Alexander Cassatt and*

the *Pennsylvania Railroad* (New York: Neale Watson Academic Publications, 1978), p. 184.

203   *"I do not give"*: "A. J. Cassatt in London," *New York Times*, May 18, 1906, p. 2.

204   *"acceptance of gratuities"*: "Gifts to High and Low on Pennsylvania Road," *New York Times*, May 19, 2005, p. 1.

204   *"the public will be strongly"*: Captain Green to A. J. Cassatt, May 18, 1906, carton 46, folder 57/22, PRR Archives, Harrisburg, Pennsylvania.

204   *"The sand oozed"*: "Air Leaks Stop Work on East River Tunnels," *New York Times*, May 20, 1906, p. 1.

205   *"It takes an enormous heap"*: Ibid.

205   *"In appearance"*: "The Pennsylvania Railroad's Extension to New York and Long Island," press release, McKim, Mead & White Papers, Department of Prints, Photographs, and Architectural Collections, New-York Historical Society, New York.

206   *"a steel skeleton"*: Hilary Ballon, *New York's Pennsylvania Station* (New York: W. W. Norton, 2002), p. 50.

206   *"stronger and better able"*: Samuel Rea to A. J. Cassatt, Feb. 27, 1906, carton 15, folder 32/20, PRR Archives, Harrisburg, Pennsylvania.

206   *"Notwithstanding Mr. Frick's"*: Ibid.

207   *"We are coming up"*: *The Reminiscences of Augustus Saint-Gaudens*, Homer Saint-Gaudens, ed., 2 (New York: Century, 1913), p. 251.

207   *"a stag event"*: Suzannah Lessard, *The Architect of Desire: Beauty and Danger in the Stanford White Family* (New York: Dial Press, 1996), p. 13.

207   *"All well"*: William Patton to A. J. Cassatt, telegram, May 22, 1906, President's Telegram Book, PRR Archives, Harrisburg, Pennsylvania.

208   *"tremendous courage"*: "Cassatt and the Pennsylvania Investigation," *Wall Street Journal*, May 22, 1906, p. 6.

208   *"It has been an open secret"*: Ibid.

208   *"It was brought out"*: "Pennsylvania Inquiry," *Wall Street Journal*, May 24, 1906.

208   *"owing to the lack of cars"*: "Pennsylvania Board Orders Full Inquiry," *New York Times*, May 24, 1906, p. 1.

209   *"As soon as I saw"*: Davis, *End of the Line*, p. 186.

209   *"the outrageous action"*: Ibid.

209   *"I suppose because"*: "Cassatt Hurries Home From European Trip," *New York Times*, May 26, 1906, p. 1.

20. "DEATH STALKS ALONGSIDE THEM"

210   *"Stalwart, deep-chested"*: "Cassatt Home to Answer," *Journal American*, June 4, 1906, p. 1.

211 *"seemed like a man on the verge"*: "Cassatt Home; Defends Pennsy Graft," *Philadelphia North American*, June 4, 1906, p. 1.

211 *"would not sacrifice"*: "Cassatt Back, Promises A Searching Inquiry," *New York Times*, June 4, 1906, p. 1.

211 *"taken the company out"*: Ibid.

212 *"the unusual number of men"*: "Coroner Shrady Demands Safety for Tunnel Men," *New York Herald*, June 4, 1906, p. 1.

212 *"that same day"*: "Tunnel Men Disagree," *New-York Tribune*, June 6, 1906, p. 9:3.

212 *"I do not see"*: Ibid.

213 *"What did you do"*: "Two RR Clerks Got $97,000 in Gifts," *New York Times*, June 7, 1906, p. 3.

213 *"Mr. Cassatt is not"*: "Frick Breaks Long Silence to Uphold Cassatt," *Philadelphia Press*, June 13, 1906.

213 *"I cannot adequately express"*: A. J. Cassatt to H. C. Frick, June 13, 1906, Archives, Frick Collection, New York.

213 *"Enough has been"*: Patricia T. Davis, *End of the Line: Alexander Cassatt and the Pennsylvania Railroad* (New York: Neale Watson Academic Publications, 1978), p. 192.

214 *"spirit of exaltation"*: "Pennsylvania's House Cleaning," *Wall Street Journal*, May 26, 1906, p. 1.

214 *"over the lavish expenditure"*: "Foreign Markets," *London Times*, May 29, 1906, p. 11.

215 *"the contractors"*: "East River Tunnels Meet the Hardest Luck," *New York Times*, June 28, 1906, p. 1.

215 *"the difficult feature"*: "Says Tunnel Delays Are Not Alarming," *New York Times*, June 30, 1906, p. 1.

215 *"Occasionally a man"*: Ibid.

215 *"Most of the alarm"*: Ibid.

216 *"the Interstate Commerce Commission"*: W. A. Patton to A. J. Cassatt, telephone message, June 22, 1906, carton 46, folder 54/40, PRR Archives, Harrisburg, Pennsylvania.

216 *"if proved"*: "May Pick Cassatt for Prosecution," *New York Times*, June 25, 1906, p. 1.

217 *"My God!"*: Suzannah Lessard, *The Architect of Desire: Beauty and Danger in the Stanford White Family* (New York: Dial Press, 1996), p. 241.

217 *"He deserved it"*: Paul R. Baker, *Stanny: The Gilded Life of Stanford White* (New York: Free Press, 1989), p. 374.

217 *"I cannot conceive"* Lessard, *Architect of Desire*, p. 241.

217 *"There is hardly a city"*: "Stanford White's Splendid Career," *New York Herald*, June 26, 1906, p. 2.

217 *"exquisitely lovely"*: Lessard, *Architect of Desire*, p. 251.

218   *"But I thought"*: Baker, *Stanny*, p. 377.

218   *"for years made life"*: Lessard, *Architect of Desire*, p. 255.

218   *"past month has been one"*: Baker, *Stanny*, p. 378.

218   *"This ship"*: Charles McKim to Margaret McKim, Aug. 4, 1906, Charles McKim Papers, Manuscript Division, Library of Congress, Washington, D.C.

21. "THE SHIELDS HAVE MET EXACTLY"

220   *"I so thoroly"*: David Nasaw, *The Chief: The Life of William Randolph Hearst* (Boston: Houghton Mifflin, 2000), p. 210.

220   *"No great discomfort"*: "Engineers Walk Through Tunnel," *New York Herald*, September 13, 1906.

220   *"cleaned out"*: "Through P.R.R. Tunnel," *Evening Sun*, September 12, 1906, p. 1.

221   *"Mr. Jacobs probably"*: Samuel Rea to A. J. Cassatt, Sept. 7, 1906, carton 21, folder 32/170, PRR Archives, Harrisburg, Pennsylvania.

222   *"Can a proper tunnel"*: Samuel Rea, *Pennsylvania Railroad New York Tunnel Extension, Historical Outline*, December 15, 1909 (Philadelphia, 1909), p. 13, Hagley Museum and Library, Wilmington, Delaware.

222   *"Would not the structure"*: Ibid.

222   *"The distance between"*: Samuel Rea to A. J. Cassatt, telegram, Sept. 6, 1906, carton 21, folder 32/183, PRR Archives, Harrisburg, Pennsylvania.

222   *"I am not satisfied"*: Samuel Rea to A. J. Cassatt, Sept. 7, 1906, carton 21, folder 32/170, PRR Archives, Harrisburg, Pennsylvania.

223   *"was suddenly submerged"*: "Through P.R.R. Tunnel," *Evening Post*, September 12, 1906, p. 2.

223   *"I sincerely believe"*: Charles Jacobs to Samuel Rea, May 17, 1906, Box 90 Penn Central Transportation Co. Records, Manuscript & Archives Division, New York Public Library.

223   *"Men of all nationalities"*: "Through P.R.R. Tunnel," *Evening Post*, September 12, 1906, p. 2.

224   *"Here we have two enormous"*: "Pennsylvania Tubes To Meet on Sept. 18," *New York Times*, September 3, 1906.

224   *"After these connections"*: " 'Pennsy's' North Tunnels a Marvel of Skill," *New York Times*, September 9, 1906, p. 2:2.

224   *"hardly short of wonderful"*: Ibid.

225   *"I am proud"*: "Through P.R.R. Tunnel," *Evening Post*, September 12, 1906, p. 1.

226   *"one of the greatest feats"*: "The North River Tube Will Be Crossed Today," *New York Times*, September 12, 1906, p. 1.

226   *"I am pleased to report"*: Charles Jacobs to A. J. Cassatt, telegram, Sept. 12, 1906, carton 21, folder 32/183 PRR Archives, Harrisburg, Pennsylvania.

226   *"You and your staff"*: "Through the Hudson Tube," *New-York Tribune*, September 13, 1906, p. 1.

226   *"The credit is yours"*: Ibid.

226   *"For the excellence"*: Ibid.

226   *"Today is the happiest"*: "Tube Engineers Cheer As River Is Crossed," *New York Times*, September 13, 1906, p. 3.

227   *"North tunnel hudson"*: Samuel Rea to A. J. Cassatt, telegram, September 12, 1906, carton 21, folder 32/183, PRR Archives, Harrisburg, Pennsylvania.

227   *"For the first time in history"*: "The Pennsylvania Opens Its Second River Tube," *New York Times*, October 10, 1906, p. 1.

227   *"This whole subject"*: A. J. Cassatt to Samuel Rea, September 12, 1906, carton 21, folder 32/170, PRR Archives, Harrisburg, Pennsylvania.

227   *"The somewhat antiquated"*: "Rapid Progress on Work Above and Below the Rivers," *New York Times*, April 14, 1907, p. R9.

228   *"our side"*: A. J. Cassatt to William Shepard, February 11, 1906, Papers of William Shepard, Special Collections, Rare Book & Manuscript Library, Columbia University, New York.

228   *"The Pennsylvania job"*: Ivy Lee to his father, November 21, 1906, box 11, folder 2, Ivy Lee Papers, Princeton University, Princeton, New Jersey.

229   *"The most deplorable"*: Editorial, *The Stockholder*, May 22, 1906.

229   *"A dozen of the best"*: "Study in Values: Pennsylvania," *Wall Street Journal*, June 29, 1906, p. 1.

230   *"Do no more financing"*: Jacob Schiff to A. J. Cassatt, June 10, 1906, carton 46, folder 57/22, PRR Archives, Harrisburg, Pennsylvania.

230   *"form for myself"*: "Acworth on Pennsylvania Railroad Finances," *Railroad Gazette*, October 26, 1906, p. 359.

230   *"the highest type"*: James. T. Woodward, *A Statistical Analysis of the Operations of the Pennsylvania Railroad* (New York: Orlando C. Lewis & Co.), pp. 10–12.

231   *"all arrangements"*: William Patton to William Loeb, May 29, 1906, Cassatt Letterbooks, PRR Archives, Harrisburg, Pennsylvania.

231   *"My best wishes"*: William Patton to William Loeb, July 31, 1906. Cassatt Letterbooks, PRR Archives, Harrisburg, Pennsylvania.

231   *"the cutting off"*: A. J. Cassatt to J. B. Thayer, August 6, 1906, Cassatt Letterbooks, PRR Archives, Harrisburg, Pennsylvania.

231   *"I am very glad"*: Samuel Rea to A. J. Cassatt, August 22, 1906, carton 37, folder 48/6, PRR Archives, Harrisburg, Pennsylvania.

231   *"corporations caught trying"*: W. A. Swanberg, *Citizen Hearst* (New York: Scribner's, 1961), p. 291.

232   *"Appeal to the dark"*: Nasaw, *The Chief*, p. 211.

232   *"ROOSEVELT CALLS HEARST"*: "Roosevelt Calls Hearst Inciter of the Assassin," *New York Times*, November 2, 1906, p. 1.

232 *"I don't like"*: "Murphy Doesn't Like Hearst," *New York Times*, November 2, 1906, p. 1.

22. "THE ONLY RAILROAD STATESMAN"

233 *"The sky-scrapers"*: H. G. Wells, *The Future in America* (New York: Harpers & Brothers, 1906), pp. 35–36.

234 *"the simple diet"*: Charles McKim to Charles Moore, July 21, 1906, Charles McKim Papers, Manuscript Division, Library of Congress, Washington, D.C.

234 *"I fear nothing"*: Suzannah Lessard, *The Architect of Desire: Beauty and Danger in the Stanford White Family* (New York: Dial Press, 1996), p. 249.

235 *"pictures, tapestries"*: Charles McKim to William Mead, July 12, 1906, Charles McKim Papers, Manuscript Division, Library of Congress, Washington, D.C.

235 *"Our sense of personal"*: Charles McKim to E. D. Morgan, July 25, 1906, Charles McKim Papers, Manuscript Division, Library of Congress, Washington, D.C.

235 *"There can be no question"*: Charles McKim to Ely, October 31, 1906, Charles McKim Papers, Manuscript Division, Library of Congress, Washington, D.C.

235 *"As quickly as the buildings"*: Lorraine B. Diehl, *The Late, Great Pennsylvania Station* (New York: Four Walls, Eight Windows Press, 1996), p. 77.

237 *"more than 300"*: "Preliminary Report of the PRR Special Investigating Committee," *Railroad Gazette* 41, no. 1 (July 6, 1906): 20.

237 *"few, if any"*: "Final Report of the PRR Special Investigating Committee, Part II" *Railroad Gazette* 42, no. 9 (March 1, 1907): 282.

237 *"I have been somewhat"*: A. J. Cassatt to William Patterson, August 11, 1906, Presidential Letterbooks, PRR Archives, Harrisburg, Pennsylvania.

238 *"It was so severe"*: Patricia T. Davis, *End of the Line: Alexander J. Cassatt and the Pennsylvania Railroad* (New York: Neale Watson Academic Publications, 1978), p. 196.

238 *"wire-rimmed spectacles"* Ron Chernow, *The House of Morgan* (New York: Atlantic Monthly Press, 1990), p. 89.

238 *"No Harriman"*: Davis, *End of the Line*, p. 196.

239 *"active duties"*: "President Cassatt's Condition Improving," *Wall Street Journal*, September 26, 1906.

239 *"Will go south"*: "Cassatt's Successor May Be James McCrea," *New York Times*, October 28, 1906.

239 *"It is a commonplace"*: "Pennsylvania," *Wall Street Journal*, December 4, 1906.

240 *"perspective of the waiting room"*: Charles McKim to A. J. Cassatt, Nov. 12, 1906, carton 15, folder 32/13–32/19, PRR Archives, Harrisburg, Pennsylvania.

241 *"It is going to be"*: A. J. Cassatt to Charles McKim, November 14, 1906, carton 15, folders 32/13–32/19, PRR Archives, Harrisburg, Pennsylvania.

241 *"thinks the whole scheme"*: Leslie Shaw to A. J. Cassatt, March 10, 1906, carton 17, folder 32/95 v. 3, PRR Archives, Harrisburg, Pennsylvania.

241 *"A strong effort"*: A. J. Cassatt to Samuel Rea, Dec. 14, 1906, carton 17, folder 32/95, v. 3, PRR Archives, Harrisburg, Pennsylvania.

242 *"movement of private car"*: A. J. Cassatt to William Patton, December 28, 1906, President's Letterbook, PRR Archives, Harrisburg, Pennsylvania.

243 *"Word was immediately sent"*: "Cassatt's Death Deposes America's Railroad King," *Philadelphia Inquirer*, December 29, 1906, p. 1.

243 *"personal dispatches"*: Ibid.

243 *"The sudden passing"*: Samuel Rea to Mrs. Lois Cassatt, December 28, 1906, from a bound letter book of condolence letters and cards loaned by Jacques de Spoelberch, Cassatt descendent.

243 *"While I knew he"*: Samuel Rea to G. Parish, January 3, 1907, Samuel Rea Papers, Accession 1810, Carton 134, Folder 15, Hagley Museum and Library, Wilmington, Delaware.

244 *"A. J. Cassatt Dies,"* "A. J. Cassatt Dies of Grief," *New York Times*, December 29, 1906, p. 1.

244 *"Many men prominent"*: "Prominent Financiers Think Cassett Died of a Broken Heart," *Philadelphia Evening Item*, December 29, 1906.

244 *"a great public servant"*: Ibid.

244 *"died of a broken"*: Ibid.

244 *"Her loss to us"*: Davis, *End of the Line*, p. 179.

244 *"He was not only,"* William G. McAdoo to Mrs. Lois Cassatt, December 28, 1906, from a bound letter book of condolence letters and cards loaned by Jacques de Spoelberch, Cassatt descendent.

244 *"was among the first"*: "Alexander Cassatt," *New York Times*, December 29, 1906, p. 8.

245 *"I don't know"*: Davis, *End of the Line*, p. 143.

246 *"Harriman may struggle"*: Steven W. Usselman, *Regulating Railroad Innovation: Business, Technology and Politics 1840–1920* (Cambridge: Cambridge University Press, 2002), p. 309.

247 *"He was a great man"*: Samuel Rea to G. Parish, January 3, 1907, Samuel Rea Papers, Accession 1810, carton 134, folder 15, Hagley Museum and Library, Wilmington, Delaware.

23. "NEW YORK CITY SHAKEN"

249 *"the supporting of streets"*: Westinghouse, Church & Kerr Company. *The New York Passenger Terminal of the Pennsylvania Railroad* (New York: 1908), p. 5.

249 *"plowed through the walls"*: "Dynamite Blast Injures Twelve," *New York Times*, May 26, 1907, p. 1.

250 *"John Fitzpatrick"*: Ibid.

250 *"This happens occasionally"*: Ibid.

250 *"firemen from all"*: "30 May Be Dead, Town Wrecked," *New York Times*, March 3, 1907, p. 1.

251 *"were awakened"*: Ibid.

251 *"looked as though"*: "Explosions Felt 20 Miles Away," *New York Times*, March 4, 1907.

251 *"It may be that"*: Session 159, March 9, 1907, Minutes of the Board of Engineers, carton 16, folders 32/47, PRR Archives, Harrisburg, Pennsylvania.

253 *"Stanford told me"*: "Evelyn Thaw Tells Her Story," *New York Times*, February 8, 1907, p. 1.

253 *"she told of awaking"*: Ibid.

253 *"This little girl's"*: Suzannah Lessard, *The Architect of Desire: Beauty and Danger in the Stanford White Family* (New York: Dial Press, 1996), p. 282.

253 *"I am afraid"*: Charles Moore, *The Life and Times of Charles Follen McKim* (Boston: Houghton Mifflin, 1929), p. 299.

253 *"The sky is blue"*: Jean Strouse, *Morgan: American Financier* (New York: Random House, 1999), p. 505.

254 *"Pennsylvania Terminal"*: Charles McKim to Larry White, February 9, 1907, Charles McKim Papers, Manuscript Division, Library of Congress, Washington, D.C.

254 *"transplanting a large"*: Charles McKim to Charles Barney, May 18, 1907, Charles McKim Papers, Manuscript Division, Library of Congress, Washington, D.C.

255 *"Since we commenced"*: "Foundations of North River Tunnels," Chief Engineer [Charles Jacobs], September 26, 1906, presented at session 137, Sept. 27, 1906, Minutes of the Board of Engineers, carton 16, folders 32/47 PRR Archives, Harrisburg, Pennsylvania.

255 *"We are faced"*: Ibid.

255 *"he had to be personally"*: "Memoir of Charles Walker Raymond," *Transactions of the American Society of Civil Engineers* 77 (December 1914): 1901.

255 *"Does Mr. Jacobs"*: "North River Tunnels," memorandum by the chairman of the Board of Engineers, Oct. 8, 1906, session 139, October 11, 1906, Minutes of the Board of Engineers, carton 16, folders 31/47, PRR Archives, Harrisburg, Pennsylvania.

256 *"re-tightened and red-leaded"*: "Behavior of Subaqueous Tunnels," session 172, June 27, 1907, Minutes of the Board of Engineers, carton 16, folders 32/47, PRR Archives, Harrisburg, Pennsylvania.

256 *"any appreciable movement"*: Samuel Rea to the Board of Engineers, session

171, June 5, 1907, Minutes of the Board of Engineers, carton 16, folders 32/47, PRR Archives, Harrisburg, Pennsylvania.

256   *"The insertion of steel"*: Ibid.

256   *"The success of the work"*: "Tunnel Tubes in Soft Material," *Scientific American*, June 8, 1907, p. 466.

257   *"Here is a question"*: "The Philadelphia Tunnels Condemned," *Philadelphia Inquirer*, June 29, 1907.

257   *"My first impulse"*: Samuel Rea to James McCrea, memorandum, July 2, 1907, carton 15, folders 32/33, PRR Archives, Harrisburg, Pennsylvania.

257   *"any movement"*: "Behavior of Subaqueous Tunnels," session 180, October 3, 1907, Minutes of the Board of Engineers, carton 16, folders 32/47, PRR Archives, Harrisburg, Pennsylvania.

257   *"The interesting fact"*: Ibid.

258   *"The actual time"*: Ibid.

258   *"That the tunnels"*: "Behavior of Subaqueous Tunnels," session 184, November 7, 1907, Minutes of the Board of Engineers, carton 16, folders 32/47, PRR Archives, Harrisburg, Pennsylvania.

258   *"In recent discussions"*: Alfred Noble, p. 44, session 196, February 14, 1908, Minutes of the Board of Engineers, carton 16, folders 32/47, PRR Archives, Harrisburg, Pennsylvania.

259   *"We ate them all"*: Strouse, Morgan, p. 576.

259   *"so that they may enjoy"*: Ibid.

259   *"as vigorously"*: "Pennsylvania Road Slows Down A Bit," *New York Times*, November 2, 1907, p. 1.

24. "THE WAY IS STONY AND WET"

260   *"When we turn"*: Charles Moore, *The Life and Times of Charles Follen McKim* (Boston: Houghton Mifflin, 1929), p. 299.

260   *"The new Pennsylvania Station"*: "The Greatest Railroad Station in the World," *Harper's Weekly*, May 9, 1908, p. 28.

261   *"Poor McKim"*: William Mead to Daniel H. Burnham, February 12, 1908, Charles McKim Papers, Manuscript Division, Library of Congress, Washington, D.C.

262   *"When he goes to bed"*: "East River Tunnels Finished," *Philadelphia Public Ledger*, March 29, 1908, p. 1.

262   *"procured a toy train"*: Wiliam Couper, ed. *History of the Engineering, Construction, and Equipment of the Pennsylvania Railroad Company's New York Terminal and Approaches* (New York: Isaac H. Blanchard, 1912.), p. 91.

263   *"who devoted so much"*: Samuel Rea to E.W. Moir, April 1, 1908, Samuel Rea Papers, Accession 1810, carton 145, folder 14, Hagley Museum and Library, Wilmington, Delaware.

263   *"There is one space"*: Charles McKim to Samuel Rea, April 1, 1907, Samuel Rea Papers, Accession 1810, carton 147, folder 19, Hagley Museum and Library, Wilmington, Delaware.

263   *"both a heavy"*: William Mead to E. B. Morris, March 11, 1908, Samuel Rea Papers, Accession 1810, carton 147, folder 19, Hagley Museum and Library, Wilmington, Delaware.

263   *"for any suggestions"*: Ibid.

264   *"not to be outdone"*: Couper, *History of the Engineering, Construction and Equipment*, p. 91.

264   *"two feet six"*: "Sand Hogs Honor Engineer," *New York Times*, March 21, 1908, p.4.

264   *"In the mud"*: "East River Tunnels Finished," *Philadelphia Public Ledger*, March 29, 1908, p. 1.

265   *"The millions of people"*: "Tunneling of East River Was a Mighty Task," *New York World*, March 29, 1908.

265   *"rolls, then pickles"*: "Sand Hog Band a Hit at Sherry's" *New York Times*, March 12, 1907, p. 16:4.

267   *"Long continued work"*: Alfred Noble to Samuel Rea, Nov. 7, 1907, Samuel Rea Papers, Accession 1810, carton 150, folder 5, Hagley Museum and Library, Wilmington, Delaware.

267   *"At 7:05 o'clock"*: "Final Blast Opens Pennsylvania Tube," *New York Times*, April 12, 1908, pt. 2, p. 5:1.

268   *"Walk From Hackensack Meadows"*: Ibid.

268   *"The Pennsylvania Railroad is"*: Samuel Rea to William Bradley, May 7, 1908, Samuel Rea Papers, Accession 1810, carton 145, folder 14, Hagley Museum and Library, Wilmington, Delaware.

269   *"it had not been possible"*: Session 204, May 6, 1908, Minutes of the Board of Engineers, carton 16, folders 32/47, PRR Archives, Harrisburg, Pennsylvania.

269   *"In my opinion"*: "Memorandum on Supports of North River Tunnels," submitted by the Chairman, November 1, 1907, Session 183, November 1, 1907, Minutes of the Board of Engineers, carton 16, folders 32/47, PRR Archives, Harrisburg, Pennsylvania.

269   *"I have, after"*: Samuel Rea to Board, May 5, 1908, Session 204, May 6, 1908, Minutes of the Board of Engineers, carton 16, folders 32/47, PRR Archives, Harrisburg, Pennsylvania.

272   *"Above the columns"*: "Granite Facade of Station Done," *New York Times*, February 21, 1909, pt. 2, p. 6.

272   *"The Manhattan terminal"*: Carl W. Condit, "Railroad Electrification in the United States," *Proceedings of the IEEE* 64, no. 9 (September 1976): 1353.

272   *"argued more strongly"*: Michael Bezilla, *Electric Traction on the Pennsylvania Railroad, 1895–1968* (University Park: Pennsylvania State University Press, 1980), p. 39.

272 *"Any serious operating"*: Ibid., p. 46.

273 *"It was decided"*: William D. Middleton, *Manhattan Gateway: New York's Pennsylvania Station* (Waukesha, Wis.: Kalmbach Books, 1996), p. 43.

273 *"showed not the slightest"*: Bezilla, *Electric Traction*, p. 40.

274 *"When you . . . come home"*: Charles McKim to Larry White, April 21, 1909, Charles McKim Papers. Manuscript Division, Library of Congress, Washington, D.C.

274 *"I think the sky line"*: Charles McKim to Larry White, May 18, 1909, Charles McKim Papers., Manuscript Division, Library of Congress, Washington, D.C.

274 *"The new Metropolitan Life"*: Ibid.

275 *"The constantly increasing"*: Ibid.

275 *"It is regarded"*: Samuel Rea to William Mead, June 22, 1909, McKim Mead & White, Penn Station papers, box 365, Department of Prints, Photographs and Architectural Collections, New-York Historical Society, New York.

275 *"It took 1,140 freight cars"*: "The Pennsylvania Railroad, Information for the Press," July 31, 1909, McKim Mead & White, Penn Station Papers, file 3, Department of Prints, Photographs and Architectural Collections, New-York Historical Society, New York.

275 *"The liberty of suggesting"*: A. J. Cassatt to Leslie Shaw, June 2, 1904, carton 17, folders 32/95, PRR Archives, Harrisburg, Pennsylvania.

276 *"Larry White was"*: Moore, *McKim*, p. 305.

25. "OFFICIALLY DECLARE THE STATION OPEN"

278 *"The conditions of"*: William Couper, ed., *History of the Engineering, Construction, and Equipment of the Pennsylvania Railroad Company's New York Terminal and Approaches* (New York: Issac H. Blanchard, 1914), p. 77.

279 *"Everyone concedes"*: Hilary Ballon, *New York's Pennsylvania Stations* (New York: W. W. Norton, 2002), p. 79.

281 *"While amply equipping"*: Ibid., p. 55

282 *"Poor health"*: Lois Cassatt to T. DeWitt Cuyler, telegram, July 18, 1910, Samuel Rea Papers, Accession 1810, carton 147, folder 21, Hagley Museum and Library, Wilmington, Delaware.

282 *"Mrs. White"*: Charles Moore, *The Life and Times of Charles Follen McKim* (Boston: Houghton Mifflin, 1929), p. 305.

282 *"the Red Cottage"*: Suzannah Lessard, *The Architect of Desire: Beauty and Danger in the Stanford White Family* (New York: Dial Press, 1996), p. 255.

282 *"For a time"*: "Architect McKim Ill," New York Times, August 20, 1909, p. 2:5.

282 *"the serene sky"*; Lessard, *Architect of Desire*, p. 255.

283 *"as we have determined"*: Samuel Rea to James McCrea, July 22, 1910,

Samuel Rea Papers, accession 1810, carton 147, folder 21, Hagley Museum and Archives, Wilmington, Delaware.

283 *"With the unveiling"*: "Remarks of President McCrea," August 1, 1910, Samuel Rea Papers, Accession 1810, carton 147, folder 21, Hagley Museum and Archives, Wilmington, Delaware.

284 *"When one considers"*: Francis Barksdale, *The Pennsylvania. Station in New York*, p. 5, Samuel Rea Papers, Accession 1810, carton 146, folder 10, Hagley Museum and Library, Wilmington, Delaware.

284 *"almost unequaled"*: Charles W. Raymond, "The New York Tunnel Extension of the Pennsylvania Railroad," *Transactions of the American Society of Civil Engineers* 68 (September 1910): 31.

285 *"I am personally,"* Samuel Rea to Charles Jacobs, August 1, 1910, Samuel Rea Papers, Accession 1810, carton 147, folder 21, Hagley Museum and Library, Wilmington, Delaware.

286 *"I am quite well"*: Samuel Rea to A. J. Cassatt, Aug. 18, 1910, Samuel Rea Papers, Accession 1810, carton 147, folder 19, Hagley Museum and Library, Wilmington, Delaware.

286 *"the severe criticism"*: Samuel Rea, *Pennsylvania Railroad New York Tunnel Extension: Historical Outline*, December 15, 1909, (Philadelphia, 1909), pp. 22–23, Hagley Museum and Library, Wilmington, Delaware.

286 *"Every agreement"*: Ibid.

287 *"the sadness"*: "Pennsylvania Station," *Architectural Record* 27 (June 1910): 519.

288 *"argued with the conductor"*: "Day Long Throng Inspects New Tube," *New York Times*, September 9, 1910, p. 5.

288 *"imperfect installation"*: Ralph Peters, Pennsylvania Railroad Company press release, September 9, 1910, Samuel Rea Papers, Accession 1810, carton 149, folder 22, Hagley Museum and Library, Wilmington, Delaware.

289 *"For some weeks past"*: Ibid.

289 *"There were no personal injuries"*: Ibid.

290 *"More people resided"*: Clifton Hood, *722 Miles: The Building of the Subways and How They Transformed New York* (New York: Simon & Schuster, 1992), p. 135.

290 *"This line"*: "PRR Vice President for 7th Av. Subway," *New York Times*, May 19, 1908, p. 5.

290 *"How red"*: "Humiliations of a Triumph," *Journal American*, September 9, 1910.

291 *"the rather cheap"*: Samuel Rea to Bert Hanson, Dec. 8, 1910, McKim Mead & White, Penn Station Papers, carton 365, Department of Prints, Photographs and Architectural Collections, New-York Historical Society, New York.

292 *"A Frenchman"*: "100,000 Persons See Penn Station on Opening Day," *New York World*, November 10, 1910, p. 1.

292   *"In thousands"*: "Thousands See Station," *New-York Tribune*, November 28, 1910, p. 1.

293   *"The dense crowds"*: Annexation of New Jersey," *New York Times*, February 3, 1907, pt. 3, p. 4:1.

294   *"Yesterday I witnessed"*: James Forgie to Samuel Rea, November 28, 1910, Samuel Rea Papers, Accession 1810, carton 145, folder marked "Celebration upon completion of tunnels," Hagley Museum and Library, Wilmington, Delaware.

294   *"Therefore permit me"*: Ibid.

295   *"Station operating"*: Samuel Rea to Charles Jacobs, telegram, November 29, 1910, Samuel Rea Papers, Accession 1810, carton 145, folder marked "Celebration upon completion of tunnels," Hagley Museum and Library, Wilmington, Delaware.

26. CODA

296   *"Few buildings are"*: Thomas Wolfe, *You Can't Go Home Again* (New York: Scribner's: 1940), p. 38.

298   *"It is not a question"*: Hilary Ballon, *New York's Pennsylvania Stations* (New York: W. W. Norton, 2002), p. 83.

298   *"take cars"*: Ibid., p. 89.

298   *"vacant or covered with"*: "Is the Pa. Station A Failure?" *New York Sun*, August 25, 1912, Sunday Real Estate front page.

299   *"The Pennsylvania did not"*: Hilary Ballon, *New York's Pennsylvania Stations* (New York: W. W. Norton, 2002) p. 92.

299   *"I find my endeavors"*: Ibid., p. 89.

299   *"Mr. Egan was"*: William D. Middleton, *Manhattan Gateway: New York's Pennsylvania Station* (Waukesha, Wis.: Kalmach Books, 1996), p. 99.

300   *"There were people"*: Wolfe, *You Can't Go Home Again*, p. 39.

300   *"The average traveler"*: Lorraine B. Diehl, *The Late, Great Pennsylvania Station* (New York: Four Walls, Eight Windows Press, 1985), p. 148.

301   *"The ambiguity"*: Lewis Mumford, *The Highway and the City* (New York: Harvest Book, 1963), p. 144.

302   *"a problem because"*: Ballon, *New York's Pennsylvania Stations*, p. 93.

302   *"The Pennsylvania Station"*: "Pennsylvania Station a Monument to Foresight," *Wall Street Journal*, November 19, 1917, p. 3.

303   *"We have had"*: "Minutes of Seventy-eighth Annual Meeting," Pennsylvania Railroad Company 1925, p. iv.

303   *"almost singular combination"*: "Samuel Rea," *Wall Street Journal*, September 23, 1925, p. 1.

304   *"I like to think"*: "Atterbury Chosen Pennsylvania. President," *Wall Street Journal*, October. 1, 1925, p. 5.

305   *"a weakness for studying"*: "Career of Samuel Rea," (Philadelphia: PRR Information, October 1925), p. 17.

305   *"Tramping and working"*: Ibid.

305   *"give us insight"*: "Samuel Rea Retires as P.R.R. Head," *Railway Age* 79, No. 13 (September 26, 1925): 566.

306   *"The ICC improvised"*: Robert Sobel, *The Fallen Colossus* (New York: Weybright and Talley, 1977), p. 341.

307   *"with the roadbeds"*: "How Not to Run the Railroads," *Wall Street Journal*, September 6, 1961, p. 16.

307   *"Government then spent"*: Henry Hope Reed Jr., "Penn Station Tour" (New York: Municipal Art Society of New York, 1962), p. 6.

308   *"a small child"*: Ballon, *New York's Pennsylvania Stations*, p. 94.

308   *"glass-domed roof"*: Diehl, *The Late, Great Pennsylvania Station*, p.25.

309   *"block access,"* Ibid., p. 144.

309   *"the great treason"*: Mumford, *The Highway and the City*, p. 144.

309   *"I lunched yesterday"*: Ballon, *New York's Pennsylvania Stations*, p. 97.

310   *"You must be wiser"*: Suzannah Lessard, *The Architect of Desire: Beauty and Danger in the Stanford White Family* (New York: Dial Press, 1996), p. 304.

311   *"People never heard"*: Diehl, *The Late, Great Pennsylvania Station*, p. 25.

311   *"You can picket"*: Ibid.

311   *"There was not"*: Ibid.

311   *"People wanted automobiles"*: Ibid.

312   *"a landmark from Philadelphia"*: "The Pennsylvania Station," *Fortune*, July 1939, p. 138.

312   *"carte blanche for demolition"*: "Architecture: How to Kill a City," *New York Times*, May 5, 1963, p. 147.

312   *"Pennsylvania Station is no longer"*: "Railroad President Says Area and Public Will Benefit," *New York Times*, August 23, 1962, p. 28.

313   *"Until the first blow"*: "Farewell to Penn Station," *New York Times*, October. 30, 1963, p. 38.

313   *"A half century of emotion"*: Diehl, *The Late, Great Pennsylvania Station*, pp. 17–18.

314   *"Still rode the comfortable"*: "Ferry to Hoboken Will Stop Nov. 22," *New York Times*, November 15, 1967.

315   *"Through it one entered"*: Vincent Scully, *American Architecture and Urbanism* (New York: Praeger, 1969), p. 169.

BIBLIOGRAPHIC NOTES

Lorraine B. Diehl's *The Late, Great Pennsylvania Station* (1985), the first history of the station, is well written and beautifully illustrated. It set a high standard. Hilary Ballon's *New York's Pennsylvania Stations* (2002) is another well researched, handsome coffee table book, and she covered both the present Penn Station and a possible future redesigned Penn Station. William B. Middleton's contribution in *Manhattan Gateway: New York's Pennsylvania Station* (1996) was his technical explanations. Steven Parissien's *Pennsylvania Station: McKim, Mead and White* (1996) with its gorgeous illustrations took a more architectural viewpoint. I enjoyed and drew on all of these earlier works.

So vast are the Pennsylvania Railroad's old business files that they had to be divided among more than a dozen institutions. Archivist Christopher Baer, leading PRR expert, led the effort to place these valuable corporate records. Baer now works at one of those institutions, the Hagley Museum and Library in Wilmington, Delaware, where the Papers of Samuel Rea proved key to writing certain sections of this book.

But I kept hoping to find the full record of the New York Terminal and Tunnels Extension up in the Pennsylvania State Archives in Harrisburg, which holds Alexander Cassatt's Presidential Papers. These gigantic Harrisburg PRR archival holdings have no detailed finding aide. Starting in 2000, I begin visiting Harrisburg trying to figure out these labryinthine records and where the Penn Station and tunnel building files might be. Finally, on October 3, 2002, I came upon them largely by accident. It was a thrilling eureka! moment as I realized that every file beginning with a 32 contained material about Penn Station and the North River and East River tunnel projects. It took two full days to work my way through all six cartons with their hundreds of files and thousands of photos just to get a general overview of the contents. As I opened one dusty folder after another to find letters, telegrams, photographs, and reports a century old, I suspected I might be the first person in decades (if not more) to look at these meticulous records. With them, I could write a new, detailed history of the monumental project that remade New York City.

Other useful archival sources were the Forgie Papers at the Smithsonian's Museum of American History, with their additional North River tunnel material and another trove of photos; the McKim, Mead and White archives at the New-York Historical Society and also at the Avery Library at Columbia University. Finally, the archives of the Pennsylvania Railroad Museum in Strasburg, Pennsylvania, yielded up a few additional materials.

The sole biography of Alexander Cassatt, Patricia T. Davis's *End of the Line: Alexander J. Cassatt and the Pennsylvania Railroad* (1978), was commissioned by his family and is workmanlike and useful. Sadly, few of Cassatt's personal papers survive, whether in any public archive or even in the hands of descendants.

As for the Pennsylvania Railroad, the only history is a corporate endeavor, George H. Burgess and Miles C. Kennedy, *Centennial History of the Pennsylvania Railroad Company, 1846–1946* (1949).

INDEX

Page numbers in *italics* refer to illustrations.